ADMINISTRATIVE DYNAMICS and DEVELOPMENT:

The Korean Experience

First Printing
Published by Kyobo Publishing, Inc.
1-1, 1-ka, Chongro-ku, Seoul, Korea

ADMINISTRATIVE DYNAMICS and DEVELOPMENT:

The Korean Experience

Edited by

Bun Woong Kim
Dongguk University

David S. Bell, Jr.
Eastern Washington University

Chong Bum Lee
Korea University

KYOBO PUBLISHING, INC.
Seoul, Korea

Administrative Dynamics and Development:

The Korean Experience

PREFACE

Innumerable laudatory statements enshroud the image of Asia's second economic "miracle," the Republic of Korea. Indeed the rapid transformation from primarily an agricultural society suffering from a stagant economy and chronic political chaos to a newly industrialized and dynamic international competitor in two decades, 1960-1980, was truly phenomenal. Faithful emulation of developed economic models, particularly the Japanese export-oriented economic model, and a single-minded national and executive devotion to economic growth produced the "miracle" and rapid industrialization. Sustained economic growth made Korean more optimistic about an improved lifestyle; but it also engendered expectations concerning the transformation of the political and social systems. However, the political and social systems remain highly centralized and personalized and despite rather cautious and tentative governmental initiatives to grant limited local autonomy, it seems highly unlikely that substantive change is imminent.

It is our conviction that the contradictions, conflicts, inconsistences, and unanticipated consequences of development and arbitrary and incautious public policy also form an integral part of the Korean "miracle" and warrant further consideration. This book therefore is an outgrowth of our belief that others may benefit not only from an exposition of the successes but also from the other side of the coin, namely, the contradictions, conflicts, inconsistencies and unanticipated consequences of development and the sometimes arbitrary and incautious public policy of the Korean experience.

January 1985
Seoul, Korea

David S. Bell, Jr.

v

ACKNOWLEDGMENTS

This volume is intended for international audiences in the belief that the Korean developmental experience is one of the most interesting and economically successful examples in the world today. We hope that *Administrative Dynamics and Development: The Korean Experience* will provide a better understanding of the multidimensional aspects of development.

We are indebted to our contributors for the preparation and timely submission of their articles. We are also greatful to *The Asian Journal of Public Administration, Journal of East and West Studies, The Journal of East Asian Affairs, Korea Journal, International Journal of Public Administration, Journal of Public and International Affairs, Journal of Northeast Asian Studies, Public Budgeting & Finance,* International Development Institute, Indiana University for giving us permission to use materials from the articles which appeared earlier in the journals.

We appreciate very much the assistance given this entire project by Dongguk University which provided research facilities, Eastern Washington University, in particular, Dr. Niel Zimmerman, Dean, School of Public Affairs, for financial assistance, and Korea University. We also wish to thank Mr. Jong Gook Park, President, and Mr. Seung Woo Lee and Mr. Moon Gil Yang, of Kyobo Publishing Company for their support of this project.

January 1985
Seoul, Korea

Bun Woong Kim
David S. Bell, Jr.
Chong Bum Lee

Contents

CONTRIBUTORS

Byong Man Ahn

Moon Suk Ahn

David S. Bell, Jr.

William W. Boyer

Gerald E. Caiden

Yong Hyo Cho

Chung Kil Chung

Myung Chan Hwang

Jong Sup Jun

Yong Duck Jung

Bun Woong Kim

Dong Hyun Kim

Dong Kun Kim

Myoung Soo Kim

Young Pyoung Kim

Young Sup Kim

Chong Bum Lee

Sung Bok Lee

Yeon Cheon Oh

Woo Suh Park

Yang Soo Rhee

Wha Joon Rho

Gilbert B. Siegel

In Joung Whang

Ahn, Byong Man, Ph.D., University of Florida, is professor of public administration at Hankuk University of Foreign Studies, where he serves as Director of the Institute of Korean Regional Studies. He has served as an invited lecturer on development problems and administration at Harvard University, Lafayette College, Rutgers University, SUNY at Buffalo and the University of Delaware (1981-1984). Professor Ahn has also served as editor-in-chief of the Korean Political Science Association (1977-1981). He served as a consultant to the Ministry of Home Affairs and the Ministry of Government Administration (1981-1983). He has coauthored several books, monographs, and research reports; and numerous articles on community development and comparative public administration in *Community Development Review, Korean Political Science Review* and *Review of the International Union of Local Authorities.*

Ahn, Moon Suk, Ph.D., University of Hawaii, is professor of public administration at Korea University. He served as the head of Software Development Laboratory, Korea Advanced Institute of Science and Technology (1968-1981). His publications include *Economics of Computers* (translated, 1982), *Research Methodologies of Social Sciences* (coauthored, 1983); and many articles on quantitative analysis of public administration, management information science, and public policy evaluation in the *Journal of Social Science, Korean Public Administration Review* and other professional Journals.

Bell, David S., Jr., Ph.D., Indiana University, is Professor of Government at Eastern Washington University. He was a Visiting Fellow at the Institute of Southeast Asian Studies (Singapore, 1975-1976), Exchange Professor at Dongguk University (Seoul, 1981-1982) and was on sabbatical leave at Dongguk University in 1984. He has lectured in Southeast Asia and in the Republic of Korea under the auspices of the United States Information Service. He has presented numerous papers at professional meetings and his articles have appeared in *The Journal of East Asian Affairs, The Asian Journal of Public Administration, Korea Observer,* and *The Korea Journal.*

Boyer, William W., Ph.D., University of Wisconsin, is Professor of Public Administration at the University of Delaware. He has served on the faculties of Kansas State University (1965-1969); Myongji University, Seoul, Korea (1973-1975); University of Malaya (1968-1969); Andhra University, India (1967); University of the Punjab, Lahore, Pakistan (1962-1964); and University of Pittsburgh (1955-1965). Professor Boyer has authored and co-authored numerous books, monographs, research reports, and journal articles. Some of his recent publications include *America's Virgin Islands: A History of Human Rights and Wrongs*(1982), "Foreword" in Charles P. Messick, *Reflections of a Public Servant; End of a Journey* (1978) and *A Report on Development Administration in Bangladesh* (1975). His articles have appeared in *Public Personnel Administration, Personnel Administration, Municipal Finance, Political Science Quarterly* and many other professional journals.

Caiden, Gerald E., Ph. D., University of London, England, graduated from the London School of Economics and Political Science, and has served on the faculties of the University of London (1957-1959), Carleton University (1959-1960), Australian National University (1961-1966), Hebrew University (1966-1968), University of California, Berkeley (1968-1971), Haifa University (1971-1975), and University of Southern California (1975-present). He has published over twenty books and monographs and over one hundred journal articles, and has acted as an editorial consultant to several leading journals in the field of public administration and as a reader for notable publishing houses. He has acted as consultant, researcher and administrator to a wide variety of public organizations ranging from the World Bank and the United Nations Organization to local authorities and public utilities. He is known best for his research in administrative reform and organizational diagnosis.

Cho, Yong Hyo, Ph.D., Syracuse University, is a Professor of Urban Studies and Political Science at The University of Akron, where he also serves as the Head of the Department of Urban Studies. He was selected as a 1977-1978 NASPAA Faculty Fellow and served as a senior policy analyst in the U.S. Department of Housing and Urban Development. He also was an elected member of the National Council of the American Society for Public Administration and served as a member of the Executive Council of the National Association of Schools of Public Affairs and Administration. He has authored and co-authored several books, monographs, and research reports as well as numerous journal articles and book chapters. Some of his recent publications include *Public Policy Outcomes in the American States: A Model for Synthesis;* and *Measuring the Effects of Legislative Reappointment.* The books to which he contributed chapters include *Cities in the 21st Century, Urban Revitalization,* and *The Political Economy of Reform.*

*Chung, Chung Kil,*Ph.D., University of Michigan, is associate professor of public administration at Seoul National University. He has coauthored *Introduction to Policy Science* (1976), *Quantitative Analysis for Public Administration* (1981) and *Policy Evaluation* (1984). Professor Chung has also published numerous articles an policy process and analysis in *The Journal of Korean Public Administration, Korean Public Administration Review* and *Korean Political Science Review*.

Hwang, Myung Chan, Ph.D., Syracuse University, professor of public administration at Kon Kuk University, where he has served as Dean of the Graduate School of Public Administration. He is now on leave as President of the Korea Research Institute for Human Settlements. He was a Regional Development Expert of UNDP, Tehran (1974) and an associate professor at the Asian Institute of Technology (1975-1976). He has served as consultant to the Premier, Ministry of Construction, and National Planning Commission Korea. He has authored *Regional Development* (1984) and has coauthored *Metropolitan Planning: Issues and Policies* (1979); and has published numerous articles on regional development planning, housing and land policies in *Journal of Korean Planners Association, Housing Science,* and *Journal of Korean Administration*.

Jun, Jong Sup, Ph.D., University of Southern California, is professor of public administration at California State University , Hayward. He has served as chairperson of the Department of Public Administration; several national committees of the National Association of *Public Administration Review, Administration and Society,* and *Journal of Comparative Administration,* and an editor of SICA occasional paper; a consultant to government agencies at the U.S. federal, state, and local levels. He is the author of *Public Administration in Change: Design and Problem Solving* (1985), *Management by Objectives in Government* (1976), and co-author of *Tomorrow's Organizations* (1973) and *Administrative Alternatives in Development Assistance* (1973). In addition, the author has published a number of articles in the *Public Administration Review, International Review of Administrative Sciences* and other professional journals.

Jung, Yong Duck, Ph.D., University of Southern California, is assistant professor of public administration at Sung Kyun Kwan University. He is the coauthor of *Korean Public Policy* (1984) and has translated many works into Korean including Arthur M. Okun's *Equality and Efficiency*. He has published a number of articles on public policy analysis and management, regulatory policy and welfare policy in the *Korean Social Science Journal, Korean Public Administration Review, Journal of Northeast Asian Studies,* and *Journal of International and Public Affairs*.

Kim, Bun Woong, Ph.D., Claremont Graduate School, is associate professor of public administration at Dongguk University. He was a visiting professor at the University of Southern California (1984); and he served as a member of the Executive Committee of Korean Society for Public Administration and Korean Political Science Association (1980-1982), and consultant to the Ministry of Economic Planning Board and Seoul City Government (1981-1983). Professor Kim is the co-editor of *Korean Public Bureaucracy* (1982) and has coauthored *Seminar in Public Administration* (1982), *Public Administration* (1981), and *Handbook of Korea* (1979). He has published numerous articles on public bureaucracy and comparative politics in the *Korea Journal, Korean Public Administration Review, Korean Political Science Review* and *Asian Journal of Public Administration.*

Kim, Dong Hyun, Ph.D., University of Missouri, is associate professor of public administration at Sung Kyun Kwan University. He was a senior fellow at the Korea Development Institute (1978-1981) and has served as a consultant to UNICEF, Seoul and several ministries of the Korean Government. He is the author of *Development Theories and Strategies: Critical Perspectives* (1984), and coauthored *Public Policy in Korea* (1984), *Public Administration Dictionary* (1984), *Understanding the Social Sciences* (1982), *Child Development Policies in Korea* (1982) and *Social Security in Korea* (1980). He has also published a number of articles pertaining to public policy and development administration in the *Korean Public Administration Review, Social Science Journal, Technology Transfer, Polity* and other professional journals.

Kim, Dong Kun, Ph.D., University of Georgia, is professor of public administration at Seoul National University. He was an associate professor at the University of Tennessee (1973-1977) and a visiting professor at the University of Chicago (1977). He served as a member of the Advisory Committee to the Economic Planning Board in Korea. He is the author of *Modern Public Finance* (1984) and has published numerous articles on public finance and budgeting, and economic policy analysis in the *Economic and Business Perspective, Public Finance & Budgeting* and *Korean Journal of Public Administration.*

Kim, Myoung Soo, D.P.A., State University of New York at Albany, is associate professor of public administration at Hankuk University of Foreign Studies, where he also serves as the Dean of Planning. He served as a member of the Advisory Committee to the Ministry of Governmental Administration in Korea. He has published numerous articles on public policy analysis and evaluation in the

Korean Political Science Review, Korean Public Administration Reivew, The Journal of Korean Regional Studies and other professional journals.

Kim, Young Pyoung, Ph.D., Indiana University, is associate professor of public administration at Korea University. He has served as lecturer of Korean Public Officials Training Institute and as research associate of the International Development Institute, Indiana University. He has published a number of articles on policy analysis and local government administration in the *Korean Public Administration Review, The Journal of Social Sciences* and other professional journals.

Kim, Young Sup, Ph.D., Myong Ji University, is professor of public administration at Han Yang University. He has served as chairperson of the Department of Public Administration; a member of Advisory Committees of the Ministry of Governmental Administration, the Ministry of Economic Planning Board and the Seoul City Government. He is the author of *Social Development Planning* (1982), and coauthored *Seminar in Public Administration* (1982) and *Public Administration* (1981). He has published a number of articles on social welfare policy and social development planning in the *Korea Journal, Korean Public Administration Review* and *International Journal of Public Administration.*

Lee, Chong Bum, Ph.D., University of Pennsylvania, is professor of public administration at Korea Universiy. He was Research Fellow at the University of Pennsylivania (1982) and served as chairperson of the Planning Committee, Korean Society for Public Administration (1981). He has published a number of articles on organization theory, research methodology, and development administration in the *Social Science Journal, Law and Administration Review* and *Korean Public Administration Review.* He has translated many works into Korean including Herbert A. Simon's *The Sciences of the Artificial.*

Lee, Sung Bok, Ph.D., Syracuse University, is assistant professor of public administration at Kon Kuk University. His primary research has been focused on city development and urban affairs in Korea. He has published journal articles pertaining to urban and regional development in *Korean Public Administration Review, Urban Affairs* and other journals.

Oh, Yeon Cheon, Ph.D., New York University, is assistant professor of public administration at Seoul National University. He was a Senior Researcher of the Korea Economic Research Institute

(1982-1983). Currently he serves as a member of the Advisory Committee to the Korea Chamber of Commerce and the Federation of Korean Industries. He has published numerous articles of financial management and taxation, and local government in the *Public Sector, Korean Public Administration Review,* and the *Journal of Korean Public Administration.*

Park, Woo Suh, Ph.D., New York University, is associate professor of public administration at Yonsei University, where he also serves as Associate Dean of the Graduate School of Public Administration. He was a Senior Research Fellow at the Korea Research Institute for Human Settlements (1980-1983) and served as a member of the Advisory Committee to the Board of Auditing and Inspection in Korea. He has authored and coauthored several books, monographs, and research reports as well as numerous articles. His recent publications include *An Analytical Study on Land Use System in Korea* (1963), *New Town Development Policy in Korea* (1980), *An Analytical Study of Recapture of Betterment in Korea* (1981), *Housing Data Book* (1981), and "The Impact Study of Urban Renewal on Local Finance" in *Environmental Study* (1984).

Rhee, Yang Soo, Ph.D., University of Southern California, is assistant professor of public administration at Yonsei University. His primary research and teaching area is organizationl behavior and management, particularly organizational psychology dealing with Korean administrative culture. He has published a number of articles on organizational theory and practices in the *Social Science Review, Korean Public Administration* and the *Journal of East and West Studies.*

Rho, Wha Joon, Ph.D., Syracuse University, is associate professor of public administration at Seoul National University. He is the author of *Public Policy Evaluation* (1983), the co-editor of *Korean Public Bureaucracy* (1982) and has coauthored *Development Planning* (1981), *Quantitative Analysis for Public Administration* (1981), *Organization and Management* (1978) and *Introduction to Policy Science* (1976). He was a fellow of the Center for Advanced Studies at the Massachusettes Institute of Technology (1978), a visiting scholar at University of California, Berkeley (1983), and editor-in-chief of *Korean Political Science Review* (1981).

Siegel, Gilbert B., Ph.D., University of Pittsburgh, is professor and Associate Dean, School of Public Administration, University of Southern California, Los Angeles. He has previously had management experience with Los Angeles County, and has served as consultant to American and foreign governments. He has authored numerous articles, *The Vicissitudes of Government Reform in Brazil: A Study of the DASP* (University Press of America, 1978); edited *Human Resources Management in Public Organizations, A Systems Approach* (University Publishers, 1974); *Breaking with Orthodoxy in Public Administration* (University Press of America, 1980); and co-authored with Michael White et al., *Management in Public Systems, Concepts and Methods* (Duxbury, (1980).

Whang, In Joung, Ph.D., University of Pittsburgh, is Director of International Development Exchange Center at the Korea Development Institute. He was professor of public administration at Seoul National University (1968-1976) and served as a senior expert with the United Nations' Asian and Pacific Development Administration Center, Kuala Lumpur, Malaysia (1973-1978). His publications include *Public Administration and Economic Development* (1970), *Management of Family Planning Programs in Asia* (1976) and *Management of Rural Change in Korea* (1981), and a number of articles on the policy sciences and social development administration in *Asian Survey, Korea Journal, Journal of Korean Public Administration* and many other professional journals.

INTRODUCTION

Until the advent of the Park Chung Hee administration in 1961, the Republic of Korea suffered from a stagnant economy and political chaos. Shortly thereafter under the tugelage of western trained economists who recognized the material benefits of unidimensional planned economic development in an atmosphere of circumscribed political liberties and blessed by a hard working literate population tired of poverty and political chaos, the Park administration engineered the dramatic reshaping of the nation. Under the guise of a single-minded national and presidential devotion to economic development, the government and a powerful and supportive cluster of leaders in the business community created a tightly organized technocratic elite drawn from the best managerial and technical talents of the civilian and military bureaucracies and the private and academic sectors. The new technocratic elite when combined with the more traditional bureaucratic elite produced an extreme degree of administrative centralization and collectivism taking its directions from the Blue House. Further the unprecedented spectacular economic successes of the 1960s reinforced the rationale for the technocratic elite's existence, demonstrated their oranizational and decision-making skills, augumented their professional and personal linkages to the president and fostered a unity of purpose for economic growth that severely restricted political liberties.

Economic growth transformed more than the economy; it produced a surfeit of rising expectations and engendered political responsibilities and liabilities. The political reforms, urged by disparate clerical, student and opposition party dissidents but ignored by the Park government were given new life in the spring and summer of 1979. A temporary economic slump had exacerbated the genuine socio-economic grievances of the urban poor. Student demonstrators in the Pusan-Masan area who were protesting Park's repressive policies were joined by large numbers of common people expressing their socio-economic grievances. A facade of calm was restored following the imposition of martial law in the area. But the potential expansion of civil unrest to other large metropolitan centers posed an immediate threat to continued economic prosperity and development and a political threat to the government. After Park Chung-Hee's assassination in October 1979, economic momentum continued unabated due to an apparent consensus among the civilian and military authorities; but the political responsibilities and liabilities were not resolved.

The Republic of Korea has weathered the death of President Park Chung Hee, massive societal unrest and General Chun Doo-Hwan's military coup d'etat. As President, ex-general Chun has continued to emphasize the economic priorities of his predecessor but the form of his succession raised serious doubts about the political legitimacy of his regime and the stability of the Republic of Korea. Even more pervasive than the problem of legitimacy, is acute public awareness of the potential of a vastly improved lifestyle brought about by sustained economic development. In the past the exigencies of economic development tempered popular responses to the harsh governmental strictures on political activities and the inequities inherent in the hierarchical national elite. However, in late 1984 there were growing indications that the middle class, students, and laborers had begun to view economic progress as a base for far-reaching political reforms. The ''just democratic welfare society'' envisioned by President Chun Doo-Hwan means a society that is responsive to the societal aspirations of a prosperous populace who want an equitable share of the economic pie and shared access to political power.

Our aim is therefore to broadly examine the successes and contradictions, conflicts, inconsistencies and unanticipated consequences of development in the Korean milieu. For that purpose we have assembled twenty one (21) scholarly articles dealing with various aspects of administrative dynamics and development. The twenty one (21) chapters are arranged in five major parts.

The first of the five parts, ''The Dilemmas of Development,'' deals with: bureaucratic elitism and democratic development; the governmental role in economic development; the human or residual factor, paticularly youth, and economic growth; and the paradoxical contradictions of rapid economic development. Bun Woong Kim and David S. Bell, Jr. view the centralized bureaucratic elite as an impediment to pluralistic participatory democracy. A complex fusion of traditional cultural/political patterns and foreign administrative practices produced a centralized system of bureaucratic thought and behavior. The authoritarian political tradition stressed popular compliance with the established leadership without question and this nutured bureaucratic elitism and impeded democratic pluralism. In this setting public policy making is the exclusive domain of the bureaucratic elite and although this may facilitate effective bureaucratic direction of economic and social development, it deters the creation of autonomous centers of authority in the political arena. The overwhelming moral and political predominance of the bureaucratic elite/technocratic elite culture over the masses is not conducive to the evolution and development of pluralistic participatory democracy. Gerald Caiden and Yong Duck Jung review Korean development concepts and strategies, assess the role of the authoritarian government in effectuating rapid economic growth, and examine the political and social trade-offs that eventuated in the directed development of the Park Chung-Hee government. Political participation was sacrificed for economic prosperity and in the short run this was highly successful. However, the liabilities were substantial and the Park government became increasingly vulnerable internally as it continued to adhere to favor rapid economic growth over political development. Further, the Park government failed to address such critical weaknesses as inflation, corruption and alienation between the privileged rich and the repressed poor. Economic growth is also a concern of Dong Hyun Kim. But economic growth is more than a function of the accumulation of material or material inputs. Income growth is also the result of other factors than just those of capital investment or material inputs. The residual or human factor is an essential condition and a major determinant of economic growth. Children and youth constitute the raw materials for the talents which constitute the human factor in economic growth. Investment in children and youth development programs is not just a program of social welfare, but rather is really analogous to investment in capital goods from an economic viewpoint. Youth development programs are instruments for economic growth and as such they have to be integrated, dovetailed and absorbed into national development strategy. Finally Jong Sup Jun focuses on the impact of economic development on the sociopsychological factors, the role of public administrators as agents for development and modernization, the organizational pathology stemming from the government's efficiency movement and the prospects for democracy. His aim is to reveal the paradoxical contradictions that exist in the process of rapid economic development. The concept of development must be reexamined in light of the requirements for democracy, equity and participation. The economic indicators employed by the Korean government and the banks clearly domonstrate that Korea has accomplished to so-called "miracle." But, he concludes, if viewed in terms of such factors as equality, justice, meaningful employment, medical care, housing for the indigent and other aspects of the quality of life, economic growth has been a failure or, at best, a partial success. Further, in order to create democracy, Jun believes that subtantial changes must take place especially in the area of centralized control of the educational processes. Democratic reform requires the implanting of the seeds of democracy in the youth through the teaching of democratic values.

The second major part "Organizational Processes," examines: socio-cultural factors and managerial styles in Korea and America; the usefulness of management theories and techniques transferred from abroad; the attempt to apply an American model to three Korean executive branch decisions; and the Korean transportation system through systemic concepts and a communication flow model. Yang Soo Rhee explores the interrelationships between socio-cultural factors and mangerial styles in the Republic of Korea and the United States. Using four socio-cultural variables, namely, familism, transitional society, formalism and environmental stability, Rhee then compares Korean and American managers in authoritarian, entrepreneurial, bureaucratic, and mechanistic managerial styles. There are differences in the two managerial styles (Korean-American) and the differences appear to be socio-culturally based. However, managerial style dissimilarities are also attributable to individual, situational and organizational differences. Accordingly, in order to gain a more accurate picture, it is necessary to explore managerial styles on the basis of socio-cultural factors and individual, situational and organizational aspects. Wha Joon Rho seeks to evaluate the usefulness of management theories and techniques transferred from abroad to the Korean administrative context and to examine the scope and magnitude of the schism between academicians and practitioners in Korean public administration. Data was collected from a questionaire sent to 130 public management academicians and 240 central government practitioners regarding the sources of management knowledge, usefulness of foreign management theories in the Korean administrative context, barriers impeding the use of the information and the ways of linking theory to practice. He found a significant information gap between the academicians and practitioners, agreement on the lack of usefulness of foreign administrative theoreis and a high degree of consensus on the objectives of research, barriers to implementation and linking theory to practice. Chung Kil Chung attempts to use Allison's conceptual models of decision-making in the U.S. executive branch in his analysis of three Korean executive branch decisions, namely, membership in the Nonaligned Movement, construction of the Seoul-Pusan highway and revolution in the educational system. All of Allison's models had some applicability but the "bureaucratic polities" and the "rational actor" models had very little applicability in explaining the behavior of either the executive or the cabinet ministers who dominated major segments of the decision-making process. Theodore Lowi's ideas were also unsuccessfully employed to explain presidential behavior and the president's role in the policy-making process. It was determined therefore that the additional observations and hypotheses provided by the author may be more useful in explaining the decision-making process in the developing nations. Most articles identifying transportation problems utilize a physical planning format, but Moon Suk Ahn and Chong Bum Lee apply systemic concepts and a communication flow model to determine administrative problems in the Korean transportation system. Extensive use was made of official in and out documents via computer tapes, and network diagrams were then constructed to determine communication flows the relevant agencies. On the basis of the data derived from their research, the authors conclude that minimal information flows between the Public Road Division and other divisions related to the traffic management. This produces a lack of coordination among the agencies responsible for network management and the cumulative result is that Seoul has a high level of traffic congestion.

In the third major part, "Budgetary Process and Fiscal Policy," two articles deal respectively with the budget as an instrument of governmental activity and the tax reform that introduced a value-added tax in the Republic of Korea. Dong Kun Kim describes Korean budgeting as a numerical expression of governmental activities which reflects political, economic and administrative decision-making. It is a public statement that attempts to link proposed expenditures to desired political, economic and administrative results. Two author's analysis identifies the budgetary institutions and the process of budgetary decision-making, reviews the scope and characteristics of the public sector, examines the budget as an instrument of economic policy, explains the development of budgetary techniques and discusses government efforts to constrain budget growth. Yeon Cheon Oh describes the introduction and implementation of a value-added tax in 1977. The importance of domestic indirect taxes to the Korean economy is indisputable and the VAT has particular importance. Not only does the value-added tax constitute an integral component of the total internal tax revenue (33% plus), but it also is a critical component (over 60%) of the total indirect tax revenue. The VAT was adopted primarily because of its administrative simplicity in comparison to the complexities of the replaced indirect tax system. However, despite its perceived administrative advantages, numerous criticisms emanated from administrative problems rather than from the anticipated controverted issues. Administrative difficulties were also encountered in the implementation process and in the intrinsic complexity of the new tax law. The success of the VAT may hinge on the extent to which administrative problems can be overcome in the implementation process and in the structural characteristics of the VAT system.

In the fourth major part, "Urbanization Policies," the thematic concerns are: the rapid transformation from a rural to a largely industrialized nation; potential rural-urban migrants; land acquisition for low income housing; the problems of squatter settlements; managed urban development; and urban overpopulation and public policy. Sung Bok Lee finds that in two decades Korea has been transformed from a rural to a primarily industrialized nation and concomitantly, per capital income has advanced from $81.00 in 1960 to $1,510.00 in 1980. In the transformation from a rural agricultural society to an urbanized and industrialized society , the author notes that people and industries have now been concentrated in major metropolitan areas and industrial estates. Byong Man Ahn and William W. Boyer utilize a cognitive behavioral approach in their research to identify potential migrants among the rural people and to consider possible strategies to decrease and/or reverse rural-urban migration to enhance rural development. They focus on four perceptions that help explain the penchant to migrate, namely, value attached to the farmland, perception of urban income, life styles of urban relatives, and the degree of comfort in urban living. Rural-urban migration can be predicted by the use of these variables: (1) the greater the attachment to the farmland, the less likely the rural resident is to migrate; (2) economic (urban income); (3) social (life styles of urban relatives); and (4) the psychological variable (adjustment and comfort); the more favorable the rural resident views variables 2,3 and 4, the more likely the rural resident is to migrate. Invariably the rural-urban migrant will seek housing and Myong Chan Hwang discusses the land readjustment project used by most urban governments in Korea to supply developed land for low income housing. However, the land readjustment project has not succeeded in supplying relatively cheap developed land for low income housing due to attempts to minimize the land reduction of the land owners and create enormous profits for them. Relatively cheap developed land remains a constant inexorable demand and he states that, either the land adjustment project has to be modified·or some alternative policy has to be used to secure developed urban land for low income housing. Frequently the new urban resident lacks the financial resources to purchase urban land and instead constructs a makeshift squatter dwelling. Woo Suh Park surveys the numerous government measures enacted to mitigate the squatter settlements; particulary in the 1960-1980 period in the capital city of Seoul. Instead of remedying the squatter problem, the government's efforts resulted in a waste of resources and the deprivation of the individual rights of squatters. The author argues that it would be both more sensible and more human to allow the existing squatter settlements to remain and allow the inhabitants to improve their lives than to risk the potentially negative effects and significant costs, both social and individual, inherent in relocating the squatters. He concludes squatter settlements in Seoul should be immediately legalized, rehabilitated and selectively redeveloped.

Nowhere in the Republic of Korea do we witness the cumulative impact of urbanization in greater magnitude than Seoul and the final two articles in this part, "Urbanization Policies," focus on the capital city. David S. Bell, Jr. and Bun Woong Kim argue that the piecemeal legislation of the last two decades will not meet the unrelenting challenges and demands of urban development. Managed urban growth is imperative and they believe. . .

"managed urban growth requires an intricately integrated and efficient system, where choices are made with full knowledge of all the variables, constraints and trade-offs and where programs and policies are synchronized for effective and timely execution."

Urban development entails a myriad of activities and in order to coordinate the activities, Bell and Kim suggest the establishment of a Ministry of Urban Affairs to be charged with the exclusive responsibility for managing and coordinating urban growth. Yong Hyo Cho and Young Sup Kim evaluate the policies developed and implemented in the last twenty years to slow down the rate of population growth in Seoul. They conclude that the previous efforts failed due to the lack of consistency and persistence in policy refinement and implementation. Since Korea is a small country with a very high population density, Cho and Kim state that priority must be given to the overall population growth and natural environment of the entire nation. The population carrying capacity of Korea is limited and the natural environment must be protected from pollution and destruction. Any policy or policies aimed at alleviating the pressure of population increases must include birth control methods. Further, policies must be developed and implemented to reduce the disparities in the political, economic, social and cultural activities between Seoul and the rest of the nation.

The final major part "Social Development," includes: two

analyses of popular participation in community development viz., Saemaeul Undong; projections of the demand-supply relationship of medical doctors; conceptions of distributive justice and equity; and a discussion of the Bureau of Audit and Inspection and its role in social development. According to Young Pyoung Kim through the launching of the Saemael Undong (New Village Movement) in 1971, the rural sector in Korea has experienced extraordinary changes in living standards and in social arrangements. Despite the absence of elaborate formal structures for rural interest articulation, the authoritarian bureaucracy, traditionally responsive only to commands from above rather than to demands from below, was induced to act in response to popular demands. In order to mobilize local people in the development program, new dynamics were infused in rural settings through the utilization of grass roots associations, viz., village organizations that have long been a part of rural cooperation in the nation. Thus the example of the Samaeul Undong provides us with information regarding the design of rural programs, the incentives to stimulate villagers, the flow of data regarding program management and the relationship between an authoritarian bureaucracy and its clients. In Joung Whang identifies and analyzes the factors and conditions underlying popular participation in the process of planning and implementing Samaeul Undong activities. Two important determinants of the extent of community participation are; the level at which participation is activated and the approach to the initiation of participation. According to the author four major factors have an impact on community participation in rural development;

"(1) individual motivation; (2) the role of leadership in responding to people's needs and in providing support for development projects; (3) the development of grass roots organizations which can accomodate individual motivation at the community level and properly aggregate and articulate community interests; and (4) government mobilization of both human and material resources for community change and regional development."

Young Sup Kim address the demand-supply relationship of medical doctors in the Republic of Korea forecasts a radical change from a heavy surplus in the early 1980s to an alarming shortage by the year 1966 and a critical shortage only five years later (2001). Current public policies and social conditions without any amendation or fluctuation will produce the critical shortage. Therefore, the forcasts of supply and demand for health care manpower must be made well in advance owing to the inelasticity of the supply of medical manpower.

Yong Duck Jung and Gilbert B. Siegel posit that the Korean concern with equity is related to one of three specific popularly held conceptions of distributive justice, namely, egalitarian, meritarian, and a needs-based conception of distributive justice. Their results indicate that the Korean people do not consider egalitarianism as a criterion of justice for economic distribution. Instead they support a meritarian principle of distributive justice by selecting occupational and educational attainment, work experience and capital investment as the major criteria for an individual's earnings. The choice of the meritarian principle however has profound consequences regarding governmental intervention in the economy and a shift to a free market oriented system. This drastic transformation must be accompained by measures to secure free competition and equal opportunities. Additional requirements include: elimination of political and administrative corruption and favoritism and the equalization of opportunities between large and small corporations and between employers and employees. Finally, Myoung Soo Kim examines the Bureau of Audit and Inspection of Korea and its auditing practices as they relate to social development. Through a diagnostic approach he suggests the BAI's role in social development can be improved by means of program evaluation and social indicators. Direct evluation of social policies and programs necessitate the use of social indicators when monitoring the conditions of various social sectors in order to pinpoint a particular sector in directing/auditing efforts and when measuring the extent to which the objectives of a social policy of program have been achieved.

Bun Woong Kim
David S. Bell, Jr.
Chong Bum Lee

Part One

Dilemmas of Development

1
Bureaucratic Elitism and
Democratic Development in Korea?

Bun Woong Kim and David S. Bell, Jr.

Korea politics and administration manifest the historical stamp of Korean political culture characterized by bureaucratic elitism and political-administrative centralism. The Korean political culture has been and still is influenced by the historical residues of Confucianism, Buddhism, Taoism, and by a high degree of ethnic homogeneity that disposes most Koreans, especially the masses to a submissive authoritarian political psychology that tends to legitimize the moral authority of the upper starta.

Traditionally, Korean public policy has been exclusively viewed as the preferences and values of the governing elite solely. The non-participatory Korean masses have long been psychologically oriented toward powerful leadership by the elite and a centralized hierarchical bureaucracy. Thus, a highly centralized elitist administration typifies the recurrent institutional essence of Korean political tradition. Despite the trauma of Westernization in recent centuries, the core values of the Korean political culture have not been substantially altered by cross-cultural fertilization. Western patterns of liberal pluralistic ideals have had some acculturative impact upon the Korean elite; however, as yet the elite political culture remains highly authoritarian and still oriented toward exclusive decision-making by a centralized elitist government.

The contemporary Korean bureaucracy is a complex fusion of Korean cultural patterns and public administration practices adopted from abroad. Chong Bum Lee has used "indigenization" to describe the forces impacting upon contemporary Korean administration. Indigenization, he states, is:

". . .the process whereby the Western science of public administration is introduced into Korean culture and takes on a new form through interactions with the existing concepts and practices in the area of public administration as well as with overall Korean cultural patterns, which leads to changes and assimilation."[1]

Indigenization, therefore, is the process of establishing a new highly adaptive system of thought and behavior which accurately reflects the social dynamics of the indigenous culture.

Korean administrative culture has been described and compared to its Western counterpart by Korean scholars in several recent publications.[2] They have concluded that Korean bureacratic change will not likely follow the developmentalist model prevalent in the West because its predominant political pattern is culturally alien to Western pluralism—democratic pluralism. However, it must be noted that the development of an indigenous theory of bureaucratic change will not obviate what Robert Dahl has labeled:

". . .the dilemma of organizational autonomy and control. Satisfactory solutions-much less ideal ones-elude both theory and practice in all technologically advanced countries. . .governed by authoritative regimes, pressures for organizational autonomy are like coiled springs precariously restrained by the counterforce of the state and ready to unwind whenever the system is jolted."[3]

Western scholars have argued that pluralist politics is the best model

1. Chong Bum Lee, "Prolegomenon to the Indigenization of Public Administration," in Bun Woong Kim and Wha Joon Rho, eds., *Korean Public Bureaucracy* (Seoul: Kyobo Publishing, Inc., 1982), p.636.

2. Wan Ki Paik, *Korean Administrative Culture* (Seoul: Korea University Press, 1981). Bun Woong Kim and Wha Joon Rho, *Korean Public Bureaucracy*, op. cit., Part II-"Administrative Culture," p.64-17. Woon Tai Kim, et al., *Korean Politico-Administrative System* (Seoul: Park-Young-Sa, 1981). Changsoo Lee, *Modernization of Korea and Impact of the West* (Los Angeles: University of Southern California, 1981). Pyong Choon Hahm, "Toward a New Theory of Korean Politics: A Reexamination of Traditional Factors," in Edward R. Wight, ed., *Korean Politics in Transition* (Seattle: University of Washington Press, 1975), pp.321-356. See also, Wha Joon Rho, "The Transfer of Knowledge in Korean Public Administration," *The Journal of East Asian Affairs*, Vol. II, No. 2, pp.375-389. See also Jong S. Jun, "Korean Public Administration: Education and Research," *International Review of Administrative Science*, No.4, 1983, pp. 413-420. Bun Woong Kim and Wha Joon Rho, eds., *Korean Public Bureaucracy* (Seoul: Kyobo Publishing, Inc., 1982). Byung Young Ahn, "Self-Referentiality in the Study of Korean Public Administration," *The Korean Political Science Review*, Vol. 13, 1979, pp. 49-66. Suk Choon Cho, "Forward," *Korean Public Administration Review*, Vol. 15, 1981, pp.i-ii.

3. Robert A. Dahl, *Dilemmas of Pluralist Democracy: Autonomy vs. Control* (New Haven: Yale University Press, 1982), p. 3.

for political and administrative development in developing nations. A working definition of pluralism is a model polity diffusing socio-political power as widely as possible throughout the society. As an ideal pluralism has been combined with "liberal-participatory" democracy, and as a public administrative system, it has merit as a means of achieving incremental change based on longterm stability. However pluralist solutions may be inapplicable to the Korean dicision-making arena because of prevasiveness of an authoritarian political culture.

Since the Republic of Korea's independence in 1945, the Western pluralist model has had a far-reaching impact on the establishment of the formal institutional framework of the Korean government. Beyond the formal structures, however, the impact has been minimal and bureaucratic elitism, perhaps more accurately stated as paralytic centripetalism, rather than democratic pluralism persists in public policy-making. We may ascribe this to the lack of socio-cultural preconditions of pluralism. The authoritarian political tradition of Korea does not nurture such pluralistic prerequisites as: 1) viable competition among individuals, elites or groups: 2) opportunities for individuals and organizations to gain input access to the decision-making process: 3) organizational mediation between elites and masses: 4) viable instruments of mass participation in political decisions such as elections and other media of influence and access: 5) democratic consensus based on "democratic creed."[4] Korea's drift to authoritarian government therefore should be viewed in part as historical-cultural determinism and in part by the absence of the pluralistic prerequisites.

The most important factor in pluralism, Tocqueville believed, was widespread individual-in-group participation in politics. In fact, however, contemporary empirical studies reveal that only a small minority of citizens, mostly from the upper socio-economic strata participate actively in American political parties and interest groups. Even the character of the voluntary associations celebrated by Tocqueville has been significantly altered by the emergence of large-scale hierarchical organizations.[5]

Critiques, of pluralist theory tend to start by noting that the gap between pluralist rhetoric and pluralist practice, and the need to revise some features of the pluralist ideal itself. C. Wright Mills launched·

---

4. Robert Presthus, "The Pluralist Framework," in Henry S. Kariel, ed., *Frontiers of Democratic Theory* (New York: Random House, 1970), pp. 289-291.

5. *William Connolly, "The Chalenge to Pluralist Theory," in William Connolly, ed., The Bias of Pluralism* (New York: Atherton Press, 1969), p.7.

a polemical critique, the class bias of pluralist theory. Mills argued that in the United States political power had become nationalized and concentrated in one inter-related economic, military, scientific-technical, and intellectual "power elite." Moreover, the pluralist system of decision-making was significantly biased toward the concerns and priorities of international corporate capitalism.[6] Henry Kariel pointed to the oligarchical tendencies of large scale organizations which function both as interest groups influencing governmental policy and as agencies making policy of great public consequence. In particular, he stated that pluralism under conditions of large scale technology conflicts with the principle of constitutional democracy.[7] Theodore Lowi emphasized the failure of interest group liberalism arguing that pluralist theory today militates against the idea of a separate government because a separate government violates the basic principle of the autonomous society; and the concluded that in the United States, the new liberal public philosophy-interest group liberalism-was corrupted by the fallacies of its primary intellectual component of pluralism.[8] William Connolly explained the bias of pluralism as:

"Pluralist politics today is one dimensional. Not only are the issues generated by competing groups constrained by established values and expectations or ideological constraints, but contemporary social structure encourages groups to organize around occupational categories while inhibiting effective political organization on the basis of other considerations. These structural constraints reinforce rather than mitigate existing ideological constraints."[9]

He added that one dimensional pluralist politics suppressed the exploration of alternatives by proliferating issues within a narrow range of concerns.

The theoretical-empirical weakness of pluralism as a model democratic ideology may help explain its dysfunctional consequences for a developing polity. Under certain pluralistic politics may even have dysfunctional effects on the rate of national development.[10] Perhaps the cultural constraints so salient in the psychocultural

---

6. C. Wright Mills, *The Power Elite* (New York: Oxford University Press, 1956), pp. 5-25.
7. Henry S. Kariel, *The Decline of American Pluralism* (Stanford: Standford University Press, 1961), pp. 3-4.
8. Theodore Lowi, *The End of Liberalism* (New York: Norton & Co., 1969), pp. 46-52.
9. William Connolly, "The Challenge to the Pluralist Theory," op. cit., p. 17.
10. Mancur Olson, *The Rise and Decline of Nations* (New Haven: Yale University Press, 1982), p. 75 and p. 150.

characteristics of the Korean people may not suppot the preconditions assumed to be necessary for pluralist-democratic government.
The unusually cohesive Korean political culture, based on a
remarkably homogenous society, does not condition environmental
time-space for the fragmentation of power or the competitive balance
of power between interest groups. The absence of natural cleavages
is not consistant with an "equilibrium" model of diverse political
groupings in balance.[11]

The elite-mass class division of Korean society tends to support
a political system maintained by domination, regulation, and not by
pluralist interest group balancing. The high degree of political cen-
tralism/or authority imposes elitist made policy upon the different
strata of the masses. Some other persistent ideological/ecological constraints in postwar Korean government also inhibit pluralistic prospects for political and socioeconomic development. These include:
1) a narrow range of individual political freedom; 2) executive
dominance of the bureaucracy, legislature and the judiciary; 3) limitations on the role and function of political parties; 4) increased role
of the military in politics; 5) the security threat from North Korea;
and 6) national planning for rapid economic growth.[12] In addition,
the Republic of Korea confronts universal dilemmas of nation-building
such as the centrifugal forces of familial ties, psychopolitical opposi-
tionalism, and other problems caused, in part, by the influence of
Western ideologies and institutions. The gradual, incremental nature
of the pluralist model with its ideal of popular participation in public
policy making may not facilitate political stability or socioeconomic
development in Korea.

Joseph LaPalombara argued that the concept of modern or modernity carries with it culture-bound assumptions of Western determinism
positing a unilinear evolution historically traceable to the social Dar-
winist model of development. He suggested that ... given certain national developments a bureaucracy that does not fully conform to
democratic norms may be more effective in bringing about certain
kinds of change than one that does manifest such conformity.[13] Fred

11. The equilibrium model is characterized by a balanced adjustment of interests that provide conditions favorable to stable government, and that tends to associate liberal democracy
with pluralism. Its antithesis is the "conflict" model. See Leo Kuper and M.G. Smith,
Pluralism in Africa, (Berkeley: University of California Press, 1969), pp. 8-15.

12. David C. Cole and Princeton N. Lyman, *Korean Development: The Interplay of Politics and
Economics* (Cambridge: Harvard University Press, 1971), pp. 240-254. See also Bae Ho
Hahn, "The Authority Structure of Korean Politics," in Edward R. Wright, ed., *Korean
Politics in Transition,* op. cit., pp. 289-319.

13. Joseph LaPalombara, "Bureaucracy and Political Development: Notes, Queries and Dilemmas," in Joseph LaPalombara, *Bureaucracy and Political Development* (Princeton: Princeton
University Press, 1963), p. 55.

Riggs advanced a similar concern.

". . .the developmental problems of the new states should be examined in their own terms, and not as possible arenas for the importation of methods and solutions which have proved useful to other countries facing a different set of problems. It is just as fallacious to think that transitional countries can or should take over intact the latest political and administrative techniques of the most developed countries as to think that they should go through the same stages of change as were experienced in the eighteenth or nineteenth century by Western nations."[14]

The Korean bureaucratic elite, a bureaucracy that clearly does not conform to democratic norms, warrants consideration as an effective instrument in facilitating economic and social developmental objectives. There are several significant ecological changes in the social-physical environment which may help in understanding how bureaucratic elitism assists development. These ecological changes are: 1) population increases and demographic mobility; 2) the impact of the Korean War on political institutions and political consciousness; 3) the effect of economic inflation on political regimes; 4) the expansion of education, urbanization, and the size and status of the military; 5) institutional changes, i.e., the growth of formal organizations, and the growth of occupational specialization; and 6) ideological changes bringing with them a positive new view of democratic ideals.[15] Widespread ecological change has had significant effects on traditional Korean social structure such as the proliferation of what Suzanne Keller termed "strategic elites" replacing to some extent, the ruling classes of the Japanese colonial period 1910-1945. According to Keller, the term "strategic elites" refers to a minority of individuals designated to serve a collectivity in a socially valued way. Their origin lies in the complex heterogeneity of modern societies-age, sex, ethnicity, skills, strength and division of labor.[16]

However, the bureaucratic elite impedes the development of

14. Fred W. Riggs, "Bureaucrats and Political Development: A Paradoxical View," in Joseph LaPalombara, *Bureaucracy and Political Development,* op. cit., p.167.
15. Hahn Been Lee, *Korea: Time, Change and Administration* (Honolulu: East-West Center Press, 1968), pp.54-68. See also the psychocultural perceptions found in Lorand B. Szalay and Rita Mae Kelly, "Political Ideology and Subjective Culture: Conceptualization and Empirical Assessment," *American Political Science Review, Vol. 76, 1982, pp.585-602.*
16. *Suzanne Keller, Beyond the Ruling Class: Strategic Elites in Modern Society* (New York: Random House, 1963).

democratic objectives. The new Korean elites tend to base their elitism on the assumption that the masses are not yet democratically acculturated and therefore incapable of making any viable national policy judgements.[17] Koreans "perceive democracy and politics in close relationship to some high ideals and principles rather than to institutionalized procedures for expressing the people's will or free choice."[18] As a consequence, public policy making is generally considered to be the exclusive domain of a few select and experienced leaders. However it seems culturally conceivable that the present anti-democratic bureaucratic elitism might become what has been termed "democratic elitism" operating in a quasi-democratic institutional framework.[19]   According to Joseph Schumpeter, democracy may be defined as elite competition, presuming that "the democratic method is the institutional arrangement for arriving at political decisions in which ... individuals acquire the power to decide by means of competitive struggle for the people's vote.[20] Thus, according to Schumpeter," ... democracy means only that the people have the opportunity of accepting or refusing the men who are to rule them ... "implying" ... government approved by the people ... "instead of" ... government by the people."[21]

The democratic elitist contends that elites must become the chief guadians of the system, viewing the political passivity of the people not as an element of democratic malfunctioning, but as a necessary condition for allowing for the creative functioning of the elite.

:efore the business of making important decisions and policies ie exclusive domain of the elites after the masses select the elites.

Korea, a great expansion of governmental institutions has taken place during the last four decades. Neverthless, by the early 1980s most sectors of the Korean polity appear to be unable to perform self-governing responsibilities. In fact, it seems that Korean political culture necessitates administrative centralization and collectivism from the core or strategic elite to maintain socio-political stability as modernization proceeds. Thus the result is that all important decisions are

---

17. B.E. Woo and C.L. Kim, "Intra-Elite Cleavage in the Korean National Assembly," *Asian Survey*, Vol. XI., No. 6, 1971, p. 55.
18. Lorand B. Szalay and Rita Mae Kelly, "Political Ideology and Subjective Culture," op. cit., p. 596.
19. A major factor that distinguishes authoritarian and democratic elitism is" ...the provision for limited, peaceful competition among members of the elite for the formal positions of leadership within the system, "Jack L. Walker, "A Critique of the Elitist Theory of Democracy," *American Political Science Review*, Vol. IX, No. 2, June 1966, p. 286.
20. Joseph A. Schumpeter, *Capitalism, Socialism, and Democracy* (New York: Harper & Row, 1975), p. 269.
21. Ibid., pp.284-285.

made unilaterally at the highest levels, viz., Presidential and ministerial, and all public employees are exhorted to work for the accomplishment of the collective objective. Jong Sup Jun states that:

". . .implementing the developmental goals, the government has achieved a great deal by appearing to the people to act cohesively in the national interest. Once administrative orders are given from the top echelon, strict obedience is expected without questions or criticisms. Since the public employees are always told that to do, it is easier for them to follow orders rather than reasoning; in case of possible failure of administrative directives, they don't have to be blamed for their disobedience or irresponsibility."[22]

This, of course, underestimates the potential conbributions of all employees below the top echelon, produces passive behavior, overemphasizes the vertical consciousness of bureaucrats and reinforces the exclusivity of the governing elite.

The present governing elite roles based upon the political passivity of the Korean masses may facilitate effective bureaucratic intervention in the economic and social areas but impedes the creation of autonomous centers of decision-making authority in the developmental process-the democratic/political area. The contemporary Korean polity has no non-bureaucratic centers capable of subjecting bureaucrats to political oversight. Korean politics and administration in the 1980s manifests bureaucratic elitism and paralytic centripetalism which gives little encouragement to any projection of democratic development. The overwhelming moral and political predominance of the elitist culture over the masses has not been conducive to the evolution of pluralist participatory democracy.

---

22. Jong Sup Jun, "The Paradoxes of Development: Problems of Korea's Transformation," Paper for the 1982 ASPA National Conference, March 21-25, Honolulu, p. 17.

2

The Political Economy of Korean Development under The Park Government

Gerald E. Caiden and Yong Duck Jung

Independence has been costly to many of the new nations who do not export oil. They have exchanged one set of autocrats for another and have suffered chronic political instability and economic deprivation. They have been split asunder by communal conflicts. Their dreams of national resurgence have been replaced by nightmares of external invasion and internal fragmentation. Contemporary events have not been at all kind to them. Korea is a case in point. It has been split into two separate identities: ideologically opposite and fearful invasion by the other; each reliant on a super power patron and diverting scarce resources to extensive military and internal security forces; and each mindful of the fate of other states similarly split. But here the resemblance between the two Koreas ends, for South Korea has far outstripped its northern neighbor in economic development. Indeed, it is one of the few nations which are not oil exporters that has been economically successful enough to be depicted (like Iran and Saudi Arabia) as a dependable ally of the United States: "dynamic, stable, forward-looking, economically progressive, and militarily strong, or at least potentially so."[1]

In less than two decades, the Republic of Korea was transformed from a marginally subsistent agricultural economy into a viable industrial power. After the launching of the First Economic Development Plan in 1961, it maintained an annual growth rate of 10 percent in real GNP with 17 percent annual growth in its industrial sector until the 1980 recession. As a result, it became a leading exporter

---

1. J. Kelly, "Of Valuable Oil and Worhless Policies" *Encounter*, June 1979, quoted by P. Lubin, "The Second Pillar of Ignorance," *The New Republic*, December 22, 1979, p. 20.

of manufactured goods, something remarkable for a small country with few natural resources. This achievement was assisted in part by international economic conditions which favored South Korea's export development strategy and by a well disciplined, literate people willing to work for relatively little reward. It had also been shaped by deliberate government planning and control, a prime example of directed modernization. Our intention is to review South Korean development concept and strategies, assess the role of government in effecting rapid economic growth, and examine the political and social trade-offs entailed in that directed development during the Park government.

Development Concepts and Strategies

In the formative years of the Republic of Korea before the Park government, issues such as autonomy, military strength, foreign assistance, and reunification necessarily dominated its politics. Even so, by the late 1950s, there was an obvious contrast between low living standards and massive, well-publicized aid which had "changed the basic character of the economy, creating new sources of wealth, new opportunities, and new problems."[2]

Dissatisfaction with the Rhee regime therefore focused more and more on his seemingly fruitless references to early reunification and his preoccupation with the preservation of his own power, while following policies and practices to the detriment of sound development programs and more honest and productive use of aid funds.[3]

The contrast cause enough, even before the unexpected 1961 military coup ended democratic freedoms, for new emphasis to be placed on economic development. The Park regime condemned the incompetence, corruption, and "politics as usual" attitude of its predecessor, and criticized its failure to advance national development. The return to authoritarian government was justified as a preparation for embarking the country on a new course of economic resurgence.

For Park, economic resurgence was an integral part of a nationalistic vision of a more independent South Korea—more independent of

---

2. D. Cole and P. Lyman, *Korean Development: The Interplay of Politics and Economics* (Cambridge, Mass.: Harvard University Press, 1971) p.79.

3. Ibid.

American aid and control and more able to stand up against North Korea. Economic development and national self-sufficiency were the keys, not only to political stability in South Korea, but also to Park's own political success. Rhee's concern with post-war reconstruction, defense, and economic gradualism gave way to emphasis on economic growth through rapid industrialization based on the expansion of exports and the attraction of foreign investment. Defense costs stabilized. The policy of encouraging import substitution through the expansion of primary production was reversed by a more ''outward-looking'' strategy that encouraged capital formation. South Korea became a national workshop, manufacturing goods for export from imported materials, drawing on its abundant, cheap labor force and both domestic and foreign investment.

Throughout the Park government, this development strategy was pursued vigorously, almost single-mindedly, once the threat of invasion faded. It produced impressive results. South Korea's real GNP grew four fold from $5.4 billion in 1961 to $23.9 billion in 1977, with per capita GNP rising threefold in the same period from $82 to $864 in current prices. The GNP grew 10 percent yearly, with rates of 18 percent in mining and manufacturing, 10 percent in social overhead capital and services (capital used for social services rather than direct industrial investment), but only 4 percent in the primary sector (agricultural, forestry and fishing). Consequently, the structure of the economy was transformed. In 1961, 40 percent of the GNP was generated in the primary sector, 45 percent in social overhead capital and services, and 15 percent in the secondary sector—mining and manufacturing. The 1977 figures were 24 percent, 46 percent, and 30 percent respectively. Within the secondary sector, heavy industries outstripped light manufactures and textiles.[4]

The emphasis on exports was reflected in the jump of commodity exports (in current prices) from $43 million in 1961 to more than $10 billion in 1977—an annual growth rate of 41 percent—while the proportion of exports to GNP increased from 2 percent to 32 percent. The share of manufactured goods rose from 22 percent to almost 90 percent. Although traditional exports continued to expand in volume, commodities demanding sophisticated production techniques, such as industrial machinery, ships, precision instruments, metal products, and chemicals, gained prominence.[5] None of this would have occurred without heavy capital formation. Investment has grown from less than 17 percent of GNP to over 26 per-

---

4. Republic of Korea, Economic Planning Board, *Korea's Economic Development* (April, 1978):31.
5. Ibid., p.32.

cent, with private domestic savings rising from 6.3 percent to 19 percent compared with foreign capital which fluctuated in the 1960s between 9 and 10.5 percent and has since fallen to below 7.5 percent.[6] Without such substantial domestic savings, rapid economic growth would not have been possible and foreign indebtedness would have been much greater.

This remarkable quantitative expansion in economic growth was a mixed blessing. Because so much was crowded into so short a time, inflation was rampant. Because so much reliance was placed on imported materials, foreign technology, and foreign trade services, there was a substantial balance of payments deficit for much of the period between 1961 and 1977.[7] This, together with accumulating foreign debts on imported capital, increased South Korea's national indebtendness from $306 million in 1966 to nearly $9 billion in 1977. Further, the whole "outward-looking" strategy made the country more vulnerable to international economic and trade fluctuations. Continued dependence on American and Japanese investment aroused internal resentment against foreign domination and ownership. Finally, rapid economic growth was not paralleled by equitable income distribution. On the contrary, regional differences and economic inequalities became more visible and, in recent years, politically unsettling.

This issue of income distribution and equitable social development was not considered that important by the Park government. It seemed pointless to worry about the redistribution of wealth until there was something to distirbute. It was thought that rapid economic growth would lead to improved conditions for everyone according to the "trickle-down" process. In any event, capital formation and a high rate of domestic investment and savings necessitated initial inequities. Such sacrifices would eventually pay off. However, when rapid economic growth took place without any easing of sacrifices or change in government socio-economic policies, the issues of income distribution and social development assumed greater importance in the minds of the disadvantaged. Eventually these inequities precipitated several labor revolts in the latter years of the Park government, despite enforced prohibitions against organized labor.

In the absence of reliable statistics, sharp disagreement exists about the extent of income inequality and relative movements in income distribution during the Park government. Adelman claims that land reform, property losses during the invasion, and increased access to

---

6. Ibid., p.36.
7. Ibid., p.35.

education tended to balance things out somewhat and therefore South Korea has not followed Kuznets' hypothesis that, as a country develops, inequality first increases and then decreases. Adelman maintains that compared with many less developed countries (and even with some more developed ones) South Korean income distribution has been relatively equitable.[8] However, some critics, citing a plethora of discriminatory government policies, rampant inflation, and inequitable distribution of foreign aid and capital, maintain that inequality has worsened.[9] Regardless of the viewpoint, blatant inequalities have existed in South Korea and still do. The rich have grown richer while large segments of the poor have remained helplessly impoverished as a result of deliberate government policy. Sooner or later, the have-nots will demand that the government live up to its slogans of the 1960s and 1970s for "long awaited, socio-economic well-being." This is particularly true in view of the fact that increased mobility and the expansion of mass media have made it easier for the poor to compare their lot with the wealthy.

The Government's Role in Economic Growth

The rapid economic growth of the Republic of Korea during the Park government was engineered by a coalition of foreign interests and a domestic elite employing the authority and machinery of the modern administrative state on behalf of guided capitalism. A crucial element was successful central economic planning, rare among less developed countries. Although planning was attempted in the 1950s, it was not effective until Park's First Five-Year Economic Plan was instituted. This, and subsequent five-year plans, avoided the weaknesses that plagued national economic planning elsewhere.

Not only were sophisticated econometric input-output and programming models constructed to assist in the formulation of the plan, a number of their results were used in the plan itself ... the administrative and institutional mechanisms for planning and plan implementation were strongly influenced by the formal planning technology, and vice versa ... the planning process led to a vast improvement in the country's data base, which, in turn, led to improved planning models.

---

8. I. Adelman, *Income Distribution Policy in Developing Countries: A Case Study of Korea.* (Stanford, Cal.: Stanford University Press, 1978).
9. See *The Dong-A Ilbo,* Aug. 6, 1979 and M. Bae, "Adelman Ui Hankook Sodeuk Bunbae Pyongdeung Non Gum To" (An Analysis of Adelman's Equitable Thesis of Korean Income Distribution), *Kyongche Nonchip,* Vol. 15, No. 4 (December 1976): 423-37.

Last, but not least, the plan appears to be successfull ... very high growth ... has been maintained, the rate of inflation has decreased, and bottlenecks that were anticipated before the plan was adopted have been much less severe than one would have expected in the absence of planning ... The entire effort was achieved with a handful of young, energetic government officials and a small of Korean academicians and foreign advisors as prime movers.[10]

Although the planning placed emphasis on the encouragement of private enterprise, the actual lead was taken by the public sector. It grew at an annual rate of 14.5 percent, absorbing around 30 percent of gross investment and 40 percent of all financial intermediation,[11] well above the norm for mixed economies. Most of the public sector growth came from new enterprises established for development purposes and intended to overcome various limitations of the private sector. It was a pragmatic, not an ideological response to market imperfections.[12]

Rapid economic growth was the primary objective of the Park government. A wide range of measures was used to direct national resources to areas that would provide the largest growth. These measures included control of bank savings and loan rates to foster domestic investment, favorable treatment for commodity export firms, the attraction of foreign capital, strict currency control, and an increasingly favorable balance of payments. A pricing policy based on profitability "released the potential for achievement that previously was frustrated and dissipated ..."[13] and, unlike other less developed countries, national economic planning paid attention to trade policy and exchange rates.

Finally, the government tried to promote local entrepreneurship. In traditional Confucian society merchants had little status, the Park government, however, elevated them to national heroes. Park personally presided over monthly export promotion meetings where top government officials and business leaders discussed economic policies and problems to remove bureaucratic bottlenecks. The annual Export Day became a country-wide celebration of "nation building

---

10. I. Adelman (ed), *Practical Approachs to Development Planning: Korea's Second Five Year Plan* (Baltimore, Md.: The Johns Hopkins Press, 1969), pp.9-10.
11. L. Jones, *Public Enterprise and Economic Development: The Korean Case* (Seoul, South Korea: Korean Development Institute 1975), p. 203.
12. Ibid., p.204.
13. G. Brown, *Korean Ruling Policies and Economic Development in the 1960s* (Baltimore, Md.: The Johns Hopkins University Press, 1973), p.268.

through exports" with awards made to leading exporters.[14] The fierce competition over the prizes attested to the government's success in changing public attitudes toward business, economic enterprise, and exports. Observers attributed South Korea's economic success to the government's firm commitment to growth and its masterly management of the economy.[15] Nevertheless, some worried that the government's regulatory powers had become excessive,[16] that the public sector had grown too fast for comfort and included less efficient businesses,[17] and that the economy had outgrown the administrative capacity of economic regulation[18] They concluded that the government would have done better to remove itself from some peripheral areas in economic policy and rely more on the free market.

There was perhaps more to worry about in the reemergence of corruption and favoritism. After the military coup in 1961, steps were taken to reduce corruption and punish offending officials for "inefficiency" and "negligence." But the so-called "four scandals" in the Park government indicated that the campaign had limited success.[19] The dominance of government over economic policy had invited abuse. The government had power to put firms out of business by shutting off their credit. It could keep them out of some fields or force them into others through its control of investment funds. Under these circumstances, officials were tempted to extract forced payments or exercise favoritism. Businessmen complained that they had to pay hidden taxes in the form of donations to the Blue House (South Korea's Presidential residence). The Samsung group, one of a number of holding companies with diverse interests, complained about favoritism in awarding major government contracts, claiming that "it is more important to be a good lobbyist than a good manager."[20] Many peo-

---

14. N. Pearlstine, "How South Korea Surprised The World," *Forbes,* (April 30, 1979): *53-61.*
15. Ibid. See also, L. Wade and B. Kim, *Economic Development of South Korea: The Political Economy of Success* (New York: Praeger, 1978).
16. J. Kim, "Recent Trends in the Government's Management of the Economy," in E. Wright (ed), *Korean Politics in Transition* (Seattle, Wash.: University of Washington Press, 1975), pp.252-82.
17. S. Han, "Saehae Yesan Kwa Chaecheong Paengchang Ui Moonchechom" *Shin Dong-A,* pp.90-101.
18. S. Cho, "Kyongche Sungchang: 1953-76," in H. Lee and T. Kwon, (eds.), *Han kook Sahoe,* Vol. 1 (Seoul, South Korea: Seoul National University, 1978), pp. 197-238.
19. The "four scandals" of the Park government are familiar to every South Korean. The first was the rigging of the stock market; the secnd involved the taking of excessive profits on a transaction for imported taxicabs; the third concerned the construction of an exclusive resort, known as Walker Hill, with foreign exchange funds that had been diverted from their original purposes; and the fourth involved the import of illegal pinball machines. For a more detailed discussion, see Han Na Bok, "South Korea: Junta's Pledge Comes True? *"Far Eastern Economic Review* (March 21, 1963): 611.
20. Pearlstine, "How South Korea Surprised the World,": 57-60.

ple felt that the new riches were obtained through corruption, perhaps an inevitable reaction in a get-rich-quick economy. The Daewoo group is an example of how fast a fortune can be amassed. Begun in 1967 with $18,000 and seven employees, with ten years it had a $2 billion business with over 60,000 employees. The Yulsan scandal seemed to confirm popular suspicions. The head of the Yulsan group of companies, Shin Sun Ho, illegally obtained $300 million in loans through the influence of friends in government to finance exports. After he went bankrupt, the government suddenly replaced the top executives of ten large government-controlled banks, but no formal charges were ever made and no one was prosecuted.[21]

This raises the question of the political and social costs of rapid economic growth favoring the business elite. The political stability of Korea was deceptive. It was achieved, in part, through political restrictions involving the denial of basic human rights, the suppression of representative institutions, severe limitations on political expression, the complete abrogation of industrial rights, and the aggrandizement of strong central controls in the military and civil bureaucracies.

Though there are exceptions, one seems naturally led to the conclusion that there is virtually wholesale repression of all basic human righst of the citizenry; that political imprisonments work, are frequent and numerous; that torture is an inseparable consequence of imprisonment; that prolonged detention incommunicado is the norm; and that political execution is the ultimate result of political imprisonment. Articles and comments on this aspect of the government in South Korea normally refer to the imprisonment and harassment of a former President of the Republic; the nation's leading poet; a Catholic bishop; a political opponent of President Park and numerous students, professors, and journalists, etc. That there have been abuses of power and gross miscarriages of justice in South Korea to the extreme detriment of some of its citizens is undeniably clear. However, it also seems undeniably clear, and equally important to note, that the government and its President have also frequently been the subject of reporting that is lacking in objectivity, or that is emotional, or that is distorted.[22]

Even so, the Park government was undeniably repressive. Such

21. W. Chapman, "South Koreans Uneasy with Changes Spawned by New Wealth," *The Washington Post* June 13, 1979, pp. A19, A22.
22. Callaway, *Korea: Future Problems, Future Policies,* National Security Affairs Monograph 77-3 (Washington, D.C.: National Defense University Directorate, Feb. 1977), p. 34.

repression was justified by public leaders who insisted that political stability was absolutely imperative for rapid economic growth and that "the temporary necessity of restricting human rights" would eventually work to the benefit of "democracy, freedom, and prosperity tomorrow."

Under the 1972 *Yushin* Constitution, basic rights and freedoms were subject to restriction when necessary, "in order to maintain public order, public welfare, or national serenity." Fear of a North Korean invasion was frequently invoked to justify such restictions on political freedom although there was little detectable subversive activity in South Korea and no apparent attempt to form an anti-capitalist party. Disorders which disrupted political calm toward the close of the Park government were aimed not at upsetting social stability and national integrity but at protesting political repression. The Park government and its predecessors had failed to build a secure and influential middle class, to develop an effective, decentralized, and democratic administrative structure and to permit mass participation in public affairs.

In order to satisfy basic needs, supply management is not enough. It is possible to envisage a perfect delivery system of basic needs, goods, and services that would resemble a zoo or a prison. It is in the area of 'demand management' that strong cooperative or local community organizations have an important role to play.... The success achieved by the Chinese, the Japanese, and the Israelis in meeting the basic needs of most of their populations within a brief period illustrates that this goal can be attained in a wide variety of political systems. These experiences also show how important broad-based participation at the local level can be for articulating the demand for meeting basic needs and for the efficient management of the services ministering to these needs. They show that representative local bodies can minimize waste, handle maintenance and also limit the amount of benefits going to the privileged groups.[23]

The Park government concentrated on supply management and neglected demand management, which in the end was its undoing.

23. P. Streeton and S. Burki, "Basic Needs: Some Issues," *World Development*, Vol. 6, No. 3, (March 1978): 411-21.

Toward Wider Political Participation

The Park government sacrificed political participation for economic wealth. In the short term, this policy of national development was highly successful. The economy was transformed. Huge capital accumulation occurred. Sizable personal fortunes were made by the business elite. Entrepreneurship was well rewarded and became eminently respectable. Strong economic performance strengthened national autonomy and made the Republic of Korea a force to be reckoned with in Asian politics. Yet as the economic gap between North and South Korea widened, the Republic became an increasingly desirable prize to capture, should its international support decline. It also became increasingly vulnerable internally as the Park government continued to favor rapid economic growth over political development and it failed to deal with such structural weaknesses as inflation, corruption, and alienation between privileged rich and repressed poor.

Understandably, the Park government could not accede to wider political representation. To have done so would have challenged, if not reversed, Park's development strategy. The restoration of democratic freedoms would have brought demands for a fairer distribution of new wealth, a reduction in the high rate of capital investment in favor of a higher rate of personal consumption, and the establishment of a welfare state entailing economic concessions by the wealthy to the poverty-stricken. It would have slowed economic growth, diverted production to domestic rather than export needs, and possibly reduced Korea's attractiveness to foreign investors. South Korea would probably have resembled Singapore more than Taiwan, for sooner or later labor organizations would have formed and attracted a large political following in opposition to privileged business interests. As voter turnout increased, more persons from the lower social classes would have exercised their right to vote and more pressure would have been exerted on them to vote for representatives of their group. As assemblies became more representative of the total population, so the government would have been expected to reduce inequalities in Korean society. Quite possibly, more militant or radical parties would have formed to vie for egalitarian policies. Among them would have been socialists and communists who might have advocated reunification and proved an international embarrassment, if not an actual security risk. None of this came to pass. The Park government, perhaps envisioning such possibilities, made no political concessions.

Nor did it make many economic concessions. The repressive

dictatorship claimed that it would use the administrative state to fashion "guided capitalism" in which, according to the First Five Year Economic Plan," the principle of free enterprise and respect for the freedom and initiative of private enterprise will be observed, but in which the government will either directly participate or indirectly render guidance to basic industries and other important fields." Whatever its original intentions, the planning machinery and economic controls it created became in time economically inhibiting and administratively burdensome. The Park government managed the economy in its own best interest, to consolidate and expand its political grip, and to build up the personal status and wealth of its leaders. Consequently, strictly economic criteria of performance were often subordinated to political criteria of performance, resulting in the aggrandizement of the public sector, the protection of inefficient producers, and the institutionalization of corrupt practices.

If the Republic of Korea is to remain socially and politically stable, some reduction in political and economic authoritarianism is required. . Both the polity and the economy could do with an injection of freedom. Political repression should be eased with the restoration of democratic freedoms and representative institutions. Economic inhibitions should be relaxed with the restoration of the market system and fair competition. More importantly, a switch in development strategy is needed—away from economic growth for its own sake, irrespective of political and social costs, and toward social equity; a reduction in the gap between rich and poor; some redistribution of wealth; and the introduction of social security programs.

Not only can the country now afford a redirection of national efforts, but it can ill-afford to follow the policies of the Park government much longer. The continued maldistribution of wealth and favoring of the privileged over the needy will only exacerbate social tensions, provoke further unrest, and possibly even invite invasion. The grievances of the under-privileged are too justified to be ignored. Because much of the present inequality was engineered by the government, it can be reversed by government action. The quickest way to more equitable distribution would be through broader participation in government and the removal of existing restrictions on basic human rights and political freedom, which in turn would do much to check corruption and favoritism in Korean society.

Could popular participation succeed in a predominantly Confucian society such as that of South Korea? Wright is skeptical.

There seems, to be a large degree of acceptance of events inKorean society—social, personal, political, economic—with 'relatively' little questioning. They (Korean people) accept the Confucian dictum that "the people should follow established leadership without question, and should not be concerned about the knowledge necessary for the exercise of leadership." In Korea ... there is no real concept of the government as "servant of the people," though "lip service is paid to such an idea." In traditional terms it is "Government high, people low."[24]

Wright further recorded that some local leaders believed that the intellectual level of ordinary Koreans was not high, that they had little longrange perception, and were quite dependent on centralized authority. They concluded that "local initiative tends to be a concept fairly alien to most Korens."[25] Admittedly, the rural population, kin-oriented and Confucianist, has been the most conservative and resistant to social change but rural migration has eroded traditional culture. In 1950, over 80 percent of the population was rural but by the mid 1970s the figure was under 50 percent.[26] Further, higher literacy has improved the prospects for popular participation and if local initiative has been alien, it may have been due to lack of opportunity and government discouragement rather than lack of talent.

The Park government resisted political liberalization, fearing that it would probably increase political instability, reduce the power of the military, and encourage the emergence of socialist and communist parties. After all, other countries had not been able to make the transition peacefully or smoothly. They had gone from periods of political repression to periods of near chaos and back to periods of political repression. Similar considerations along with the current economic recession have so far prevented the new government from making more than token gestures to liberalization. With economic recovery, the time may be propitious to proceed with political and economic liberalization. A redirection of national development efforts would not end economic growth and might speed recovery. The Republic of Korea is still relatively poor. It still needs to grow economically and to maintain sufficient economic and political strength to deter aggression from its neighbors. The objective is not growth or redistribution but growth with redistribution. For this, domestic social stability is essential.

---

24. Wright, *Korean Politics in Transition,* p.7.
25. Ibid.
26. Callaway, *Korea: Future Problems,* p. 40.

3

The Development of Human Resources and Economic Growth in Korea

Dong Hyun Kim

I. Human Factors in Economic Growth

It is a matter for regret that, in the economic development plans that have been formulated or implanted in developing countries, insufficient importance has been given to the role of the human factor in economic growth. It is seldom realized that economic growth is not just a function of the accumulation of material, or of material inputs. Undoubtedly, there must be material inputs for maximizing production as well as the necessary infra-structure. But what emerges from a study of the economic history and an analysis of the economic growth of the developed countries is the fact that it is not possible to explain their economic growth merely in terms of the capital investment that has gone into their economies. A large fraction of the rise in income that has taken place is due to reasons other than capital investment or material inputs: and those reasons have been summed up by economists as what is called "the residual factor". This residual factor has subsequently become identified with what is now called the human factor. Human resources development is both an essential condition and a major determinant of economic growth. It is the human being who operates the economy, and uses the instruments of production and other material and natural facilities of production. He must have the knowledge, the skills, the physical, mental and emotional fitness, and the necessary motivation and discipline to get maximum advantage out of the facilities placed at his disposal by programmes of economic development. This connection may well be phrased as "the response ratio of the human factor to production opportunities."

Considering that the response ratio of the human factor is one of the major instruments for economic growth, it is legitimate to ask, what is the human factor? What determines the response ratio of the human factor to the production activities. What is it that determines the development of human resources? Obviously, human resources depend upon what is done with the young.

It is the child and the youth who constitute the raw materials for the talents which constitute the human factor in economic growth. It is the kind of training that we give them; it is the kind of opportunity that we give them; it is the kind of attitudes, skills, etc., that we are able to evoke among the children and youth that ultimately determine what kind of adults they grow up to be in terms of skills, in terms of talents, in terms of techniques, in terms of attitudes, and in terms of all the other factors, ponderable and imponderable, that make up what we call the ratio of human response to production opportunities. It is futile to tackle children and youth problems is isolation. These have to be treated as an integral, inseparable and vital part of the total national development programme. The separate treatment of children and youth in development planning has an obvious drawback. It is neither feasible nor desirable to divide a population into age groups and have separate plans for each. In any case, children and youth are not outside the development programmes but are equal beneficiaries of development elsewhere. If the parents' income rises, does not the child benefit? Does not its health problem become less acute? Does not its nutrition problem bcome less grave? Does not its education problem become less serious? Similarly, when development is taking place in agriculture, industry or transport, the interests of children are also being served. Therefore, I venture to suggest that investment in children and youth developmental programmes is not just a programme of social welfare, but is really analogous to investment in capital goods from the economic standpoint.

True, the period of gestation of this investment is long. In fact, almost all the major types of plant, machinery or material investment that so conspicuously impress people with their productivity, have long periods of gestation. In this respect, they all stand parallel to the period of gestation which is involved in children and youth development programmes, which are initiated to develop the adult into the kind of person who give a higher ratio of human response to production opportunities, note a smaller ratio. But I must add the warning that it is not the length of the gestation period by itself which brings about productivity and increase in yield. It is only when the length of the gestation period is combined with the development of production opportunities and the improvement of quality, that a long gestation period yields us larger results than the shorter period.

If this thesis is right that human resources development is esentially and fundamentally a part of economic development, then child and youth development becomes an instrument of economic development, not something which is to be taken up after economic development has been completed. In fact, child and youth development programmes of the appropriate character form an instrument for economic growth and therefore they have to be woven into the strategy of economic growth. They have got to form a part of development planning and not be set aside as something which can be taken up after economic development has been achieved. This is not the same as suggesting that all child and youth development programmes constitute factors whcih in their entirely are responsible for human rsources development in the narrow economic sense that I have used it. Like education, human resources development has two sides: it has a production and investment aspect, and a welfare aspect. One would not say that there should be no child and youth welfare programmes unless they stand a rigid and acid test of what they do to promote the development of human resources. There is always room and place for child and youth development programmes which constitute welfare. All the same, child and youth development programmes do constitute a fundamental element of human resources development and therefore of economic development: and attention must be paid to those aspects of child development which will bring about the kind of results that we are talking about.

Then, there is one more aspect of child and youth development programmes which perhaps has not received sufficient emphasis. We all agree that there must be equalization of opportunities and no widening of the gap between the income of the few and the income of the many. We want to bring about social justice in our distribution system, not only in terms of ultimate consumption, but also in terms of production opportunities. I suggest that child and youth development programming is one of the most effective ways of dealing with this distributional problem. Child and youth development programmes give opportunities to children to develop the potentials which they otherwise would not have achieved because of low parental income. Thus, child and youth developmental programmes constitute a very important non-violent distributional instrument and therefore are ethically and morally superior to other distributional instruments.

To sum up, child and youth development programmes have three aspects:

(1) The first is the aspect of investment and development of children in order that the adult may develop into an efficient human being

and have a high human response ratio to production opportunities.

(2) The second is the utilization of the child and youth development programme as a distributional tool.

(3) The third is the welfare aspect which also deserves attention, while one may vary one's emphasis, depending upon the stage of economic development one's country has reached, the constraint of resources, and other factors too numerous to mention, nevertheless all these factors have an immediate place in child and youth development programmes.

In sum, child and youth development should be integrated, dovetailed and absorbed into developmental programmes and into the developmental strategy. It should form part of economic and social development.

II. Social Welfare Services for Integrated Approach

The integrated approach implies that planning must be continuous and widely diffused process. Thus, it cannot be equated with the periodic elaboration of a national plan. On the contrary, an orientation towards planning and an effective planning discipline need to be disseminated throughout the multiplicity of agents who, from the central to the lowest local level, are engaged in making decisions affecting the direct delivery of services.

One way is to base it simply on the welfare-humanitarian aspects of the question: children with unsatisfied basic needs exist in great numbers and therefore efforts have to be directed towards the satisfaction of these needs.

Another alternative is to base the advocacy efforts by equating resources used for social purposes, including for children and youth, with investments, that is, with additions to the stock of capital of a given society or country. "Social development" planning becomes then human resource development planning. Planning for the delivery of services for children and youth becomes "young human resource development planning." An earlier definition of the approach is worth quoting:

Human resource development is the process of increasing the knowledge, the skills, and the capacities of all people in a society. In economic terms, it could be described as the accumulation of human capital and its effective investment in the development of an economy. In political terms, human resource development prepares people for adult participation in political processes, particularly a citizen in a democracy. From the social and cultural points of view, the development of human resources helps people to lead fuller and richer lives, less bound by tradition.[1]

This point of view is appealing, not least because it gives the impression of providing a unified focus on which to base developmental actions. However, it is also misleading because fundamentally, it represents atttempts to enlarge the concept of capital building, due to the recognition that a large part of the explanation of the economic growth of today's developed nations could not be explained in terms of inputs of physical capital only.

As a matter of fact, needs vary according to the stage of development of the child. These needs could be classified on a sectoral or functional basis, into different groups such as family care; environmental, social and cultural needs; health needs; nutritional needs; education and schooling needs; training needs for participation in economic life of the community, etc.

Needs vary not only by age groups but also by the circumstances in which children and youth are placed. These circumstances could be classified by sex (boys or girls); locale (urban or rural); socioeconomic strata (children of low-income families or high-income families, or children and youth in families of special categories, for example, tribal and underprivileged families which suffer from initial handicaps, etc.) and by special requirements (physically and mentally handicapped children or "gifted" children.

Each need would have to be analyzed, keeping in mind the types of ameliorative measures and the degree of the relative impact of these measures on the growth and development of the child in terms of physical, emotional, social and economic factors. Ameliorative measures for fulfilling the needs of children could be classified as follows:

a) Curative measures with the accent on the cure of overt disorders from normality.

b) Preventive measures which, if implemented beforehand, would make curative efforts either unnecessary or easier to succeed. These measures could also be considered as protective both in the social as well as the health sense.

c) Positive promotional measures, which relate to the over-all environment conducive to the development of the child.

---

1. Frederick Harbison and Charles A. Myers, *Education, Manpower and Economic Growth: Strategies of Human Resource Development,* (New York: McGraw Hill Series in International Development, 1964), p.2.

In actual terms, the advocacy of appropriate and increased attention to the specific needs of children and youth has to be put in terms of a combination of political and ideological, social justice, social change, and economic imperatives.

The political and ideological imperative is connected with the question of human rights. Thus, the United Nations Declaration of the Rights of the Child states that "the child shall enjoy protection, and shall be given opportunities and facilities, by law and by other means, to enable him to develop physically, mentally, morally, spiritually and socially in a healthy and normal manner and in conditions of freedom and dignity."[2] This is, of course, an over encompassing statement, but which has the important characteristic of being genuinely accepted by all societies as a general principle. Its major importance is that it justifies attention to the problemes of children and youth as an end in itself, independently of the functional values and permeates all advocacy planning efforts for children and youth.

The point made above does not imply a rating of the imperatives we have listed above. Thus, it is important to stress, as does Hans Singer, that "if development means the introduction of social change, children are the prime agents through which important cultural and normative changes can be brought about" and that "ultimately, it is the improvement in the quality, and the productivity of the next generation of producers which well enable the poor countries to reach to a higher level of economic activity."[3]

III. Current Situations in Korea

1. *Overview of Demographic Trends*

The population of Korea during the past twenty years has been characterized by rapid increase, geographic redistribution, and urbanization. Since the end of the Korean War, there has been a sharp decline in mortality unaccompanied by a commensurate decline in fertility. Table 1 presents recent trends in population size and growth rates. Although the intercensal rate of growth has been decreasing, the population will continue to grow substantially for some decades as a result of the age structure.

---

2. United Nations, *Declaration of the Rights of the Child.* Principle 2 (New York: United Nations, 1959).

3. Hans Singer, *Children in the Strategy of Development,* United Nations Center for Economic and Social Information, Executive Briefing Paper No. 6 (New York: United Nations, 1972), pp. 14-15.

Table 1: Total Populations as given in the Census of Korea,
1960—78 and Intercensal Growth Rates
(Population in thousands, Growth Rates in percentages)

Year	Population/a	Intercensal Growth Rate per Annum
1960 (December 1)	24,989	2.64
1966 (October 1)	29,160	1.87
1970 (October 1)	31,435	2.38
1975 (October 1)	34,681	3.40
1976 (October 1)	35,860	1.61
1977 (October 1)	36,436	1.60
1978 (October 1)	37,019	

/a Population as given in the censuses; no adjustment has been made for
underenumeration. Census figures exclude foreigners.

Source: Population Censuses of Korea, 1925—1970. Another figures are
from Economic Planning Board.

Sex and Age Structure

The percent distribution of the age-sex structure for Korea from
1955-1975 is presented in Table 2. Sex ratio for the total population
have remained in balance over the period, but the age specific sex
ratios reveal a considerable excess of males over females. This is a
marked contrast to the typical pattern of sex ratios which normally
reveals a predominance of males at birth which subsequently evens
out, showing only minor fluctuations until the older ages when the

Table 2: Percentage Distribution of the Population by Age and Sex
Composition as Given in the Censuses of Korea, 1960–1975

	Percentage Distribution														
	1960				1966				1970				1975		
			Sex				Sex				Sex				Sex
	Total	Males	Females	Ratio	Total	Males	Females	Ratio	Total	Males	Females	Ratio	Total	Males	Females	Ratio
0–4	14.2	14.5	13.9	105.3	15.4	15.8	14.9	107.3	13.73	14.13	13.33	106.8	12.7	13.2	12.2	109.4
5–9	15.1	15.6	14.6	107.4	15.8	16.3	15.3	107.6	14.42	14.89	13.94	107.6	12.7	13.0	12.3	107.5
10–14	11.3	11.8	10.8	110.4	12.3	12.6	12.0	107.2	13.98	14.42	13.54	107.3	12.9	13.3	12.5	107.9
15–19	9.5	10.0	9.1	110.1	9.3	9.5	9.0	106.9	9.82	9.97	9.68	103.8	12.4	12.7	12.0	107.1
20–24	9.1	9.4	8.9	106.5	7.9	8.2	7.6	109.9	8.03	8.23	7.82	106.1	8.9	9.0	8.7	104.7

Source: Economic Planning Board, Censuses of the Population, 1955-1970. The percentages for 1975 are based on the
Preliminary Release of the 1975 Population Census.

Table 3: Selected Demographic Measures of Changes in the Age Composition of the Korean Population: 1960–1978

	1960	1966	1970	1975	1976	1977	1978
Total	24,989	29,160	31,435	34,679	35,860	36,436	37,019
Ratio	100	100	100	100	100	100	100
age, 0–4	4,365	4,481	4,316	4,227	4,392	4,255	4,160
Ratio	17.5	15.4	13.7	12.2	12.2	11.7	11.2
age, 5–9	3,482	4,613	4,532	4,454	4,528	4,577	4,584
Ratio	13.9	15.8	14.4	12.8	12.6	12.6	12.4
age, 10–14	2,840	3,590	4,393	4,527	4,523	4,459	4,398
Ratio	11.4	12.2	14.0	13.1	12.6	12.2	11.9
age, 15–19	2,370	2,708	3,088	4,147	4,491	4,559	4,667
Ratio	9.48	9.3	9.8	12.0	12.5	12.5	12.6
age, 20–24	2,184	2,290	2,522	3,123			
Ratio	8.7	7.9	8.0	9.0			

Source: EPB, Bureau of Statistics, *Korea Statistical Yearbook*, 1978

differential male and female death rates result in a pronounced excess of women at the older ages. A number of explanations have been advanced to account for the predominance of males. In a society known for its strong son preference, there is probably underenumeration of females; parents are likely to be quit careful in recording their male children and less concerned with the accurate enumeration of their female offspring. In situations where the survival of an infant is threatened, it is possible that greater efforts would be expened to ensure the life of the male infant.

Table 3 summarizes some of the salient indicators of changes that have taken place in the age composition of the population over the past twenty years. The proportion of dependent children, aged 0-14, reached its peak in 1966 reflecting the impact of the post-war baby boom. The decline in the proportion 0-14 since 1966 represents a drop in fertility which can be attributed to a number of causes, among them the governments vigorous family planning program, which was inaugurated in 1961, a rising age at marriage, as well as the rapid urbanization which has taken place during the past ten years.

2. Health

Korea's rapid economic growth has been obtained in part by sacrificing development of social services—most notably social insurance, health care and housing. In contrast with many developing countries the government has committed very modest quantities of resources to these sectors. However, in spite of the apparent neglect of social development, Korea has made rather spectacular strides in improving health in particular. This contradiction is explainable by

two sets of facts. First, a substantial private health care sector exists
and second, the improvements in income per capita have contributed
substantially to the improvement of nutritional status, housing quality
and sanitation. The number of qualified physicians has quadrupl-
ed. There has been a five-fold increase in the quantity of sanitary
water supplied over this same fifteen years. The death rate attributable
to epidemics dropped from an average of 2.7% in the first half of
the period to less than .05% since 1971. Similarly, the estimated crude
death rate fell from a level of 13-15 per thousand population in the
early 1960s to 8-9 by 1970. These highly selected statistics strongly
suggest that substantial gains have been made in improving health
in spite of the modest scale of direct government initiatives; and it
might be added that this experience is throughly consistent with the
widespread belief that the environmental and nutritional improvements
that accompany economic development are highly signficiant factors
affecting health status.

Any aggregate level assessment of health conditions obviously masks
the tragedy of morbidity and mortality for victims. The impressive
accomplishments that Korea has made in dealing with its health problems are still overshadowed by considerable amounts of easily preven-
table disease. The scale of losses attributable to unnecessary disease
remains large and for the poor, particularly in rural areas, health problems are still of considerable dimensions. The rapid economic development of Korea and the parallel rises in per capita income are certain
to heighten intolerance to unnecessary disease and to produce still
more rapid increases in private health care expenditures. The policies
that are put into effect in anticipation of the growth in private demand for health services will substantially influence the productivity
of future private and public outlays. And finally, the development
of a national scheme of health insurance would have profound implications for the demand for health resources and for equitable access to care.

3. *Education*

From Table 3 it can be seen that the period of rapidly rising
numbers at primary school age is well past; these numbers will begin
to rise again only with the children of parents born in the baby boom
in the late 1980s. More details of the structure of the population of
school age are given in Table 4. They show how Korea already
benefits from age cohort sizes that differ very little between ages 6
and 18. In consequence, most new educational investment can be
directed to enlarging the proportion of the population enrolled in school

Table 4: 1975 Educational Enrollment Ratios By Age and Sex

Age	Males Educational Enrollment/a	Populations/b	% Population Females	Enrolled Educational Enrollement/a	Population	% Population Enrolled/b
6	408,525	469,676	87.0	377,387	440,738	85.6
7	455,927	456,722	97.6	417,127	430,129	97.0
8	456,842	453,663	100.8	430,766	422,450	102.0
9	457,988	456,760	100.3	427,528	424,935	100.6
10	469,469	453,047	103.6	432,451	420,656	102.8
11	479,739	469,264	102.2	447,932	432,889	103.5
12	340,559	488,511	69.7	290,035	451,395	64.3
13	404,696	483,473	83.7	305,612	449,171	68.0
14	404,667	490,282	82.5	305,612	456,497	66.9
15	333,035	497,845	66.9	241,777	462,702	52.3
16	256,400	474,148	54.1	176,902	440,321	40.2
17	207,545	446,443	46.5	138,436	416,296	33.3
18	137,558	420,772	32.7	72,326	394,818	18.3
19	71,684	400,803	17.9	33,329	380,121	8.8
20	52,412	381,470	13.7	23,907	361,802	6.6
21	38,496	338,858	11.4	16,368	316,958	5.2
22	25,051	310,917	8.1	9,200	290,349	3.2
23	16,984	288,898	5.9	3,498	279,632	1.3
24	9,721	251,282	3.9	1,382	255,256	0.6

Notes:

/a April 1

/b Mid-year estimate based on preliminary census data. There has been no adjustment for under-enumeration, which may explain the apparent discrepancies between observed enrollment and population size and primary school ages,

Source: Population Bureau of Statistics Economic Planning Board, *Korean Population Projection, 1975-1985.*

Enrollment: Ministry of Education, Korea *Statistical Yearbook of Education* 1975.

Table 5: Growth in Educational Enrollment

	Primary School				Secondary School						Tertiary School					
								General				Vocational				
Year	Total	% Rate of Increase	% Enrollment Rate	% Female	Total	% Enrollment Rate	% Female	Total	% Rate of Increase	Total	% Rate of Increase	Total	% Rate of Increase	Total	% Rate of Increase	% Female
1950	2,669,494	—	83	—	436,175	16	19	380,829	—	55,346	—	36,385	—			11
1960	3,621,267	3.1	96	45	875,249	29	26	749,500	7.0	125,749	8.6	101,041	10.8			17
1965	4,941,345	6.4	100	46	1,201,207	34	35	1,005,436	6.1	195,771	9.3	141,636	7.0			25
1970	5,749,301	2.2	97.0	48	1,935,192	41	38	1,634,175	10.2	301,017	9.0	201,436	7.9			24
1971	5,807,448	1.0	97.6	48	2,201,259		39	1,886,666	14.2	334,593	11.2	214,653	6.6			25
1972	5,775,880	-0.1	97.5	48	2,437,748		39	2,055,871	10.1	381,877	14.1	228,976	6.7			26
1973	5,692,285	-1.6	98.1	48	2,695,053		40	2,243,198	9.1	451,855	19.1	251,017	9.6			27
1974	5,618,768	-1.3	97.5	48	2,936,042		40	2,460,152	9.7	475,890	5.3	273,479	9.0			27
1975	5,599,074	-0.4	97.2	48	3,176,154		41	2,674,974	8.7	501,182	5.3	297,219	8.7			27

Source: Korea Ministry of Education, *Statistical Year Books of Education* and UNESCO *Year Books.*

and in raising expenditures per pupil.

The high enrollment rates (shown in Table 4) reflect an impressive growth of enrollment at all levels of education (Table 5). Growth after 1945 was dramatic; enrollments in primary school rose extremely rapidly and secondary and tertiary education systems were built up from virtually nothing. Primary education (six years) was made compulsory in 1949 and virtually full enrollment at that level had been achieved by the early 1960s. Since then the main growth point of the educational system has been in secondary education. In the 1960s the three-year middle schools grew particularly fast, and now provide a primarily academic education to a very substantial proportion of the 12-15 year age group. There remain only a few romote rural areas not yet reached by middle school.

In the last few years the most rapidly growing educational institutions have been at the higher secondary level. For several years before 1973, vocational school enrollments were growing much faster than those of general high schools. This trend has been dramatically reversed and general high schools are now growing much more rapidly. Between 1973 and 1975, enrollment in general high schools increased 57.7% (reflecting primarily the opening of several new schools); that in vocational high schools grew only by 8.8%. Although the children participating in this very rapid expansion were born during the post-war baby boom, the growth in enrollment has been much faster than in cohort size.

Kindergarten is the only existing formal educational institution for preschool children in Korea. Table 6 shows the number of institution and enrollment from 1970 through 1978.

Table 6: Number of Kindergartens and Enrollments

Year	Number of Kindergartens	Enrollments	Number of Teachers
1970	484	22,271	1,660
1971	512	22,207	1,694
1972	531	22,466	1,800
1973	548	25,339	1,880
1974	588	27,774	2,013
1975	611	32,032	2,153
1976	635	37,197	2,288
1977	665	41,866	2,415
1978	721	47,571	2,561

Source: Ministry of Education, 1978

Although the number of institutions and enrollment, as shown in Table 6, indicates a steady increase over the past years, it still remains at the beginning stage of preschool education. The enrollment rate among eligible children reached to the level of meager 2.8%, which clearly reveals that kindergarten education is only available for those from will-to-do family, who can afford high cost.

Table 7 provides the statistics regarding the geographical distributions of Kindergarten which indicates that a great majority are located in urban areas.

Table 7: Geographical Distribution of Kindergartens, 1978

Area	Number of Kindergartens	Number of Children
Seoul	242	19,052
Pusan	67	5,168
Kyŏnggi	87	4,461
Kangwŏn	37	1,678
Ch'ungbuk	18	947
Ch'ungnam	44	2,290
Ch'ŏnbuk	23	1,426
Ch'ŏnnam	40	2,048
Kyŏngbuk	100	6,657
Kyŏngnam	54	3,209
Ch'eju	9	635
Total	721	47,571

Source: Ministry of Education, 1978

The relatively low enrollment rate is the utmost problem in the present conditions of kindergarten education in Korea. For the past ten years, the rate of increase of kindergarten enrollment is 46%, while elementary and secondary schools showed an enrollment increase rate of 17.5% and 11.1% respectively. However, the fact that the kindergaten enrollment rate is 2.8% of the eligible population, is a good index of the limited opportunities for preschool education. It seems imperative that kindergarten education in Korea be given special attention in order to provide wider opportunities for preschool children.

4. Welfare Services

Viewed from a nation-wide perspective, the most urgent needs to be met in the field of social welfare are the basic physical needs of individuals and families. Important as they may be, social and emotional needs for human welfare are inevitably given lower priority. Thus most of the nation's resources are being used up at present for emergency and temporary care or survival needs, leaving little room

Table 8: Number of Institutions for Children and Inmates

Area	Number of Institutions	Number of Inmates
1970	430	42,155
1971	400	39,731
1972	376	34,469
1973	333	31,782
1974	323	30,921
1975	313	29,323
1976	307	27,896
1977	293	25,887
1978	271	23,805

Source: Ministry of Health and Social Affaris, 1978

Table 9: Juvenile delinquency

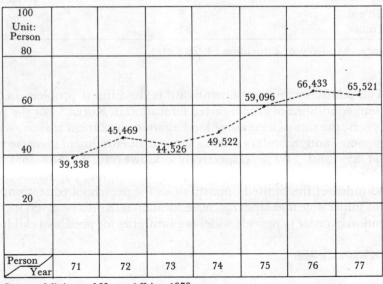

Source: Ministry of Home Affairs, 1978

for the long-term development of social services.

The following Table 8 shows a slightly declining trend in the number of institutions for children and inmates.

In addition to the orphaned, abandoned, and vagrant children, there are increasing numbers of juvenile deliquents (Table 9).

To help these children realize their potential abilities, vocational training (thereby securing job opportunities) and other constructive measures have been given serious consideration by the Government as well as voluntary agencies.

To carry out the welfare service programme benefiting children and youth, the following plans and programmes have been established:

(a) Study and guidance to promote child welfare.

To improve the welfare of children throughout the country, the National Child Welfare Committee was set up at the national level while at the city and/or provincial levels, Child Welfare Committees were organized. The functions of the Committees are to study, examine, and guide children with respect to their needs, as well as provide necessary services to pregnant women and their families.

(b) Child placement service.

The Government has put emphasis on foster-care placement and adoption, with the conviction that a child should be brought up in a healthy family atmosphere for normal growth and development. Foster-care placement is divided into three categories: paid foster care (care money paid), unpaid foster care, and employed foster care. Some foreign voluntary agencies are participating in this programme very actively.

(c) Guidance of juvenile delinquents and vagrants.

In order to guide and protect juvenile delinquents and vagrants, the Protective Countermeasure Committee for Children and Youth was organized in the Office of Prime Minister. On this Committee experts and scholars were also included. In dealing with this category of young persons, efforts are made to send them to their own homes under the guardianship of parents, or to assign them to institutional care or settlement projects, or, more often, to provide them with the necessary guidance.

(d) Programme for destitute families.

Measures taken by the Government to help destitute families include free relief programmes for the sick and aged, dependent children, and other handicapped persons. Secondly, there is an emergency help service through which various work-projects and self-help projects are provided for those families

who are unemployed or destitute. Another programme undertaken by the Government is to assist the dependent children
of bereaved families of military forces and policemen by providing scholarships for the children, medical services, and other
necessary services to maintain family life.

(e) Institutional care.
Apart from the various institutional programmes for children
and youth undertaken by the Government and private agencies, the Government also operates correctional schools, protective facilities for vagrants, special schools for the mentally
retarded, and vocational schools for orphaned youth. The
Government endeavours to provide as much vocational training as possible so that the children can help themselves through
their own efforts. The Government also gives financial aid to
institutions for physical therapy, occupational therapy, and
other services for handicapped children.

(f) The National Social Workers' Training Center.
Because the limited number of graduates from the schools of
social work cannot meet the requirements and needs of the people, the Government established the National Social Workers'
Training Center in 1958.

In urban areas, the lack of recreational facilities for the increasing
number of children is a serious problem. It is necessary to expand
the existing recreational facilities on the one hand, and to establish
new facilities on the other.

IV. Recommendations and Strategy for Long Range Policy

1. *Recommendations*

The immensity of the problem posed by the current size of the
children-and-youth population is further enhanced by the appalling-
ly low stage of their current development in terms of ante-natal and
maternity care, infant health, nutrition, school health, extent and
quality of primary education including the vexing phenomenon of
school drop-outs, and stagnation, and the acquisition of skills and the
inculcation of attitudes oriented towards production and economic
development. Though the problem is immense and may have to be
tackled only by stages, there is no doubt that it has to be tackled both
in the interests of economic development and of human welfare.

Hence we have the need for the formulation of a long-term national policy for children and youth in Korea.

Any long-term national policy for children and youth must make provision for the following items:

a) Mother care. This includes knowledge and practice of contraceptives suited to local economic and sociological considerations, pre-natal treatment, and postmaternity nutrition. Maternity welfare is an essential condition for child and youth welfare programmes directed at human resource development.

b) Infant care. This includes innoculation, nutrition, and preschool education.

c) Child development. This includes school health, midday meals, free supply of textbooks, slates and pencils, and a system of primary education that interests the student, gives the pupil an orientation towards dignity of labour and productive activity, and reduces incidence of wastage, stagnation, and drop-outs.

d) Youth development. This includes:

   i) Provision of continuation classes at suitable times for those who leave school at an early stage.

   ii) A system of elementary education that inculcates the scientific spirit, an attitude of rationality, and a development orientation based on work experience.

Several factors are involved in the implementation of a national policy that will take care of all these items. In the first instance, there has to be national recognition of the problem. Secondly, arrangements will have to be made at the governmental level for the establishment of institutions and agencies that can take care of the various requirements. Thirdly, suitable legislative and policy measures will have to be undertaken for facilitating the implementation of these programmes. Finally, a scheme has to be devised by which the beneficiaries of these programmes, especially those relating to mother, infant and child welfare, get involved in the programmes not only as recipients but also as participants. It is also important to underline the fact that all this is a long-range programme, to be executed in stages, the phasing depending upon the enthusiasm, resources, and administrative efficiency.

To begin with, there should be a Government Resolution outlining the objectives and components of a national long-range policy of child and youth development. This statement should clearly underline the crucial role of these programmes as an investment in the development of human resources for the promotion of economic and social growth. It must also draw attention to their redistributional and welfare implications. Having done this, it must go on to list the major programmes that are needed for the fulfillment of this policy such as mother care, infant care, child development, and youth development. It must then spell out the respective responsibilities of governments, the beneficiaries, the public, and voluntary agencies for the implementation of these programmes. It must end with an appeal to the people to undertake the development of their children and youth in a planned manner and reaffirm the determination of governments to do everything they can to assist in the process.

Planning for the Better Health of Children and Youth as an Aspect of Public Health Planning.

Here the accent should be on the methodology of public health planning as it relates to services for children and youth, in terms of priorities, targets, long-term and short-term strategy, as well as indirect measures for fulfilling their health needs. The creation of basic health services in rural areas, environmental sanitation, control over communicable diseases as well as specialized services for children would have to be considered. The question of integration of child health with community health in areas where basic community services themselves are absent is an important aspect. However, in urban areas specialized services for mothers and children could be supported for economic as well as other reasons.

The non-health aspects of health planning or the relationship between health and other sectors, need to be emphasized. Educational, nutritional and environmental factors in planning for better health also require attention. This is an aspect of cross-sectoral planning and co-ordination. The criteria of allocation of resources to programmes for the better health of children and youth in resources devoted to public health, need analysis.

The first requirement of the programme is the establishment of a network of maternity and child welfare centers throughout the country, especially in the rural areas where private institutions catering to these needs are bound to be negligible in number. These centers should help the married couples to go in for family planning by offering them advice, in formation, and facilities for the purpose. Hospitals where possible, and camps where necessary, should be established for sterilization operations and loop insertions. They should provide pre-natal care facilities for pregnant women, especially in those cases where they have either already taken up, or are prepared to take up, family planning. Facilities for safe delivery should be provided to these expectant mothers, as also nutritional and other facilities both during pregnancy and after delivery. Similar facilities should also be provided for the newly-born infants.

Economic policy can help in this process by encouraging the production of loops and other contraceptives, and of protein foods for mothers and infants. Provision could also be made for controlled distribution, subsidization and other incentives where necessary. Educational policy can also help by providing facilities for increases in the number of medical and nursing personnel, education in the implications of a sound population policy, and guarantees of good quality education for the children whose numbers could become manageable because of the adoption of family planning. Social policy can also help by building up social pressures against large families and encouraging an ideology of small families for maximizing both economic development and human welfare.

Planning for the Better Nutrition of Children and Youth as an Aspect of National Food and Nutrition Planning.

The younger age groups, particularly preschool children, have special nutritional needs which, if unmet, will have long-term deleterious consequences for their physical growth and mental development. The need is particularly felt in respect of protein-rich or body building foods as well as vitamin foods. The accent here is on the production and utilization as well as distribution aspects of foods in general, and protective foods in particular, and the role of supplementary feeding programmes in correcting the nutritional deficiencies amongst pre-school as well as school-age children. The setting of nutritional targets which include the nutritional needs of children, crop planning for the production of nutritive foods, particularly the production of low-cost protein-rich foods for the use of low-income groups in urban and rural areas, establishment of priorities in food distribution including indirect policy measures for facilitating more intake of protective foods for children, for example, the allocation of milk for use of children, and above all, the cost of nutrition services for families and children, are essential elements of nutrition planning.

The next, and perhaps the most difficult item in the programme, relates to the requirements of the pre-school child. While infants have continuous protective care from their mothers, and the school-age child can be reached through the school, the pre-school child is often without adequate attention and also difficult to reach. Malnutrition is widespread in this age group as a result of inadequate supplies of protective, especially protein-rich foods. Rigid food habits and mother's ignorance of nutritional needs also hamper the pre-school child's development.

It is also a fact that theirs is an age group that is most vulnerable to disease, and yet their health-heeds remain largely unattended. At the same time, there is an almost insoluble administrative problem involved in reaching them through community institutions, quire apart from the financial implications of catering to the requirements of the large numbers involved. Programmes in the field should, therefore, partly be general in terms of education in the nutritional field and partly indirect by being aimed at the mothers of pre-school children rather than directly at the children themselves. Thus the items in this programme should be:

a) Measures aimed at improving the levels of living of the whole family especially in environmental sanitation, that will have an important impact on the pre-school child.
b) Measures aimed at the nutritional education of the present generation of mothers through appropriate adult literacy programmes and of the future generation through its inclusion in school curricula and the curricula of teacher training institutions.
c) Establishment of a programme of health visitors who could pay periodic visits to private homes and encourage nutritional and psychological care of pre-school children. Voluntary agencies could play an important role in the implementation of this programme.
d) Establishment, or encouraging the establishment, of children's wings in hospitals, and children's centers, including crèches, play-centers, and kindergartens which could also be used for providing pre-school education programmes.
e) Provision of more and better trained personnel programmes for those professionally engaged in pre-school child care, and extensive adult education programmes in subjects related to the protection and development of the pre-school child.

Planning for the Educational and Schooling Needs of the Younger Generation.
The bulk of investment on human resources is in the field of education, which prepares children to partake eventually in national life, both as citizens and more importantly, as members of the productive labor force. The basic schooling needs arise mainly in respect of primary and secondary education. The allocation of resources to secondary education, particularly over the longterm period, has to be justified in relation to the changing perspective of occupational and employment opportunities. The main objective here is to avoid wastage in education and to shape the educational system in such a manner as to subserve the economic interest.

A question of utmost importance in Korean circumstances is the recuperation of out-of-school or uneducated youth, that is those who are left out of the educational stream. The orientation of education in rural areas towards more realistic participation in rural economic life is another aspect of planning. The structuring of the educational system in order to give more emphasis to science and technical subjects and to prevocational guidance aspects, is also an important element. The integration of education of handicapped children with the normal schooling system is an issue worthy of consideration. The criteria of allocation of resources to the various educational programmes in national and local budgets need to be analyzed. In this connection, unit costs of educating the school child, with a clear distinction between costs of building, teaching equipment and training of teachers under the special circumstances of Korea, would provide an important tool of forward educational planning in concrete terms.

The important thing needed in our primary education if we want to modernize our society, is an inculcation of the knowledge of science and logic. Science does not merely mean teaching chemistry and physics, for the essence of science is that everything has an explanation, nothing is supernatural; and all phenomena have a rational explanation. It is that kind of science that has got to be taught at the primary educational stage, although how it should be done is a matter of detail for experts. Unless education in the primary school has in it an element of what may be called a knowledge of the essence of science, it will not be possible to modernize our society; and if we do not modernize our society, we would not be able to bring about necessary economic development.

Then there is the need for inculcating logic, because logic is something which one often misses in both elementary and secondary education. Intellectual curiosity and the use of the mind are very important. What is education meant for it is does not stimulate the use of the mind and make it agile and able to pierce through appearance to reality? The primary education that we give children in our developing societies should have positive orientation.

Preparing the Younger Generation for Productive-economic Activities in Long-Term Manpower Planning.

This is the end-product, as it were, of all the preceding types of investments intending to prepare the child to contribute to the economic life of the community and enabling it to become a national asset or resource and not a liability. The planning of a vocational stream for the younger generation has three aspects: early vocational guidance, vocational education, and vocational training in specific skills. Organization and financing of vocational guidance and employ-

ment information services, youth vocational courses and appren-
ticeship schemes for youth are therefore, integral aspects of manpower
training and planning.

Family and Child Welfare Services in Social Welfare Planning.

An important stage in the planning process for meeting the needs
of younger age groups consists in developing a strategy for shaping
the social and physical environment conducive to their development
and imparting a sense of stability and security to them. Adequate
facilities in terms of housing, parks, playgrounds, sports and recreational activities, etc., are some of the essential components of planning a healthy physical environment since they provide constructive
opportunities for self-development and self-adjustment as well as in-
culcate team spirit amongst younger people.

The attitude to the bearing and rearing of children which conditions the attention that a family could give to children, is one aspect
of the social environment. Cultural and religious factors in the value
system of societies have an important bearing in shaping the character
of the younger generation.

Three more subjects need to be covered in order to complete the
picture of the long-range national policy and planning of child youth
development. These are organization, research and training, and
finance.

As regards organization, it is not possible to have a separate sector or a ministry for the purpose of child and youth development.
And it would be necessary to get the planners and the commissions,
wherever they operate, to recognize child and youth development as
part of human resources development, and indicate in the plans how
child and youth development programmes have been integrated in
the general developmental programmes for human resources.

In many ways the most important aspect of the organizational problem in regard to child and youth development relates to the relationship between voluntary organizations and the government. The
voluntary organizations always complain of bureaucratic procedures
causing unnecessary delays and imposing irritating financial objections. Undoubtedly resources have got to come from the government.
But it should not be directly involved in the support of voluntary
organizations, as it would inevitably lead to bureaucratic procedures
and delays. In any case bureaucracy is not the right agency for the
promotion or guidance of voluntary organizations which have got to
find their own guides; where necessary they might have professional
persons to help them. Therefore, it is suggested that an autonomous
body like the child and youth development board be accompanied

by a larger body which would be a forum for interested public opinion. It could meet once in six months enabling the people to make their criticisms and suggestions. The Commissioner for Child and Youth Development should be a member of the autonomous board for the promotion of child and youth development programmes in the voluntary sector. Such a board should function in the cabinet secretariat and under the prime minister, so that the prestige of the prime minister's office could be used advantageously for resolving problems and effecting co-ordination of all child and youth development work.

It is also important to provide for adequate, suitable, and competent research work in the many problems that are involved in the child and youth development programmes. Sociologists, psychologists, economists, health specialists, nutritionists, doctors and educationalists are all involved if there is to be an integrated programme of research for child and youth development; and it is not easy to bring them together on a research project. New institutions are needed that will have as their primary objective co-operative, integrated, and multi-discipline research on problems of child and youth development. If we cannot set up new institutions, we should encourage inter-disciplinary research in existing institutions, universities departments and other specialized institutions.

To conclude, while there is research on individual topics, an integrated, inter-disciplinary approach is obviously lacking and this is what has got to be remedied if we are to have well-planned programmes of child and youth development.

Finally, there is the all-important problem of finance. It is well known that almost by definition, inadequate financial resources constitute the greatest constraint on the developmental programmes of the developing countries. Nevertheless, these countries have no escape from spending on development programmes and they must find the necessary finance partly by governmental mobilization of resources and partly by encouraging private mobilization of resources. The important thing is to see that the planners and the governments of the developing countries attach the necessary priority to the human resource development in their economic planning, and further that, in this sector, they give high priority to child and youth development programmes. This should be supplemented by funds raised on a voluntary basis from the community at large, by non-official institutions and agencies interested in the promotion of child and youth development.

2. Strategy

In arriving at an appropriate strategy of planning adequate services to the younger generation, it may be desirable to develop three types of approaches: (a) the normative or "ideal" approach; (b) the "minimal" requirements approach; and (c) the "optimal" approach.

The normative approach should yield the ideal or theoretical requirements in health, food and nutrition, education and schooling, etc. Norms or standard of requirements in terms of various services for the full development of children as established by technical specialists form the basis on which the needs of children could be quantified. It would be necessary to establish minimal levels which, while not meeting the ideal situation, would ensure adequate minimal support necessary for the younger generation. In view of the limited resources, it may be necessary to aim, initially at least, to reach a certain minimal standard of services on the way to achieving the more ideal level of requirements.

Under the resources conditions of many developing countries, it would be impossible to fulfil the ideal requirements within a short span of time. Can the requirements be met within a generation or so? If it is not possible, it is desirable to settle for something less than ideal. The targets for the medium-term then, would have to be based on fulfilling at least the minimal requirements and for the long-term, to meeting the greater priority needs to the extent feasible.

In any strategy of developing concrete programmes and services for children and youth, a distinction would have to be made between three types of services: (a) community services; (b) joint services; and (c) specialized services. Community services are those which benefit the community, children as well as adults. In other words, all groups of population irrespective of their age, benefit from these services. Joint services are those which are economical to provide to adults and children jointly; for example, maternal and child health services may be organized as a part of rural health services in order to economize on scarce resources and trained personnel. Specialized services are those which exclusively benefit children; for example, day-care centers, school feeding programmes, etc., provided for one specific age group.

Since the different requirements of children are interlinked, there is an advantage in co-ordinating the organization of services; for example, while schooling is the responsibility of the ministry of education, the school itself could become the nucleus for the organizations of school health, school nutrition, school sanitation, health education, etc. The extent to which such integration or co-ordination can be effected depends on the administrative arrangements in health, food, welfare, and other departmental services in rural and urban areas.

V. Conclusions

In the foregoing, an attempt has been made to trace the steps in the planning process for taking into better account the needs of children and youth in national development, which are necessary for evolving a long-term national policy for the development of the younger generation as an integral aspect of long-term development. It is obvious that planning for meeting the needs of the younger age group is a complex matter involving the inter-weaving of the needs of children and youth into planned objectives. Just as physical resource development requires pre-investment, that is, investment in pre-project surveys, applied research and training of manpower, similarly human resource development also requires pre-investment, that is, the development of children to the stage where they become vessels and carriers of human investment.

4

The Paradoxes of Development: Problems of Korea's Transformation*

Jong Sup Jun

After years of rapid economic growth, daring planning, and political turbulence, Korea is reorienting its course of national development. Since the implementation of the First Five Year Economic Planning in 1962, the country has been transformed from an agricultural society to a semi-industrial one. Korea exported goods worth $41 million in 1961 and $20 billion in 1981. The gross national product has grown an average 10 percent annually between 1962 and 1977.[1] In recent years, however, the country has experienced its worst economic setback in nearly two decades. This economic downfall was characterized by rampant inflation and a negative 5 percent GNP growth in 1980.

Anyone who has visited Korea during the 70's must have sensed a great deal of developmental euphoria among the Korean people. Government officials, business leaders, intellectuals, urban citizens, and farmers, all had expressed their optimism toward development and modernization. However, their feelings were also accompanied

* The preparation of this article was supported in part by a grant from the Social Science Research Council in New York.

1. Some recent studies on Korean development include: David C. Cole and Princeton N. Lyman, *Korean Development: The Interplay of Politics and Economics.* Cambridge, Mass.: Harvard University Press, 1971; Noel F. McGinn, et al., *Education and Development in Korea.* Cambridge, Mass.: Harvard University Press, 1980; Anne O. Krueger, *The Developmental Role of the Foreign Sector and Aid.* Cambridge, Mass.: Harvard University Press, 1979; Kwang Suk Kim and Michael Roemer, *Growth and Structural Transformation.* Cambridge, Mass.: Harvard University Press, 1979; Chong Kee Park, ed. *Human Resources and Social Development in Korea.* Seoul, Korea: Korea Development Institute, 1980; Parvez Hasan, *Korea: Problems and Issues in a Rapidly Growing Economy.* Baltimore, Md.: The Johns Hopkins University Press, 1976; Parvez Hasan and D. C. Rao, *Korea; Policy Issues for Long-Term Development.* Baltimore, Md.: The Johns Hopkins University Press, 1979.

by an uneasiness toward high inflation, rapid urban sprawl, excessive pollution and environmental deterioration, lack of political freedom, and world political and economic situations. Economic growth inevitably produces many contradictions and perplexities that lead to societal conflicts and unanticipated consequences. It also generates pluralistic changes in such elements as institutional differentiations, beliefs and values, political consciousness, religious groups, rising expectations toward equity and equality, interest groups, and union movements. Ironically, most of the current problems stem directly from what has been Korea's rapid achievement in economic growth. Yet the accomplishment of the country's economic growth has been widely publicized and uncritically accepted. The problems of today's economic and social transformation require social scientists to do some critical reflection on the past experiences.

In the following sections I shall (1) offer some critical comments on the impact of economic development, with particular attention to the socio-psychological factors; (2) argue the role of public administrators as one of the main forces for development and modernization; (3) point out some organizational pathology as a result of the government's efficiency movement; and (4) speculate about the prospect of democracy in Korea. My principal aim here is to point out the paradoxical contradictions that exist in the process of rapid economic development I shall not argue with the utility of a particular theory of development. I shall suggest, however, that the concept of development must be reexamined in light of democracy, equity, and participation.

Social Implications of Economic Success

The basic goal of economic development is to achieve better living conditions and to meet the basic needs of people in a society. The means for accomplishing this task is different between capitalism and socialism. Since Korea is a capitalistic system, the government encourages a free economy and competition. Goods are produced and owned by the people (or the capitalists). Capitalist development centers on the notion that once a small proportion of the entire population reach a developed level of economic output, then the supposed benefits of development such as personal income, improved education, health care, housing, consumer goods, and others will slowly filter down to the rest of population. The rationale for this "trickledown theory" has come under critical reexamination.

Economists emphasize the measurement of development in terms of aggregate growth rates such as overall and per capita GNP as an index of development. The economic indicators developed by the government and banks seem to demonstrate that Korea has certainly accomplished a so called "miracle" for the past two decades. But viewed in terms of equality, justice, meaningful jobs, medical care, housing for the poor, and other aspects of the quality of life, economic growth has been a failure or, at best, only a partial success. Irma Adelman and Cynthia Morris, in describing "Who Benefits from Economic Development?" have stated that economic growth brings greater inequality and "typically" an absolute decline in real income for most of the population.[2]

Korea is becoming a newly industrialized society in a socially pathological manner. As the level of income rises, so do people's expectation for material satisfaction. Spending sprees invariably indulge in luxury goods and speculation in investment . The good life depicted in the soap operas on the television screen, movies, and new fashions reinforces the quest for high consumption, and the import liberalization policy in recent years has certainly benefitted the rich more than the poor. Despite this apparent sign of affluence, most average citizens can hardly afford to make ends meet, for inflation reduces the value of wages especially for those who belong to the lower income brackets. Furthermore, wage increase for workers has always lagged behind the rate of inflation. According to the Ministry of Labor, the average with a family of five was earning 55 percent below the monthly minimum living cost in 1978—an average earning of 97,000 won compared to minimum living cost of 190,000 won. Growth has also produced significant psychological effects on people's value perception. The upper-calss people always go for the best leisure life, the big house or modern apartment, the best gadgets and automobile, and expensive goods available in the society. The behavioral impact of the rich on the people at the middle and lower classes is unmeasurably high: many try to emulate the life style of the rich beyond their ability. Economists call this heated consumption as an inflationary psychology and "demonstration effect."[3]

Economic growth provides benefits in many different ways. It has provided productive employment opportunities, improved agricultural

---

2. Irma Adelman and Cynthia Taft Morris. *Economic Growth and Social Equity in Developing Countries.* Palo Alto, Calif.: Standford University Press, 1973.
3. On the discussion of socio-psychological problems as a result of economic growth, see: John Kenneth Galbraith, *The Affluent Society.* London: Hamish Hamilton, 1958; Fred Hirsch. *Social Limits to Growth.* Cambridge, Mass.: Harvard University Press, 1978; William Leiss. *The Limits to Satisfaction: An Essay on the problem of needs and commodities.* Toronto: University of Toronto Press, 1976.

products, accelerated educational growth, and improved the living conditions of many people. Unlike Middle-Eastern countries where 95 percent of the oil profit goes to the top 3 to 5 percent of elites in the society, Korea seems to have a better distribution of income. However, income disparity is still a serious problem: according to the report of Korea Development Institute, the top 20 percent of families received approximately 46.7 percent of the income in 1978 (41.8 percent in 1965 and 41.6 percent in 1970). The bottom 40 percent of families received only 15.5 percent of the income (12.2 percent in 1965 and 19.6 percent in 1970). Proportionally speaking, the upper-class people are highly benefited by the rest of the population.

Korean people are more or less resigned to accepting spiraling inflation as a fact of life. According to the *U.S. News and World Report,* the compounded annual inflation of Korea from 1970 to 1978 was 14.4 percent, the 12th highest among 50 non-Communist countries in the world, with a 28.9 percent price increase in 1979, the 9th highest. The inflation rate in 1980 was 40 percent. Later the government changed the figure to 29 percent. However, statistical figures don't mean much to ordinary citizens, and practical consumer price increase is always far above the announced figure.

To continue sustained economic development, savings must be accumulated. One of the reasons for Japan's enormous economic success has been the propensity of the people to save even during inflationary times. The statistics released by the Bank of Korea in March, 1979 indicated that the consumption propensity of Korea was far higher than that of Japan when she attained $1,000 per capita GNP. Korean civil consumption in 1978 was 61.2 percent of the GNP, but Japan's consumption was only 55 percent of its GNP in 1965 when she attained a per capita GNP of $1,000. Another striking comparison was that Korea's per capita savings ratio was 9 percent in the same year in comparison to the 18 percent Japan recorded in 1965. One major characteristic feature of Korea's consumption pattern is that consumption is not led by the general public as is the case with Japan and the United States but by high income bracket people. The Commercial Bank of Korea in 1979 also reported that the rich saved less than the middle and lower income groups. In fact, it is very common for the rich people to deposit their savings with foreign banks overseas. The government's campaign to encourage the people to save money has been rather belated due to the sharply heightening mood of consumption. The campaign for savings affects the low-paid workers more than the rich entrepreneurs. The parodoxical result is that in order to sustain economic growth and share the benefits in the long-run, the rich must pump a substantial portion of their income into the national economy. In the early 1970's an average income earner could afford to purchase a residential home with three year salary savings, but now in the early 80's, it is bearly possible to do that with seven years of savings.

The social malaise can also be analyzed in terms of social inequity. The rich have better access to government agencies, policy and administrative information, banks, and business opportunities, thereby enjoying higher social mobiliby and economic gains. Favorable government policies toward big corporations contributed to slow growth in small and medium sized businesses. The government has also offered special bank loan privileges to growth industries and large corporations. Social mobility in professional occupations for the poor is limited due to escalating costs for higher education. At the same time, the educational policy tends to favor the rich more than the poor. For example, since 1981, wealthy college students can enjoy a short-term study tour abroad during the summer vacation—approximately 4,000 rich kids went aborad costing each a minimum expense of $5,000 for four weeks.

Government economic reports, including social development plans published by the Economic Planning Board, always contain optimistic statistical projections. And yet, when the life of the ordinary citizens is observed, one cannot help but see why the people have been experiencing so much pain. It seems clear to the majority of the people that GNP growth rate as well as the high export volume is not, in itself, a major indicator that the national economy is healthy, that the people are more well off than before, and the quality of work life has improved. The citizens are indifferent to government statistics if they do not trust them. Industrial workers and farmers are asked to pay the price in blood and sweat now in order to enjoy the affluent life in the future. The government emphasizes the austere and frugal lifestyle to cope with the worsening scarcity of available materials and sources of energy. The truth is that the poor cannot contribute much to economic sacrifice and national savings. But they do have emotions and a common sense knowledge about the problems of society and community. As Peter Berger has pointed in his book *Pyramids of Sacrifice,* policy makers must demonstrate more sincere effort to understand the "realities" as perceived by the ultimate beneficiaries of development strategies.[4] This has to be the most important strategy for the Korean leaders in order to maintain sustainable growth in the 1980's.

---

4. Peter L. Berger. *Pyramids of Sacrifice: Political Ethics and Social Change.* New York: Anchor Press, 1976.

Beleaguered Public top Administrators

Despite their loyalty and dedication to economic development goals, public employees are least appreciated by the public and little known in the economic success stories of the country. Rather business entrepreneurs and top policy makers are frequently pictured as the main forces of economic growth. Without the commitment of public administrators, however, economic development plans could not have been accomplished. Public administrators have been the main force for social change particularly in the process of implementing developmental programs and projects throughout the provincial and local agencies. They are responsible for mobilizing human and material resources toward the realization of the collective purpose of the administrative state. To a great extent, efficiency in accomplishing the development goals is also attributed to the relatively high degree of professionalization and manpower in the civil service system. The government administration employs 596,000 civil seervants of which 200,000 were recruited during the rapid development period between 1967 and 1977. A recent study on the background of the higher civil servants indicates that 87 percent of the sample survey involving 174 officials above the third grade (the mid-management level under the old system) received some college education.[5]

Public administrators have played the most important role as change agents in implementing developmental projects. Once developmental priorities and planning goals are established and approved by the president, it becomes the responsibility of the ministers, bureau chiefs, and their subordinates to execute them throughout the provincial agencies, and local officials are obligated to produce some tangible results whatever means they adopt. Since almost all public servants have completed military duty prior to their government job, they are accustomed to a militaristic chain of command. Many employees working at the provincial and local levels have long workdays without pay for overtime. During the agricultural season, the county and village officials frequently work in the fields to help the farmers or supervise the progress toward the New Community Movement projects mandated by the central government. Due to the shortage of manpower, they work day and night including Sundays and holidays.

Despite their dedication toward developmental goals, public administrators have not been benefitted much by the outcome of economic growth. Korean public employees are poorly paid as com-

---

5. Jung Hyun Rho, "Survey of the Value Characteristics and Profile of Korean Elite Bureaucrats, *Korean Public Administration Review*, Vol. 13 (1979), pp. 5-59.

pared to those in the private sector and in relation to the cost of living. The average monthly salary of public employees amounts to approximately 60 percent of the average business employee. Salaries and official bonuses meet only about two-thirds the amount which most people need to sustain their families' monthly standard of living and the cost for their children's education. When a college graduate after the completion of the traditionally competitive Higher Civil Service Examination enters into the middle level of the government hierarchy, that person will earn approximatley $250 per month after taxes as compared the possibility of earning $350 in the business sector with his educational background. This person has to pay over $500 to buy a 15 inch color television set. A government employee who can afford other necessities such as a refrigerator, modern apartment, modern furnitures, and a child's college education is supported by his parents or by other means. Wages for public employees are unquestionably a major determinant for the quality of government employees. A recent report by th Ministry of Government Administration pointed out that 17 percent of the persons on the government payroll were still receiving salaries that fall short of minimum living expenses.

A Westerner might ask the question why a public employee's wife does not work to supplement her husband's income. In general, the housewife in Korea does not work—in part because she could not earn enough to pay someone to take care of her children and house chores. Furthermore, the opportunities for work and women's rights are not recognized yet in the society. Traditionally, Korean bureaucrats have enjoyed prestige and power—this was one of the incentives for working in the government. As the society becomes industrialized, the private sector offers more challenging job opportunities with better pay. The annual increases in the resignation rate of public employees and the deterioration of the general quality of applicants are obviously indicative of the declining level of appeal public positions offer. The problem is far more severe in the area of technical, engineering, and other professional jobs.

Among other factors, low salaries of the civil servants have caused excessive corruption. During the rapid growth period, practices of favoritism and graft have become commonly accepted behavior among politicians, judges, businessmen, public bureaucrats, and even journalists. The government first launched an anticorruption move in the public bureaucracy in the early 1970's which began with the Yushin administration (the Revitalizing Reform) during the late President Park's administration to eliminate various irregularities involving the handling of civil petitions and licenses. The government dismissed a total of 331 officials in April, 1974, including 52 section chiefs and above. In March, 1977, a total of 420 public employees involved in irregular acts were purged. In 1976, the administration launched another anticorruption drive; more than 15,000 officials were reprimanded and brought under other sanctions. One of the sanctions applied was that when an employee accepts petite bribery (let's say $5.00), his immediate supervisor is subjected to a serious disciplinary action. This policy was an impractical rule and impossible to implement. Despite these sanctions, corruption became more apparent toward the end of the Park administration. Soon after the assassination of President Park in October, 1979, the Special Committee for National Security Measures headed by then the army general Chun Doo Hwan announced the purge of 4,760 puiblic employees with the rank of the third grade (the middle management level the grade 5 being the lowest rank under the old system) and below, involving the officials from the central and provincial agencies, policemen, fire fighters, tax collectors, and customs officials. In July, 1980, the 232 top executives with rank of the second grade and up including a cabinet minister and six vice ministers were also dismissed.

Since President Chun officially became the President in September, 1980, he has renewed his strong determination to ferret out corruption involving politicians and higher government officials in an effort to create so called a "clean society." After the massive purge of public employees, President Chun has introduced various antigraft systems to "purify" the public services; for example, high ranking bureaucrats are required to register their properties as an institutional device to prevent them from gaining illegal wealth by taking advantage of their positions. The government has also introduced a system of informing about proposals and requests for political or administrative favors and influence-paddling made to politicians, ranking civil servants and similar public office holders. Both the giver and the taker are equally responsible and accountable for such reciprocal acts of injustice, irregularity and crime. In April, 1981, the entire cabinet, led by Prime Minister took an oath of service in front of President Chun, and all civil servants had to swear that they will shun requests for personal favors and refrain engaging in any influence peddling at a rally in each agency. Finally, the government also established an ethics law for public officials to award "clean and exemplary officials," and to improve legal and systematic structures to clean up the bureaucracy. The government strongly insists that its anticorruption campaign has contributed much to the establishment of political and social stability and to the foundation for the establishment of a "justice soceity" which is one of the main policies of the present government. So far, President Chun's administration is lenient toward the military and the business sector; a favorable policy toward them is necessary to maintain national security and stable economy. The policy makers need the continuous support of the military generals to maintain the political power and of the business entrepreneurs to increase exports and industrial production.

We may draw two conlcusions from the above discussion. As a new civilian-military government emerges, the vulnerability of the public bureaucracy is anticipated by the government bureaucrats. When the incumbent president begins to lose public support for his policies, one way of making headlines is to crackdown on the public bureaucracy (or to provoke the public with a national security issue). Another observation may be made in terms of the behavioral change on the part of public employees. The Korean case is a classic example of an organization theory which states that as an organization experiences deviant behavior of its members, more rules and regulations are introduced to control such behavior.[6]

Ironically, the bureaucrats do not always behave rationally according to new rules, and irrational behavior becomes more latent in everyday activities. The rules are perverted by subtlety. As a result, most organizations are not able to deal with the side-effects of the new organizational policy. It is frequently mentioned by Korean people and in the newspapers that the government's purification policy has produced more pathological behavior by bureaucrats. The public employees in general are only concerned with the routine tasks and have an "easy-going attitude;" rigid rules and regulations are strictly applied against the client's request, and they become the means for evading their responsibility. At a time when the public bureaucracy needs to be more flexible and responsible in dealing with complex problems and services, the system is becoming more rigid, uncooperative, formalistic, and impersonal. This bureaucratic phenomenon certainly poses a dilemma for the policy makers. To increase the level of employee's morale, the government should begin with the problem of adequate employee welfare. But considering various budget constraints, such as the continuously increasing defense budget (36 percent of the total budget in 1981) and the expansion of social welfare development plans, comparable salary increase is a most difficult task for the policy makers and budget planners.

No one will question the importance of honesty, integrity, and

---

6. Robert K. Merton. *Social Theory and Social Structure.* Revised and enlarged edition. New York: The Free Press of Glencoe, 1957.

dedication on the part of public employees. However important such dedicated behavior may be for them, it would be unreasonable to press them to do so without providing them with adequate remuneration. The establishment of the "just society" the government is planning to achieve is not likely to be realized by neglecting the improvement of the quality of public administrators.

The Limits of Efficiency and Rationality

Since the mid 1980, the government has exhibited a strong movement toward the improvement of efficiency and rationality in the public bureaucracy. In addition to the eradication of corruption, the government has also attempted to reduce red tape as a way of preventing irregularities. As the functions of the government expand in a rapidly changing society, a great deal of demands were put on government agencies. Thus to prevent possible loopholes in administrative procedures, each agency over the years has developed cumbersome documentary requirements. Citizens who seek agency services have to go through unpleasant obstacles such as filling out complex forms, approval delays, interaction with unfriendly officials, and submitting the same papers to several other agencies. Recently, the policy makers seem to be serious about streamlining agency red tape. However, while a reduction in red tape may help the clients to some extent, the improvement of the bureaucratic climate prevailing in government agencies requires much more profound changes.

The revised Civil Service Law of 1981 seems to be the specific administrative policy designed to improve public administration. The basic aim of the law is to ensure efficiency in personnel administration, job security for the career civil servants, and professional independence of the civil service system. First, the law has changed the old rank system of personnel administration (five ranks in the career system) into a nine grades system (the first grade being the top executive position). It has also strenghened the power of the Ministry of Government Administration over the employment of civil servants in such functions as testing, hiring, and dispatching new employees to other ministries. Since the change gives little power to other ministries concerning personnel matters, a great deal of interministerial conflict has been created.

This new policy is designed to help administrative agencies recruit university professors or other professionals in such specialized areas as atomic power, scientific research, and environmental studies. The idea of recruiting expertise from outside the civil service system provides an opportunity for injecting some new perspectives into the stagnant bureaucracy. But this also tends to generate strong hostility among career bureaucrats toward the newcomer who takes a lateral appointment without going through open competition. Another change introduced is the emphasis on the interchange of officials among government ministries. Such interchanges are designed to broaden the range of an official's experience and to increase interministry cooperation and coordination. The creation of the Grievance Screening Commission is a significant provision for protecting public employees from arbitary dismissal and other discriminatory steps by the government and their superiors; employees can submit complaints and petitions on personal grievance to the Committee. Considering the undemocratic and unilateral decision-making process of Korean bureaucracy, how well the rights of the employees will be protected remains to be seen.

The most unprecedented movement toward efficiency in government was the restructuring of the government bureaucracy in October, 1981. The reshuffling of the 531 positions held by officials with the rank of the fourth grade and up was the largest reduction in the Republic's history. They accounted for 10.5 percent of 5,037 officials with ranks higher than the fourth grade—223 officials were from the central organizations in Seoul, 253 people from subordinate agencies and 56 from other organizaitons. Four advisory agencies established during the Park administration were also abolished permanently; they included the Administrative Improvement Commission, the Office of Planning and Coordination, the Secretariat of the National Security Council, and the Secretariat of the President's Council on Economic and Scientific Advisors. As a result, 24 first grade executives were forced to resign. The reorganization plan has also reduced the size of the three offices, 41 bureaus, and 135 divisions and branches.[7]

The latest administrative reform to improve efficiency and rationality in government is the introduction of zero-base budgeting system (ZBB). The new budgeting system is supposed to be introduced for the preparation of the 1983 budget beginning with the calendar year. Traditionally, the Korean government has relied on incremental budgeting, a process that aims at marginal changes to previous allocations. The Economic Planning Board (EPB), which is the most influential agency and largely responsible for the change, intends to combine the advantages of both the Planning Programming Budgeting (PPB) and ZBB systems. With the implementation of ZBB, the

---

7. *Dong A Daily Review*, October 16, 1981.

Economic Planning Board officials hope to maximize efficiency, reduce waste, improve priority setting, and thereby economize the overall budget. They would also like to see the systematic evaluation of individual development projects. This is a wishful thinking on the part of planning and budget experts.

The Korean government like other developing countries has a tendency to emulate the Western management models without critically reflecting on the context of its own administrative conditions. The government is undoubtingly emulating the U.S. model of budgeting used in the executive branch of the federal government and some state governments. Whatever their motives are, practitioners and academics educated in the United States are usually inclined to advocate new approaches while disregarding the unique administrative environment of Korean public administration. Thus far, the use of ZBB in the United States faces many problems such as excessive time demand, reams of paperwork, little change in budget priorities, and resistance by program managers (although ZBB is an efficient management tool for the budget directors). It is worthwhile to point out here that despite the use of ZBB during the Carter administration, the U.S. federal government has failed to control the annual budget, and was never able to use the evaluation process of different public programs applied to the budgetary review process.[8]

The Korean bureaucracy is already too impersonal, inflexible, formalistic, ritualistic, and mechanial. Through the application of ZBB, the Economic Planning Board will obviously enjoy more power and influence in controlling other ministries. However, the agency will become a more centralized, scientific, professionalized enterprise and be further removed from realities of local problems. The bureaucrats at the central and provincial levels are likely to complain about the complexity, time, paperwork, and priority setting procedures. From their point of view, administrative time should be spent more efficiently for serving the citizens and working on the developmental projects. The top policy makers and experts should not assume that the people under them will behave rationally as they are expected, or that they can make rational choices based on systematic and quantitative information prepared by their followers. Regardless of the future impact of a new budgeting system, priority setting will always be performed at the higher level as has been the

---

8. On the discussion of the problems and progress of ZBB, see: a special symposium on "Budgeting in an Era of Resources Scarcity," *Public Administration Review*, Volume 38, No. 6, (November/December 1978); Frank D. Draper and Bernard T. Pitsvada, "ZBB— Looking Back After Ten Years," *Public Administration Review*, Vol. 41, No. 1 (January/February 1981), pp. 76-83.

case in the past. It is doubtful that inputs provided by the provincial and local county agencies will make a significant difference in the budgetary process.

Democracy, Politics and Administration

The idea of democracy is frequently discussed among political leaders and intellectuals. To the eyes of the ordinary citizens, their emphasis on democracy is largely seen as political rhetoric and has little meaning to the reality of the political situation. The issue of democracy in Korea is the most perplexing one to every new president. Internally, the president must allow reasonable freedom for the people since the Republic was founded on the ideals of liberal democracy. In addition, the country is a non-communist society, and has to think about the pressures of the U.S. government. Over the years, the Korean people lost their confidence in political leaders mainly due to their deceiving tactics, corruption, frequent revision of the constitutions at their convenience, and long-term authoritarian regimes.

The First Republic was born in 1948 following the U.N. supervised election. The fragile and corrupt civilian government led by President Syngman Rhee was brought down by the student demonstration in April, 1960. A year later, his successor John M. Chang proved to be a weak leader and ineffective in solving economic and social problems was overthrown by a military coup. Chung Hee Park, then an army general and the President of the Third Republic ruled until late 1979. During his rule, the country set records for economic growth mainly at the expense of individual freedom; political opportunities for opposition leaders were severely restricted. In 1971, he proclaimed martial law and called for a new constitution that gave him strong power, reduced the power of the National Assembly, and place new restraints on civil liberties. Opposition to Park grew with the imposition of the Yushin system (the so called Revitalizing Reform) which virtually guaranteed the life time rule of President Park. With the emergency decrees in 1974, President Park prohibited any criticism of the constitution and his policies. He was assassinated in October, 1979 by his close subordinate and ex-general. The lesson to be drawn from Park's demise was that the Korean people wanted a change, demanded flexibility in government, and wished to have more political opportunities. The current President, Chun Doo-Hwan, another ex-army general, has emerged as a strong leader.

During the political turmoil of the later part of 1979 and most of

1980, the government was largely controlled by ex-generals and their colleagues in the military. This was the period of a massive purge of politicians, government bureaucrats, and journalists, the integration of broadcasting and communication systems, the consolidation of newspapers, the abolishment of numerous journals and magazines, and crackdowns on critical church leadership.[9] As a result, many domestic problems were compounded at once: the 40 percent inflation rate in 1980 discouraging foreign investors, a high rate of bankruptcies by heavily indebted companies, a decrease in export volume, labor unrest, rising wages, a 25 percent decline in industrial production, rising unemployment, and negative GNP growth. In summary, one may conclude that the political and economic turmoil during this period was largely related to the military intervention.

The Fifth Republic since 1981 has emphasized the promotion of a "welfare democracy and justice society" that is, the society must build a firm democracy suited to Korea's historical and cultural background, build a welfare society benefiting each citizen, and create a just society through broad and continuous social reform. Certainly all the good words are expressed in many of President Chun's speeches. But political uncertainty stems from the present governments efforts to create welfare democracy and to establish democratic political processes with the intervention of military. Many intellectuals think that democracy is an impossible dream as long as the country has powerful military involvement in civilian politics. On the other hand, those who support the military role think that only a leader with the military background can lead the country considering the continuous threat of North Korea and the need for social stability to sustain, economic development. As the country approaches 1988, the year of the presidential election (and the Olympics in Seoul), the attention of the public will increasingly focus on the election of a new leader. The future political burdens seem to be on President Chun's shoulder.

The problem of democratization may also be described in the context of public administration. The Korean public administration can be characterized as having high administrative centralization and collectivism; all the important administrative decisions are made unilaterally at the Presidential and ministrial levels; public employees are commanded to work toward the accomplishment of the collective goals. In implementing the developmental goals, the government has

---

9. The political situaiton in 1979 and 80 was well described by Gregory Henderson in his paper "The Fifth Republic's Military-Politics," presented at the Association for Asian Studies held at Toronto, 1981.

achieved a great deal by appearing to the people to act cohesively in the national interests. Once administrative orders are given from the top echelon, strict obedience is expected without questions or criticisms. Since the public employees are always told what to do, it is easier for them to follow orders rather than reasoning; in case of possible failure of administrative directives, they don't have to be blamed for their disobedience or irresponsibility. Obedience is a virtue of being a good employee. The late President Park once said that "Why do I have to be concerned with all the details of running the government?" And yet, he was unable to delegate the authority to and trust his subordinates. He demanded absolute obedience, and was not able to tolerate any criticism against his policy. Passive behavior is also a cultural trait; it is wrong to question and criticize the leader. In this administrative culture, the administrators become reactive, uncritical, and conditioned into a dehumanizing bureaucracy. As a consequence, the stagnant bureaucracy does not provide much room for initiative, creativity, and innovation. In essence, the leaders discourage individual's exercise of "critical consciousness" in which one critically examines his administrative activities and attempts to clarify the meanings of them. Paulo Freire in describing the Brazilian society has pointed out that through the use of critical capacity of a person, the individual can learn democratic life.[10]

The strong bureaucracy dominates the process of policy making and planning. Staffed with highly educated experts, the central bureaucracy also tends to rely heavily on the use of rational tools, functional analysis, and factual (statistical) knowledge in making administrative choice. When policy proposals prepared by experienced bureaucrats, planners, and economists, are submitted to the National Assembly, the expedient and incompetent legislators tend to approve them without serious debate and scrutiny. Since the united and majority ruling party supports every policy proposals submitted by the president, political opposition has never been a serious issue as long as they are congruent with the ideological goals of the government.

The centralized process of rational-comprehensive planning puts a major emphasis on hierachical coordination in carrying out developmental projects. Unity toward developmental goals is always stressed as opposed to the diversity and distinctiveness of localities. The central planners and bureaucrats underestimates the local (village) situations where particular needs and implementation issues are

---

10. Paulo Freire. *Education for Critical Consciousness.* New York: The Seabury Press, 1973.

relevant. The developmental plans established by the experts generally include unrealistic target-setting to be accomplished by the provincial officials. It also neglects the availability of regional resources as well as the psychological commitment of county officials and rural people. In fact, there has been little attempt to decentralize the planning process by recognizing the local and regional differences as well as to design different programs to help local needs.

Development Reconsidered

Emphasis on the economic development program will be continued because under the rationale of national security, social welfare still has symbolic appeal and the power to persuade the people that they have to accept pragmatic goals. However, since economic development affects many aspects of the society, we need to examine critically the economists's conception of development. The theoretical assumptions and problem-solving methods of the planners, economists, and top policy makers must be carefully examined; their paradigmatic assumptions determine the outcome of explaining and interpreting the social problems and their solutions. Development depends largely on complex elements which cannot readily be analyzed with the tools of rational-economic theory. Economists are good at making theoretical assumptions, projections, and quantitative description, but they are rather poor in understanding the intangible and tacit knowledge that exists in human phenomena. My scepticism about overdependence on the economists and their rational-comprehensive planning does not imply that their approach has been total failure. On the contrary, they have played an important role, but their contribution has inherent limitations and must be complemented by other perspectives.

Development is a complex and evolving process which displays some obvious progress by following designed plans, but is also characterized by contradictory functions, conflicts, and psychological issues which are difficult to anticipate and plan in advance. Numerous unpredictable behavior is likely to emerge in the process of human participation in implementing the programs and projects. To understand various paradoxical phenomena, the concept of development has to be broadened, and this requires broadly based knowledge in addition to economic knowledge and administrative techniques. We cannot assume that "more GNP is better than less." Increased production and sale of automobile is added into GNP, but it also generates many social costs (externalities) such as pollution, traffic congestion, and the construction of additional roads.[11] Moreover, the country may still have the real problem of inequity and poverty despite the triple increase in per capita GNP. This is certainly not a balanced or a people-oriented development. The benefits of development depend partly on their effects on the total society and partly on the development of the people in socio-psychological, economic and political terms.

To cope with the complex problems of the society, a new orientation in Korean development is needed. This need is aptly described by Michael P. Todaro:

Development must, therefore, be conceived of as a multidimensional process involving major changes in social structures, popular attitudes and national institutions as well as the acceleration of economic growth, the reduction of inequality and the eradication of absolute poverty. Development, in its essence, must represent the entire gamut of change by which an entire social system, tuned to the diverse basic needs and desires of individuals and social groups within that system, moves away from a condition of life widely perceived as 'unsatisfactory' and towards a situation or condition of life regarded as materially and spiritually 'better.'[12]

In my opinion, Korean development can succeed only if the policy makers and experts realize that it can also fail. They have been overly optimistic about the prospect of development, and did not pay enough attention to societal conflicts, developmental inconsistencies, and unanticipated consequences that occur in the process of economic development. Their future responsibility should be beyond the task of comprehensive planning and centralized control of administrative functions. They need to reorient developmental strategy toward more participative planning (transactive planning) in which the developmental process facilitates regional and local involvement, institutional autonomy, criticisms and mutual learning, and meaningful dialogue.[13] This can be only accomplished through the careful design of decen-

---

11.   Elliott D. Sclar, "Social Cost Minimization: A National Policy Approach to the Problems of Distressed Economic Regions," *Policy Studies Journal,* Vol. 10, No. 2 (December, 1981), pp. 235-247.

12.   Michael P. Todaro. *Economic Development in the Third World.* New York: Longman, 1977, p. 62; and also see Denis Goulet's analysis of the problems of development in his book, *The Cruel Choice: A New Concept in the Theory of Development.* New York: Anthenium, 1971.

13.   John Friedmann and G. Abonyi, "Social Learning: A Model for Policy Research," *Environment and Planning,* Vol. 8 (1976), pp. 927-940; John Friedmann and Barclay Hudson, "Knowledge and Action: A Guide to Planning Theory," *AIP Journal* (January, 1974), pp. 2-16.

tralized sturctures, interaction processes, and communication networks. The decentralization in development also involves the reorientation of power structures and decision making opportunities in order to provide the context for people's collaboration over their hard work and for the control of scarce resources.

Conclusion

The peril to the Korean government lies not in the immediate danger of North Korean threat, but rather in the mismanagement of economic growth that could generate further problems into political and social chaos. A critical examination of the side-effects of economic development and administrative centralization is necessary to reorient the developmental strategies toward more participative, decentralized, and democratic alternatives. The following is a list of some concluding observations:

1. In reviewing the literature on Korean development, I have quickly discovered that most studies have been intensely preoccupied with economic issues. The studies also exhibit a systematic bias which seems to reflect either the legitimation of government economic development plans or the intellectual satisfaction of economists. Many seminars, symposiums, conferences and public meetings held in Korea in the past 20 years were largely designed to rationalize and publicize the government policies.

2. Social problem-solving calls for the application of various disciplines to study the interactions among complex variables. Each discipline employs a set of assumptions, theories, concepts, or methods, and thereby, offers a different perspective toward the same problem situation. Thus the interdisciplinary or multidisciplinary approach is desirable in order to understand the dynamics of social phenomena.

3. In a society where only quantitative growth is sought, the quality of life is overshadowed by the pursuance of material interests. Life should mean not only economic affluence but also individual freedom and power.

4. Uncontrolled growth produces many undesirable socio-psychological effects such as depersonalization, alienation, overheated consumption, inequality, urban sprawl, crime, and many others.

5. The society must be concerned with the quality of work life as it is developing rapidly into a skill intensive economy from a labor intensive economy. As workers gain more economic power, they demand better working conditions, sense of community, and opportunity for participation.

6. The government planning process must reflect the possibilities of meaningful community change within the context of local realities. Developmental policies in the past were far too government-oriented and centrally controlled. In the future, decentralized people-oriented projects should be designed in order to facilitate more relevant change for the people in the community.

7. The policy makers and experts should not assume flawless, high morale, discipline, loyalty, ethical responsibility of all employees. Not all individuals behave rationally according to administrative orders. The leaders must try to learn and appreciate the diversity of human motivation, desire, and conflicts.

8. The government reorganization projects and efficiency drive will hardly achieve its basic aims unless accompanied by various organizational changes and development projects such as the improvement of administrative climate, better reward systems, training and education, job security, openness and confidence, and career opportunities.

9. The institutional processes are not conducive to the development of democratic government. Public administration being excessively centralized underestimates the potential contributions of employees at the lower echelons. The passive behavior of public employees is not the result of low intelligence or even meager education, but rather is due to stifled consciousness in rigid hierarchical bureaucracy. Emphasis on vertical consciousness of the people reduces the possibilities of mutual learning and continues "unitary democracy."

10. The government has not only been controlling social and political criticisms of intellectuals and activists, but also has depoliticized the citizens by diverting their attention from political issues to national stability and economic prosperity. As a result, the citizens have become politically passive, and apathetic toward government policy and administration.

11. The Korean people want to be free from administrative and political control, but at the same time, they want to be led by a strong leader who has the qualities of charismatic personality, honesty, integrity, forcefulness, futuristic vision, and fortitude. This is a dilemma in building democracy since the ideals of democracy are in opposition to the values of an autocratic leader.

12. To create democracy, educational institutions must teach democratic values. Students must learn the meanings of participation, equality, mutual learning and caring, individual realization, and freedom of choice. Since the institutional processes involving educational curricula, programs and majors, and faculty appointments and

tenure decisions are centrally controlled by the Ministry of Education, college and university professors are reluctant to be creative and discouraged to exercise their critical consciousness. They tend to spend more time in controlling student demonstration on campus and less in developing a learning community. The seed of democracy must begin in the educational institutions and its processes.

Part Two

Organizational Processes

5

A Cross-Cultural Comparison of Korean and American Managerial Styles: An Inventory of Propositions

Yang Soo Rhee

Introduction

The purpose of this study is to present what interrelationships exist between socio-cultural factors and managerial style. The format used in this presentation is an inventory of propositions. This inventory presents propositions on the relationships between managerial style and socio-cultural variables and illustrates them based upon cross-cultural comparison between Korean and American managerial styles.

Comparative management theorists focusing on cross-cultural study of organizational functioning have utilized three different approaches on the basis of explanatory variables.[1] First, economic development orientation; the basic premise of this approach is that management practice is highly correlated to the stage and pace of economic development or industrialization. Theorists using this approach argue that since all modern societies, by necessity, must obey the logic and imperatives of industrialization, differences in managerial behaviors and practices among nations can best be explained by their level of economic development.[2] They assert that managers operating in

---

1. England et al. divide conceptual and methodological approaches into three different groups: economic development; environmental approach; and behavioral approach. See G. W. England, A. R. Negandhi, and B. Wilpert, *Organizational Functioning in A Cross-Cultural Perspective* (Kent, Kent State University, 1979), pp. 2-3. Ajiferuke and Boddewyn classify comparative management studies into four explanations groups; cultural explanations; economic explanations; psychological explanations; and sociological explanations. See M. Ajiferuke & J. Boddewyn, "Culture and Other Explanatory Variables in Comparative Management Studies," *Academy of Management Journal,* 13 (1970), pp. 153-63.
2. Ajeferuke & Boddewyn, op. cit., p. 154.

similar economic environments will tend to behave alike, while those working in dissimilar economic environments will tend to behave differently.[3] This approach is essentially a macro or aggregate approach and, accordingly, concentrates on the examination of basic trends of managerial practices at the micro or firm level.[4]

Second, the behavioral approach or psychological explanation; the premise of this approach is that such personality traits as achievement motives and inferiority complexes, account for managerial differences among nations more than other factors.[5] This approach to cross-cultural management studies attempts to explain behavioral patterns between individuals and groups in organizational settings by using such psychological factors as attitudes, beliefs, value systems and need hierarchies. The basic assumption of this approach is that attitudes, beliefs, value systems, and need hierarchies are functions of a given culture. Therefore, by establishing relationships between these concepts and managerial practices, one can deduce the impact of cultural variables on management practices and effectiveness.[6] In this sense, it can be said that the behavioral approach is really an extension of the next socio-cultural approach.

Third, socio-cultural environmental approach or cultural explanations; this is the major approach in cross-cultural management studies. The basic contention of this approach is that the sociological or cultural environment of a given country has a considerable impact on the ways in which firms and their personnel carry out their functions.[7] Therefore, the underlying hypothesis of this approach is that managerial practices and effectiveness are the functions of socio-cultural environmental variables and, accordingly, interfirm differences in both practices and effectiveness can be explained on the basis of differences in socio-cultural environmental conditions facing firms in different locations and/or countries.[8]

Nowotny's study comparing American and European management philosophy is a good example of this approach.[9] In his study, Nowotny found that socio-cultural and environmental factors are responsible for the differences in management philosophy between the two regions. However, among the comparative management studies

---

3. Ibid.
4. England et al., op. cit., p. 2.
5. Ajiferuke & Boddewyn, op. cit., p. 158.
6. England et al., op. cit., p. 3.
7. R. N. Farmer & B. M. Richman, *Comparative Management and Economic Progress,* Homewood, Richard D. Irwin, 1965, p. 109.
8. England et al., p. 2.
9. O. H. Nowotny, "American vs. European Management Philosophy," *Harvard Business Review,* vol. 42, no. 2 (1964), pp. 101-108.

using a socio-cultural explanation for managerial differences, there is a varied and widely divergent array of conceptions because, as Ajiferuke and Boddewyn have stated, "culture is one of those terms that defy a single all-purpose definition, and there are almost as many meanings of culture as people using the term."[10]

By the way, in this inventory cultural explantions will be utilized as a methodological approach to cross-cultural study. For operational purposes, notwithstanding its ambiguity, the term "culture" in this inventory corresponds to either tradition, social customs and attitudes, language, religion, or a combination of any of these elements, and the terms "sociological" and "cultural" are used synonymously, although these terms defy precise definition. In this context, culture can be referred as "social character." Social character is defined by Fromm in the following manner:

. . . It is the function of the social character to shape the energies of the members of society in such a way that their behavior is not left to conscious decisions whether or not to follow the social pattern but that people want to act as they have to act and at the same time find gratification in acting according to the requirements of the culture. In other words, the social character has the function of molding human energy for the purpose of the functioning of a given society.[11]

Here, culture is the basis for judgements as to "what ought" and "what ought not" to be and the basis for evaluation, and positive and negative sanctions.[12]

As such, an understanding of the culture of a given country is critical for administrative and organizational behavior. As Thompson notes, complex organizations in a given country bear the stamp of its culture in spite of the similarities of their core technologies.[13] Complex organizations in the United States, for example, bear the stamp of American culture, and those in Korea, the stamp of Korean culture. Therefore, culture can act as a constraint in the society geared to complex organizations as well as in the transitional society.[14] Ad-

---

10. Ajiferuke & Boddewyn, op. cit., p. 154.
11. Erich Fromm, "Psychoanalytic Characterology and Its Application to the Understanding of Culture," in S. S. Sargent and M. W. Smith, eds., *Culture and Personality*, New York, Viking Fund, 1949, p. 5.
12. D. R. Domm, R. N. Blakeney, M. T. Matteson, and R. Scofield, *Thd Individual and The Organization*, New York, Harper & Row, 1973, p. 37.
13. J. D. Thompson, *Organizations in Action*, New York, McGraw-Hill, 1967, p. 103.
14. Ibid.

mittedly, this inventory acknowledges that culture is not uniform and static but is continually reshaped by individuals as social changes occur in a given society, and as individuals learn values in their parent culture.

American Culture and Its Impact on Management Practices

The United States has been called a melting pot because so many alien group have been blended into a society with a common language. Many customs have developed that are common to the nation.[15] As a result, the United States has become a heterogeneous society. Thus, American culture has often been described as pluralistic, meaning that there are actually many cultures contributing to national life. These differences in custom and national origin are cherished by U.S. society, which passionately believes in the right of each individual to choose for himself the way that he shall go.[16] In other words, pluralism has been associated with individualism. Therefore, these two related concepts, pluralism and individualism, widely reflect American society.[17]

Pluralism stresses the appropriateness of group organization as a means of securing protection for broad group interests in society. Page states:

. . . Pluralism, as a theory and practice, assumes that groups are good: that citizens have the right to organize to advance their interests; that groups with differing interests will bargain and compete; and that the result of bargaining and competition among group interests is the interest of the whole community or nation—the public interest.[18]

On the other hand, in America individualism has its roots in the precepts of religion, that is, the Protestant ethic emphasizes self-reliance and the welfare of the individual. Emphasis on the individual is evident in the protections of civil rights and liberties, but individualism also implies the right and responsibility to participate meaningfully

15. W. A. Long and K. K. Seo, *Management in Japan and India,* New York, Praeger Publishers, 1977, p.222.
16. Ibid.
17. R. S. Page, "The Ideological-Philosophical Setting of American Public Administration" in Dwight Waldo, ed, *Public Administration in a Time of Turbulence,* New York, Chandler Publishing Co., 1971. p.61.
18. Ibid. This is not necessarily only way to view the public interest.

in the political process in pursuit of the goals one considers important.[19] In America, the ideas of democracy have been grounded in
a philosophical setting of individualism. A major political value in
America thus has been "democracy," and increasing emphasis has
been placed on democratizing the political process by increasing direct
participation in making and administering important decisions by
those most directly affected.[20]

Directly, related to individualism and pluralism is the notion of
political and economic competition, with minimal involvement of
government.[21] This notion is very suitable for capitalism. Political
and economic competition generally emphasizes how things are
accomplished more than what is accomplished. Namely, American
values stress the importance of means, not ends; the ends do not justify
the means; procedures are rather valued for their own sake.[22]

A complex technology provided by the scientific and industrial
revolutions, an accompanying reverence for the scientific and the
abstract, emphasis on individual independence and mobility, and value
placed on competition and achieved status tend to isolate an American
from his concrete relation to others.[23] The United States is described as a universalistically oriented society. Parsons notes:

. . . the American occupational system is universalistic and achievement oriented. . . Compared with other possible ways of organizing the
division of labor, the predominant norms which are institutionalized
in the American society and which embody the predominant value
orientation of the culture give rise to expectations that occupational
roles will be treated by their incumbents and those who are associated
with them universalistically. . .[24]

In a universalistic society, friendship which is generally stressed
in a particularistic society, tends to be expedient and manipulative,
and valued mainly in terms of material or status gain.[25] Within a
universalistic work structure the employee is expected to be imper-

19. G. J. Gordon, *Public Administration in America,* New York, St. Martin's Press, 1978, p.34.
20. Page, op.cit., pp.60-61.
21. Gordon, op.cit., p.34.
22. Ibid., p.35.
23. This notion comes from Erich Fromm, *Escape from Freedom* (New York, Farrar and Rinehart,
     1940), David Riesman, *The Lonely Crowd: A Study of the Changing American Character* (New
     Heaven, Yale University Press, 1950) and Martin Buber, *I and Thou* (New York, Charles
     Scribner's Sons, 1970).
24. T. Parsons, *Essays in Sociological Theory,* Glencoe, Free Press, 1954, p.79.
25. Y. A. Cohen, "Patterns of Friendship" in Y. A. Cohen, ed., *Social Structure and Personali-
     ty* (New York, Holt, Rinehart and Winston, 1961), pp.353-54.

sonal in his relations with other employees and with clients or customers, to put loyalty to the company ahead of other loyalties, and to value the external motivators of status and achievement above the rewards of interpersonal relations.[26]

Characteristics of American management practices shaped by American culture can be summarized briefly as follows:[27] personal emphasis on individualism; interpersonal relationships that encourage independence; worker participation in an atmosphere of competition and elitism; preference for the specialist rather than the generalist; decision-making from the top down, with decision being made quickly by individuals; emphasis on conflict management, with a desire for all conflicts to be surfaced and confronted; verbal and written communications stating explicit instructions and politics; making changes when required in an abrupt, complete, and surgical manner; employment, retention, and promotion based on individual merit with little or no regard for length of employment; and little sense of belonging to the organization, with a consequent low degree of loyalty.

Korean Culture and Its Impact on Management Practices

Korea is a society in transition, gradually transforming itself from a premodern state into a modern nation, from a traditional, agrarian society into an industrial society. Korea, like other traditional societies in Asia, has experienced the rise and fall of dynasties for more than 2,000 years according to the earliest available historical records. Korea is a homogeneous society having unique people, language, and customs. This homogeneous Korean society was originally rooted in and developed from familism which stresses family relationships based not on the concept of equality but on the hierarachical concept, and a village-centered clan organization.[28]

Familism in Korea, however, has been either consciously or unconsciously conceived and embedded in Confucianism.[29] Thus, it is a wellknown fact that the traditional Korean culture has been

26. L. A. Zurcher, Jr., A. Meadow, and S. L. Zurcher, "Value Orientation, Role Conflict, and Alienation from Work: A Cross-Cultural Study," *American Sociological Review*, vol. 30, no. 4 (1965), pp.539-48.
27. M. K. Kobayashi and W. W. Burke, "Organization Development in Japan," *Columbia Journal of World Business*, 11, no. 2(1976), p.116.
28. Seong-Hi Yim, "Changing Patterns in Korean Family Structure," *The Korea Journal*, vol. 6, no. 8 (1966), pp.4-9.
29. Ibid.

influenced decidedly by Confucian ideas since the Yi dynasty
(established in 1392). Confucianism basically consists of the following
five cardinal virtues.[30] First of all, the relationship between father
and son must be part of filial piety of the son for his father and the
love of the father by his son. In its patriarchal family system, the
authority of the father is not only the highest, it is absolute. Secondly,
the bond between husband and wife must be linked with love, the
concept and teaching of which were more or less ritualized, formalized
and meaningless. Thirdly, social orders must be arranged in accordance with seniority: the subordination of the younger to the older and
the humanity of the older to the younger. Fourthly, mutual trust
between friends must be permanent in times of hardship and adversity
just as they are in times of joy and glory. This is the key to all human
relationships, leading to the final sense of humanity and solidarity.
Finally, the loyalty of the subject to the lord is held as unconditionally
sacred and respected just as it should be between son and father.

A characteristic of Confucianism is to look upon human relations
not as those between men of euqal rights and duties but as those between superiors and subordinates. Among the five major human
relationships in Confucianism, only that of "friends" has been considered as a horizontal relationship.[31] Here, Korean cultural values
are predominatingly particularistic, which is a value orientation toward
institutionalized obligations of friendship.[32] As a result of Confucian
upbringing, the Korean people on the one hand developed an
authoritarian attitude and, on the other failed to develop into self-
reliant individuals, that is, Confucianism was responsible for preventing the people from becoming independent and progressive.[33]

Korean culture was also strongly influenced by the antimaterialistic
philosophy of Taoism and Buddhism, which lead Korean people to
suppress their acquisitive instincts and hedonistic desires by seeking
refuge in the mystical doctrine of Buddhism and fatalistic quietism

30. Confucianism, though originally introduced in 221 A.D., replaced Buddishm as the
    predominant religion with the coming of the Yi dynasty in 1392. See K. P. Yang and
    G. Henderson, "An Outline of History of Korean Confucianism," *Journal of Asian Studies,*
    vol. xviii, no. 1 & no. 2, pp. 77-101 and 259-76.
31. Tae-Gil Kim, "How to Harmonize the Traditional Moral Value and Present-Day Needs"
    in *Report on the International Conference on the Problem of Modernization in Asia* (Seoul, Asiatic
    Research Center, Korea University, 1966). pp. 114-26.
32. "Universalism vs. Particularism," one of the pattern variables, postulated by Parsons
    and Shils in their general theory of action: see T. Parsons and E. A. Shils, eds., *Toward
    a General Theory of Action* (Cambridge, Harvard University Press, 1959), pp. 76-77.
33. Hyun-ki Paik, "The Korean Social Strulcture and Its Implications for Education,' *The
    Korea Journal,* vol. 8, no. 3 (1968), pp. 11-15.

of Taoism.[34] In such a taste, assertion of political and economic equali-ty by the populace was not conceivable. Koreans placed trust in the ruling body to provide their guidance and protection. The inevitable result of such a situation was the continuation of paternalism.[35]

The thirty-six years of Japanese rule (1909-1945) significantly influenced Korean culture and society although only limited segments of Korean life were affected. Japanese influence was most evident in the administrative, legal, and educational fields.[36] Substantial in-flows of Japanese administration and capital brought changes to Korea's administrative, economic, and educational structures through the introduction of Japanese systems and new agricultural practices. The impact of the Japanese was limited, however, by the restrictions placed on Korean participation in economic and political planning and management, and the customs and structure of Korean society as a whole were not deeply affected.[37] It should be noted that in socio-cultural aspects, Japanese society is very similar to Korean soceity, and both societies are homogeneous societies.

Since the establishment of the Republic of Korea as a democratic nation in 1948, Confucianism and traditional culture have incrementally weakened and changed in the process of the nation's modernization and urbanization. Urbanization as a phenomenon came close to representing the cumulative social change that occurred after liberation from Japanese rule in 1945.[38] The ideology of democracy and Western culture (particularly, American culture) have also influenced Korean social change.[39] In current Korean society there are three different groups of people, each with a different way of thinking. The first group is people age sixty-five or over belonging to what we may call the Yi-dynasty stratum. The second contains people those between sixty-five and forty-five involved in the Japanese stratum. And the third includes people those under forty-five involved in the stratum with its educational background rooted in the imported Western ideology of democracy.[40] Since the behavioral patterns of man

34. H. Sunwoo & Se-Jin Kim, "Historical Perspective on Korean Politics" is Se-Jin Kim & Chang-Hyun Cho, eds., *Government and Politics of Korea* (Silver Spring, The Research Institute on Korean Affairs, 1972), pp. 15-24.
35. Ibid., p. 18.
36. P. Hasan, *Korean*, Baltimore, Johns Hopkins University Press, 1976, p. 26.
37. Ibid.
38. Hahn-Been Lee, *Korea: Time, Change, and Administration*, Honolulu, East-West Center, University of Hawaii, 1968, p. 60.
39. Man-Gap Lee, "Rural People and Their Modernization" in *Report on the International Con-ference on the Problems of Modernization in Asia* (Seoul, Asiatic Research Center, Korea Univer-sity, 1966), pp. 665-78.
40. Paik, op. cit., p. 12.

emanate from his culture,[41] naturally there is considerable disagreement among the above three groups formed under different but dominant cultures. There is bound to be some difference between generations in any society, but the differences and conflicts existing among the three strata of Korean society have an intensity beyond the mere conflict of generations observable in other societies.[42] Thus, it can be said that the managerial thinking of the three different groups also are different in many ways due to differences not only in generation but also in culture. Nevertheless, there has been relatively little change in the fundamental characteristics of Korean society. Vestiges of traditional ideas and habits and Confucianism are still very much alive in Korean society and in the Korean mind.[43]

As previously noted, socio-cultural factors of a given society have considerable impact on organizational behavior and functionings.

Fig. 1. *The Socio-Cultural Determinants of Managerial Style.*

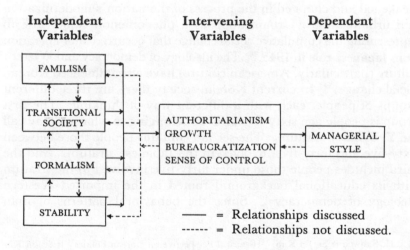

Independent Variables

Intervening Variables

Dependent Variables

FAMILISM

TRANSITIONAL SOCIETY

FORMALISM

STABILITY

AUTHORITARIANISM
GROWTH
BUREAUCRATIZATION
SENSE OF CONTROL

MANAGERIAL STYLE

———— = Relationships discussed
------ = Relationships not discussed.

41. Parsons and Shils explain that in any given social situation the actor's cultural background will influence his choice between the horns of the dilemma presented by each pattern variable: see Parsons & Shils, op. cit., p. 79.

42. Paik, op. cit., p. 12.

43. Ibid.

Korean management practices have been impacted by Korean culture which has been influenced by familism, Confucianism, and Japanese and Western cultures. Characteristics of Korean management practices could be summarized briefly as follows:[44] a pervasive organizational paternalism; authoritative relationships between superiors and subordinates; a unique, group decision-making; distinctive interpersonal behavior growing out of deep emotional sensitivity; preference for the generalist rather than the specialist; a Tabooed materialism; a high degree of sense of belonging and loyalty; emphasis on agreement management; risk averision; nonverbal and implied communication; desire for all conflict to be avoided or melted; and excessive formalism.

In this inventory familism, traditional society, formalism, and environmental stability are selected intentionally as the socio-cultural variables for a comparative management study between Korea and the United States. These socio-cultural variables will be defined and illustrated in relevant proposition. The proposition of familism will be illustrated first and then traditional society, formalism, and environmental stability in that order. Figure 1 depicts in highly abbreviated way relationships between socio-cultural variables and managerial style which will be illustrated in this inventory.

Proposition 1. KOREAN MANAGERS WHOSE SOCIO-CULTURAL FACTORS HAVE BEEN IMPACTED BY FAMILISM ARE MORE LIKELY TO HAVE AN AUTHORITARIAN MANAGERIAL STYLE THAN AMERICAN MANAGERS WHOSE SOCIO-CULTURAL FACTORS HAVE BEEN IMPACTED BY INDIVIDUALISM.

Definition & introduction Socio-cultural factors may be defined as the dominant human attitudes, values, and beliefs in a given society or country and the way they tend to influence the motivation, behavior, and performance of individuals in organizations.[45] As noted earlier, however, the terms "sociological" and "cultural" are used synonymously in this inventory. Familism may be characterized as follows: the family is the basic unit of society; the whole picture of social life may be represented in the family system in a society; it stresses the loyalty that should exist between superior and subordinate

---

44. This summarization is mainly based upon Suk-Choon Cho, *Han-Guk Haeng Jeong Hak* (Korean Public Administration), Seoul, Bark Young Sa, 1980, pp. 134-54.

45. This definition of socio-cultural factors is adapted from Farmer & Richman, op. cit., pp. 109-110.

46. Paik, op. cit., pp. 11-15 and Long & Seo, op. cit., p. 13.

in all social and family relations; relations among members of a family are not based on the concept of equality but are strictly hierarchical.[46] In Korean society familism was embedded in Confucianism. The outstanding characteristic of familism is, therefore, the authoritarian role of the head of the family who is absolutely obeyed. Hence, the rules that govern relationships between subordinates and their superiors are the same as those that govern relationships between father and son.[47] The terms "paternalism" and "groupism" are sometimes used as a synonym for familism. "Particularism" is also associated with familism.

As previously noted, individualism stresses self-reliance, i.e., the individual is assumed to be both self-sufficient and capable of self-governing: individual rights and liberties; interpersonal relations are based on the concept of equality; and society exists to provide fulfill-ment for the individuals.[48] In American society individualism was, therefore, associated with the ideology of democracy.[49] Individualism also corresponds to universalism.

An authoritarian managerial style may be defined as a managerial style which has the following characteristics:[50] (1) the relatively high degree of power wielded by the superior over the work group; (2) reliance on authority to accomplish the work of the organization; (3) an authoritative manager tends to centralize his authority in his own hands; (4) both power and all decision-making functions are concen-trated in the person with authority; and (5) the subordinates are highly dependent upon the superior, and they feel their performance is judged by their obedience to the superior's directives. In the management literature the opposite of an authoritarian managerial style has been presumed to be a participative or democratic managerial style. A more authoritarian managerial style in this inventory corresponds to a less participative or democratic style.

This inventory suggests that Korean managers influenced by familism are likely to have an authoritarian managerial style. Sung-Chick Hong's study of values of the three Korean population strata, Woo-Kon Yoon's study, and Joseph's cross-cultural study of

---

47. Long & Seo, op. cit., p. 13.
48. Page, op. cit., pp. 60-61 and Long & Seo, op. cit., p. 15.
49. Page, ibid.
50. These characteristics of an authoritative managerial style are based upon Rensis Likert, *New Patterns of Management* (New York, McGraw-Hill, 1961), pp. 222-36, and S. M. Sales, "Supervisory Style and Productivity: Review and Theory," *Personal Psychology,* vol. 19, no. 3 (1966), pp. 275-286.

managerial practices illustrate this proposition.[51]

Illustration Hong's study attempts to ascertain empirically the current values of Korean farmers, businessmen, and professors within the framework of economic development. Data were collected by face-to-face interviews with 352 farmers, 261 businessmen, and 392 professors. Questions included cover the following topics: attitudes toward traditional family system: attitudes toward status vs. money; and self-conceptions of Korean character. Research results indicate that in Korea the traditional family orientation is still strong. A majority of interviewees still consider the traditional family-oriented (familism-oriented) person more respectable than the business-oriented (individualism-oriented) person. A great majority of the three population strata also respond that they would prefer a job that is more respected even if it means a little less pay. These results corroborates the fact that Korean people tend to be exceedingly status conscious. The study concludes that regardless of population strata the majority of them share an authoritarian character.

Yoon's study of Korean bureaucratic behavior explores the fundamental cause of administrative problems by determining the influence of personality structure on bureaucrats' behavior. One of his findings is that the analysis of the Korean socio-family system and cultural values of raising children on the basis of previous empirical observations showed a large probability that Korean people as a whole have a high degree of authoritarianism in common.

Meanwhile, findings of Joseph's cross-cultural study of managerial practices indicate that U.S. managers followed a democratic style of leadership in performing directive functions.[52] That is, participation in the decision-making process was encouraged at all levels. Various upward and downward communication techniques were used in getting feedback, i.e., suggestions and sending information from top to bottom levels. Superiors perceived their subordinates as trustworthy and confident. They also felt that the average human being will

---

51. Sung-Chick Hong, "Values of the Farmers, Businessman, and Professors" in *Report on the International Conference on the Problems of Modernization in Asia* (Seoul, Asiatic Research Center, Korea University, 1966), pp. 789-802; Woo-Kon Yoon, *Bureaucratic Behavior in the Case of South Korea,* unpublished doctoral dissertation, New York University, 1972; and P. M. Joseph, "A Cross-Cultural Comparison of Managerial Practices: India and The United States," *Quarterly Journal of Management Development,* vol. 4, no. 2 (1973), pp. 73-82.

52. Most cross-cultural comparative studies state same notion. For example, in their world-wide comparative surveys of managerial behavior Barret and Bass indicate that managers in the U.S. subsidiaries as well as American organization have a democratic style: see G. V. Barret and B. M. Bass, "Comparative Surveys of Managerial Attitudes and Behavior," *Quarterly Journal of Management Development,* vol. 4, no. 1 (1973), pp. 1-28.

exercise self-direction in the service of objectives to which he is committed. In other words, American managers believe in self-reliance which is a key concept of individualism. American managers whose socio-cultural factors were impacted by individualism are thus less likely to have an authoritarian managerial style than Korean managers.

Proposition 2. KOREAN MANAGERS WHO ARE IN A TRANSITIONAL SOCIETY ARE MORE LIKELY TO HAVE AN ENTREPRENEURIAL MANAGERIAL STYLE THAN AMERICAN MANAGERS WHO ARE IN AN ADVANCED SOCIETY.

Definition & introduction   A transitional society may be defined as a society which is in the state of passing from one place, condition, or action to another.[53] For example, as noted earlier, Korea is a transitional society transforming itself from a traditional agrarian society into an industrial society. Fred Riggs refers to the countries seeking to speed up their own industrialization as transitional societies.[54] Riggs also characterizes a transitional society as a prismatic society in an effort to identify and analyze a particular kind of social order of wide prevalence and importance.[55] He states:

. . . The transitional countries are influenced by external models of standards. It is easier to adopt by fiat or law a formal organizational structure with a manifest administrative function than it is to institutionalize corresponding social behavior. Hence many formally administrative structures in transitional societies turn out to be mere facades, while the effective administrative work remains a latent function of older, more diffuse institutions.[56]

"Developing" or "less developed" countries are sometimes referred to as transitional societies.

An advanced society may be defined as a society which is already completely developed or industrialized.[57] Needless to say, the United States belongs to an advanced society. Riggs regards the United States

---

53. This definition of transitional society is based upon *Standard College Dictionary* (New York, Harcourt, Brace and World, 1963).
54. F. W. Riggs, *Administration in Development Countries,* Boston, Houghton Mifflin Co., 1964. p. 4.
55. Ibid., p. 34.
56. Ibid.
57. This definition of advanced society is based on *Standard College Dictionary,* op. cit.

as a diffracted society which is composed predominantly of functionally specific structures.[58] It should be noted that in this proposition the definitions of transitional society and advanced society are focused on the degree of economic development or growth.

An entrepreneurial managerial style may be defined as a managerial style which has the following characteristics: (1) bold, risky, aggressive decision-making; (2) charismatic leaders; (3) a strong commitment to growth; (4) an emphasis on administrative flexibility; and (5) reliance on intuitive judgements rather than those based on elaborate technical analysis, and not too strong a belief in institutionalized participatory decision-making.[59] Khandwalla illustrates this style as follows:

. . . Since the practitioners of this style are in the habit of seizing opportunities before all the facts about them are known, they put a premium on managerial flexibility so that the organization rapidly adapts to the evolving situation. They are not very comfortable with technocratic and participative modes of decision-making because they find them cumbersome and time consuming. Since bold moves imply frequent major organizational changes, the entrepreneurial management may occasionally be quite coercive, especially if there is resistance to such changes from the rank and file. But if such resistance is not there, such managements may not be coercive.[60]

This inventory suggests that Korean managers who are in a transitional society are quite likely to have an entrepreneurial managerial style because of a strong commitment to growth. This inventory also suggests that with respect to organizational structural variables (specialization, formalization, and centralization) Korean managers are more likely to have an entrepreneurial managerial style. Because organizations in transitional countries have in general a low degree of personal specialization, a high degree of formalization, and a high degree of centralization,[61] there are substantial barriers to a participative managerial style.

Unfortunately, the inventory contains no studies which provide an illustration for this proposition. However, there are several studies which partly illustrate the characteristics of Korean managers' en-

58. Riggs, op. cit., p. 31.
59. P. N. Khandwalla, "Some Top Management Styles, Their Context and Performance," *Organization and Adminsitrative Sciences,* vol. 7, no. 4 (1976/77), pp. 21-51.
60. Ibid., p. 25.
61. Riggs, op. cit., pp. 15-19, 45-49, 181-84, 250-55, and 280-83.

trepreneurial style. For example, Suk-Choon Cho notes that reasons for success of Korean economic development are strong commitment to growth, bold decision-making, and strong execution.[62] In their cross-cultural comparative study, England and Lee indicate that Korean managers place greater value on organizational growth than on organizational efficiency and profit, while American managers are much more concerned about organizational efficiency and profit maximization than organizational growth.[63]

Proposition 3. KOREAN MANAGERS WHOSE SOCIO-CULTURAL FACTORS HAVE BEEN IMPACTED BY A HIGH DEGREE OF FORMALISM ARE MORE LIKELY TO HAVE A BUREAUCRATIC MANAGERIAL STYLE THAN AMERICAN MANAGERS IMPACTED BY A LOW DEGREE OF FORMALISM.

Definition & introduction   Formalism may be defined as scrupulous observance of prescribed forms, as in social life.[64] Riggs characterizes a situation which does not represent reality as "formalistic."[65] For example, he states:

. . . If you find an organization chart which purports to describe the structure of a government department, with elaborate statements of the duties of each unit and post in the department, you will hold this chart formalistic if you find the real people and units in the department doing different things from those mentioned in the chart.[66]

If normlessness is widespread and a high degree of overlapping in administrative organization occurs, considerable formalism may be expected.[67] Riggs asserts that formalism is more prevailing in the poly-normative state which is characterized not only by overlapping, fossilization, and attenuation of the more vigorous norms of the fused and refracted models, but also by a condition of normlessness.[68] Particularly, in Korea, people traditionally preferred formalism

---

62. Cho, op. cit., pp. 334-49.
63. G. W. England and R. Lee, "Organizational Goals and Expected Behavior among American, Japanese, and Korean Managers: A comparative Study," *Academy of Management Journal*, vol. 14, no. 4 (1971), pp. 425-438.
64. This definition of formalism comes from *Standard College Dictionary*, op. cit.
65. Riggs, op. cit., p. 15.
66. Ibid.
67. Ibid., p. 15 & p. 183.
68. Ibid., p. 181.

because of its consistency with teaching of Confucianism.[69] Formalism is also both cause and consequence of lack of consensus. According to Riggs, in transitional (prismatic) society poly-normatism carries dissensus as a corollary.[70] He states:

. . . When there is little agreement about what the goals of the state should be, or on who should have the right to rule, control is grasped by coercion, by violence, by money, or by 'charismatic' leaders, but not by legitimate authority. When legal and constituional procedures and forms are invoked, they prove unenforceable.[71]

One result of formalism is therefore the twin phenomena of over-conformity and non-enforcement. That is, ritualistic insistence on overconformity can be used to raise the price for non-enforcement; what the right hand insists on, the left hand ignores.[72] Riggs goes on to point out:

. . . in this context, goal oriented administrators are trapped by red tape and proceduralism as the lack of clear-cut political and policy guidance leaves them bemused and floundering. . . . meanwhile, legalistic bureaucrats, less concerned with goals than with textual intricacies, manipulate the rules to their own advantage. The free-wheeling makeup of the prismatic society's juridical superstructure offers dizzying joyrides to a bureaucratic elite.[73]

A bureaucratic managerial style may be operationally defined as a managerial style which has the following characteristics:[74] (1) the manager accepts his role as one which puts himself and others into narrowly prescribed roles; (2) its stresses a tidy show as a condition of executive competence. A tidy show means personal or administrative cleanliness; (3) it emphasized regularity which is an outgrowth of the need to practice personal or administrative cleanliness. Regularity means basically punctuality. A punctuality pattern is one of a high degree of routine. A high degree of routine results in flexibility. Routine regularity is found in the attempt to routinize the behavior of subordinates, (4) accurate reports and files are necessary

---

69. Man-Gap Lee, op. cit., pp. 670-75.
70. Riggs. op. cit., p. 183.
71. Ibid.
72. Ibid.
73. Ibid.
74. This definition is based on E. E. Jennings, *The Executive*, (New York, Harper & Row, 1962), pp. 164-95.

for communication; (5) conscientiousness in the performances of petty duties is an ingredient in the bureaucratic style. Rules and regulations are essential in keeping the whole system together in working order; and (6) impersonality and bureaucratic vindictiveness are dominant in managerial practices because of the loss of objectivity due to ritualistic observance of rules.

In Korea, one of the dominant values governing bureaucratic behavior is regarding human relations as characterized by hierarchical order.[75] As previously noted, Confucianism was most influential in forming such values in the traditional culture. Hence, the most important criterion governing human relations remains hierarchical role. Subordinates are likely to obey the superior's decision-making even when their judgement of the task requirement does not agree with that of the superior's.[76]

This inventory suggests that a high degree of formalism makes it more possible for managers to have a bureaucratic managerial style by increasing bureaucratization. This inventory also suggests that a higher degree of formalism is associated with a high degree of formalization of individuals' work roles. Dong-Suh Bark's study of policy making in the Korean executive branch and Hae-Dong Kim's study provide an illustration of this proposition.[77]

Illustration   The results of Bark's study reflect Korean bureaucratic behavior. Namely, the results of structured interviews with 126 higher civil servants indicate that a majority of them believe that legal bases determine the authority and influence of administrators in their superior-subordinate relations. This means that they regard rules and regulations as essential elements for human relations. The interview results also indicate that subordinates are reluctant to disagree with superiors in meetings where policy issues are discussed and where their superiors are present. Accordingly, it indicates that such bureaucratic behavior routinizes hierarchical roles in the organization and increases bureaucratization.

In his study of formalistic attitudes of Korean bureaucrats, Kim explores whether Korean bureaucrat's formalistic attitude is related to their desire for success in life and personal needs in the organization. He asserts that formalistic attitudes begin to appear

---

75. Suk-Choon Cho, "The Korean Bureaucracy; Authority and Policy Formulation Process," *Korean Journal of Public Administration,* vol. viii, no. 1 (1970), pp. 153-64.
76. Ibid.
77. Dong-Suh Bark, "Policy Making in the Korean Executive Branch," *Korean Journal of Public Administration,* vol. 4, no. 2 (1966), pp. 207-42, and Hae-Dong Kim, "A Study on Formalistic Attitudes of Korean Bureaucreats," *Korean Journal of Public Administration,* vol. xii, no. 2 (1974), pp. 40-59.

psychologically when people only seek to meet their success needs and personal needs through the organization regardless of the effects on achievement of organizational goals, and that formalistic attitudes result in such behaviors as bureaucratic vindictiveness, overconformity, laziness and opportunistic attitudes. Therefore, formalistic attitudes make it more possible for Korean managers to have a bureaucratic managerial style.

Proposition 4. KOREAN MANAGERS WHOSE ENVIRONMENTAL CONDITIONS HAVE A LOW DEGREE OF STABILITY ARE MORE LIKELY TO HAVE A MECHANISTIC MANAGERIAL STYLE THAN AMERICAN MANAGERS WHOSE ENVIRONMENTAL CONDITIONS HAVE A HIGH DEGREE OF STABILITY.

Definition & introduction Environmental conditions include socioeconomic, educational, political, legal, and cultural factors which impinge upon the organization's internal operation but are external to the organization.[78] In this inventory environment is thought of as the totality of physical and social factors that are taken directly into consideration in the decision-making behavior of individuals in the organization.

If environmental conditions remain the same over time, these conditions would characterize a high degree of stability. On the other hand, if environmental conditions are in a continual process of change, these conditions would characterize a low degree of stability. A high degree of "change" or "variability" is a term which means approximately the same thing as a low degree of stability. And a low degree of "change" or "variability" is a term which means approximately the same thing as a high degree of stability.

A mechanistic managerial style may be defined as a managerial style which has the following characteristics:[79] (1) stress on hierarchic structure of control, authority and communication (high centralization); (2) precise definition of rights and obligations and technical methods attached to each functional role (high formalization); (3) a tendency for interaction between members of the concern to be vertical,

---

78. This definition of environmental conditions comes from A. R. Negandhi, "A Model for Analyzing Organizations in Cross-Cultural Settings" in A. R. Negandhi, *Modern Organizational Theory* (Kent, Kent State University, 1973), pp. 285-312.
79. This definition of a mechanistic managerial style is based on T. Burns and G. M. Stalker, *The Management of Innovation*, London, Tavistock Publications, 1961, pp. 119-120.

i.e., between superiors and subordinates; (4) a tendency for operations and working behaviors to be governed by the instructions and decisions issued by superiors; (5) specialized differentiation of functional tasks into which the problems and tasks facing the concern as a whole are broken down; (6) insistence on loyalty to the concern and obedience to superiors as a condition of membership; and (7) greater importance and prestige attaching to internal than to general knowledge, experience, and skill. Under a mechanistic managerial style, management is strongly risk aversive in its external strategy. Presumably, coercion is high in unstable circumstances in order to maintain stability but low in stable environments. As part of its conservatism, this style also tends to discount technocracy and participation.

A study indicates that managers who encounter turbulent environmental conditions will react by "pulling in the reins," resorting to a mechanistic style in order to gain a sense of a control over the situation rather than to face the perceived risks inherent in delegation and "loose" structure.[80]

Korean socio-cultural environmental conditions have been more turbulent than that of the United States. In the present century alone, for example, Korea has undergone a series of historical upheavals. During the first decade of this century, Korea was annexed by Japan and remained under its colonial rule for 36 years. Then, there was the liberation from Japanese rule in 1945. As previously noted, Japanese rule significantly influenced Korean culture and society. Particularly, the administrative, legal, and educational systems were changed by Japanese influence. Since 1945, Korea has been divided into two countries and experienced a devastating war. Korea has recently experienced two revolutions. And she is still experiencing political upheaval and frequent changes in the administrative, legal, and educational system.

This inventory therefore suggests that Korean managers who have a low degree of stability in environmental conditions are more likely to have a mechanistic managerial style in order to gain a sense of control or stability.

England and Lee's comparative management study and Dong-Suh Bark's previously cited study of policy making in the Korean executive branch illustrate this proposition.[81]

---

80. See L. J. Bourgeois, III, D. W. McAllister, and T. R. Mitchell, "The Effect of Different Organizational Environments upon Decisions about Organizational Structure," *Academy of Management Journal,* vol. 21, no. 3 (1978), pp. 508-14.
81. England & Lee, op. cit., and Bark, op. cit.

Illustration The purpose of England and Lee's comparative management study is to explore the linkage between perceptions of organizational goals and expected organizational behaviors of managers from Korea, Japan, and the United States. The study was conducted by Personal Value Questionnaires (PVQ) which is based on the rationale that meanings attached by an individual to a carefully selected set of concepts will provide a useful description of his personal value system, which, in turn, will be related to his behavior in understandable ways.[82] In their study one of the eight organizational goals which is most apt to influence behavior is organizational stability. England and Lee postulate that the higher the behavioral relevance score, the greater the expected influence the concept will have on behavior.

The results of their study indicate that Korean managers have higher behavior relevance scores on organizational stability than American managers. The relatively high scores of Korean managers for organizational stability may reflect a higher value being placed on stable environmental conditions. In other words, Korean managers who are under turbulent environmental conditions naturally try to gain a sense of control for stability.

The findings of Bark's study indicate that Korean managers prefer a mechanistic managerial style. Namely, Korean managers seem to attach considerably more importance to interpersonal relations between superiors and subordinates, and human relations take precedence over competence. Another finding is that career civil servants emphatically confirm the paramount role of higher authorities in administrative decision-making.

Implications

This model of socio-cultural variables in relation to managerial style can be complicated in four ways: first, the interdependence between the results can be systematically examined; second, additional propositions can be specified; third, additional intervening variables can be specified; and fourth, the mechanisms can be ranked according to the degree they impact on managerial style. These complications are required to bring the model into closer correspondence with reality. The strategy of this inventory, as in model building in general, is to simplify now and complicate later. The test of this simplified model is, not the impossible standard of perfect correspondence with reality,

---

82. England & lee, Ibid., p. 428.

but the inclusion of objective variables which influence managerial style. This inventory attempts to present variables pertinent to managerial style, and it does not attempt to make value judgement about each managerial style.

This inventory disregards the reverse situation of each variable and the dysfunctions. This inventory, therefore, assumes that the mechanisms are basically functional for the managerial style, but the generality of mechanisms can not be asserted.

Finally, there are differences between Korea and the United States in managerial styles. These differences appear to be largely socio-culturally based. It would be naive to advocate one model of managerial style as being optimal for two countries. The widely advocated American model of participative managerial style, for example, may not be optimal for the Korean culture and, in fact, may be dysfunctional. However, this inventory acknowledges that differences in managerial style are accounted for by individual, situational, and organizational differences. Therefore, managerial style should be explored on the basis of not only socio-cultural factors but individual, situational, and organizational aspects.

6

The Transfer of Knowledge in Korean Public Administration

Wha Joon Rho

I. Introduction

In recent years there has been increased interest in the indigenization of public administration and in the effective and efficient transfer
of administrative theory to practice.[1] The indigenization problems
were brought in because administrative theories developed abroad
are not adequate in explaining Korean administrative phenomena
in terms of theory and practice. On the other hand, the problems
of the transfer of administrative knowledge were raised because the
lack of effective communication and understanding between scholars
and practitioners was identified as one of the most critical obstacles
to be overcome in building up Korean public dministration as an
indigenous discipline.

Despite the importance of closely related issues in the developmental
process of administrative science and administrative practice, there
have been no attempts to examine these issues on the basis of
empirical data. The purposes of this essay are; to evaluate the
usefulness of management theories and techniques transferred from
abroad to the Korean administrative context, and to examine the scope
and magnitude of the schism between academicians and practitioners

---

1. Dong Suh Bark, "Trends in the study of Public Administration in Korea: A Critical Assessment," *The Korean Political Science Review*, Vol. 12 (1978), pp. 63-72; Wan Ki Paik, "On
   the Problems of Building up Korean Public Administration as a Discipline: A Scientific
   Approach," *Ibid.*, pp. 73-92; Byung Young Ahn, "Self-Referentiality in the Study of
   Korean Public Administration," *The Korean Political Science Review*, Vol. 13 (1979), pp.
   49-66; Chong Bum Lee, "A Prolegomenon to the Indigenization of Public Administration," *Korean Public Administration Review*, Vol. 11 (1977), pp. 203-220.

in Korean public administration.

In an attempt to obtain systematic data on these problems, a questionaire[2] was mailed to 130 public management academicians and 240 central government practitioners in May and June, 1981. The samples of the public management academicians were chosen by clustered sampling from the files of the professors of departments of public administration. The samples of the government practitioners were chosen from the Economic Planning Board, the Ministry of Home Affairs, the Ministry of Agriculture, the Ministry of Government Administration, and the Department of Planning and Coordination for Premier. The survey instrument administered to each group was identical. Usable questionaires were received from 98 academicians (75 per cent of the samples) and from 197 practitioners (82 per cent of the samples).

Table 1 through Table 4 present the backgrounds of the respondents.[3]

The academicians tended to be somewhat older than their government counterparts while practitioners tended to serve longer than their academic counterparts. Among the respondents about 43 per cent

Table 1: Ages

Age	Respondents	
	Academicians (N = 98)	Practitioners (N = 197)
under 35 year	19.4(%)	36.6(%)
35 year—under 40 year	24.5	15.2
40 year—under 45 year	30.6	26.9
45 year—under 50 year	15.3	19.8
50 year or older	10.2	1.5
Total	100.0	100.0

2. Most of this questionaire was adapted from the study of Duncan and Bowman. W. Jack Duncan, "Transferring Management Theory to Practice,' *Academy of Management Journal*, Vol. 17 (December, 1974), pp. 719-723; James S. Bowman, "Managerial Theory and Practice: the Transfer of Knowledge in Public Administration," *Public Administration Review*, Vol. 38, No. 6 (November/December, 1978), pp. 563-570.

3. In the central government of Korea, the administrative positions of rank 5 are for the sub-sections of rank 4 or equivalents. The administrative positions of rank 4 are for the section chiefs or equivalents and the administrative positions of rank 3 and rank 2 are for the bureau chiefs or equivalents.

Table 2: Length of Tenure

	Respondents	
Tenure	Academicians (N = 98)	Practitioners (N = 197)
under 5 years	28.6(%)	21.3(%)
5 ycars—under 10 years	35.7	18.3
10 years—under 15 years	15.3	20.3
15 years—under 20 years	12.2	22.8
20 years or more	8.2	17.3
Total	100.0	100.0

Table 3: Present Position

Academicians (N = 98)		Practitioners (N = 197)	
Position	Percentage	Position	Percentage
Full time Lecturer	26.5	Rank 5	70.6
Assistant Professor	26.5	Rank 4	23.3
Associate Professor	25.5	Rank 3	3.6
Professor	21.5	Rank 2 or above	2.5
Total	100.0		100.0

Table 4: Length of Training Abroad

	Respondents	
Education	Academicians (N = 98)	Practitioners (N = 197)
none	40.8(%)	71.0(%)
under 1 year	16.3	18.3
1 yesr—less than 3 years	14.3	5.6
3 years—less than 5 years	10.2	1.0
5 years or more	18.4	0.0
no response	0.0	4.1
Total	100.0	100.0

of the academicians were trained abroad for more than one year. However, only about 7 per cent of the practitioners were trained abroad for more than one year.

II. Sources of Professional Knowledge in Korean Public Administration.

In order to identify the sources and the developmental processes of professional knowledge in public administration in Korea, the following five questions were asked to determine preferred sources

Table 5: Sources of Management Information

Sources	Respondents	
	Academicians (N = 98)	Practitioners (N = 197)
University teachers and researchers	7.1(%)	15.7(%)
Government and private industry research and development	1.0	20.8
Research foundations	0.0	2.0
Practioning managers	1.0	30.6
Management consultants	0.0	2.5
Professional and academic societies	3.1	1.5
Foreign books and journals in the field of public administration	86.8	21.3
Others	1.0	4.6
No response/opinion	0.0	1.0
Total	100.0	100.0

of knowledge in the field. The first question concerned general sources of information. The second and third questions concerned the types and significance of literature. And the other two items were about foreign language books of references and the practical usefulness of public management theories developed abroad.

The most important sources of knowledge in the field of public management were the foreign books and journals in the field of public administration. As shown in Table 5, 86.8 per cent of the academicians selected foreign books and journals as "the most important source of management knowledge." This choice was followed by university teachers and researchers and professional and academic societies. Unlike the academic respondents, public managers ranked practitioners as the prime source of knowledge. Foreign books and journals in the field of public administration, and government and private industry research and development were judged as the second and third best sources of knowledge. University teachers and researchers, however, were regarded as only the fourth best source of information.

In short, academicians view foreign counterparts as the single most relevant base of information while public managers think their own peer groups are the most important base of management knowledge.

When asked to list two professional journals published in Korea as well as abroad that are important to them as a professional in public administration, both the academicians and practitioners recorded a large number of periodicals. A total of 26 different journals were mentioned by the academicians.

Among the 26 different journals mentioned, 3 journals were written in Korean, 19 journals were in English, 2 journals were in Japanese, and the other 2 journals were in French. The most frequently mentioned journal (70 citations) was *Public Administration Review,* and the other frequently mentioned journals were *Administrative Science Quarterly* (29 citations), *Korean Journal of Public Administration* (19 citations), *Korean Public Administration Review* (17 citations), *The American Political Science Review* (13 citations) *Policy Studies Journal* (4 citations), and *American Sociological Review* (4 citations). The other journals were cited less than three times.

The practitioners cited a total of 23 different journals. Among these journals, 8 journals were written in Korean, 9 journals were in English and the remaining 6 journals were in Japanese. Among the 23 journals, *Korean Journal of Local Administration* was the most frequently cited journal (31 citations) and this was followed by *Korean Journal of Public Adminsitration* (20 citations), *Public Administration Review* (7 citations), *Korean Public Administration Review* (6 citations) and *Urban Affairs* (Japanese Journal, 5 citations). The other journals were cited less than three times.

Public Administration Review, Korean Journal of Public Administration and *Korean Public Administration Review* were read very widely by both groups.

Another important characteristic is that the leading scholarly journals such as the *Administrative Science Quarterly, The American Political Science Review* and *American Sociological Review* were read by the scholars while the more practitioner oriented journals such as *Korean Journal of Local Administration* and *Urban Affairs* (Japanese Journal) were preferred by the practitioners. These tendencies are somewhat different from those of the United States in which significant parts of scholars tended to read *Public Management,* a practitioner oriented magazine, while many of the practitioners preferred. *The American Political Science Review,* the leading scholarly journal of political science.[4] These tendencies in Korea might be an indication of the lack of communication and understanding between scholars and practitioners. And this lack of communication, in turn, might have blocked the development of an indigenous administrative discipline in Korea.

What are the most significant contributions to the literature in Korean Public Administration? Survey participants were asked to list up to three books including foreign books which they perceived "greatly influenced management" thought in Korea.

What are the most significnt contributions to the literature in Korean public administration? Survey participants were asked to list up to three books including foreign books which they perceived "greatly influenced management" thought in Korea.

A total of 99 different books were indicated by the 75 academicians and a total of 87 different books were cited by the 103 practi-

Table 6: Books Greatly Influencing Management Thought in Korea
(By the Order of the Citation Frequencies)

Academicians	Practitioners
1. Herbert A. Simon, *Administrative Behavior* (New York: Free Press, 1945).	1. Dong Suh Bark, *Korean Public Adminsitration* (Seoul: Bubmoon Sa, 1975).
2. Dong Suh Bark, *Korean Public Administration* (Seoul: Bubmoon Sa, 1975).	2. Hoon Yu, *Public Administration* (Seoul: Bubmoon Sa, 1970).
3. James G. March and Herbert A. Simon, *Organizations* (New York: John Wiley & Sons, Inc., 1958).	3. Moon Ok Park, *Public Administration* (Seoul: Barkyoung Sa, 1971).
4. F. W. Riggs, *Administration in Developing Countries* (Boston: Houghton Mifflin, 1964).	4. Dou Chang Kim, *Administration Law* (Seoul: Barkyoung Sa, 1971).
5. Hoon Yu, *Public Adminsitration* (Seoul: Bubmoon Sa, 1970).	5. Suck Choon Cho, *Organization and Mangement* (Seoul: Bubmoon Sa, 1964).

---

4. Bowman, *op. cit.,* p. 565.

tioners. Among the 99 books indicated by the academicians, 15 books were written in Korean, 80 books were in English, 2 were in Japanese and the other 2 were in French. On the other hand, among the 87 books mentioned by the practitioners, 47 books were written in Korean, the other 30 books and 10 books were in English and Japanese respectively.

The most frequently cited five volumes are listed in rank order in Table 6. The academicians cited foreign scholars more frequently than Korean scholars while the practitioners cited only Korean scholars.

The other cited books which did not appear in Table 6 were mentioned less frequently than five times. One of the important common characteristics is that Korean books cited are all university textbooks.

The evidence presented so far shows that Korean public administration is still in the stage of importing management technologies developed abroad. If this is the case then what are the most important foreign languages to transfer foreign management technology to Korean public management? How useful are they in the Korean administrative context? Survey participants were requested to list one foreign language in which their most important foreign reference books were written and to evaluate the practical usefulness of management theories developed abroad.

There was great agreement among university and government respondents regarding important languages for the foreign reference books. The foreign languages indicated are listed in rank order in Table 7. Both groups listed the most important languages for foreign

Table 7: Important Language for the Foreign Reference Books

	Respondents	
Language	Academicians (N = 98)	Practitioners (N = 197)
English	92.9(%)	57.9(%)
Japanese	5.1	30.5
German	0.0	0.0
French	1.0	0.5
Others	1.0	0.0
No response	0.0	11.1
Total	100.0	100.0

Table 8: Practical Usefulness of Management Theories Developed
          Abroad

| | Respondents | |
Usefulness	Academicians (N = 98)	Practitioners (N = 197)
Very useful	6.1(%)	4.1(%)
Useful	42.9	47.7
Almost not useful	43.9	46.2
Not useful	3.1	1.5
Others	2.0	0.0
No response	2.0	0.5
Total	100.0	100.0

reference books as English and Japanese. However, more than 90
per cent of the academicians tended to prefer administrative literature
written in English while more than 30 per cent of practitioners tended to prefer Japanese books as the second most important source in
contrast to only 5 percent of the academicians.

There was also great agreement about the degree of usefulness of
foreign management theories in the Korean administrative context.
Only about half of the respondents regarded foreign management
theories as either useful or very useful (Table 8).

The results of this evaluation on the usefullness of public management theories developed abroad indicate the needs and justify the
movement to indigenize public administration in Korea.

III. The Information Flow between Academicians and
Practitioners

In an effort to facilitate the indigenization of public administration in Korea, Korean public administration should be built up as
a discipline on the basic of common efforts and mutual understanding between academicians and public managers. These common
efforts can be more effective when the direction of the efforts is clearly understood. Survey data suggests that scholars and managers mostly agreed about the objectives of academic inquiry as shown in Table
9. Both groups, academicians and practitioners, considered the practicality and usefulness of research to be most important. In addition, academicians were particularly concerned about empirical

Table 9: Preferred Characteristics of Management Research

| | Respondents | |
Characteristics	Academicians (N = 98)	Practitioners (N = 197)
Practicality and usefulness	64.3(%)	57.9(%)
Logical preciseness	11.2	3.0
Saving money	2.0	0.0
Applicability to specific situations	9.2	18.8
Empirical validity	11.3	14.2
Ease of implementation	0.0	2.6
Others	2.0	3.0
No opinion	0.0	0.5
Total	100.0	100.0

validity and logical preciseness while practitioners were more concerned about applicability to specific situations and empirical validity.

If there is a general consensus on the objectives of administrative
research, what are some of the significant obstacles in the transfer
of research findings into administrative practice? Respondents were
asked to indicate the most important barrier to the effective flow of
knowledge between the academic society and the practical world. Some
of potential impediments to this conversion process are condensed
in Table 10. The three most frequently listed barriers cited by both
groups were overreliance on established procedures, insufficient incentives to develop and implement new ideas, and communication
and status problems. These findings parallel the barriers indicated
in other studies that legal oriented administrative procedures in Korean
administration, and insufficient incentives to develop and implement
new ideas were important barries to the utilization of management
knowledge.[5]

In sum, the result of these questions reveal that there is a great
consensus within the public administration profession in building up
Korean public administration as an indigenous discipline. Both
academicans and practitioners share agreement about the important
characteristics of research and the kinds of obstacle that tend to inhibit development and utilization of this work. Given this general
agreement about the characteristics of research and the barriers to

5. For the legal oriented administrative procedures in Korea see Hahn Been Lee, *Korea:
Time, Change and Administration* (Hawaii: East-West Center Press, 1968).

Table 10: Important Barriers to the Utilization of Management
Knowledge

| | Respondents | |
Barriers	Academicians (N = 98)	Practitioners (N = 197)
Overreliance on established procedures	29.6(%)	30.1(%)
Communication and Status Problems	12.2	21.8
Mistrust of outsiders	3.1	1.5
Inability of outsiders to communicate	2.0	2.0
Economic restraints	6.1	5.1
Insufficient incentives to develop and implement new ideas	27.6	24.4
Inherent residence to change	4.1	5.1
Fear of effects on organization's image from innovation	5.1	5.1
Others (Please specify)	8.2	3.9
No opinion	2.0	1.0
Total	100.0	100.0

the development and utilization of management knowledge, how can
these barriers be overcome? What specific methods might be useful
to link theory to practice in Korea?

IV. Toward More Effective Ways of Linking Theory to Practice

More than 40 per cent of the academicians said that increased participation in decision-making was the single most important way that
barriers could be surmounted as shown in Table 11. The development of official programs to stimulate creativity, and the use of rewards
for developing and implementing new ideas were also perceived as
effective ways by the academicians.

Increased participation in decision-making, and the development
of official programs to stimulate creativity also were regarded as the
first and second most effetive ways by the management circles.
However, practitioners saw new organizational forms to overcome
the hierachy and the encouragement of employee identification with
professional and subject matter groups to be more important ways
to overcome communication barriers than the remaining other ways.

Table 11: Importance of Various Methods of Overcoming Conversation Barriers

| | Respondents | |
Methods	Academicians (N = 98)	Practitioners (N = 197)
Use of rewards for developing and implementing new ideas	11.2(%)	7.1(%)
Development of official programs to stimulate creativity	18.4	17.3
Increased participation in decision-making	40.8	36.0
New organizational forms to overcome the hierarchy	6.1	17.3
Increased use of outside change agents	9.2	3.0
Encouragement of employee identification with professional and subject matter group	9.2	15.7
Others (Please specify)	5.1	2.0
No opinion	1.0	1.5
Total	100.0	100.0

In sum, each group seems to believe that barriers can be overcome
in various ways, particularly participation in decision-making processes, and development of official programs to stimulate creativity.

Both academicians and practitioners regarded in-house training programs as the most important linking agents between the academic
society and the practical world as shown in Table 12.

However academicians believe university-sponsored training programs were equally as important as in-house training programs, while
practitioners saw that professional and academic journals were the
second best linking agents. Consulting firms, and professional and
academic societies also were regarded as important linking agents between the two worlds even though their emphases were slightly different. The preference for training programs by both groups coincides
with other studies.[6] It is also noteworthy that practitioners saw pro-

6. *Research Report on the Reform of the Training and Development Institutions for the Government Of-*
ficials (Seoul: Graduate School of Public Administration, Seoul National University, 1980).

Table 12: Importance of Various Linking Agents Between Academicians and Practitioners

| | Respondents | |
Linking Agents	Academicians (N = 98)	Practitioners (N = 197)
Consulting firms	14.3(%)	10.7(%)
Professional, Academic societies	9.2	12.7
Professional, Academic journals	6.1	24.4
In-house training programs	24.4	30.0
University-sponsored training programs	24.4	6.6
University-based consultants	10.2	7.1
Trade magazines	3.1	1.0
Textbook publishers	1.0	1.5
Others (please specify)	4.2	5.6
No opinion	3.1	0.5
Total	100.0	100.0

fessional societies and their publications programs as good aids in
transferring administrative theory to practice. Actually in Korea, only
a few journals are published in the professional societies of public
management.[7] Furthermore, only a few government officials have participated in the activities of professional societies.[8] In order to facilitate
interactions between academicians and practitioners, professional
societies in the field of public management should be more active.

In short, the results of our data reveal that there are high degrees
of consensus between the academic and practical worlds on the importance of methods of overcoming conversation barriers, and the
importance of linking agents between academicians and practitioners.
These can be summarized in the following knowledge flow system
(Figure 1).

---

7. The two most important journals in public management in Korea are *The Korean Political
Science Review* published by the Korean Political Science Association, and the *Korean Public
Administration Review* published by the Korean Society for Public Administration. These
journals are published annually. There are a few other journals published either once
or twice in each year. For example *Korean Journal of Public Administration* has been published
twice a year by the Graduate School of Public Administration, Seoul National University.

8. The total number of membership in the Korean Society for Public Administration in 1981
was 476. Among them 65 were public managers. This was only 13.6 percent of the
total KSPA members.

Figure 1. The Knowledge Flow System

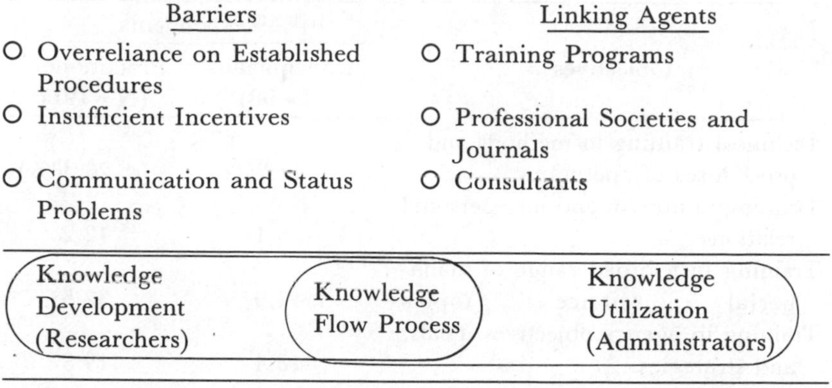

Barriers	Linking Agents
O Overreliance on Established Procedures	O Training Programs
O Insufficient Incentives	O Professional Societies and Journals
O Communication and Status Problems	O Consultants

Knowledge Development (Researchers)	Knowledge Flow Process	Knowledge Utilization (Administrators)

Source: Adapted: W. J. Duncan, "Knowledge Transfer in Administrative Science," *Public Administration Review,* Vol. 40, No. 4 (July/August, 1980), p. 345.

V. Toward More Effective Ways of Training

If training courses are the most effective way to link theory to practice, what should be the objective of such training? What media is most effective in transferring theory to practice in these programs? On the whole, how beneficial are training programs in integrating administrative science and administration?

Respondents were asked to select what they believed to be the essential purpose of management education. The data reveal that academicians as well as practitioners believe that training in a "broad range of management science topics" and in agency objectives, goals, and strategies is more important than training in human and interpersonal relations. It is interesting to note that academicians perceived training in broad governmental principles and objectives as the prime objective of training programs while practitioners believed technical training in methods and procedures of operations to be the prime objective of training programs.

In addition to exploring objective of training, the respondents were asked their preferences about the forms that it should assume. Academicians selected small group encounters as the most important training method while practitioners saw on-the-job training and job rotation as the most important training method in transferring theory to practice. Seminars, and role playing and simulation were ranked

Table 13: Objectives of Management Training Program

	Respondents	
Objectives	Academicians (N = 98)	Practitioners (N = 197)
Technical training in methods and procedures of operations	11.2(%)	20.3(%)
Training in human and interpersonal relations	5.1	12.2
Training in a broad range of managerial science topics	44.9	32.5
Training in agency objectives, goals, and strategies	18.4	19.8
Training in broad governmental principles and objectives	19.4	11.2
Others(Please specify)	1.0	3.0
No opinion	0.0	1.0
Total	100.0	100.0

Table 14: Effectiveness of Training Methods

	Respondents	
Methods	Academicians (N = 98)	Practitioners (N = 197)
On-the-job experience and job rotation	23.4(%)	48.7(%)
Seminars	18.4	12.7
Conferences and conventions	4.1	4.6
Role playing and simulation	8.2	8.6
Textbooks, articles, handbooks	7.1	5.1
Programmed instruction materials	4.1	2.5
TV, films, and/or tape recording	1.0	2.0
Small group encounters (sensitivity training)	29.6	12.7
Others (Please specify)	3.1	2.0
No opinion	1.0	1.0
Total	100.0	100.0

second and third best methods by each group.

Given the general agreement about the objectives and types of training programs, how beneficial are they? Both groups believe that training experiences in general are either "beneficial" or "somewhat
beneficial." On the whole, both groups have generally positive feel-
ing about the efficiency of management education. These views support the below finding that training programs are the most effective
linkage mechanism for transferring theory to practice. Only very small
numbers of academicians and practitioners believe that training is
not beneficial as a method to cope with the interface challenge.

Table 15: Value of Management Training

Value	Respondents	
	Academicians (N = 98)	Practitioners (N = 197)
Very beneficial	14.3(%)	10.7(%)
Beneficial	35.7	37.1
Somewhat beneficial	48.0	50.2
Not beneficial	1.0	1.0
No opinion	1.0	1.0
Total	100.0	100.0

In summary, scholars and managers believe that the most effective way to link theory to practice is through the use of training programs. They further perceive that the objective of management
development activities should focus on training in a broad range of
managerial science topics that will enhance the participant's career
prospects.

This type of learning should occur in the form of on-the-job training and job rotation, small group encounters, and seminars.

VI. Conclusion

The purposes of this study were to examine the usefulness of
management theories and techniques transferred from abroad to
Korean public management, and the perceptions of academicians and
practitioners with respect to the interface problems in Korean public

administration. These issues were explored by analysing the sources of management knowledge, usefulness of foreign management theories in the Korean administrative context, barriers to the use of information, and the ways of linking the theory to practice in Korea.

The first part of this paper dealt with the sources of knowledge and usefulness of foreign public management theory in the public administration profession. It was found that academicians tended to see foreign books and journals in the field of public management as the most significant source of information while practitioners tended to identify managers as the most significant source of information. However, managers also regarded foreign books and journals, government and private industry research, and university teachers as important sources of information. The implication of this finding is that there may be a significant information gap between administrative theory and management practice in Korea. The main reason for this interpretation is that scholars were concentrating their efforts to transfer foreign administrative theories instead of constructing management theories rooted in the Korean administrative settings while managers tended to rely more upon their own experiences. Furthermore, about half of the academicians and practitioners had doubts about the usefulness of borrowed management theories in the Korean administrative context. Management research and effective utilization of management knowledge are urgently needed in this situation. The second part of this study dealt with the preferred characteristics of management research and the flow of research information. Both researchs and managers believed that practicality and usefulness were the most preferred characteristics of management research in Korean administration. There was also a high degree of consensus regarding the types of obstacles in the transfer of research into practice. Scholars and managers in public management felt that overreliance on established procedures, insufficient incentives to develop new ideas, and communication and status problems were important barriers in the conversion process.

The final part of the study concerned the methods used to link theory to practice. Both parties agreed that increased participation in decision making, and development of official programs to stimulate creativity were the most important ways to overcome barriers in the communication of theory to practicing managers. The specific institutional arrangements chosen to accomplish this purpose were in-hosue and university training programs.

In conclusion, there was a significant information gap between the academic society and the practical world in Korean public management. However, both parties agreed that borrowed administrative theories were not so useful in the Korean administrative context.[9] They also showed high degrees of consensus on the objective of research, barriers to its implementation, and the methods to link theory to practice. Therefore there needs to be more active interaction theory and practice, and more efforts by both parties to build up public administration as a discipline rooted in the Korean administrative setting.

---

9. For a discussion of the question of an indigenous administrative discipline, see Marn-Jai Cha, "Is Indigenous Korean Public Administration Possible?: A look at American Public Administration, *The Korean Political Science Association and The Association of Korean Political Scientists in North America,* August 10-12, *1981* (Seoul, Korea, 1981).

7
Policymaking in the Executive Branch - Application of An American Model to Three Korean Cases

Chung Kil Chung

I. Introduction

I may not be the only one who is tempted to utilize decisionmaking theories or models found in developed countries like U.S. to explain concrete cases of decision making in developing countries. Also, I may not be the only one who has been frustrated by an unsuccessful effort of such kind. This paper is a report of such an effort.

However, it may be very useful for some scholars to know what aspects of the decisionmaking process can or cannot be explained by existent decisionmaking theories or models. And also helpful may be some hypotheses or assertions about the decisionmaking process which can be obtained from the effort.

I began with Allison's Models: I briefly introduce them and then apply them to three Korean cases of decisionmaking within the Executive Branch. Those cases were selected partly because they were very important and partly because they were finally decided by the President after much debate.

Allison's Models, though applicable to the three cases, could not explain important aspects of decisionmaking patterns discerned in the cases. Thus, I tried to explain those aspects with other concepts and ideas.

Finally, some observations and hypotheses were drawn from the cases and other materials which may better explain the governmental decisionmaking process of the developing countries. Those hypotheses may not be much better than common sense, but they are the kind of aspects which can hardly be expected from existent decisionmaking or policymaking theories explored in developed countries like U.S.

Cases selected were those decided during President Park's era, and thus, explanations, observations or assertions all have limited applicability. Still, those may become some parts of current policymaking models.

II. A Brief Review of Allison's Model

1. Allison's Model as A Model

Professor Allison suggested three distinctive models for the explanation of the decisionmaking precess and utilized them to explain why President Kennedy and his secretaries finally chose, among many possible alternatives, to block Soviet shipments of missiles to Cuba in the Cuban Missile Crisis in 1962.[1] The three models are Rational Actor Model (Model I), Organizational Process Model (Model II), and Bureaucratic Politics Model (Model III), This paper, first of all, *ries to apply these three models to some decisionmaking cases of the Korean government. These models were selected because of two different reasons, and these two different reasons must be mentioned to clarify the purpose and scope of this paper.

First, this paper deals with certain aspects of the decisionmaking process within the executive branch where the president is the final decisionmaker and Allison's three models have similar purposes. This paper will focus on the internal decisionmaking process of the executive branch of the Korean government. Thus, the role, influence and behavior of the National Assembly, parties, interest group, mass media or the general public will not be analyzed. They will be briefly mentioned only when it is necessary. The emphasis on the executive branch can be justified from the fact that the Executive Branch now dominates policymaking process in many countries, developed or developing.

The second reason why we start from Allison's model is that the three models in fact are not Allison's personal invention, but rather a synthesis of major decisionmaking theories developed till 1970. The synthesis has been highly regarded, if not very successful, as some

---

1. G. T. Allison, "Conceptual Models and the Cuban Missile Crisis," *American Political Science Review* (APSR), September, 1969 and G. T. Allison, *Essence of Decision* (Boston: Little, Brown and Company, 1971)

scholars point out, for its inclusion of many important theories and models which prevailed at that time. This is true even now, almost a decade after his book was published, simply because better breaking—through synthesis or new important models have not been offered since. There are some exceptions of course, and the Garbage Can Model[2] is a very important decision-making pradigm which appeared after Allison's Model. However, some new or old models not covered in Allison's framework and the Garbage Can Model can be subsumed in Bureaucratic Politics Model (Allison's Model III), obviously enriching the latter model. In short, Allison's models can be a summary of decisionmaking theories or models developed in the U.S. with the purpose of describing, explaining and predicting decisionmaking process in the Executive Branch.

Before we move on, one point must be clarified. The title of this paper indicates the ''Policy'' making process as the major target of discussion, and yet, Allison's models and following cases are largely about the decisionmaking process. Usually a policy is made through many decisions. Policymaking is a process composed of many decisionmaking points. Thus, there is no essential difference, at least in explanatory or predictive nature, between decisionmaking and policymaking models.

2. Contents of Allison's Models

This is no time to fully discuss the contents of selected models. They are notoriously complex. Yet, it is nonetheless necessary to introduce the models to continue our discussion. Thus, I will try to summarize the major contents of Allison's models as briefly as possible, emphasizing some aspects directly relevant to our later discussion.[3]

Rational Actor Model (Allison's Model I) assumes that a national policy or decision is a choice to maximize national goals under given constraints. Organizational Process Model (Model II), however, conceptualizes a nation's decision as the output of some organizations in the government, while Bureaucratic Politics Model (Model III) regards a governmental decision as a resultant of a political game among various power holders in the government.

---

2. M. Cohen, J. March & J. Olsen, "A Garbage Can Model of Organizational Choice," *Administrative Science Quarterly*, No. 1, 1972

3. I once tried to summarize the contents of Allison's Model which may be helpful. See Chung-Kil CHUNG, "Critical Review of Allison's Models," *Research Review of Kyungpook National University*, Vol. 20, 1975, pp. 189-198.

In Model I, government is assumed to be an organism well-coordinated by a very rational head. Thus, a governmental decision is regarded as one coordinated rational choice of an individual whose head is the chief of the government or a group of leaders who share the conmon goal of maximizing national interest.

According to Model II, government is a set of loosely allied semi-independent sub-organizations which cannot be well coordinated or appropriately controlled by the head or leaders. Suborganizations have their own SOP's and program repertories, which, in turn, decide how to define problems, how to collect and process information, what kind of alternatives to consider and how to choose among different alternatives.

In Model III, a government is composed of many political players who have their personal goals as well as the goal of the government. A governmental decision is nothing but a result of compromises or bargains among participants in the political game.

One important concept, goals of decisionmakers, further distinguishes Model I, Model II and Model III. In the Rational Actor Model, leaders of the government (or participants in decision-making) have a common goal or a set of common goals: that is, national interest in foreign affairs, social welfare or public welfare in the domestic area, or any name which indicates the goal of government as a whole. Leaders of the government in the Organizational Process Model belong to some sub-organizations as head or member and therefore, have two-conceptually different goals. In addition to the goal (or goals) for the government as a whole, sub-organizations like many departments or agencies have their own objectives. They have to maintain their own sub-organizations, to satisfy to some extent the aspirations of their members, etc. Moreover, they redefine the governmental goals from their points of view. Governmental leaders, in Bureaucratic Politics Model, have the goal of government as a whole as a leader of the government, the goal of sub-organization as its member and personal goals as an individual. Thus the degree of goal-sharing among governmental leaders is the highest in Model I and the lowest in Model III.

The three models are different also in the rules and the power locus of decisionmaking. All powers or authorities for decisionmaking are concentrated at the center (or head) of the government in Model I. Governmental leaders decide what to do, just like the brain of animal does. But, in Model II, sub-organizations within government are semi-independent from their superiors or governmental leaders. Here, sub-organizations can be an agency or a department like DOD, CIA, FBI, Army or Navy. Governmental leaders include President, secretaries or other politically appointed staffs or career officials. In Model II, sub-organizations have their own patterns of organizational behavior: They work according to SOP and, when confronted with the necessity of choice, usually try to find out good alternatives from their program repertories, set of alternatives or programs considered and tried in thc past.

Model II is essentially a synthesis of organizational decisionmaking models or theories such as Firm Model (by R. Cyert and J. March). Thus, in Model II, the sub-organizations decide important phase of decision and leaders can only trim the edge, or sub-organizations limit the scope of alternatives to consider such that governmental leaders have no other choise than to choose one alternative among those offered by the sub-organization. In this way, Model II emphasizes the dominance of the sub-organizations.

Model III is clearly contrasted with Model II in two aspects of the power locus. First, the power-problem in Model III is not only vertical but also horizontal, while it is vertical in Model II. Governmental leaders play political games against superiors or subordinates (vertical aspect) and also against others of the same level of formal position in the government (horizontal aspect). Second, governmental leaders are all players of the game with certain shared power, and even the President is only one of the powerful players. The focus, therefore, is not on the sub-organization or heads of sub-organizations but on the players who have more power. The power resources of each player include not only the formal power specified in laws and constitution but informal power of any kind. Thus, rules of game are very important to guarantee "fair play" and it also have many sources such as constitutional law, laws, customs, political morals, etc.

III. Applying the Models to Some Korean Cases

1. Cases Selected

The political systems of developing countries have frequently been characterized by such aspects as the over-concentration of power in the Executive Branch (against other branches and other groups) and, within it, in the hands of top governmental leader. Every important decision is made, according to the above-mentioned assumption, by the top leader. If such is the case, Allison's Model II has no room in the policymaking process in developing countries. For the power of sub-organization is in inverse relationship to the power of the governmental head.

If the above-mentioned assumption is valid, Allison's Model I can hardly be applied to the developing countries. This is so, simply because a few leaders cannot rationally solve many complex problems without real help from buraurcratic experience and manpower for appropriate collection, process and analysis of information and for searching, assesing and comparing a wide variety of alternatives to solve problems.

If all the important decisions arc made by the top leader, Allison's Model III will not explain any important aspect of decisionmaking, since Model III can best be applied to the pluralistic situation where the president can become only a member of cabinet meeting.

Are the models really unable to explain decisionmaking process of important issues in developing countries? Is the top leader really dominating every important decision? If the answer is no, then what is the underlying mechanism of the decisionmaking process in the Executive Branch? In order to answer some of these questions, I selected three very important decisionmaking cases of late 1960's and early 1970's where President Park, as strong leader, is directly involved. Those cases are neither representative nor typical Korean cases. (In fact, we do not know what the typical case is). Those cases are selected for the simple purpose of carefully examining the above-mentioned assumptions.

2. Applying for Membership in the Non-aligned Movement

A. Outline of Case[4]

One early morning in March, 1975, all personnel in the United Nations Affairs division of the Ministry of Foreign Affairs hurried to their office. The division chief had received in his bed a very urgent overseas cable from the Korean Embassy to the U.N. The cable informed him that North Korea applied for membership of the Non-aligned Movement of the Foreign Ministers' Conference of the Coordination Member Countries held in Havana, Cuba. The cable also indicated that the conference gave its unanimous approval to recommend North Korea's admission to the Ministerial Conference of the Movement which will be held in Lima in August, 1975.

The division chief immediately relayed the news on the phone to the bureau chief, associate vice-minister and vice-minister (the

---

4. Summarized from Ik-Sik Kim, "The Korean Foreign Policy Toward the Non-alignment Movement," Master's Thesis, Graduate School of Public Administration (GSPA), Seoul National University (SNU), 1982, pp. 76-104.

Minister was in Europe at that time). The division also began to operate according to regular procedures: gathering information from new and old information sources which includes old documents; defining problems they must solve; looking for alternatives from old precedents; and most importantly, preparing a briefing chart, getting signatures from the superiors in opposite hierarchical order, and holding meetings. The bureau chief ordered the division chief to outline the contents of the major alternatives which were reported to the Associate Vice-Minister and Vice-Minister. The three alternatives written in a typical briefing chart were also reported later to the Minister of Foreign Affairs (after he returned from travel to Europe and later to the U.N. in New York). Among the three alternatives two received intensive examination. They had the same goal to block North Korea's admission to the Non-aligned Movment. But, they differed in strategies and so in predicted consequences.

The first alternative suggested that the Korean government also apply for the admission and it was predicted to achieve the goal more successfully, but it might bring serious damage to the national image if North Korea is admitted and South Korea is not. The second alternative suggested that the government try everything to block the admission but not apply for membership and this was predicted to avoid the damage of the first alternative but with less probability of goal attainment. When the Minister chaired the final meeting of the Ministry, he decided to go with the first alternative, predicting an optimistic result that the first alternative will not fail.

The Ministry of Foreign Affairs brought its dicision together with other alternative to the President's Office where President Park himself presided over the meeting. Participants at the meeting were not very optimistic about the result of the first alternative: that is, Korea also apply for membership. In fact, Special Advisor to the President in Foreign Affairs and the chief of the Korean C.I.A. opposed the alternative. However, President Park finally relied on the minister's opinion. Some people say that President Park at that time largely depended on career official's ideas on foreign affairs. In addition, the minister's persuasive talk along with his optimistic prediction might have appealed to President.

B. Explaining the Case with the Models

The decision-making to apply for membership of the Non-aligned Movement has several characteristics which are very similar to the Cuban Missile Case. First of all, both were dealing with some unexpected foreign affairs (unexpected, at least, by top decisionmaker).

Second, the President as top-decisionmaker was directly involved. Third, participants had different ideas in both cases. These common factors may account for the very similar pattern of decisionmaking in both cases. Therefore, all three of Allison's Models can be utilized for the explanation of both cases.

However, there are some important differences between the two cases, also. The Cuban Missile Case was much more serious in its probable impact: It might have triggered the Third World War to destroy the earth or at least limited nuclear war to kill millions of U.S. citizens and Soviet citizens. The Cuban case was also very urgent: the U.S. had to do something before the Soviet missiles in Cuba became operational (they spent thirteen days to choose an alternative strategy). These differences may be one of the reasons why the participants of Non-aligned Movement Case showed a lower degree of goal-sharing than the participants of Cuban Missile Case.

One of the reasons why the Minister of Foreign Affairs strongly argued for the first alternative (submission of Korean application for membership in the Non-aligned Movement) might have been his judgement that, regardless of who recommended which strategies, he himself must be responsible for the final result and that the critical result to the President is whether the Ministry of Foreign Affairs could prevent North Korea from getting membership in the Non-aligned Movement. He and his staff in the ministry were definitely sure that the first alternative was the best way to prevent North Korean membership. Thus, more broad and long range national goals and means for them were not given very much attention. Moreover, the probable damage which may result from the failure of the first alternative was continuously under-estimated.

If the Minister had been cool and rational, he would have sensed (he was a very successful career bureaucrat) that the danger of failure was highly probable. This is not an ex-post-facto explanation (unlike the minister's arguement and exactly as his opponents worried, North Korea succeeded to get membership while Korea did not). Many people recognized that Korea was probably in a weak diplomatic situation at that time in 1975 due to many events: domestic and foreign. The minister might have made a better prediction. It looked like wishful thinking disturbed his shrewd calculations. In short, the Rational Actor Model (Allison's Model I) has only limited explanatory power in this example.

Allison's Model III (Bureaucratic Politics Model) provides a better explanation than Model I. As mentioned above, participants in the final decision stage at the President's office seemed to have different goals, or at least differently perceived national goals in mind, not to mention the minister's personal goal. They played a political game sometimes in president's presence and sometimes in his absense. The game ended when the President finally decided to support the minister's idea.

However, all things considered, Allison's Model II (Organizational Process Model) seems to more accurately depict the case. From the time the division chief of Ministry of Foreign Affairs received cable from Korean Embassy to U.N., the ministry moved according to pre-established regular procedures to finally produce three alternatives for the Minister to choose. The activities followed typical SOP's and utilized program repertories. Although not introduced here, the ministry also followed their SOP's after the final decision by the President was made: first they contacted strong allied countries like U.S.A. and then, asked the help of friendly non-aligned movement member countries, and then tried to get additional support from neutral non-aligned countries, etc.

Even though the minister's decision to go with the first alternative was somewhat dominated by his strong personality within the ministry, his motive or goal was not his own but largely the goal of M.O.F.A. as a sub-organization (the ministry must take final responsibility, if North Korea is admitted to the Non-aligned Movement).

Moreover, President Park's final decision was to accept the choice of the ministry. Further, it is said that President Park's decision was partly based on the idea that in foreign affairs, expertness based on long career experience must play its role in decisionmaking: the value of functional authority is well recognized by the top decisionmaker.

All in all, Model II, the Organizational Process Model, can explain important aspects of decisionmaking in the Non-aligned Movement Case.

3. Construction of the Seoul-Pusan Highway

A. Outline of the Case[5]

Around 400Km in length the Seoul—Pusan Highway is the first real expressway Korea has ever constructed.[6] The Construction began in 1968 and it was the largest construction project Korea had ever tried. Hot debate and much opposition was quite natural. The

---

5. The case is much publicized but for the objectivity of the stories I largely depended upon two cases. They are: GSPA, SNU, *Public Administration Cases in Korea,* Seoul: Bub-moon-sa, 1980, pp. 214-232, and, Song-Ho Lee, "A Study of Policy Making Process," Master's Thesis, GSPA, SNU, 1982, pp. 51-65.
6. Seoul-Inchon Highway was built earlier, but it is only around 50 km.

opposition was so strong that Cho-sun Ilbo, after President Park died, named the construction project as "The President's Lone Decision Against the Whole Nation's Opposition"

However, President Park was not the only person who strongly supported the construction project. Quite understandably, the Ministry of Construction spent 6 months in 1965 on a survey and feasibility study. But the tremendous amount of project cost discouraged the effort. Early the following the year, IBRD (International Bank of Reconstruction and Development) was invited to perform feasibility study.

Apart from the unsuccessful effort of Ministry of Construction, President Park was reported to be deeply interested in the German highway system in 1964 and he ordered a special report by one of his highest ranking staff member in the Presidential office in 1966. The following year President Park as a presidential candidate seeking re-election, promised in his campaign platform, the construction of Seoul—Pusan Highway along with other important large—scale projects. President Park was very active in the construction of the Seoul—Pusan Highway after his re-election: He gave specific orders to MOC (Ministry of Construction) and appointed as the new Minister of MOC a highway specialist with whom he frequently met. He also met several times with the Chairman of the Hyundai Construction Company to check on the possibility of cost reduction.

When the plan of the project was first discussed in the Administration—Party Joint Committee, the opposition was rather vocal until everyone found out that this was President Park's firm intention. Opposition to the project also burst out when the plan was publicly announced. The mass media, big business, not to mention opposition parties, all spoke out so loudly that whole the nation seemed to oppose the project. Yet, President Park repeated his firm belief in the necessity of the project for economic development, and national defense. Naturally, President Park was deeply involved in the implementation process of the project, sometimes persuading and sometimes enforcing even career bureaucrats.

B. Explaining the Case with the Models.

Quite distinct from the former case, we cannot find any important aspect of Allison's Model II, the Organizational Process Model, in the decision to construct the Seoul—Pusan Highway. It is true that Ministry of Construction had once initiated the idea of the construction project. But the ministry had abandoned the idea. It is probable that President Park might have gained some idea from

the ministry's early effort (this is not clear), but it is much more
probable that the president was collecting ideas from other sources
and had slowly built a firm belief in the project. Thus, SOP's and
program repertories within MOC did not make any significant contribution to the decision.

It is not, however, clear which of the models Model I or Model
III can better explain the case. There are some aspects which Model
III can explain. Governmental leaders, before the final decision was
made, were divided. The Minister of Construction, and some other
ministers supported the project partly because of their own personal
and sub-organizational goals, and partly because of the national goals
they perceived. Many opposed: the Minister of Finance and the
Economic Planing Board worried about the huge construction costs
and its impact on other projects. Doubtlessly, there was coalition—
building, at least. But the explanatory power of Model III stops here.
President Park's domination was too much for Model III to explain
(Recall that Model III assumes the President is only one of several
strong players).

As far as the overwhelming influence of top decisionmaker is
concerned, the construction project case looks much more like Model
I where the top leader's idea is supposed to dominate. Some cabinet
members and party leaders first opposed the idea but quickly changed
their minds, when they confirmed the president's firm intentions.
Yet, the rationality of decision, which should be the core element of
Model I (Rational Actor Model), is not apparent to many people.

Although Allison himself is not clear, there can be two distinct
criteria to evaluate the rationality of a decision: end—result—oriented
and process—oriented. Objectively speaking, a decision can be said
to be "rational" when the chosen alternative creates the best result.
The Seoul—Pusan Highway construction must have seemed the best
alternative means of transportation then considered, if the construction can be regarded as rational. Readers will quickly recognize
conceptual vagueness with the use of the term rationality expressed
in this sense: the best result for the 1970's will not necessarily be the
best result for the 1980's or the 1990's, etc. No one will know the
best alternative in this situation. Thus, we must look for another,
additional or alternative, criterion for the rationality of the decision.
If the decisionmaker tries his best and believes that his choice is the
best one for given goals and constraints, then his decision can be
regarded as rational. The final decisionmaker, President Park, had
a firm belief that he made the best decision to construct the highway.
Moreover, rumor has it that President Park had probably done his
best to reach the decision. In short, Model I explains the case better.

However, how can we explain the people's opposition to the project? Can it be labelled rational even when it is opposed by the people? When and why do the top leaders act like President Park in the highway construction project? It is obvious that Allison's model cannot give us good answers to these questions. Now, let us turn to a case quite different from the highway case.

4. Revolution in Educational System

A. Outline of the Case

Educational policies and systems may have been the most hotly debated issues among Koreans. Around 1965, the debate began to focus on notoriously competetive entrance examination for good middle schools. Graduates of first-class middle schools could pass the entrance examination for first-class high schools and then pass another entrance examination for first-class universities. This kind of chain was so strong that everyone tried whatever one can do to pass the entrance examination for good middle school. Quite naturally, many serious problems arouse: curricula of the primary schools were crippled; extra-curricular teaching created numerous problems; children's physical growth was stunted, not to mention psychological pressure. Teacher's associations and mother's associations among others were very active seeking to change the examination system and the mass media did not lose any time to report many dramatic events and problems related to the entrance examinations.

The Korean Teacher's Association was the most active group, and in October, 1967, recommended the random assignment of students to middle schools, completely abolishing the entrance examination. After receiving a negative answer from Ministry of Education, the KTA in early 1968 held a series of public hearings against the entrance examination and payed for research carried out by famous professors in the field of Education. Based on the research, KTA recommended a more concrete and specific plan of a no examination system. The recommendation was not only widely publicized, but also received support from many groups. But governmental response was immediate and negative: MOE announced several reasons why the recommended idea was not better than the existent system.

Many people openly supported KTA's recommendation of a no examination system. The whole nation seemed to support the no examination system. If there were some opponents to the new idea, they did not speak out much. This kind of atmosphere continued till around a month after KTA's open recommendation. President

Park shuffled his cabinet and appointed a new Minister of Education. Minister Kwon was Minister of Justice when he was appointed. He had a nickname "Bulldozer" due to his strong personality. Many people guessed that President Park wanted a strong minister to decide what to do with the entrance examination.

The new minister began to work immediately but very secretly. He treated his subordinates harshly to keep it secret. He permitted only three high ranking officials to work on the secret task force. He seemed to have an idea very similar to KTA's recommendation. A month after he took his new position, he reported to President Park that he was examining alternative systems for entrance to the middle schools. And President Park was quoted as saying "Do something to free children from an entrance examination." Apparently encouraged by the president's favorable reply, the minister pushed his task force to finish an analysis of three alternatives among which the no entrance examination alternative was the new minister's pet one. After a week, the Administration—Party Joint Committee discussed the MOE's new proposals, but it was split on the new idea of no examination with no first-class middle school. However, the minister was not at all discouraged. He reported the new idea to President Park and succeded in getting the President's affirmative decision with a promise of support after almost four hours talk. At the next Administration-Party Joint Committee three days later, the minister let others know that the new idea had the President's approval and pushed it without any difficulty.

B. Explaining the Case with the Models

In the above case again, Allison's Model II (Organizational Process Model) can hardly be applied. Althoug, the task force (composed of a division chief, bureau chief, and an associate-vice-minister-level official) prepared the proposal at the final stage, the proposal was not an output of regular SOP's and program repertories. Rather, MOE, as an organization, continuously showed negative response to the new idea of no entrance examination system, until it changed its stand dramatically after the new minister took office.

What about Model I (Rational Actor Model)? This model is not very helpful either to explain the case. It may be that governmenttal leaders, though with split ideas at first, finally agreed on the new idea, believing that the new idea was the best alternative. However, this element of rationality can hardly be identified in this case. Rather the following seems to be a more correct picture of what really happened. Problems of the notoriously competitive examinations for entrance to the middle schools were so hotly discussed that both pros and cons of the new idea wanted a decisive governmental decision. President Park selected a strong man as a new minister who felt that President also wanted some new ideas.

Finding that other alternatives discussed publicly were only temporary amendments to the existing system, and no-examination system was getting very popular, the minister decided to go with the new system. Did he have a firm belief that the new system was the best alternative for the nation as a whole? It seemed unlikely. His choice looked much more like the one which pleased both President and the general public (He might have sensed that he could not do anything but accept the most popular, at least overtly, and revolutionary one.) As for President Park, he also had no firm belief in the new idea except that something must be done. In short, top leaders did not seem to have a firm belief in the rationality of the new idea.

Moreover, other governmental leaders did not act like cells of an organism at all. When the minister first offered the new idea as one of three alternatives they strongly opposed it. Some governmental leaders had different ideas. But the new minister with the support of some leaders and public opinion and most of all with the President's personal confidence pushed the new idea. The whole picture looked very much like the political game in Model III.

However, there are some other parts of Model III that do not fit well. There is, for example, no sign of compromise or bargaining among participants which is so typical in Model III (Bureaucratic politics Model). Moreover, the new minister was dominating the political game except when President was directly involved. When he received the President's personal confidence and support for his new idea, he dominated the other players. Model III assumes more or less equal power resources among the players. And it was not so in the above case.

IV. Some Lessons and Further Explorations

1. Allison's Model and Korean Cases

(1) The first lesson from our case studies is drawn from the case of Applying for Membership of the Non-aligned Movement. Recall in the Non-aligned case the Ministry of Foreign Affairs succeeded in pushing its choice. Thus it is obvious that the President, or the top decisionmaker, does not always dominate the decisionmaking process in developing countries. Although it was not introduced here,

many case studies indicate the arguement is correct. When the Pusan City Government planned to construct a large scale urban industrial highway, President Park accepted the idea and supported almost half of the construction cost from national treasury. The highway construction project was an output after extensive preparation of the bureau of city planning.[8] As for the many decisionmakings involved in the implementation process, we can easily conclude that the bureaucracy dominates in Korea.[9] As mentioned earlier, career officials at Ministry of Construction pushed their choice even against President Park's original order in choosing among the different routes from Tae-gu to Pusan during the implementation of the Seoul-Pusan Highway construction project.

Thus, unlike naive expectations, sub-organizations have some power and the President does not dominate in many cases of decisionmaking (But, this does not necessarily mean that the suborganizations always follow established SOP's and utilize program repertories). Some surveys indicate that the bureaucrats feel that they themselves make the essential ingredients of public policies.[10]

(2) The three cases examined indicate that all of Allison's three models can compete with other models or theories applicable to Korean cases. As can be remembered, Model I can be applicable to Seoul—Pusan Highway Construction case, Model II to the Non-aligned case and Model III to Educational Revolution case. Although the three cases are neither typical, nor representative Korean cases, this does not invalidate the argument that Allison's Models can be applied to Korean cases.

(3) However, Allison's models have very limited explanatory power in some aspects of the cases. For, example, the overwhelming domination of President Park in the Seoul-Pusan Highway case in fighting against the whole nation's opposition as the President himself perceived the correct option and the over-all pattern of the political game in the Educational Revolution case where the rules of the game were

---

7. This case is also well publicized. I used the same sources as those in footnote 5. See, GSPA, SNU, op. cit. (1980), pp. 164-183 and Song-Ho Lee, op. cit., pp. 79-94.

8. Kwang-Soo Lee, "The Applicability of Allison's Model in the Policy-making Process," Ph. D. Dissertation, School of Graduate Studies, Kyung-pook National University, 1983, pp. 88-146.

9. See for example the many cases treated in two volumes: GSPA, SNU, *Policy Implementation Cases,* Research Report, 1983 and 1984.

10. Two similar surveys with almost twenty years interval show interesting results. See Dong-Suh Park, "Policymaking in the Korean Executive Branch," *Korean Journal of Public Administration,* GSPA, SNU, Vol. 4, No. 2, 1966, pp. 229-236. Also, see Dae-woon Park, "The Role of Korean Bureaucrats in Policy Process," Ph. D. Dissertation, Kun-Kuk University, 1984, pp. 120-143.

changed according to signals from President who was formally sitting back from the game.

In short, aspects of the President's domination and its changing faces cannot be well explained by the three models. It seems true that the President dominates in many decisionmaking cases, at least, it is true in our two cases.

It also seems correct that Allison's three models cannot explain why the President sometimes actively dominates and sometimes passively sits back or relies on career officials. Thus, we must look for some other models or ideas.

2. Some Other Ideas and Hypotheses

Why did President Park act as he did in the three cases? He was in the front for the construction of Seoul-Pusan Highway, knowing that he was the target of critical public opinion. He was depending on the Ministry of Foreign Affairs in the Non-aligned case. He was sitting back, but continuously and carefully watching the process of decision in the Educational Revolution case.

One answer comes quickly to mind: the seriousness or importance of the issues determines the top decisionmaker's attitude and behavior. This hypothesis is highly plausible, since many miscellaneous and trivial issues during the implementation process were normally left to career bureaucrats to decide (Someone observed that the bureaucrats in the Ministry of Construction could push their own idea on the route from Taegu to Pusan of the Seoul-Pusan Highway against the President's idea).

It is quite logical that with limited time and energy the top decisionmaker must concentrate his effort on more fundamental and serious issues and leave other matters to expert career officials. Thus, this hypothesis may explain why President Park was passively accepting the idea of the ministry in the Non-aligned case. Maybe the issue was not so serious or at least the President perceived it to be not as serious as the other cases.

However, the hypothesis does not explain why the President sat back from the front-line and let the new Minister of Education dominate the decisionmaking process in the Educational Revolution case. The issue was very important and serious, maybe much more serious than Seoul-Pusan Highway case. Moreover, the new minister was not an educational expert, and the same idea as his final choice had been repeatedly rejected by the same ministry before he became the minister.

In sum, the importance of the issues can only partly explain whether the top decisionmaker will rely on bureaucratic agencies and their SOP's.

(2) Some may try to explain President Park's behavior in the Educational Revolution case, with T. Lowi's framework.[11] T. Lowi suggested that patterns of policymaking are determined by types of policies. Among his four types of policy, one is relevant to our present discussion. Regulatory policy intends to regulate people's behavior or limit liberty and give benefit to some others as a consequence.

Labor laws usually specify what the employer and employee can and cannot do; some regulations permit some commodities to be imported and some not; some regulations prohibit a certain kind of commercial advertisement. All those regulations have common characteristics: the beneficiary group and the regulated group can be in open conflict in the policymaking process. Lowi argues that compromise is inevitable to build a majority coalition, and that regulatory policy is thus pluralistically made. One implication is that the President cannot play influential role.[12]

Now in the Educational Revolution case there are some aspects which are clearly regulatory. If the government abolishes the entrance examination, middle school teachers, students and parents must follow the decision, and there will be losers and winners. Thus, we may expect that the case was hotly and openly debated and the President could not play on influential role. However, there are many cases which are not introduced here, which clearly indicate that President Park himself, though not openly, killed ideas proposed by career officials to regulate air pollution, water pollution[13] and unfair competition caused by big monopolistic companies.[14]

3. Some Further Hypotheses

A.O. Hirschman once suggested two different types of policymaking processes which we can find in Latin America.[15] On of them is a

---

11. T. Lowi, "American Business, Public Policy, Case-Studies, and Political Theory," *World Politics,* July 1964, pp. 677-715.
12. Lowi also indicated this, "(President's) access to public opinion and use of lofty rhetoric are resources that simply do not spend well in the regulatory area," in T. Lowi, "Four Systems of Policy, Politics, and Choice," *PAR,* July/August 1972, p. 303.
13. In-Sik Nam, "A Study on Nondecision-making of Pollution Issue in Korea," Master's Thesis, GSPA, SNU, 1983, pp. 38-79.
14. Byung-Kee Chung, "A Study on Types of Policy and Policy Process—The Case of Korean Fair Trade Act—," Master's Thesis, GSPA, SNU, 1984.
15. A. O. Hirschman, "Policymaking and Policy Analysis in Latin America—A Return to Journey—," *Policy Science,* 1975, pp. 385-402.

process where governmental leaders push their ideas even against public opinion. Leaders do this because of their firm belief in their ideas. Hirschman's suggestion gives us some explantion of President Park's behavior in the three cases we discussed. Thus, we can hypothesize that President Park was

(a) largely dominating when he had a confident and firm belief in his own ideas on important issues;

(b) largely relying upon the expertness of career bureaucrats when he did not have a firm belief or when he perceived that issues at hand were trivial;

(c) largely trying to find some reliable person to play this role when he had neither a firm belief in his ideas nor in the expertness of the bureaucrats or others, when the issues at hand were important.

The Seoul-Pusan Highway Construction belongs to category (a). As mentioned earlier, the Non-aligned Movement case and many technical decisions in the implementation process will belong to category (b), or Allison's Model II (Organization Process Model).

As the President spends more time on certain issues, he or she will gain more concrete knowledge of them, thus dominating the decisionmaking process more and more. This might have happened in President Park's later days. For example, the technical economic issues once regarded as under economic technocrats' monopolistic jurisdiction might have become more and more dominated by President Park.

Going back to category (c), whoch most probably describes President Park's behavior in the Educational Revolution case, it needs a rather lengthy explanation such as follows. Even when the President has a firm belief in some idea, not to mention when he does not, he will never consider it wise to be perceived by the people as an authoritarian dictator who frequently acts against public opinion. This is plausible especially when the President is not very popular as was the case with President Park at the time due to many factors such as the challenge to his regime's legitimacy and its repressive activities, etc.

What can a President do in such a situation? Three options are potentially available. First, he may give up his belief and follow whatever public opinion dictates. But this strategy has two serious problems at least in important issues. First, it is not easy to grasp public opinion. One typical reason why this is so is that the majority of the people usually keep silent till they know what the government intends to do about a certain issues. It is highly probable that if the Ministry of Education had announced its intention to accept the new "No Examination System" before the new idea got popular, public opinion might have turned against the new system. (This may be one reason why the new Minister of Education forced his task force to keep it secret). Second, the President, if he gives up his own ideas, will lose many strong supporters, since nobody can rely on him on important issues. It is true that some Presidents will easily give up their ideas. But President Park was a man with strong will and he is believed to have had a firm belief (so firm that some say it was an ideology) in economic development, this was partly due to the continued challenge to the legitimacy of his presidency.

Thus, President Park might have relied more on the second and third strategies to get involved in important decisionmakings but not to antagonize the general public. The second strategy seems to be what President Park did in the Educational Revolution case as category (c) indicates. Sensing that something fundamental must be done to change the entrance examination for the middle schools and that the President himself lacked the time and knowledge, and most importantly, that public opinion might abruptly change in an unpredictable direction if the government became openly committed to the most to the most promising idea too early, President Park might have delegated his authority to a strong reliable man who could play the President's role. In such a case, the selected person plays the role of "acting President". One of the most important elements of the role is to act as a scapegoat when things turn our badly. He must also receive blame from opponents to governmental decisions. This is probably one aspect of what was expected from the new minister in the Educational Revolution case. President Park could not waste his political resources by antagonizing latent opponents, especially when he was already very unpopular due to his lonely fighting for the construction of Seoul-Pusan Highway.[16]

When will the President select his "acting President"? The types of policy or issue can be a determinant. As discussed earlier, regulatory policy always has supporters and opponents. Front-line leaders of any alternative in the regulatory area will antagonize people on the opposite side. Thus, the President might have left to others those important issues in regulatory policies.

Then why did President Park himself kill many regulatory policies as mentioned earlier? To answer this question, we must turn to the third strategy which a President can employ to avoid unpopular involvement in important issues. The third strategy is to contain issues and not to arouse public attention or debate and decide the issue as

---

16. The two cases were decided during almost the same period of time.

quietly as possible. This strategy usually takes two patterns. One is to kill issues but not to let out any news about the fact that President himself decided, and try other measures to prevent issues from expanding to the general public. This pattern has been mentioned very frequently in many non-decision cases in the U.S. in which powerful groups kill issues before they receive big attention.[17] This pattern could be seen in some issues where President Park be believed they would hurt economic development, as mentioned before. In some instances the issues were so critical, as President perceived them, that he left them to others. And yet, if those issues become targets of hot public debate, the President could have not killed them without antagonizing many people.

Another pattern is to choose some policy means, which President thinks best, to solve policy problems and then, to persuade general public to believe that the selected means are the best. This pattern is what Cobb, Ross and Ross mentioned as their "Mobilization Model."[18] This pattern fully exploits the "follower mentality"[19] of the people by making people believe that the President can choose he best option. Usually the government announces a policy all of a sudden, explaining advantages (normally very exaggerated and over-estimated) and disadvantages (normally under-estimated) of the selected policy.

Both of the above two patterns can be effective only when complete secrecy is kept: the general public must know neither who did what in the case of killing the issues, nor what other kinds of alternatives and their merits in the case of persuading the people. This is one of the reasons why the decisionmaking process of developing countries tends to become closed and secret.

We tried to explain some aspect of decisionmaking process in three important cases: Why President Park and his staffs behave as they did in the three cases? Till now, we focused on aspects which can be explained when we assume the President's rational calculation. The whole picture can be clarified when we examine the rational calculation of presidential staffs and secretaries. But, this job is too much for this paper, so it is left for another paper.

---

17. R. Cobb and C. Elder, *Participation in American Politics* (Boston: Allyn and Bacon, 1972).
18. R. Cobb, J. Ross, and M. Ross, "Agenda Building as a Comparative Political Process," *APSR*, 1976, pp. 126-138.
19. J. Mueller, *War, Presidents and Public Opinion* (New York: John Wiley and Son's, 1973), pp. 122-140.

V. Concluding Remarks

Starting from Allison's Model for the explanation of the decision-making patterns in Executive Branch of Korean Government, we have tried to see whether decisionmaking theories found in developed countries like U.S. can explain Korean cases also. We have selected three important cases in which President Park was directly involved during late 1960's and mid 1970's. Although the three selected ones are neither typical nor representative Korean cases, they nontheless clearly indicate several facts.

First, sub-organization sometimes had real power to decide the final output just like the Organization Process Model indicates. Thus, the strong top decisionmaker had not dominated all the important decisionmakings.

Second, all of Allison's three models could be applicable. However, the Bureaucratic Politics Model and the Rational Actor Model have very limited explanatory pwoer. More specifically, they could not well explain behavior of the top decision maker and his important ministers who dominated major phases of decisionmaking in two of our three cases.

Leaving Allison's Model at this point, we tried to explain why and when President Park dominated (and therefore, why and when the President's men or sub-organization dominated) decisionmaking process. We tried to borrow ideas from T. Lowi's types of policy. Our effort was partly successful in that the decisionmaking process of regulatory policy could explain some part of President Park's behavior. Unsatisfied with the results of our earlier effort to explain President Park's behavior, we tried another explanation, focusing on President's viewpoint. Assuming that President Park behaved very rationally, (this assumption will most probably be valid in important issues), we hypothesized as follows: the President relied on bureaucratic suborganizations when he was confident in their expertness or when the issues were trivial. When the President had a firm idea, he himself dominated the decisionmaking process. When the situation was different from the above two cases, President Park selected, a reliable man as his "acting President." In the case of regulatory policies which triggered big conflict among groups, the "acting President" usually became very active, while the President sat back, the carefully watching and saving his political resources.

The President's role in the policymaking process depends on many other factors not explored here such as, personality, length of term, age, etc. Moreover, the hypotheses or observations we made here must be supplemented by other important observations.

The above hypotheses or observations are based on the expected behavior from the President's rational calculations. They must be complemented and enriched, by (1) the behavior of Presidential secretaries, ministers or higher rank bureaucrats and by (2) the influence or the activities of important groups, party leaders, Assembly men and mass-media which are outside of the formal decisionmakig process within the Executive Branch.

The first (1) aspect mentioned above is particularly important, since the President's decision to delegate or not to delegate his authority to the sub-organizations, or to a reliable man and the President's behavior to control his subordinates during decisionmaking process are the greatly influenced by the responses or reactions of his subordinates. Moreover, the President's subordinates sometimes dominate the decisionmaking process independent from the President's intention. When and why do they accept the authority delegated to them and the role of "acting President" including the role of scapegoat? How do they treat their subordinates and other participants? How do they check the President's conflidence in them and the President's idea which may change during the decisionmaking process? How do they exploit the opportunity of "acting President" in one issue area for issue areas of other sorts and how do they exploit the strict secrecy, required by the President, of some decisions? Answers to these questions are very important to explain the decisionmaking process in developing countries. However, this job is left for another paper.

8

A Network Analysis of
Interorganizational Relations:
A Case Study of the Transportation System
in Korea

Moon Suk Ahn and Chong Bum Lee

1. Introduction

The purpose of this study is to analyze the communication patterns among government agencies in the field of transportation in Korea.

In the first part, the transportation system is defined together with its supra-system and subsystems.

In the second part, some communication patterns among the system-related agencies will be derived from the communication analysis.

Finally, some policy implications will be discussed from the fact-findings shown in the previous parts.

2. Transportation System

The transportation system can be defined as a system of integrating landuse functions scattered over seperate spaces. In broader terms, exchanges of information among different locations, which is considered to perform important linkage roles, can legitimately be included in the transportation system.

The transportation system of the study, however, is confined to the movements of persons and goods among spaces.

When we follow the above definition, landuse planning becomes

---

* This study was sponsored by IBRD via the Korea Advanced Institute of Science and Technology.

the supra-system to the transportation system. National physical planning, special region planning and urban planning are included in this category.

The subsystems of the system can be classified into two areas, i.e., the demand subsystem and the supply subsystem. The supply side consists of road or railroad network, vehicles and traffic flow controls. The demand element consists of customers who use the supply subsystem.

The government agencies relevant to the transportation system are as follows:

Supra-system ...... Ministry of Construction (Landuse planning)
Subsystems ...... Ministry of Construction (Road construction)
                    ...... Ministry of Transportation (Railroad construction)
                    ...... Seoul Special City (Subway construction)
                    ...... Ministry of Transportation (Vehicle administration)
                    ...... National Police Headquarters (Driver's licence administration)
                    ...... National Police Headquaters (Traffic flow controls)
                    ...... Economic Planning Board (Transportation price)

In the following section, the inter-relationships among those organizations will be discussed from the standpoint of information exchanges.

3. Communication Analysis

The degree of cooperation among the relevant agencies can be measured through the communication frequencies revealed in the registration book of offical documents kept in each department.

3-1. Ministry of Transportation (at the level of central government) and Seoul Metropolitan Government (at the level of local government) are selected as the object agencies of communication analysis.

Vehicle technology, Guidance, the Passenger and Cargo Transport and Urban Transport Divisions of Land Transport Bureau, Transport Coordination and Transport Management Divisions of the Transport Coordination Bureau, Inspection & Safety Control Office, Planning and Management Office, and Transportation Inconvenience Report. Center which are recognized as administrative agencies related to the transportation function in the Ministry of Transportation are selected as the target agencies.

Also in the case of the Seoul Metropolitan Government, Transportation Administration I, Transportation Administration II, Transportation Planning and Subway Divisions of the Transportation Bureau and Public Road Division of the Construction Management Bureau are selected as the target agencies of the study.

The registration books which keep recording all the official documents in and out from the target agencies were analyzed in a one year period except in the case of the Transportation Administration Division II of Seoul. The period for this particular agency was selected to be four months for convenience of collecting data. The study periods are as follows:

1982. 3. 6 — 1982. 5. 3 : two months
1982. 6. 24 — 1982. 8. 24 : two months

For the remaining agencies, the period covers from January 1, 1982 to December 1, 1982.

The following is the format of the registration book for incoming official documents used for this study.

1	2	3	4	5	6	Appendix		9	Distribution	
				Classification				Manage-		
	Accep-	Dispat-	Enfor-	Symbol		7	8	ment	10	11
No.	tance	ch	cement	Document	Subject			Official		
	Date		Date	No.		Title	Volume		Transferer	Receipter

Item numbers 2, 3, 6 and 9 among the items listed in the above table were selected to be stored into computer magnetic tapes for analysis.

The format of the registration book for outgoing official documents is as follow:

1	2	3	4	5	Appendix		Distribution Method		Original	
	Dispatch	Accep-	Classification		6	7	8	9	10	11
No.	Date	tance	Symbol Docu-	Subject			by Mail	by	Chief	Receipter
			ment No.		Title	Volume		Someone	official	

Item numbers 2, 3 and 5 were memorized in the computer tape for this study.

The total number of records for incoming and outgoing documents were 28,915 and 20,452 respectively.

3-2. Results of communication analysis of the Ministry of Transportation.

The following communication patterns are the results of this study.
1) *Results from the analysis of the Incoming Official Documents*
    A. The main source of inputs to the Urban Transport Division
       of the Land Transport Bureau are Provincial Governments
       of Seoul, Daegu and Inchon. The Urban Transport Division
       receives information from the Ministry of Home Affairs (19),
       Joint Civil Affairs Office (21) and Federation of Bus Associa-
       tion (11). Information flows to the Urban Transport Division
       are shown in Figure 1.

Figure 1. Information Flow to Urban Transport Division

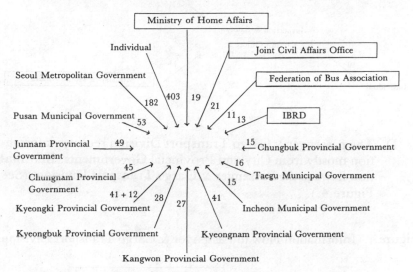

    B. The main sources of information to the Transport Coordina-
       tion Division are Economic Planning Board (20) and the
       Ministry of Construction (14) of the central government.
       Figure 2 shows information flows to the Transport Coordina-
       tion Division.

Figure 2. Information Flow to Transport Coordination Division

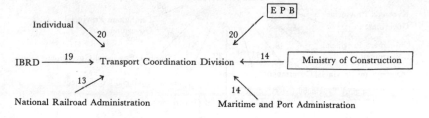

C. The Agency sending the most frequent information to the Inspection & Safety Control Officer is the Safety Public Corporation. And it receives information from the Ministry of Home Affairs (11) and National Railroad Administration (13). Figure 3 shows information flows to the Inspection & Safety Control Officer.

Figure 3. Information Flow to Inspection & Safety Control Officer

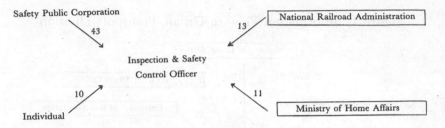

D. The passenger & Cargo Transport Division receives information mostly from City and Provincial Governments. Information flows to the Passenger & Cargo Transport Division. (See Figure 4.)

Figure 4. Information Flow to Passenger & Cargo Transport Division

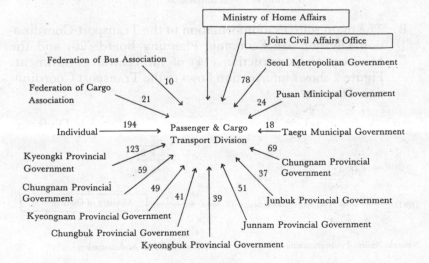

E. The Vehicle Technology Division of the Land Transport
Bureau receives information from the Ministry of Commerce
& Industry, the Ministry of Home Affairs, the Economic Plan-
ning Board, the Ministry of Energy and Resources and the
Joint Civil Affairs Office. And it relates to the Hyundae Motor
Vehicle Corporation (18) and the Kia Industrial Corporation
(13). But the agency with the most information input to the
Vehicle Technology Division is the Traffic Safety Promotion
Corporation (54). (See Figure 5.)

Figure 5. Information Flow to Vehicle Technology Division

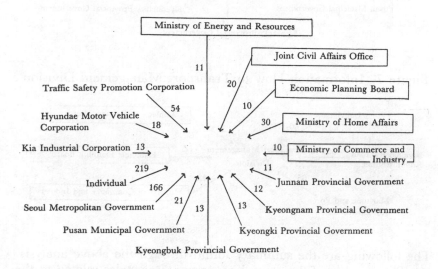

F. The Guidance Division of the Land Transport Bureau receives
information from the Ministry of Home Affairs and the Joint
Civil Affairs Office of the central government. Figure 6 shows
information flows to the Guidance Division.

G. Transport Management Division of the Transport Coordination Bureau accepts information from the National Railroad
Administration and the Maritime & Port Administration of
the Ministry of Transportation, and is related to the Ministry
of Foreign Affairs, the Economic Planning Board and the
Ministry of Commerce & Industry of the central government.
(See Figure 7.)

Figure 6. Information Flow to Guidance Division

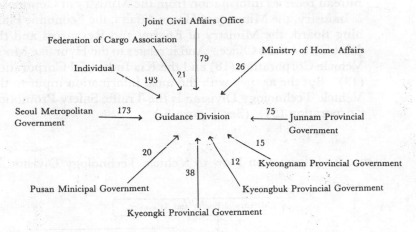

Figure 7. Information Flow to Transport Management Division

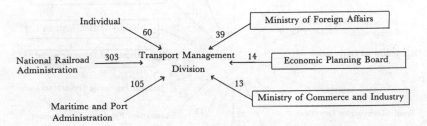

The following are the summary found through the above analysis.

(1) The number of the central government agencies related to the Vehicle Technology Division is 5. Most of the divisions relate to two agencies.

(2) The agencies related to the local governments are the Urban Transport Division, Passenger & Cargo Transport Division, Vehicle Technology Division and Guidance Division.

(3) The divisions related to private sectors are as follows:
   - Urban Transport Division — Federation of Bus Association
   - Passenger & Cargo Transport Division
     — Federation of Bus Association
     Federation of Cargo Association
   - Guidance Division — Federation of Cargo Association

(4) The divisions related to IBRD are Urban Transport Division and Transport Coordination Division.

(5) The divisions related to the Ministry of Construction, the Ministry of Home Affairs, the Economic Planning Board, the Ministry of Finance and the Ministry of Commerce & Industry are as follows:

- Ministry of Home Affairs

  26/19 Guidance Division
  (Land Transport Bureau)

  Urban Transport Division
  (Land Transport Bureau)

  11 Inspection & Safety Control Officer

  10 Passenger & Cargo Transport Division
  (Land Transport Bureau)

  30 Vehicle Technology Division
  (Land Transport Bureau)

- Economic Planning Board

  20 Transport Coordination Division
  (Transport Coordination Bureau)

  10 Vehicle Technology Division
  (Land Transport Bureau)

  14 Transport Management Division
  (Transport Coordination Bureau)

- Ministry of Construction —14→ Transport Coordination Division
  (Transport Coordination Bureau)

- Ministry of Commerce and Industry

  10 Vehicle Technology Division
  (Land Transport Bureau)

  13 Transport Management Division
  (Transport Coordination Bureau)

- Ministry of Energy and and Resources —11→ Vehicle Technology Division
  (Transport Coordination Bureau)

- Ministry of Foreign Affairs —39→ Transport Coordination Division
  (Transport Coordination Bureau)

The following table reflects the communication patterns dominating the Ministry of Transportation at the Central Government level.

	Number of Related Division	Number of Relations
Ministry of Home Affairs	5	96
Economic Planning Board	3	56
Ministry of Commerce and Industry	2	23
Ministry of Construction	1	14
Ministry of Energy and Resources	1	11
Ministry of Foreign Affairs	1	39

(6) There are two channels for individual citizens to have contacts with the Ministry of Transportation. One is to contact the Ministry via the Joint Civil Affairs Office of the Ministry of Government Administration, and the other is to have direct contact with the relevant divisions of the Ministry of Transportation. The communication flows showing the direct contacts are described in the following figures:

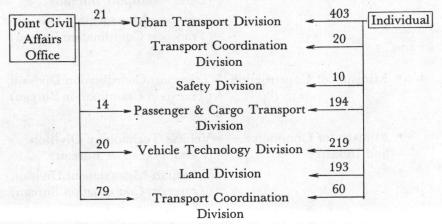

2) *Results from the analysis of the outgoing official documents at the Ministry of Transportation*

Here, the units of analysis are the Land Transport Bureau, the Transport Coordination Bureau, the Inspection Safety Bureau and the Transport Inconveniences Report Center of the Ministry of Transportation.

Figure 8. Information Flow from Land Transport Bureau

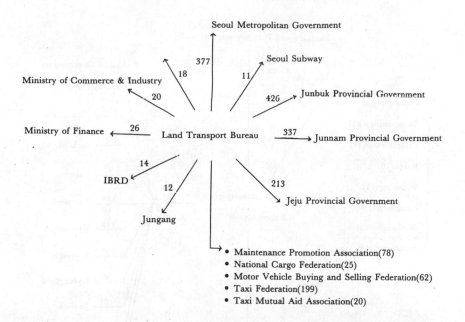

Figure 9. Information Flow from Transport Coordination Bureau

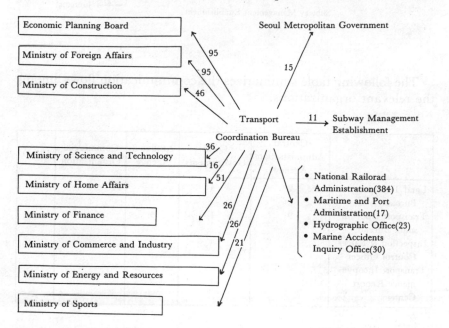

Figure 10. Information Flow from Transport Inconvenience Report Center

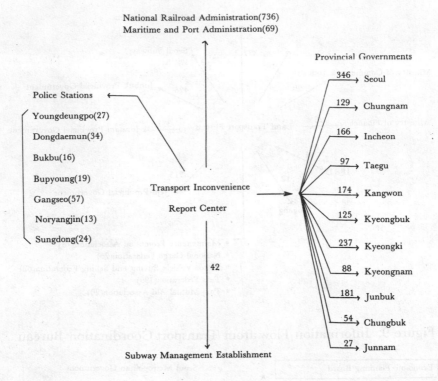

The following table summarizes the communication flows among the relevant organizations.

	Central Administration Agency	Local Governments	Affiliated Agency	Commercial Organization	IBRD
Land Transport Bureau	2	4	1	6	1
Transport Coordination Bureau	9	1	4	.	.
Inspection & Safety Control Officer	.	.	3	.	.
Transport Inconvenience Report Center		11	2	.	

3) *Conclusions of the network analysis at the level of the Central Government.*
The in-and-out flows of information existing at the Ministerial levels
of central government can be summarized in the following figure.

Figure 11. Information Flow among Agencies

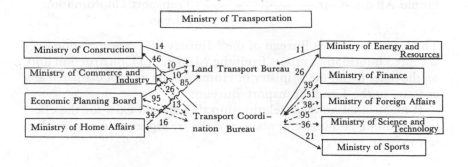

It is said that when communication flows between two agencies
is mutual, the two agencies are in a stable relation in communication
analysis. It can be said that two agencies are in an unstable relation
when communication flows are one-sided.

A. The Land Transport Bureau does not seem to have a stable relation with any agencies. It only receives information inputs from
the Ministry of Construction, the Ministry of Commerce and Industry, the Ministry of Energy and Resources and the Ministry
of Home Affairs.

B. The Transport Coordination Bureau has inputs of communication flows only in relation to the Ministry of Home Affairs and
the Ministry of Energy and Resources. And it has outputs only
in relation to the Ministry of Science and Technology and the
Ministry of Sports. The agencies which have mutual flows of communication with the Transport Coordination Bureau are the
Ministry of Commerce & Industry, the Economic Planning Board,
the Ministry of Finance, that is, the agencies related to economy
and administration, and the Ministry of Foreign Affairs. It can
be seen that information from the agency outnumbers information into the agency in the Transport Coordination Bureau. The
Transport Coordination Bureau keeps stable relations with agencies related to economy and administration, and unstable relations with the Ministry of Home Affairs and the Ministry of Energy
and Resources.

C. Communications among the three main organizations in charge of the transportation system administration are found to be highly unstable. The following figure shows the relationships.

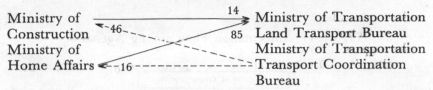

Ministry of Construction
Ministry of Home Affairs

Ministry of Transportation
Land Transport Bureau
Ministry of Transportation
Transport Coordination Bureau

The Land Transport Bureau of the Ministry of Transportation only accepted information inputs from the Ministry of Construction and, on the other hand, the Ministry of Home Affairs did not distpatch any outputs to the Land Transport Bureau.

It means that an ideal relationship that should exist for the effective planning and implementation of the transportation system does not exist in reality.

3-3. Summary of the communication patterns at the level of Seoul City Government.

The same analysical method was applied to the study of the communication patterns at the level of local government. Seoul City was selected as a target agency. Divisions related to the transportation system administration at the city government were chosen for this study. Those are the Transportation Administration Division I and II, the Subway Division, the Transportation Planning Division and the Public Road Division.

1) The following table was derived from the analysis of the registration books of the incoming official documents held at the divisions.

	Central Administration Agency (Bureau)	Transportation Bureau (Division)	Construction Management Bureau (Division)	Ward Office	Commercial Organization	Police Station	Police Bureau	Transportation Company	Near City and Provincial Government
Transportation Administration Division I	2	2	2		4			47	1
Transportation Administration Division II	1	2			6			40	4
Subway Division	4	2	3						
Transportation Planning Division	3	2	3		2				
Public Road Division	5	2	2						

It can be seen from the above table that Public Road Division of the Construction Management Bureau has relations with 5 Central Government agencies and the Subway Division has relations with 4 Central Government agencies. The divisions which accepted information inputs from Police Bureau were Transportation Administration Division I, Transportation Administration Division II and Public Road Division. And the division related to Police Stations of Seoul City was Transportation Administration Division II.

The division related to the Kyeonggi Provincial Government, the Incheon Municipal Government and the Kangwon Provincial Government within the Metropolitan area was Transportation Administration Division II.

2) The results derived from the analysis of the outgoing official documents are summarized in the following table.

	Central Administration Agency (Bureau)	Transportation Bureau (Division)	Construction Management Bureau	Police Bureau	Police Station	Joint Civil Affairs Office	Remarkable Agency
Transportation Administration Division I	1	1	1				
Transportation Administration Division II	1	2					Fine Collection Officer
Subway Division		1					
Transportation Planning Division	2	2					Police Coordination Officer
							Korea Electric Energy Corporation
Public Road Division	2	1	2				Korea Electric Communication Corporation

The above table shows that Transportation Planning Division and Public Road Division had contacts with relatively more agencies.

3) Combining the two analytical results described above, we get the following information flows among the relevant agencies at the Seoul City level. (See Figure 12)

(1) There were no contacts between divisions of the Transportation Bureau and the Public Road Division.

Figure 12. Document Flows between Administration Agencies
related to Transportation at Seoul City Government

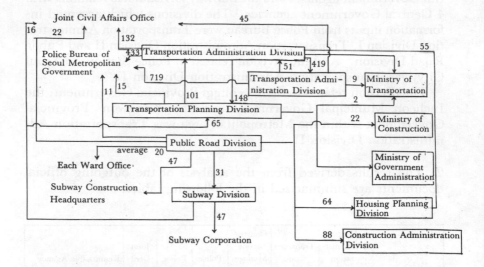

(2) Inputs into the Central Government Agencies were very weak.
(3) Joint Civil Affairs Office was the window for contacts with the
    Public.
(4) Subway Division acted as a connecting point between the Public
    Road Division and the Transportation Planning Division.
(5) City Planning Bureau which takes charge of urban planning func-
    tions accepted inputs from the Transportation Bureau. But it
    didn't accept any information from the Public Road Division.
(6) Police which takes charge of traffic order and safety actively ac-
    cepted inputs from all divisions.

4. Policy Implications of the communication analysis

First, the strength of the communication among the transportation administration agencies at the central government level is found
to be very weak. That is, the information flows among the Ministry
of Construction (in charge of transportation network), the Ministry
of Transportation (in charge of vehicle administration) and the Police
Headquaters (in charge of traffic control) seem to be unstable.
Particularly, there were few contacts between the Ministry of Construction and the Ministry of Transportation.

It means that the supra-system of the transportation system, i.e., the landuse functions dominate other functions. It may reduce the possibilities that the landuse planning reflects the problems of vehicle administration and traffic controls.

Second, in case of the Ministry of Transportation, work volumes related to the direct contacts with citizens outnumber that of planning works. Poor quality of transportation planning may be attributed to this phenomenon.

Third, at the level of local government, the Seoul City receives large volume of information from the central government, mainly from the Ministry of Construction and the Ministry of Transportation. On the contrary, the city government sends very little information to the central government.

Minimal communication between the central government and the local government may cause heavy damages to the local transportation system.

Fourth, the director of the Public Road Division of the Seoul City government reports directly to the Bureau Chief of the Construction Management Bureau. It means that he has no responsibilities regarding traffic flows. Extremely little information flowed between the Public Road Division and other divisions related to traffic management as was shown in our analysis. The lack of coordination among the agencies responsible for network management and other functions is considered to be one of the main reasons that Seoul has a high level of traffic congestion.

5. Conclusions

Most of the articles dealing with transportation problems approach transportation problems from the physical planning standpoint. In this article, we applied system concepts and a communication flow model approach for finding the administrative problems in the transportation system in Korea.

The registration books of the in-and-out official documents that must be kept at each organizations were analyzed extensively via computer programs.

Network diagrams were then derived from the raw materials and policy implications were discussed.

The lack of communication among the relavant system elements were believed to be the main factors that result in the poor quality of transportation services in Seoul.

Part Three

Budgetary Process and Fiscal Policy

9

The Budget System and Structure in Korea

Dong Kun Kim

Introduction

Korean budgeting as a numerical expression of governmental activities reflects political, economic, and administrative decision making in Korea. It is a record of the past and also a statement about the future which "attempts to link proposed expenditures with desirable future events."[1]

This paper is divided into five parts. Part I describes budgetary institutions and process in Korea. Part II reviews the scope and characteristics of the public sector; the budget as an instrument of economic policy is analyzed in Part III. Part IV explains the development of budgetary techniques. Finally, government efforts to constrain the growth in the budget are discussed in Part V.

BUDGETARY INSTITUTIONS AND PROCESS IN KOREA

The budget system in Korea is governed by four important documents: the constituion, which has a few significant general provisions on the national budget; the Budget and Accounting Law, which lays down in great detail budgetary procedures of ordinary government agencies; the Budget and Accounting Law for Government Enterprise; and the Budget and Accounting Law for Government Invested

---

1. Aaron Wildavsky, *Budgeting: A Comparative Theory of Budgetary Process* (Boston: Little, Brown and Company, 1975), p. 3.

Corporations, which is somewhat similar to the Government Corporation Control Act of 1945 in the United States. Under these laws, the following budgetary institutions and process can be identified.

Budgetary Institutions

Four institutions are involved in the budget cycle.

Bureau of Budget, Economic Planning Board. In 1961 the Korean government established the Economic Planning Board (EPB) for the purpose of formulating and executing economic development plans. The first five-year plan was duly introduced in 1962 and the country embarked on its fifth plan in 1982.

The Bureau of Budget in the EPB, which is analogous to the Office of Management and Budget (OMB) in the United States, has functions such as reviewing the ministerial budget estimates, preparing a centralized and comprehensive government budget bill, and submitting the budget bill to the National Assembly. While the U.S. Office of Management and Budget has responsibility for improving administrative management and legislative affairs in addition to the traditional budgetary functions, the Bureau of Budget is concerned only with budget-related matters. In 1981 the bureau was reorganized in order to strengthen its policy-making role.

Ministry of Finance. The Ministry of Finance, which assesses and collects taxes, has the task of revenue budgeting. It controls the execution of the authorized budget in accordance with the government's financial plan and closes the accounts of revenues and expenditures. It also manages the national treasury accounts which deal with government securities and properties.

Board of Audit and Inspection. The Board of Audit and Inspection, which is directly under the Office of President, is a functionally independent, constitutional agency. The board inspects the closing of accounts of revenues and expenditures at the end of the fiscal year[2] and in the following year reports the results to the president and the National Assembly.

National Assembly. The National Assembly has the right to deliberate and decide upon the national budget bill and to authorize the closing of accounts of revenues and expenditures submitted by the Board of Audit and Inspection. But the National Assembly cannot, without the consent of the executive, either increase the sum of any item of expenditure or add any new item to the budget. The major func-

---

2. The fiscal year begins on January 1 and ends on December 31.

tions of the National Assembly concerned with budget are as follows.[3]

- *Inspection of Government Activity.* Before the 7th Amendment of the constitution in 1972, the National Assembly inspected government activities prior to deliberating on the budget. The purpose of this inspection was to draw on past budgetary experience for the purpose of formulating the new budget. This right was repealed by the 7th Amendment in 1972 but subsequently reestablished by the 8th Amendment in 1980. Whereas formerly the inspection involved a formal review, it is now a right which may be exercised in order to inspect specific matters of state affairs individually.
- *Special Committee on Budget and Account.* The current National Assembly Act stipulates that the Special Committee on Budget and Account is the agency fully responsible for budget deliberation. Since the budget bill resolved by the Special Committee is usually passed in the plenary session, it plays an important role in budget authorization. But this committee is not a standing committee and there is no specialized standing committee regarding budget deliberation in the National Assembly. Moreover, due to the fact that few members of the National Assembly are reelected, the Special Committee on Budget and Account is short on experience and specialized knowledge.

Thus, the influence exerted by the National Assembly on budgetary issues is weak and it rarely challenges the proposals put forward by the executive. The record for the 1970s shows that, on the average, the National Assembly has cut the budget bill submitted by the executive by less than one percent.[4]

Budgetary Process

The budgetary process in Korea may be described in four steps.

Preparation of the Budget. By March 31 each year the minister of the Economic Planning Board sends the guiding principles for budget preparation to the heads of all ministries and agencies, requiring them to submit their budget estimates by May 31 to the Economic Planning Board. The Bureau of Budget then begins reviewing and revising these estimates in consultation with the agencies involved. Once agreement is reached on budgetary allocations, they must be deliberated

---

3. Unlike the U.S. budget, the budget in Korea is not treated as a law or an appropriations act. The budget is authorized by legislative resolution.
4. National Assembly Secretariat, *The History of National Assembly in Korea,* 1977.

by the State Council and approved by the president. After his approval has been obtained, the budget bill is prepared and submitted to the National Assembly within ninety days before the beginning of the fiscal year. In actual fact, budget preparation begins earlier than March. The Bureau of Budget collects the necessary data and prepares possible alternative budgeting standards in line with the president's New Year's Address and his approach to economic policy.

Authorization of the Budget. The authorization of the budget by the legislative body is an important constituent of the democratic system. Such actions of a legislative body represent the formulation of policy as well as the oversight of administration.[5]

Submission of the budget bill to the National Assembly takes place no later than October 2 and is followed by the policy speech of the president in the plenary session. The National Assembly then refers the budget bill to the Special Committee on Budget and Account. Questions raised by members of the Special Committee must be answered by the relevant ministers and the Special Committee can establish several subcommittees, if necessary, to investigate certain aspects of the bill in more detail. The National Assembly's deliberations must be completed thirty days before the fiscal year begins on January 1.

Execution of the Budget. Upon receipt of a spending program from each ministry and agency and a consolidated funding plan from the minister of finance, the minister of the Economic Planning Board prepares the quarterly apportionment plans for all ministries and agencies. After each ministry and agency receives its quarterly apportionment, the actual execution of the budget is carried out by the financial attachés.

Accounting and Auditing. The Ministry of Finance closes all accounts of revenues and expenditures by March 20 of the following year as the preparation of the new budget is undertaken. A comprehensive report covering all the financial operations of the fiscal year is then prepared by the minister of finance and submitted to the president through the Board of Audit and Inspection by June 30. The board audits this and sends its own report to the minister of finance, who submits it to the National Assembly at least ninety days before the beginning of the next fiscal year.

As the above account indicates, the budget cycle in Korea has a life of three years, consisting of a first year for budget preparation and authorization, a second year for budget execution, and a third year for budget audit and approval.

---

5. Jesse Burkhead, *Government Budgeting* (New York: John Wiley & Sons, Inc., 1956), p. 308.

THE SCOPE AND CHARACTERISTICS OF THE PUBLIC SECTOR

The Scope of the Public Sector

The public sector in Korea consists of a government sector and a nongovernment sector which includes banking institutions and government-owned corporations. The government sector, in turn, is subdivided into central and local governments. The central government budget is categorized into general accounts and special accounts, the latter being designed to implement special projects outside of the general account.[6]

The proportion of the central government budget to GNP in Korea remained around 22 percent throughout the 1970s, as illustrated by Table 1. But the ratio began rising in 1980 and reached 26.4 percent in 1981. The general account of the central government budget makes up about 16-18 percent of GNP, while the total budget, which includes local government expenditures, reached 34 percent in 1981 as compared to 25.8 percent in 1970.

Table 1: The Size of the Government Sector in Korea

	1970	1975	1977	1979	1981	1982*
GNP (billion dollars)	7.8	20.2	35.2	60.7	63.3	67.4
Per capita income ($)	243	574	966	1546	1636	1713
Total size of government sector (as % of GNP)	25.8	25.3	26.0	29.4	34.0	30.3
A. Central government	22.3	21.7	21.8	22.2	26.4	22.4
General account	16.4	15.7	16.1	17.4	18.3	17.4
Special accounts	5.9	6.0	5.7	4.8	8.1	5.0
B. Local government†	3.5	3.6	4.2	7.2	7.6	7.9

* Estimated original budget.

† Includes general account and special accounts.

Source: Economic Planning Board, *Summary of Budget for Fiscal Year 1982.*

---

6. There were a total of seventeen special accounts in 1982. The most important ones are the Monopoly Enterprise S/A, and the Communication Service S/A.

7. Ministry of Finance, *Government Finance Statistics in Korea (1982).*

Expenditure

The various components of the general account of the central government budget are shown in Table 2.

Table 2: Expenditure Structure by Function of Central Government
(General Account Only)

	1962-66 (average)	1967-71 (average)	1972-76 (average)	1979	1981	1982*
General administration	12.1	11.7	10.2	9.0	11.1	10.5
Defense	29.0	24.7	30.2	30.3	33.8	34.4
Social development	23.9	23.5	20.3	22.5	23.9	26.9
Economic development	27.0	26.0	23.0	27.5	18.6	17.6
Grants to local government	3.4	11.4	9.0	6.4	6.5	7.5
Repayment of government debts and others	4.6	2.7	7.3	4.3	6.1	3.1
Total expenditures	100.0	100.0	100.0	100.0	100.0	100.0

* Estimated original budget.
Source: Economic Planning Board, *Summary of Budget for Fiscal Year 1982.*

One significant feature of the expenditure pattern is the excessively high proportion of defense expenditure. The total defense expenditure in Korea accounted for about 6 percent of GNP or 33.8 percent of total expenditures in 1981. Another important characteristic is that the proportion of social development expenditure is still low. The ratio, which was about 24 percent in the 1960s, fell to 20 percent in the 1970s and is expected to average 25 percent in the 1980s. In addition, most of the social development expenditure was allocated to education, which accounted for 76 percent of the total social development expenditure or 18.2 percent of total government expenditures in 1981. As a result, other areas of social development such as social security, housing, and medical care were given relatively little attention.

Economic development expenditure was the second largest item in both the 1960s and the 1970s. However, the ratio has declined to less than 18 percent in the early 1980s. The decrease of economic development expenditure reflects the shift in economic development policy from government initiative to the private sector. General administration expenditure accounts for 10.5 percent in 1982 and is decreasing slightly. It is still high compared with other countries, chiefly because public services are centralized in the national government.

Lastly, the structure of expenditure has been quite rigid. Defense and education expenditures were 52 percent of the total budget, limiting the availability of funds in other sectors. If other statutory expenditures such as labor costs, grants to local governments and repayments of government debts are added, almost 75 percent of the total budget in 1981 was more or less fixed. This rigidity in expenditure interferes with the budget's adjustment function for economic stabilization.

Revenue

One of the most serious problems in the revenue structure is its excessive dependence on tax revenue. The proportion of tax revenues to the total revenues was 90.0 percent in 1970 and is expected to soar to as high as 95.9 percent in 1982, which makes it very difficult to acquire additional funds for more flexible budget operation (see Table 3).

Another problem in the revenue structure is that revenues from indirect taxes are very high compared with those from direct taxes. No such difference existed between the two taxes before the value

Table 3: Central Government Revenues (in percent)

	1970	1975	1977	1979	1981	1982*
Tax revenues	90.0	90.6	87.7	86.4	88.8	95.9
Internal taxes†	70.0	65.9	56.0	55.1	56.2	58.3
Customs duties	12.6	11.8	12.9	13.3	10.9	12.9
Defense surtax	—	4.1	11.4	11.5	13.4	14.3
Education tax‡	—	—	—	—	—	2.5
Monopoly profits	7.4	8.8	7.4	6.5	8.3	7.9
Borrowing and other						
nontax revenues	10.0	9.4	12.3	13.6	11.2	4.1
Total revenues	100.0	100.0	100.0	100.0	100.0	100.0

* Estimated original budget.

† Internal taxes consist of the personal income tax, corporation income tax, inheritance and gift tax, value added tax, liquor tax, special consumption tax, etc.

‡ Adopted in 1982 as an earmarked tax.

Source: Economic Planning Board, *Summary of Budget for Fiscal Year 1982.*

added tax was introduced in 1977, but the gap has since widened rapidly, with the tax system becoming centered on indirect taxes. The proportion of indirect tax revenue to the total internal taxes was 50.5 percent in 1970 but rose to 63.4 percent in 1981. Moreover, if customs duties and the defense surtax are added, total indirect tax revenue reaches as high as 67.8 percent of total tax revenues in 1981.

The government prefers to rely on indirect taxes to meet its revenue needs because such taxes are cheaper to collect and encounter less resistance. Indirect taxes, however, generally have a single tax rate and are regressive in nature. They play little role in redistributing income and on occasion have been instrumental in raising prices.[8]

The third problem in the structure of revenue is that local government revenue is too small and too heavily dependent on the central government. In 1981, for instance, local taxes accounted for 40.3 percent of the total and local nontax revenues for 16.2 percent. Hence, the central government had filled 43.5 percent of local government needs.

THE BUDGET AS AN INSTRUMENT OF ECONOMIC POLICY

Tax Policy

The Korean tax structure leans heavily on indirect taxes for the sake of administrative convenience, as noted above, but considerable progress in improving direct tax collection has been made since the establishment of the Office of National Tax Administration in 1966. The agency was established to achieve non-arbitrary tax administration as well as to increase tax revenue by eliminating tax evasion and other forms of corruption. However, it is undeniable that tax policy has concentrated on tax collection rather than economic stabilization and income redistribution.

The annual rate of increase in tax revenue far exceeded 30 percent during the period of 1975-79 except in 1977, as shown in Table 4. This rapid growth of tax revenue was caused primarily by inflation and the increase in imports. It was generally acknowledged that the tax rate was not sufficiently progressive and its revenue was not elastic

---

8. An indirect tax, especially a consumption tax, may be more favorable to saving than a direct tax. Thus, the use of a consumption tax can be advocated in developing countries where saving is needed to expedite economic growth. See Richard A. Musgrave and Peggy B. Musgrave, *Public Finance in Theory and Practice*, 3rd edition (Tokyo: McGraw-Hill International Book Company, 1980), pp. 670-671.

Table 4: Annual Percentage Rate of Increase in Tax Revenue

	1975	1976	1977	1978	1979	1980	1981	1982*
Rate of increase	51.7	49.3	27.9	38.4	30.9	22.7	23.8	25.8

* Estimated original budget.
Source: Ministry of Finance, *Government Finance Statistics in Korea (1982).*

in relation to the national income; therefore, the automatic stabilization function in the fiscal system was not effectuated. Rather, tax revenue fluctuated in proportion to prices due to its dependence on indirect taxes centering on the value added tax. High tax effort as well as a high tax rate inevitably increased the tax burden. As illustrated in Table 5, the ratio of the tax burden to GNP showed a continuous rise to 19 percent in 1980.

Table 5: Tax Burden as A Percentage of GNP

1975	1976	1977	1978	1979	1980	1981	1982*
15.8	17.4	17.4	17.9	18.4	19.2	18.8	18.6

* Estimated original budget.
Source: Ministry of Finance, *Government Finance Statistics in Korea (1982).*

On the other hand, the continuous increase of exemptions to direct taxes, particularly the corporation income tax, and tax favors extended to certain industries (such as the chemical industry) in support of economic development seriously compromised tax neutrality and the balances of the tax burden. Moreover, the separate and preferential tax treatment given to interest and dividend income increased the inequity of the tax burden.

Government Investment

Government investment, like business investment, has a very favorable influence on economic stabilization and growth with its multiplier effect on national income. The Korean economy began moving rapidly at the beginning of the 1960s and maintained its momentum of development through the 1970s, with average annual growth rates as high as 9.9 percent. The investment in domestic fixed capital also grew 19 percent annually during the period of

1962-78, and government investment accounted for more than 6 percent of GNP throughout the 1970s.[9]

Table 6: Government Investment as Percentage of Total Domestic Investment*

	General Government	Government Enterprises
1962-66 average	12.6	10.3
1967-71 average	17.3	6.2
1972-76 average	12.7	5.3
1977-81 average	13.6	6.8
Average, 1962-81	14.0	7.2

* Based on current prices.
Source: Bank of Korea, *Economic Statistics Yearbook* (1982).

Table 6 shows the proportion of government investment to total domestic investment during the period 1962-81. As shown in the table, government investment constituted an average of 14 percent of gross domestic capital formation. If the government enterprise investment of 7.2 percent is included, the figure rises to 21.2 percent.

In view of the above, it can be said that the expansion of the industrial base and production aided by the government's active investment has played a crucial role in achieving Korea's astonishing economic growth. But the excessive dependence on the public sector for rapid economic growth brought an expansion of the money supply and, thus, high inflation. The average annual rate of increase in the money supply in the 1970s was 28.6 percent. This explains the average annual rise of wholesale prices by 20 percent during the same period.[10]

Money Expansion in the Government Sector

The government budget shows that the general account has shown a surplus every year, while a deficit has been accumulated in the special account and in the area of nonbanking public enterprises. This has been caused mainly by the grain price support system which the government has used to raise the incomes of farmers. The government subsidization of the deficits of public sector corporations in order

---

9. Bank of Korea, *Economic Statistics Yearbook* (1982).
10. For the relationship between Money supply and wholesale prices in Korea, see *National Budget and Policy Goals* published by the Korean Development Institute (1981).

to ensure public welfare also contributed to the budget deficit. These deficits have mostly been financed by borrowing from the central bank (the Bank of Korea), causing a direct money expansion.

The expansion of money supply in the public sector was particularly noticeable during 1972-75. During that period, tax revenue dropped due to the recession triggered by the worldwide energy crisis, while the government expanded the budget deficit to break through the economic difficulties. The public sector was responsible for 59 percent of money expansion during this period.[11]

Table 7: Compensatory Financing in the Unified Budget
          (in billion won)

	1979	1980	1981
Total unified budget	6,210	8,455	11,481
Budget deficit	440	1,174	2,127
(as % of total			
unified budget)	(7.1)	(13.9)	(18.5)
Borrowing from the Bank of Korea	– 156 (– 35.5)	265 (22.6)	576 (27.1)
Borrowing from the deposit			
money banks	– 30 (– 6.8)	317 (27.0)	423 (19.9)
Borrowing from abroad (net)	266 (60.5)	318 (27.0)	460 (21.6)
Government bonds issued and others	360 (81.8)	274 (23.4)	668 (31.4)
Total	440 (100.0)	1,174 (100.0)	2,127 (100.0)

Source: Ministry of Finance, *Government Finance Statistics in Korea (1982).*

Table 7 illustrates the size of the budget deficit based on the unified budget and compensatory financing during 1979-81.[12] The size of the deficit in 1981 reached 18.5 percent of the unified budget, and 47 percent of this deficit was financed by the Bank of Korea and the deposit money banks.[13]

THE DEVELOPMENT OF BUDGETING TECHNIQUES

The Korean budget system made some progress in the analysis and evaluation of the budget with the reclassification of the budget based on the *UN Manual* at the end of the 1950s, but the real advance took place in the 1960s. Budgeting in the 1960s was characterized by the

---

11. Bank of Korea, op. cit., (1972-81).
12. The unified budget system began in fiscal year 1979.
13. Deposit money banks are equivalent to commercial banks.

provision of the Budget and Accounting Law that suggested the possible introduction of a performance budget. The Ministry of National Defense independently adopted the performance budget in 1962, and some other ministries also attempted to apply this system to a limited number of projects. Unfortunately, the system was abandoned in 1964 due to conceptual problems with the system itself and a shift in the leadership in the Bureau of Budget.

As a result, the Korean budget is modelled on the so-called line-item budget, which is classified by objects of expenditures. It is designed mainly for administrative control, with the tendency to follow the previous year's budget aggravating the inflexibility of the budget and, thereby, hampering the effective allocation of resources. Furthermore, there has been no effective linkage between planning and budgeting. Continuous government efforts were made throughout the 1970s to eliminate these kinds of problems, such as attempts to introduce Planning Programming Budgeting System (PPBS) and Zero-Based Budgeting (ZBB).

PPBS

The Ministry of National Defense (MOND) independently planned to launch the PPB system and organized a PPBS Research Committee in 1971. The plan was pursued with the objective of building up the foundation of the management system on which the self-reliance of national defense is realized rather than attempting to transplant the American system to Korea without modifications. In February 1974 the decree of MOND was issued, and efforts for introducing the PPB system were continued in 1974-75 at the preparation stage and 1976-78 at the implementation stage. Major documents were compiled in 1980, and the system is now being partially implemented by MOND.

ZBB

In 1981 the Bureau of Budget in Economic Planning Board reported to the president plans for improving the budget system based on ZBB and acquired presidential support for it. The plans were designed to break from the convention of following the previous year's budget, to eliminate waste and ineffectiveness in the budget, and thus to achieve more flexible budget operation.

The 1983 budget has been compiled partially based on the ZBB approach. Its major procedures are as follows: First, the decision units have been selected and classified. The cards and data for evaluating the effects of budgetary projects are being compiled. Second, educational materials have been prepared and in-service training has been given to the officers concerned with the implementation of ZBB. Third, the Budgetary Reform Committee and field investigation teams have been organized. The field investigation team has drawn up a comprehensive diagnostic report based on its study of the key projects of each ministry, which is reflected in the guiding principles for 1983 budget preparation.

GOVERNMENT EFFORTS TO CONSTRAIN THE GROWTH OF THE BUDGET

As illustrated in Table 1, the proportion of budget to GNP is expected to decrease in 1982. It is estimated that the increase rate of the 1983 budget bill will be the lowest since the 1960s (except 1973). The annual rate of increase in the general account budget of the central government was about 30 percent, which was as high as the rate of money expansion, during the 1960s and 1970s. The rate dropped to about 20 percent in the 1980s and is expected to be further lowered to 9.8 percent in 1983.[14] The constraint on budget expansion is in part the result of a reduction in revenue due to the recession, but it also reflects the firm policy of the government to prevent fiscal inflation and to eliminate the waste of public resources.

Some of the most important efforts to constrain the expansion of budget are described below.

The Reshuffling of Central Government Organization

The administrative machinery of the central government was made up of 12 ministries and 4 offices in 1960, but by 1979 it had expanded to 2 boards, 15 ministries, and 16 offices. Accordingly, the number of officers also drastically increased from 230,000 in 1960, to 400,000 in 1970, and to over 500,000 in 1979.

After the death of President Park, the government decided to restructure the administrative machinery in 1981 under the slogan "Simple and Clean Government." The reshuffle aimed at eliminating budgetary waste by reducing the complexity of the administrative machinery as well as by simplifying administration procedures.

The restructuring covered both the central and local governments and, thus, was quite extensive in its scale. One of its major results was the abolition of some agencies at the level of the ministry, such

---

14. Economic Planning Board, *1983 Budget Bill* (1982).

as the Administrative Innovation Committee (AIC) and the Office of Planning and Coordination (OPC). The workload among ministries was also rearranged.

The Implementation of the Budgetary Reform Plans

Some budgetary reforms are being carried out in support of a movement towards frugal government with the objective of strengthening the efficiency of public investment. The first is the introduction of ZBB. Since the system is still in its infancy, the effects remain to be seen.

The second is the medium-term fiscal plan. The plan is designed to analyze and establish the efficient allocation of fiscal resources by strengthening, through a rolling plan, the link between the five-year economic development plan and the annual budget. The medium-term plans (3 to 5 years) are set up to reflect changes in economic conditions, and the annual statutory budget is compiled and implemented on the basis of the plan.

The third is the strengthening of the public investment screening system. The system is intended to evaluate the effects of government projects currently under implementation and set up a priority ranking of future projects based on the analysis of their effects. The Bureau of Project Evaluation was established in the Economic Planning Board in 1978, and since then its screening function that utilizes cost/benefit analysis has been strengthened. The bureau plans to develop the manuals and methodologies required for the feasibility analysis and to computerize its data base.

The Reestablishment of Functions between the Public and Private Sectors

The key factor in the attempt to constrain the budget will be a reestablishment of functions between the public and private sectors. In other words, a clear line must be drawn between private sector activities and those of the public sector so as to ensure a gradual cutback in government activities. Efforts should be made to avoid the development plan implemented under the initiative of the government and to encourage private entrepreneurs to exercise their creativity by revitalizing the function of markets. By the same token, the public corporations, the major cause of the budget deficit in Korea, may adopt a more responsible management system and be transferred to the private sector.

10

Administrative Effects of the Tax Reform: A Value-Added Tax in Korea

Yeon Cheon Oh

1. Tax Reform and Introduction of the VAT System

In December 1976, the Korean government carried out an overall tax reform on a grand scale, including the introduction of a value-added tax and a special excise tax in the field of indirect taxation. Eighteen tax laws were newly enacted or amended under the reform, aimed at meeting the fiscal demand required for the effective administration of the 4th Economic Development Plan, and developing the tax system to a modern format. The 1976 tax reform for the VAT and special excise tax came into force on July 1, 1977. The VAT reform reflects such authoritative proposals as were prepared by Dr. J.C. Duignan, Professor Carl S. Shoup, and Dr. Alan A. Tait.

Eight existing indirect taxes including the cascade type business tax were replaced by the consumption type VAT and the supplementary special excise tax, in an effort to simplify the indirect tax system and its administration, and to promote export and capital investment. Table 1 illustrates the present indirect tax system which is composed of the VAT, special excise tax, and three minor taxes (liquor tax, telephone tax, and stamp tax).

Korea is heavily reliant on domestic indirect taxes, which account for more than 60% of the total internal tax revenue (excluding tariffs) since 1977. The two principal indirect taxes (VAT and the special excise tax) after the tax reform comprise a little over 50% of the total internal tax revenue. The VAT in particular constitutes a major component of the revenue system in Korea, where it represents more than one-third of the total internal tax revenue, and approximately 60% of the total indirect tax revenue.

Table 1. Outline of the Indirect Tax System

Before Change(11 taxes)	After Change(5 taxes)
Business Tax	Value-Added Tax
Commodity Tax	
Textile Products Tax	
Petroleum Products Tax	
Electricity and Gas Tax	
Travel Tax	Special Excise Tax
Adminission Tax	
Entertainment & Food Tax	
Liquor Tax	Liquor Tax
Telephone Tax	Telephone Tax
Stamp Tax	Stamp Tax

2. Administrative Aspect of the VAT Reform

Many proponents of VAT believed that the measure offers the advantage of administrative simplicity as compared with other general taxes for which it is a likely substitute. Thomas S. Adams, who proposed the VAT for the first time in the United States, indicated that the VAT would be easier to administer than a tax on gross turnover with differentiated rates.[1] Martin Bronfenbrenner insisted that the VAT is superior to the single stage retail sales tax chiefly because of its ease of collection and difficulty of tax evasion.[2]

The administrative efficiency of a VAT, which was one of the important considerations of adopting the VAT system in Korea, will be the topic of this paper. The administrative characteristics of the VAT will be compared with those of previous indirect tax system. This paper will be concerned with evaluating how the structure and procedure of the indirect tax system have been simplified because of the tax reform. This study will not be concerned with the issue of economic efficiency (input-output ratio) resulting from the adoption of VAT. The problems of VAT administration will be viewed from the angle of tax administration as well as taxpayers' compliance. A particular interest of the administrative issue will be on the structural

---

1.   Adams, Thomas S., "Fundamental Problems of Federal Income Taxation," *Quarterly Journal of Economics*, Vol. 35 (Aug. 1921), p. 552.
2.   Bronfenbrenner, Martin, "The Japanese Value Added Sales Tax," *National Tax Journal*, Vo. 3 (Dec. 1950), p. 299.

characteristics such as the rate and exemption structure, and treatment of small taxpayers. Besides, the number of taxpayers, the computation of the tax base, the frequency of payment, and other procedural characteristics will be discussed.

3. Structural Characteristics

(1) The Tax Rate Structure

The most important facet of the VAT that has direct influence on its administration is its tax rate structure. The single rate (10%) has been used since the introduction of the VAT in Korea.

While the single rate VAT is much simpler to administer than a multiple rate VAT, a number of countries have adopted multiple rates for equity and revenue purpose. Two types of problems caused by the use of multiple rates were pointed out in a report submitted to the U.S. Congress: first, the rate categories may not be sufficiently defined so that a product may fit into more than one category; second, the categories themselves may be based on criteria for which information is not readily available.[3] Multiple rates also cause particular problems for small businesses, especially retailers, dealing with goods covered by various rates. It may be extremely time consuming for such businesses to separately account for the various tax categories in the daily receipts. It is further argued that the single rate VAT can serve as a check on tax evasion while multiple rates may give taxpayers the opportunity to evade the tax by a miscalculation of goods and services.

In addition to the administrative advantages, the government is able to vary and utilize the single VAT rate as an economic stimulator or brake with far more predictability than a multiple rate VAT. The Korean government allowed adjustment of the normal rate (13%) with the limitation of 3% point, where deemed necessary due to changes in economic situations. The VAT has been implemented so far at the minimum level of 10%.

Korea had suffered from the previous indirect tax system with its very complicated rate structure. The business tax, which was a major target of the tax reform, had six differentiated rates ranging from 0.5% to 3.5% depending upon the categories of business. As shown in Table 2, the previous indirect system had more than 50 rates ranging

---

3. The Comptroller General of the U.S., "The Report to the Congress: *The VAT in the European Community*," (Dec. 1980), p. 11.

Table 2. Comparison of Tax Rates Between the Previous and New Tax Regime

Tax	Previous Tax Regime			New Tax Regime			
	Number	Tax Rates Maximum (%)	Minimum (%)	Tax	Number	Tax Rates Maximum (%)	Minimum (%)
Business	5	3.5	0.5	VAT (General) (Special)	1 2	10.0 3.5	2.0
Commodity	17	100.0	2.0				
Textile Products	7	40.00	10.0				
Petroleum Products	4	300.0	10.0	SET	13	180.0	10.0
Admission	12	250.0	5.0				
Travel	3	20.0	5.0				
Electricity & Gas	1	15.0	15.0				
Entertainment	4	20.0	2.0				

Source: The Ministry of Finance, Korea, *The Survey and Report on the Value-Added Tax* (April 1980), p. 48.

from 0.5% to 300%. This background led to a strong desire to simplify the tax structure, and consequently, to adopt a uniform rate of the VAT. Due to the VAT reform, the rate structure of the indirect tax system has been considerably simplified. Though Korea adopted the single rate VAT with 10%, it provided for special treatment to small taxpayers: small taxpayers whose total sales are less than 24 million Won a year are not subject to the 10% VAT, but they are subject to 2% tax on turnovers. These small taxpayers account for about 6% of the total VAT revenue. The problem of small taxpayers and special taxation will be discussed in detail in the next section.

There is a disadvantage in the single rate VAT which must be mentioned. It is not able to treat favorably those items which form a much greater proportion of low income household expenditures, and against those items which are bought mainly by the better-off households.[4] Multiple rates are used primarily to lighten the tax burden on necessities and to impose a very heavy tax burden on luxuries. Under the single rate VAT, exemptions on necessities play an important role in reducing the regressivity of the value-added tax. Even if increasing the progressivity of VAT is indispensable, it is more efficient to have a single rate which could yield a high revenue and to use that revenue to redistribute income to lower and needy groups, than to have multiple rates. Many of European countries which have used multiple rate VAT are moving to simplify their tax rate structure.[5]

In relation to a single rate VAT, it is argued that the tax base which makes possible a relatively low effective tax rate is likely to have an administrative advantage over one which requires a higher rate of tax because high rates create an incentive to tax evasion and intensify competitive inequities, especially when a tax is new.[6] This implies that for a given revenue yield, a tax which utilizes a measure of wide scope and thereby permits a low rate is, in principle, preferable to one imposed on a limited base and a high rate. In this respect, the government effort to lower the VAT rate to 10% may have contributed to alleviating administrative burdens and compliance problems.

---

4. But there is a powerful argument in favor of differential VAT rates, at least to start with. The introduction of the VAT nearly always means a broadening of the tax base, taxing some items which were untaxed. To soften the transition, low rates can be used for those items which are associated with high expenditure in low income households. See Tait, Alan A., *Value Added Tax* (McGraw-Hill: London, 1972), p. 60.
5. The United Kingdom, Belgium, and Ireland have decreased the number of VAT rates they used.
6. U.S. Treasury Department, "Federal Manufacturer's Wholesale and Retail Sales Taxes," *Hearings, Revenue Revision of 1943*, I, p. 349.

Finally, frequent rate changes are cited as causing administrative and compliance problems because they are likely to increase record keeping costs for both government and business sectors.[7] The fact that the 10% VAT has been maintained since the introduction of the VAT in 1977 may have positive implication on tax administration.

In summary, the rate structure has been simplified due to the adoption of the integrated form of VAT. It is the single rate VAT that has remarkably contributed to reducing the administrative and compliance problems.

(2) Exemptions

Exemption is one of the ways of adjusting a VAT to accomodate special considerations. The Korean VAT allows a variety of exemptions. They are based on classes of products, classes of services, classes of taxpayers, and stages in the production-distribution process for social, political and administrative reasons.[8]

First, exemptions are made for equity purposes. The most important one is exemptions on necessities like unprocessed agricultural products, which play a critical role in reducing the regressivity of the VAT burden distribution. Exemptions on medical and dental care, mass transit, educational services, non-profit social services, and similar services, are granted for social reasons.

Second, exemptions of classes of services, such as banking and insurance, are made and reflect the difficulty in applying the concept of value-added to these areas.[9] The value-added by banks and insurance is difficult to calculate under the indirect subtractive (tax-credit) method as used in Korea. The exemptions on service oriented businesses such as educational institutions, medical organizations, and lawyers are also applied to this category.

Third, some goods and services are exempt from the VAT because they are taxed in some other way. Supplementary separate taxes are imposed on telephone services, postage stamps, and liquors (telephone tax, stamp tax, and liquor tax, respectively).

Fourth, goods and services supplied to the government are also

---

7. Sullivan, Clara: *The Tax on Value Added* (Columbia University Press: New York, 1965), p. 222.
8. The Comptroller General, op. cit., p. 9.
9. "For financial services, the inputs could be considered as money deposits, but these would have no VAT content; the output could be repayments, but if these were taxed at the full VAT rate with no credit offset (because no VAT was credited on the input) clearly inequity would be created." Tait, Alan, *Value Added Tax*, p. 21.

exempt from the VAT. In addition, government monopoly goods such as cigarettes and ginseng are not liable to the VAT.

Fifth, certain classes of taxpayers are exempt from the VAT for reasons of administrative smplicity. A special treatment is given to this small group of taxpayers, either by exempting the VAT or by taxing them under special provisions. The problems of small tax-payers will be discussed in detail in the next section.

Sixth, certain goods and services are not only exempt but also zero-rated; that is, not only is no VAT levied on their sale, but the business producing them is reimbursed for VAT paid on its purchases. The zero applies to exports and international transportation by ship and aircraft. The question of zero-rating on export goods will also be discussed in the following section.

It is argued that exemptions facilitate the administration of the VAT. This is true of exemptions for small taxpayers and certain ser-vices such as financial services and professional services (e.g., doc-tors, lawyers, accountants, artists, researchers, and so on). On the other hand, it should not be ignored that excessive exemptions com-plicate administrative problems because of the difficulty of distinguishing taxable from nontaxable transactions, the more detailed records and invoices, and the opportunities provided for tax evasion and avoidance. Furthermore, if the reduction in the tax base raises the necessary tax rate to obtain a given amount of revenue, it may intensify administrative problems and inequities among the remain-ing taxpayers.[10]

It is recommended that exemptions be kept to a minimum in order to not only keep the VAT base broad but also minimize administrative problems and distortions in the economy.[11] The rule of thumb for criteria minimizing exemptions is as follows. First, the exemptions designed to make the VAT more equitable should be maintained. Second, exemptions of certain classes of taxpayers are more desirable than those of services and products. Third, where determination of value-added is difficult, the revenue potential of services and products subject to exemption must be weighed against the additional ad-ministrative and compliance burdens due to exemptions.

Let us discuse some issues regarding exemptions. First, it may be worth discussing whether the exemption of financial services from the VAT can be justified. In the light of rapid expansion of finan-cial services in the Korean economy, the extension of VAT to finan-

---

10. Sullivan, op. cit., p. 253.
11. IMF Fiscal Affairs Department (prepared by Alan A. Tait, Angelo G. Faria, and Peter S. Heller), *Korea: Taxes in the 1980's* (July 26, 1979), p. 152.

cial services, in an attempt to increase tax revenues, has been suggested. It is generally agreed that the VAT is not well adapted to financial services, especially banking and insurance under the indirect subtractive method. But the taxation on financial services is feasible by employing the additive method and applying the tax to total payrolls and profits after depreciation allowances. [12] In addition to the revenue increase, the idea would have some desirable distributional characteristics. Since most financial services are met by large corporations which can absorb the accounting and procedural requirements of the VAT with ease, administrative burdens resulting from imposing the VAT on the financial services will be minimized.

Second, it is desirable to incorporate the supplementary taxes imposed on telephone services, postage stamps, and liquors within the VAT network in terms of simplifying the indirect tax structure.

Third, although the government gets sizable revenue from the profits of its monopolies, and their prices are entirely under government control, there has been a strong argument for making the monopoly goods such as cigarettes and ginseng subject to the VAT. [13] The potential extension of the 10% VAT to tobacco and ginseng could yield approximately 7% increase on the VAT revenue based on 1983 and 1984 estimations. The extension of the VAT base to monopoly goods does not seem to result in much administrative burdens, either, because they are wholly controlled by the government.

Finally, exemptions pose administrative problems, particularly for such businesses as department stores and food chains, where a wide variety of taxable and nontaxable goods are handled. For example, a store might elect to be unregistered on farm products and conduct a business selling agricultural machinery which would be liable to VAT. The question may be raised: How do you apportion those purchases which will be allowable as offsets against VAT liability and those which will not? The appropriate solution in this case is to allow current and capital inputs in the ratio of the proportion of sales taxed to sales untaxed over the year. [14]

(3) Methods for Computing the Tax

There are three basic, alternative methods for computing the VAT: the addition method; the subtraction method; and the invoice

---

12. Lent, op. cit., pp. 330-31.
13. IMF Fiscal Affairs Department, op. cit., pp. 148-49.
14. Tait, op. cit., p. 32.

method.[15] The addition method calls for adding up all the payments made by the business for the production services it uses—its payroll and profits—and subtracting from that amount the change in inventories and capital outlays. The subtraction method requires the taxpayer to calculate his total net sales and receipts and to subtract from this total all of his purchases from other businesses including his capital outlays.

The third method, the invoice method, is the one used in Korea and virtually all of the countries having a VAT. Under this method, the taxpayer applied the VAT rate to the amount of his sales and shows this amount of tax as a separte item on his sales invoice. Every business making purchases from other businesses, therefore, finds the amount of the tax on each purchase separately stated on the invoice he receives. To compute the amount of tax he pays the government, he adds up all the VAT he has charged his customers, subtracts all the VAT his suppliers have charged him and the remainder is his VAT liability. The principal advantage claimed for this method is that it is self-enforcing. To establish the correctness of his own VAT liability each taxpayer would have to show the amount of tax he paid on his purchases from other businesses. And he would want to be sure that he passed on to his customers the amount of tax owing on his sales, which his customers presumably would insist on seeing separately on their purchase invoices for the same reason. When exemptions are widely allowed as in Korea, compliance may be less burdensome under the invoice method than other two methods.

The attachment of invocies to every transaction, and the checking of those invocies both by the purchaser and by the tax authority may represent a large potential administrative burden, particularly if accounting is manual[16] Experience has shown that small retailers and artisans greatly resist issuing invoices, not only for the administrative complexity that they imply but also to avoid registering total sales.[17] The major problem remains of how to deal with small businesses, where books are not kept in sufficient detail for the tax due on sales or reclaimable on purchases to be proved. This problem will be discussed in detail in the next section.

15. Ture, Norman R., "Economics of the VAT," *Value-Added Tax: Two Views* (American Enterprise Institute for Public Policy Research: Washington, D.C., 1972), pp. 74-75.
16. National Economic Development Office, *Value-Added Tax* (Her Majesty's Stationery Office: London, 1971), p. 19.
17. Lent, op. cit., p. 347.

(4) Number of Taxpayers

The number of taxpayers is one of the factors responsible for a considerable portion of administrative and compliance costs. On this count, the VAT has a great advantage over taxes assessed directly on individual incomes.[18] But the VAT's advantage is not expected over a general turnover tax. In Korea a changeover to the VAT has not involved a substantial increase in taxpayers because the multistage business tax already embraced most wholesale and retail firms.

Table 3 clearly shows that the number of taxpayers has not significantly changed following the introduction of the VAT. In reality, the number of taxpayers under the VAT has slightly decreased compared to that under the business tax, and increased gradually as a result of the growing economy.

The problem of the number of taxpayers has to be viewed with caution when only a small percentage of taxpayers affects the revenue significantly. In developing countries, the large number of small businesses accounts for only a small proportion of the revenue. We can estimate the number of taxpayers, if it is assumed that the small taxpayers are those who are treated as special taxpayers, as those whose total sales are less than 24 million Won a year.[19] Tables 4 and 5 indicate that special taxpayers account for a majority number of taxpayers. They represent approximately 80% of the total taxpayers. In contrast to the number of taxpayers, the revenue importance is placed on general taxation. The revenue from general taxation represents approximately 93% of the total VAT revenue while that of special taxation represents only 7%. The special taxpayers are most likely concentrated in small retailers.[20] Even though the control and audit of small taxpayers may be kept at a minimum, their number alone poses problems of registration, filing returns, and tax collection that could impede the efficient administration of the entire tax system.[21] The cost of administering the large numbers of relatively unproductive small taxpayers must be weighed against considerations of revenue and equity. If the administrative burden outweighs their revenue potential, such small businesses had better be exempt from the VAT.

---

18. Sllivan, op. cit., p. 215.
19. IMF Fiscal Department, op. cit., p. 145.
20. This special treatment consists of a 2% tax on turnover but this turnover can be checked by the cash receipts retailers are supposed to issue.
21. Lent, op. cit., p. 346.

Table 3. Number of Taxpayers

period (½ year)	76.2*1 the business tax		77.1		77.2		78.1		78.2 VAT		79.1		79.2	
	number	%	number	%	number	%	number	%	number	%	number	%	number	%
Total	846518	100	914901	100	824192	100	853277	100	878429	100	914366	100	933475	100
General Taxation subtotal					156949	19	173184	20	203290	23	201036	22	205603	22
cor-poration	17112	2	17715	2	19182	2	20622	2	22042	2	23763	3	25167	3
individual	819406	98	897188	98	137767	17	152562	18	181248	21	177273	19	189436	19
Special*2 taxation					667243	81	680093	80	675139	77	713330	78	727872	78

Sources: Ministry of Finance, Korea, *Major Tax Statistics (1980)*, p. 210; and author's estimates.

*1 The number of taxpayers for the commodity and other major previous indirect taxes was approximately 9000 in 1976.

*2 The special taxation is a form of VAT taxation which applies to small taxpayers like small retailers whose total sales are less than 24 million Won (as to June 1980) a year. This treatment consists of a 2% tax on turnover instead of 10% VAT.

Table 4. The Revenue of VAT depending upon General and Special Taxation, 1979 and 1980

(unit: hundred million Won)

Year Classification		79		80	
		revenue (Won)	percentage	revenue (Won)	percentage
General Taxation	Corporation	6046	72.4	8276	76.1
	Individual	1752	21.0	1830	16.8
	Subtotal	7798	93.4	10106	92.9
Special Taxation		553	6.6	771	7.1
Total		8351	100.0	10877	100.0

*Source: The Ministry of Finance, Korea, *Major Statistics of Korean Taxes* (1981).

Table 5. Ratio of Taxpayers by Industry Under General and Special Rates
of VAT in the year of 1982

unit: percentage

Industry	General Taxation	Special Taxation
Mining	0.6	0.0
Manufacturing	28.2	3.5
Wholesale	21.0	0.1
Retail	25.9	58.0
Construction	3.3	0.2
Hotels & Restaurants	4.3	17.3
Transfers	4.6	8.3
Other*	12.0	12.5
Total	100.0	100.0

Sources: The Office of National Tax Administration, *Statistical Yearbook of
National Tax* (1983).
*"Other" includes agriculture, electricity, gas, water, real estate, finance
and insurance, and community and personal services.

The other approach to minimize the problem of numbers of taxpayers, who keep inadequate records or none at all, is to limit the
VAT to firms with annual sales in excess of a specified minimum,
a policy that is generally practiced in Europe. For example, in the
Republic of Ireland, retail units with annual sales of less than £12,000
and persons providing services of less than £1,800 are not obliged
to register.[22] In Korea, small taxpayers with annual tax amount
payable less than 10,000 Won are excluded from the VAT.

(5) Treatment of Small Businesses

One of the criticisms of the VAT has been of the burden on
businesses, particularly small businesses as mentioned above to keep
books and render returns to the tax authorities in a prescribed format. Taxpayers' records must show clearly not only total sales and
the taxes payable but also his purchases and the taxes paid. Large
or medium-sized enterprises can absorb the accounting and procedural
requirements of the VAT with relative ease. On the other hand, the

---

22. Lent, op. cit., p. 346.

problems have arisen with the large numbers of small businesses like artisans, traders, and peddlers, where books are not kept in sufficient detail for the tax due on sales or reclaimable on purchases to be proved, who comprise an important proportion of total businesses in terms of numbers.[23]

One of the various solutions to the problem of administering the VAT on these small firms is to use the forfait (i.e., flat rate charge) type of assessment, which is the French system of bilateral agreement on tax liability between the small taxpayer and the government.[24] This system is widely used for small businesses and in those firms that are larger than those within the exempt category. Developing countries like Korea with large numbers of retailers, many of them with small turnovers, sometimes ill-educated, and often non complying, need to have the option of levying a simple turnover tax at a low rate instead of the more complicated VAT which requires the presentation of invoices and the calculation of the tax content of purchases.[25] A variant of this forfait system is used in Korea with a special turnover levy, in an effort to help administer small businesses, which might not be able to cope with the more difficult concept involved in the VAT. Those small businesses whose sales are less than 24 million Won a year are taxed on the basis of 2% of turnover. This turnover can be checked by the cash receipt that retailers are supposed to issue. But retailers tend to avoid issuing recepts to purchasers, who are not familiar with asking for receipts in their daily commercial transactions. Under this situation, a determination of total receipts of small businesses relies heavily on the tax authorities.[26] For this reason, the special treatment for small businesses may be subject to arbitrary decisions on the part of the administration and to collusion between taxpayers and tax inspectors. In such countries like Korea in which political influence or other disruptive factors characterize tax ad-

---

23. Ibid., p. 348.
24. It may be worth noting that the forfeit system is employed in the French speaking West African countries. "There, small taxpayers are required to submit an annual declaration of gross turnover, purchases, number of employees, wages and salaries paid, and the value of inventory. On the basis of these data tax authorities estimate taxable sales and assess the taxpayer, who has 20 days to accept or reject it. If the assessment is rejected, the tax department negotiates a mutually acceptable assessment. If no agreement is reached, the case is referred to an ad hoc commission composed of the director of the internal tax department, representatives of the Ministry of Finance, and the taxpayer. Unless the taxpayer chooses to appeal to the courts, this assessment is final and is generally valid for two years." Lent, op. cit., p. 353.
25. Tait, Alan A., op. cit., p. 35.
26. For small retailers, checking the total turnover by the cash receipts is very difficult. Actually the receipt plays no role for small retailers. Therefore, sales by peddlers, taxis, and street stalls are already exempt from the obligation to issue a receipt.

ministration, the forfait system might tend to perpetuate such problems.[27]

This flat rate turnover type tax superimposed on the VAT is likely to have a cascade effect and may reduce the simplicity and neutrality of the VAT. As a minor disadvantage, use of the forfait technique tends not to encourage the use of invoices and improvements in accounting. This special treatment of small taxpayers should be temporary until small retailers are able to keep accounting records of their dealings. It is important to emphasize that the public should be accustomed to the practice of asking for and receiving receipts.

As pointed out, another possible solution to relieving small businesses is to exclude small businesses from the taxable object by limiting the VAT to those firms which have a yearly turnover above a specified level. It seems indispensable that the very small taxpayers be exempt from the VAT. By excluding those taxpayers with small turnovers, the government can reduce administrative and compliance problems. But this advantage, in principle, should be weighed against other considerations like the revenue potential of those small businesses and the neutrality of a VAT. Those small taxpayers whose annual tax amount payable is less than 10,000 Won are not subject to the VAT, in Korea.[28] The actual value added of a small business with the amount of tax payable less than 10,000 Won per year is so small that the administrative costs of collecting it may not be covered by the tax.

Finally, the fundamental difficulty with respect to the problem of small businesses is to determine which taxpayers should be considered small. Faced with this problem Korea has set a limit on total yearly turnover (W24 million) as an appropriate dividing line. But it is extremely difficult to obtain an accurate report of total sales from small businesses. Small taxpayers tend to try to adjust their total sales to fall within or outside the scope of the VAT, according to their interests. The tax authorities find it difficult to control such a situation. It is argued often that the amount of limit is arbitrary and it is difficult to justify why two taxpayers should be in different situations only because one has a turnover that slightly exceeds the fixed limit and the other is barely below this limit. Therefore, it will be desirable to incorporate in the definition of a small business other objective elements such as value of total assets, value of inventory, or number of employees.[29]

---

27. Lent, op. cit., p. 354.
28. Ministry of Finance, Korea, *Korean Taxation* (Seoul, 1980), p. 163.
29. Lent, op. cit., pp. 354-55.

4. Procedural Characteristics

(1) Registration and Data Processing System

In order to efficiently administer the VAT, partiularly in handling millions of transactions based on the invoice method, one must have a proper registration and data processing system.[30] Taxpayers have been registered and given a number that has been valid only for the VAT. There has been some criticism that this numbering system has led to lack of coordination of the information about each taxpayer. In fact, a registration and numbering system, called the master file system, in which each taxpayer is given a number that identifies him for the VAT and other taxes like the income tax is ideal for administering the VAT, as it makes possible efficient control of tax collection.

For effcient tax administration, a data processing system is used. It has been designed to analyze returns of the VAT, with respect to amount of value added, relation of purchases to sales, etc., and for preselectig cases for audit. The use of the computerized file system is valuable in obtaining statistics on input and output of business and in reducing tax evasion.

Table 6 shows the number of total transactions, nonmatching (i.e., sales and purchase invoices are not consistent), and error (i.e., sales and purchase invocies match but details like taxpayer numbers do not match) data for each half year covered by the data processing unit of the Office of National Tax Administration.[31] The number of transactions covered by the computer system has expanded from 24.7 million for the business tax in the first half of 1977 to 52.2 million for the VAT in the second half of 1977, reflecting the fact that the VAT requires more transactions than the business tax did.

As the economy expands, the administrative burden of processing this input and output data is expected to increase.[32] But transactions for the first half of 1979 have decreased compared to the previous years because the annual tax amount payable which is not subject to taxation has increased from 7,500 won to 10,000 won in 1979. Table 6 also shows that the ratio of nonmatching cases (sales invoices are not matched with purchase invocies) of the total transactions has gradually decreased from 7.2% in the second half of 1977 to 3.0% in the first half of 1979. It reflects that business' ability to deal with

---

30. Lent, op. cit., p. 347.
31. IMF Fiscal Affairs Dept., op. cit., p. 143.
32. Ibid., p. 146.

Table 6. VAT Tax Nonmatching and Error Data

		In Thousands			In percent	
		Data Total	Nonmatching	Error	Nonmatching/Total	Error/Total
1977/2	Total	52245	3761	3363	7.2	6.4
	Output	34128	1566	2201	4.6	6.5
	Input	18117	2195	1164	12.1	6.4
1978/1	Total	55490	2428	2223	4.4	4.0
	Output	35713	897	1508	2.5	4.2
	Input	19777	1531	715	7.7	3.6
1978/2	Total	56649	1909	1430	3.4	2.5
	Output	35304	699	1002	2.0	2.8
	Input	21345	1210	429	5.8	2.0
1979/1	Total	51523	1554	954	3.0	1.9
	Output	32338	460	705	1.4	2.2
	Input	19185	1094	249	5.7	1.3

Source: The Ministry of Finance, Korea, *Major Statistics of Korean Taxes* (1979); Tait, Alan A., Angelo G. Faria, and Peter S. Heller, *Korea: Taxes in the 1980's* (July 26, 1969), p. 143.
*The total number of data of the business tax in 1976 was 4946900.

sales and purchase invoices has been gradually improved, in other words, the VAT has been settled. It is interesting to note that output invoices have caused less difficulties than input invoices; this might be expected as it is by maximizing input claims that VAT liability is minimized. It is ecouraging to see that the percentage of mismatched input invoices has fallen from 12.1% to 5.8%. By the same token, error data, when sales and purchase invoices match but details (for example, taxpayer numbers) within invoices do not, have fallen from 6.4% of total operations to 1.9%. As these percentages of errors and nonmatching data fall, the government may be able to move to a less problematic data processing system. At the same time the government can make its tax administration more efficient by investigating identified particular problem areas, and possibly, firms which might need special attention.

(2) Frequency and Means of Tax Payment

The administrative and compliance problems also vary with the frequency of tax payment. The taxable period for the VAT varies considerably both with countries and to categories of business. The VAT normally requires monthly or quarterly payment. A monthly period for filing and payment can become a burden to the taxpayer as well as to the tax administration by increasing administrative and compliance costs, presenting the advantage of a close check on taxpayers. As was indicated by Professor Neil H. Jacoby, the monthly payment increases the amount of paperwork of receiving, opening checking remittances, auditing and filing necessary compared to the quarterly payment.[33] He argued that the extra cost can be justified if better enforement results from the more frequent collection, and less evasion occurs on the part of seasonal and transient merchants. The EEC Commission suggested in article 12(3) of the Second Directive that any taxable person file a declaration (showing tax liability on sales and tax credits on purchases) each month.[34] Each country, however, can have its own particular system for dealing with the taxable period.

The Korean VAT requires quarterly payment and returns as a general rule. The payment is due by the end of the month following the last month in the quarter. The quarterly payment has been favored because of administrative convenience with respect to paperwork of

33. Jacoby, Neil Herman, *Retail Sales Taxation* (Chicago, 1938), p. 271.
34. Tait, op. cit., p. 128

receiving, invoicing, auditing, filing, and so on, while it may have
a minor disadvantage in dealing with financially unstable and seasonal
businesses. The quarterly payment of Korean VAT has provided
more simplified procedure in contrast to the two-month taxable period
employed for the previous business tax.

This quarterly basis needs to be flexible for very small businesses
with low annual turnovers and lack of accounting techniques. Longer
taxable periods are employed in some countries for small taxpayers.
Semiannual or yearly payment for those small businesses will alleviate
their burdens as well as those of the tax administration. Sweden, for
example, provides a tax payment period of two months, but with the
permission of the tax authorities a small firm may file in a period
of four, six, or even twelve months, depending on the size of its annual turnover. Under these rules, most farmers can be expected to
report their taxes only once a year.[35]

The criteria of determining the tax amount has been improved
because the tax amount payable or refundable is basically based on
taxpayers' reports under the VAT. It had been determined previously
by the tax authorities under the now defunct business tax. There
are two steps in the tax payment and return. First, taxpayers are
required to furnish to the tax authorities a preliminary return on the
tax base and tax amount payable or refundable within twenty-five days
from the date of termination of each preliminary return period.[36] Second, taxpayers must confirm to the tax authorities a final return on
the tax base and tax amount payable or refundable in respect of each
taxable period within twenty-five days after the expiration of the taxable period concerned. Taxpayers are required to submit tax invoices
at the time of preliminary or final return concerned.

The means of payment should be as simple as possible. The ideal
means of payment, as is used in Denmark involves reporting under
a simple VAT system. Each firm is required to give a minimal amount
of information such as its total sales and purchases, with and without
the VAT, and the net VAT payable.[37] All the required information
can be put on a postcard. It is not only an extremely simple documentation procedure but also a way to guarantee a considerable volume
of business for the state postal (so called Giro) System.[38]

---

35. Norr, Martin, and Nils G. Hornhammer, "The Value-Added Tax in Sweden," *Colum-
     bia Law Review* (March 1970), p. 410.
36. Ministry of Finance, Korea, *Korean Taxation* (1980), pp. 155-56.
37. Smith, Dan Ghrop, James B. Webber, and Carol M. Cerf, *What You Should Know About
     the Value Added Tax* (Dow Jones-Irwin, Inc.: Homewood, Illinois, 1973), p. 29. Also, Tait,
     op. cit., pp. 127-28.
38. Wheatcroft, G.S.A., "Some Administrative Problems of an Added Value Tax," *British
     Tax Review* (Sept., Oct., 1963), pp. 349-52.

A scheme suggested by Professor Wheatcroft deserves discussion with regard to efficient collection.[39] Though it is in the context of administering an account type of VAT, it is applicable to other forms. The idea revolves around the creation of special bank accounts by firms, into which they pay all money receipts for taxable goods and services and from which they make all payments for taxable goods and services. When the account is cleared the determined tax rate of the account is transferred to the revenue authorities and the remainder to the non-tax account of the taxpayer. At any given time, if the tax accounts were in debit, either the debit could be carried forward or the account could be cleared by a transfer of funds from the revenue authorities.

(3) Transitional Problems

In every country, start-up costs are considerable when a new tax, especially one which replaces the well-known taxes, is imposed. The costs to government and business of administering the VAT tend to be greatest in the initial years because new procedures have to be adapted and possibly new staff employed, or existing staff retrained. But start-up costs are mainly of a transitional nature.

The Korean government operated extensive orientation programs prior to the introduction of VAT to minimize transitional problems. These included training the technical personnel who would administer the VAT, with respect to the new procedures and requirements necessary for controlling it. Educating the taxpayers and the general public about the characteristics of the new tax, as well as about the new requirements with which taxpayers would have to comply were also important dimensions of this procedure. The orientation program included the special transitional provisions which mainly covered the treatment of investment goods and inventory on hand.[40]

The lack of adequate personnel training has been indicated as one of the weaknesses of the tax administration services in developing countries that adversely affects the efficient administration of their whole tax structure, especially the implementation of any new tax scheme. The intensity of training depends on the previous experience of the personnel in administering more or less complex forms of taxation. In this respect, the fact that there were a number of personnel who

---

39. Wheatcroft, G.S.A., "Some Administrative Problems of an Added Value Tax," *British Tax Review* (Sept., Oct., 1963), pp. 349-52.
40. Lent, op. cit., pp. 357-58.

were in charge of administering the very complicated business tax and other indirect taxes has made the personnel training much easier. The government has trained 64,000 public officials for 449 times during 1976-77 period, with respect to the new procedures and requirements for the VAT.[41]

The general public was afraid that the new tax would be more complicated and burdensome than the previous system. Therefore, educating the general public and the taxpayers about the features of the VAT was of great importance to its adequate implementation. Since it was a change from the turnover-type business tax and other consumption taxes, it was not only a matter of teaching the new technique but also of explaining the merits of the VAT in contributing to the fairness of the indirect tax system, even if it sometimes entailed initial hardship for some taxpayers.

Most orientation programs implemented by the government prior to the imposition of the VAT were designed to inform the business community and the voting public of the new tax systme and how to comply with it.[42] There were extensive training programs for taxable persons. Public relations through the mass media like TV, radio, movies, and newspapers were arranged for educating and informing the general public about the new tax system. The government also provided taxpayers with individual guidance to the bookkeeeping, return, and payment proceudres, covering about 590,000 taxable persons. But it must be pointed out that there was a lack of necessary contact between the government and organizations of taxpayers or of professionals who devote themselves to tax problems. Direct contacts with trade unions, consumer groups, association of lawyers, accountants, etc., should have been made for the better administration and compliance of the new tax. In addition to that, special attention should have been paid to small businesses, especially retail outlets and self-employed individuals for whom compliance with the VAT was extremely difficult because they could not afford adequate bookkeeping records. Nationwide tryout exercises for filing return were carried out three times before the changeover to the VAT.[43] They revealed that taxpayers were afraid of the possible upward change of price due to the introduction of the VAT, especially the psychological factor of the general public regarding the new tax. Taxpayers did not clearly understand taxable persons subject to special

---

41. Ministry of Finance, Korea, *Introduction of Value Added Tax into Korea,* (November 1977), pp. 11-12.
42. Ibid., p. 12.
43. Ministry of Finance, Korea, op. cit., p. 13.

taxation for small businesses.

Another important administrative problem was that of applying the special transitional provisions. These provisions, which dealt with investment goods and inventories, were necessary because these items have borne some form of previous taxes before the introduction of the VAT. Taxpayers were allowed to take credit for previous taxes that had already been paid on inventories on the date of the changeover.[14] Since the taxes replaced were of the multistage turnover variety, a difficult problem arose in determining the effective tax rate cumulatively on the many types of goods in inventory. The government imposed the average rate on each item in inventory.

5. Summary and Conclusion

The VAT appeared to possess the important administrative advantages over the previous indirect taxes. Despite the administrative advantages, a majority of criticisms on the VAT resulted from administrative problems rather than other controversial issues like regressivity. We found that the great administrative difficulties were associated not only with the intrinsic complexity of the tax law but also with the implementation process. This suggested that the success of the VAT largely depended on the extent to which the administrative problems could be reached or overcome. Therefore, an emphasis should be placed on the implementation process of the new tax system as well as the structural characteristic of the new tax system, particularly in developing countries.

It is commonly agreed that the fundamental difficulty in administering the VAT is the problem of coping with small taxpayers, which include a large percentage of retail and service enterprises.[45] In Korea, special treatment was provided on a forfait basis, in an effort to help those small businesses, which might not be able to cope with the more difficult concepts involved in the VAT. But the special treatment falls short of eliminating the fundamental problem. A more effective method for dealing with the problem is to exclude these taxpayers from the requirement of the VAT at the expense of decreases in tax revenues. Then the problems of administering the VAT would be greatly reduced. This would have the effect of decreasing the number of taxpayers by up to 80% with only a small decrease of 6% in the

---

44. No attempt was made by most European countries to mitigate this double taxation. Rather, it was left to be worked out in the market process. Lent, op. cit., p. 359.
45. Lent, op. cit., p. 374.

VAT revenue.

The severity of the administrative problems depends upon the range of tax rates and exemptions, the frequency of payment, the complexity of documentation, and the extent to which the new tax system could be automated and computerized.[46] Undoubtedly a VAT with multiple rates and many exemptions (on consumption items) presents greater difficulties of administration and compliance then does a single-rate tax with few exemptions. The VAT introduced to Korea has a uniform rate, which contributed to reducing administrative burdens. The merit of simplicity both for taxpayers and administrators may be offset by the wide range of exemptions. In principle, exemptions must be as few as possible to minimize the administrative complexity of the VAT. It should be borne in mind though that exemptions provided on the grounds of equity have such a strong political appeal that their elimination based on tax administrative efficiency is highly unlikely.

As a means of simplifying the tax administration, the master file system should be designed for efficient registration and control of tax collection for both the VAT and the income taxes.

We discussed the administrative considerations of the VAT with respect to the scope of tax, the degree of its complexity in terms of rate structure and exemptions, VAT techniques and procedures employed, and treatment of small businesses. But the ability to administer the VAT is also a function of the degree of literacy, the size of monetary economy, nature and size of industrial and trade establishments, adequacy of record keeping, attitudes toward taxation and tax administration, and efficiency of tax administration services. Though those elements are not reviewed in this paper their importance should not be ignored in evaluating the tax system.

---

46. NEDO, op. cit., p. 59.

11

Implementation of Urban and Regional Policy in Korea

Sung Bok Lee

Introduction

Over the past two decades Korea has undergone a profound transformation from rural to urban, from primarily agricultural to primarily industrial, and from low to moderate per capita income. Although the transformation in Korea displays many special features, it is in part following a process that began in advanced countries with the Industrial Revolution and that brought urbanization, economic development, and social change. In a short period, Korea has experienced a dramatic and thorough transformation: rapid urban and industrial growth and a strong concentration of population and industry in major metropolitan areas and industrial estates. Because the transformation to an urbanized and industrialized society has now been largely completed in Korea, the time seems propitious to review the metamorphosis.

Higgins attempts to describe economic development as a way of solving the population problem and low production which consequently generate poor livelihood.[1] Hoselitz points out that economic development is a process which affects the entire social, political, and cultural fabric of a society. When the rapidly "explosive" take-off occurred, Hoselitz observed, social institutions were created which allowed capital formation and made available a number of highly skilled and specialized services.[2]

---

1. B. Higgins, "The Dualistic Theory of Underdeveloped Areas," *Economic Development and Cultural Change*, Vol. 4, No. 2, 1956, pp. 99-115.
2. Bert F. Hoselitz, "Economic Growth and Development: Noneconomic Factors in Economic Development," *American Economic Review*, Vol. 47, 1957, pp. 28-41.

Urbanization is sometimes, but not always, a consequence of industrialization. Tangri asserts that urbanization is neither a necessary nor sufficient condition for economic development. It can be a desirable condition for development, but under certain conditions it can be a factor which slows it down. Reminiscent of the sociologists of previous generations, he contends that the role of urbanization cannot be determined without estimating the costs of such urban phenomena as anomie, political and ideological ferment, and transformation of cultural and social values.[3]

The processes of economic development and urbanization are highly interrelated. The inter-sectoral shifts from a subsistence agricultural base to a market economy based on the production of nonagricultural goods and services are paralleled by spatial shifts in the distribution of economic activity and population that involve urbanization.[4]

The process of economic development and growth in Korea involves a dramatic reallocation of resources both sectorally and spatially. The task of an economic policy is to facilitate and promote this allocation.

Both industrialization and urbanization in Korea have been extremely rapid since 1963 as shown in Table 1, with the beginning of the first five year economic development plan, 1962-1966.

Urban growth is an essential element in the process of economic, social, spatial, and political development in Korea. It accompanies the transformation of rural, agricultural economies into industrial, urban economies, and it is a transition from tradition to modernity. An increase in the level of urban growth usually leads to an increasing openness of the system of social power and hence to an increase in the frequency of innovation.

In Korea, the average annual growth of urban population between 1960-1980 was 5.6 percent during the first, second, third, and fourth five-year economic and social development plans. In 1980, 25.7 million people or 68.7 percent of the total population lived in 138 urban areas with population over 20,000.

The massive transformation of the occupational structure in Korea has been accompanied by profound changes in the economy, society, politics, patterns of living, culture, and education. But perhaps the most conspicuous changes have been in urbanization and related

3. Shanti Tangri, "Urbanization, Political Stability, and Economic Growth," in Jason L. Finkle and Richard W. Gable, eds., *Political Development and Social Change* (New York: John Wiley and Sons, Inc., 1971), pp. 212-226.
4. Harry W. Richardson, *City Size and National Spatial Strategies in Developing Countries,* World Bank Staff Working Paper, No. 252 (Washington, D.C.: World Bank, 1977), p. 3.

Table 1: Major Economic and Regional Indicators, 1955-1980

Indicator \ Year	1955	1960	1970	1975	1980
GNP per Capita (US $)	66	81	242	532	1,510
Urbanization Ratio (%)	24.4	28.3	43.1	50.9	57.3
Labor Force Participation Rate			55.9	56.5	57.6
Number of Automobiles		29,100	126,500	193,927	637,548
Total Population (in million)	21.5	25.0	31.4	34.7	37.4
Farm Population (in million)	13.3	14.6	14.4	13.2	10.2
Share of Total (%)	61.9	58.3	44.8	38.2	27.3
Share of Agriculture in GNP (%)	43.9	35.9	26.2	24.0	15.8
Percent of Non-Agricultural Farm Household Income			24.1	18.1	28.6
Exports (US million $)	18.0	32.8	835.2	5,081.0	17,500.0
Imports (US million $)	341.4	343.5	1,984.0	7,294.4	22,300.0

Source: Bank of Korea, *Economic Statistics Yearbook*, 1980.
Korea Development Institute, *Long-Term Prospect for Economic and Social Development, 1977-1991*, 1976.
Working Committee for the Transport Sector Plan for the Fifth Five-Year Economic and Social Development Plan, *The Transport Sector Plan*, Seoul, Korea, 1976.

industrialization. Economic development consists in substantial degree of rising real income per capita and of a related shift of labor and other productive resources from primary to secondary and tertiary activities. Secondary and tertiary activities are largely, and for good economic reasons, concentrated in urban areas.

The movement of agricultural population out of rural areas has been extremely rapid in Korea since the early 1960s, more rapid than any country at a comparable stage of economic development. The share of farm population fell from 58.3 percent of the total employment of 1963 to 27.3 percent in 1980. In the same period, the share of manufacturing employment rose from about 7.0 percent to 23.0 percent. In general, agricultural employment is less than 20 percent of the total employment in developed countries. In Japan, agricultural employment is presently less than 15 percent of the total. The Korean government's economic policy can be expected to continue to encourage the movement of workers out of agriculture for many years to come.[5]

The total population growth rate averaged 1.87 percent per year from 1945 to 1980, and urban population grew at an average annual rate of 5.9 percent. Until recently the natural increase has been less in urban than in rural areas because urban birth rates have been much lower. Therefore, more than two-thirds of postwar urban growth has been due to rural-urban migration. It has been estimated that about two-thirds of the population of Korea's largest cities was born elsewhere.

The trend and pattern of Korean urbanization appears to be closely associated with the national development strategies and national characteristics of Korea, namely, the export-oriented industrialization strategy, the high population density resulting from large population size and small national land (98,965 square kilometers), poor resource endowments, the South-North division of the nation, and the extensive intervention in the economic plan by the government.[6]

Urban and Regional Policy Trends

Urban and regional strategies have been a part of economic develop-

5. Byung-Nak Song, "The Role of Small and Intermediate Size Cities in National Development: The Korean Case," in *Expert Group Meeting on the Role of Small and Intermediate Size Cities in National Development,* United Nations Centre for Regional Development, Nagoya, Japan, January 26-February 1, 1982, pp. 10-12.
6. Ibid., p. 13.

ment policies in Korea since the late 1960s and have been reflected
in the first ten-year land development plan and the third five-year
economic development plan. The most important goals of each
development plan have been to slow the rate of urban population
growth in Seoul and to control the pace of rural to urban migration.
The third goal has been to develop the manufacturing sector as
quickly as possible. The final goal has been to use land, growth pole
and rural integrated development programs to overcome the most
serious and visible disparities in development among regions.[7]

The major urban and regional development strategies at various
time periods were as follows: primate city growth in the early 1960s,
countermagnet city growth in the early 1970s, new towns policy in
the mid 1970s, and regional growth center development in the mid
1970s.

Until the first five-year economic development plan, urban and
regional development policies remained ill-focused. Unrelated and
unplanned efforts to develop public works, industrial and social welfare
projects were imposed and financed by the central government. The
policies consisted mostly of education, water service, and housing projects of narrow scope.[8]

In the first five-year economic development plan, the Korean
government had tried to implement industrial location and region
development policies. The basis for regional planning was found in
the law concerning general planning for national construction in 1963.
This policy was concerned with "fundamental long-term plans which
will become the targets and guidelines with regard to land locations
and scales of facilities to be carried out by the central government."[9]

In 1964, the government adopted a metropolitan control policy.
The policy consisted of several measures such as i) the decentralization of secondary government agencies; ii) the development of new
towns; iii) the control of industrial location in the Seoul area; and
iv) the location of educational and cultural facilities in other non-
metropolitan areas. It is significant that the problems of metropolitan
concentration were recognized for the first time in the government's

7. Dennis A. Rondinelli, "The Role of Intermediate Cities in Regional and National Development: The Experience in Korea," paper for conference on Urban Planning and Regional
   Development in a Rapidly Changing Society, Princeton University, May 1982, p. 3.

8. Bertrand Renaud, "Regional Policy and Industrial Location in South Korea," *Asian Survey*,
   Vol. 14, 1973, p. 458.

9. Myong Chan Hwang, "A Search for a Development Strategy for the Capital Region
   of Korea," in Yung-Hee Rho and Myong-Chan Hwang, eds., *Metropolitan Planning: Issues
   and Policies* (Seoul: Korea Research Institute for Human Settlements, 1979), p. 7.

regional policies.[10]

Industrial location and regional development were to be promoted through the industrial estate law (1964), the law for the establishment and management of a free trade zone (1970), the law on provincial industrial development (1971), the tax reduction control law (1971), the corporate tax law (1971), and the provincial government tax laws (1971).

When rapid industrialization began in the early 1960s, Korea's infrastructure was concentrated in and near Seoul and Busan and was therefore unable to support a spatially diffused pattern of industrialization. Throughout the 1960s, government economic and regional policies were aimed at the promotion of export-oriented industrialization through support of labor intensive manufacturing enterprises in Seoul, Busan, and a few industrial estates. Due to export-oriented industrialization and primate city development policies, the problem of overcrowding and regional imbalance was most acute in the Seoul region.

At this time, the government saw the need to formulate a national comprehensive land development plan in order to solve Seoul's over-concentration and to improve the environment. The government was also concerned with promoting an equitable distribution of industries in such a way as to strengthen both agriculture and industry, and to balance development between urban and rural areas. The government prepared a new ten-year national land development plan for the period 1972-1981 which would coincide with the third and fourth national five-year economic development plans. The development policies of this plan were: i) establishment of a large-scale industrial base; ii) expansion of transportation and telecommunication networks and water resources and energy supply networks, and iii) strengthening of regional functions for the development of depressed areas.[11]

In 1972, the national land use and management law was enacted to support long-range development plans. The law provided the government with various planning and policy tools such as the application of the standard land price system. At the same time, the amended urban planning law gave the government the power to designate greenbelts around major urban areas.

In 1973, the citizen tax law was enacted to control the growing in-migration and the development of new industries in the large metropolitan areas. This policy also included differential property tax rates to be applied to newly established factories in large

10. Bertrand Renaud, "Regional Survey ...," p. 460.
11. Ministry of Construction, *First Ten-Years National Land Development Plans,* Seoul, Korea, 1971.

metropolitan areas.

Other policies and actions taken to address development problems were the farm land conservation act (1972) to prevent farm land from being used for non-farm purposes, the industrial base development act (1973), and the agricultural land expansion and development act (1975) to provide estates for heavy and chemical industries and to provide for the expansion and development of farmland and promotion of uncultivated land development. The urban renewal act (1976), the housing construction promotion act (1977), the environment conservation act (1977), the parking area act (1979), and the urban park act (1980) also sought to control national land development.

At the same time the Korean government implemented a number of programs for restricting the flow of migrants to Seoul and for redirecting people and educational, industrial, commercial, bank, public and private institutional activities to secondary urban centers. The government restricted the expansion of colleges in Seoul and required branches of major universities to be located in cities outside of the Seoul metropolitan area.[12]

To promote industrial relocation, the government enacted the industrial distribution law. The law, partly amended in December 1981, sought to contribute to balanced national economic growth and enhance social welfare by providing appropriate industrial location criteria and by promoting relocation of plants to prevent industrial over-concentration. This policy affects four regions: i) the relocation region for promoting relocation of plants; ii) the consolidation region; iii) the inducement region; and iv) other regions. The relocation region comprises Seoul and its immediate surrounding areas including Euijeongbu. The consolidation region consists of the cities of Busan, Daegu, and Incheon and surrounding areas, and the relocation regions are in Gyeonggi province, including Suweon, Seongnam, Anyang, Gwangmeong, and Bucheon. Establishments of new plants, plant expansion, and development of industrial land are prohibited with a few exceptions within the relocation and consolidation regions. The government identifies inducement regions based on the following criteria: i) low industrial density, ii) high accommodation effect of population and industry, iii) linkage with existing industry, and iv) convenience for supplying industrial land, water, and power. Plant relocation is supported by national and local governments through preparation of plant sites and the consolidation of existing land. Tax

---

12. Son-Ung Kim and Peter J. Donaldson, "Dealing with Seoul's Population Growth: Government Plans and Their Implementations," *Asian Survey*, Vol. 14, No. 7, 1979, pp. 663-667.

exemptions, financial support and administrative controls are methods used to implement their policy.[13]

The government announced other strategies in the second ten-years natinal land development plan in 1980:[14]

i) to control further growth of Seoul and promote regional growth centers;

ii) to promote the growth of regional service centers to stimulate the economies of small towns and rural areas;

iii) to balance spatial development with optimum spatial allocation of industrial activities;

iv) to improve and expand the transportation network;

v) to raise the quality of life for citizens by improving the living environment.

The government's plans for balanced urban growth call for the creation of eight planning regions in which twenty-six intermediate cities would be strengthened to serve both rural and urban residents. The country would be divided into twenty-eight "integration service-provision areas" to be developed on the basis of their spatial and functional relationships, socio-economic characteristics and physical and economic comparative advantages. Four types of centers have been proposed.

i) National Metropolitan Centers—Seoul and Busan—in which central management functions and highly specialized social and economic activities would continue to be concentrated;

ii) Regional Metropolitan Centers—Daegu, Gwangju, and Daejeon—in which high-level commercial and administrative functions would be located and which would enhance Seoul's social, economic, culture, and educational level and to which some of the population now migrating to the largest metropolitan centers might be attracted;

iii) Urban Growth Centers—Chuncheon, Gangneung, Weonju, Chungju, Cheonan, Yeongju, Andong, Cheongju, Jeonju, Mogpo, Suncheon, Namweon, Jinju, Jeju, Pohang, Jeongju, and Jecheon—in which central place functions would be encouraged to serve both urban and rural residents; and

iv) Rural Service Centers—Yeongweol, Hongseong, Gangjin, Geochang, Jeomchon, and Seosan—in which small-scale commercial, manufacturing, agro-processing and marketing activities would

---

13. Korea Research Institute for Human Settlements, *Draft on Second Ten-Year National Land Development Plan*, Seoul, Korea, 1981.
14. Ministry of Construction, *Second Ten-Year National Land Development Plans*, Seoul, Korea, 1981.

be strengthened to serve the rural population.

In addition, some cities—Incheon, Suweon, Anyang, Bucheon, Seongnam, Euijeongbu, Songtan, Gwangmeong, Dongducheon, Masan, Changweon, Ulsan, Chungmu, Jinhae, and Kimhae—are to be developed as satellite centers for Seoul and Busan and would be encouraged to perform supplementary social and economic functions for the largest metropolitan centers and relieve some of the population pressures on their core areas.

Urban and Regional Development Patterns

Seoul's share of the national population increased from 7.3 percent in 1955 to 22.3 percent in 1980. Much of the increase was due to migration. Seoul's population in 1981 was 8,676,000 according to government statistics, an increase of 3.7 percent from a year earlier, whereas national population growth during the same period was 1.57 percent.[15]

The urban and industrial transformation of Korea has produced a massive migration across prefectural lines from peripheral, largely rural prefectures to the major metropolitan center of Seoul. This migration involves mostly young persons in search of employment, higher incomes, education and urban amenities found in a large metropolitan center. At the time of the heaviest migration, there were very large income differentials between rural and urban dwellers and also between jobs in traditional small-scale industries and those in large-scale high technology industries that were largely concentrated in the metropolitan center.

The high concentration of human and economic activities in Seoul has played an important role in the rapid economic growth of Korea during the last two decades. The dominance of Seoul's economy over the rest of the natioin can be seen as a result of its initial advantages as a center of innovation and economic concentration.

Industries historically preferred advantages in prospering areas like Seoul where there are cumulative, self-reinforeing effects between the provision of urban infrastructure and other locational economies.

In 1981, Seoul's gross product was 12,489.8 billion won ($179 million), about 29 percent of the gross national product. Adjusted for the prices of 1975, according to government statistics, the capital's output was 4,547.3 billion won ($65 million). Seoul's output show-

---

15. Ministry of Home Affairs, *Municipal Yearbook, 1981, 1982*, Seoul, Korea, 1981, 1982.

ed an 8.1 percent growth whereas the national growth rate was 7.1 percent.

About 43 percent of the nation's value added by manufacturing, 33 percent of the nation's total industry employment, 64 percent of the nation's total savings, 62 percent of the nation's total loan capital, and 39 percent of the nation's total existing marketing facilities were accounted for by Seoul alone. Almost all insurance companies, stock exchange offices, headquarters of business firms, and research facilities can be found in the national capital.[16]

Theorists explain similar findings in terms of agglomeration economies and the concentration of social capital in the largest cities.[17] Among the more important agglomeration economies are the opportunities for face-to-face contact, the availability of ancillary services such as accountancy, insurance, and banking, centralized policy-making process and the existence of an experienced labor pool. Seoul is similar to the generally accepted model of a primate city in these aspects.

There are other reasons for Seoul's predominance. About 44 percent of colleges and universities, 40 percent of medical doctors, and 36 percent of medical facilities are located in the capital city.[18] In addition, the concentration of political resources and power has strengthened the city's position in the settlement hierarchy.

Agglomeration economies, access to bureaucracy, ties with other commercial operations, the diversity of urban infrastructure as well as superstructure, and skilled labor have favored newly located industries in Seoul. Industrial location and job opportunities have affected the continuous migration of population towards Seoul and, therefore, the concomitant expansion of service activities.

Korea has experienced rapid simultaneous urbanization and industrialization leading to a high level of concentration of population and economic activity and structure in Seoul. Nevertheless, there are several important reasons why industrial dispersion should be adopted as a policy for decentralizing population from Seoul. First of all, interregional inequality resulting from the excessive agglomeration in Seoul has become a growing concern, not to mention a national defense problem. Secondly, the polarization results in very harmful effects on regional income distribution and the growth of other

16. Korea Commerce and Industry Chamber, *Special Report on Overconcentration in Seoul,* Seoul, Korea, December 1982.
17. Won-Yong Kwon, "A Study of the Economic Impact of Industrial Relocation: The Case of Seoul," *Urban Studies,* Vol. 18, 1981, pp. 82-83.
18. Ministry of Home Affairs, *Municipal Yearbook,* 1981.

regional economies. Presently, the per capita income of Seoul is
$2,113, nearly 30 percent higher than the national average.[19] Such
income disparities have attracted more migrants. Finally, the rapid
growth and the gigantic size of the Seoul metropolitan area have
resulted in many urban problems: excessive commuting time; congestion on roads, highways, and narrow streets and roads; shortages
of housing units and their small size with hardly enough space to accommodate the consumer goods that Koreans now can afford to buy
and are buying in large numbers; environmental problems of air and
water pollution, noise, and noxious waste materials; weak infrastructure of commercial, social, cultural, and recreational facilities, of parks
and open spaces, and of public facilities and utilities; and very high
land values.

Psychological stresses doubtlessly occur as the traditional values
of home ownership are difficult to satisfy because of high land costs.
High population densities favor the construction of apartment
buildings. With prosperity and higher living standards, attention is
being turned increasingly to the quality of life, healthier living conditions, a more beautiful landscape, and social amenities in general.
Therefore, the Seoul municipal government has recently encountered
serious urbanization diseconomies.[20] Among these is the rapidly expanding expenditure on the provision of urban services due to the
continuous inflow of people.

The growth of diseconomies in the primate city may lead to additional pressures on the balance of payments and may actually retard
the rate of national economic growth.[21]

Korea has not escaped problems resulting from industrialization,
even though the aims of a high rate of economic growth and industrialization were achieved during the 1960s. Bipolar concentration of economic activities and population in the Seoul and Busan
metropolitan areas, for example, has become an urgent problem in
view of both economic efficiency and equity. As the result of this
policy, in the early 1970s over 60 percent of educational resources,
71 percent of wholesale establishments and more than half of transportation services were located in Seoul and Busan, with Seoul having
the largest portion.

The problem with countermagnet policies in Korea is the danger
of replicating the social and congestion costs of the primate city by

19. Korea Commerce and Industry Chamber, *Special Report* ....
20. Son-Ung Kim and Peter J. Donaldson, "Dealing with Seoul's...," pp. 651-669.
21. Won-Yong Kwon, "A Study of the Economic Impact of Industrial Relocation: The Case
     of Seoul," *Urban Studies...,* p. 80.

failing to keep infrastructure and populated growth in step. The key element in countermagnet strategies is the idea of using a form of polarized development to compete with polarization towards the primate city. Thus, it represents a very limited type of decentralization.

An industrial relocation policy is not commonly regarded as an influential factor in its own right. Rather, an industrial relocation policy is viewed as one factor that reinforces others. Capital may be made cheaper in certain locations by making it available at preferential rates, or the disadvantages of a distant location may be mitigated by a subsidized transport rate, or in more extreme cases, certain locations will be forbidden and others may be made mandatory by government decree.

The Korean government has developed several industrial estates including Gumi, Changweon, Yeocheon, and Ulsan to promote heavy industry and improve the industrial structure. Also, a number of local industry promotion areas in middle-sized cities were established to encourage dispersion of industries across the nation.

The Korean government's industrial location policy is designed to reduce urban-rural income disparities. The industrial location policy has been formulated and implemented as a part of regional planning for economic growth and social equity; however, it also has the objective of slowing down the expansion of industries into the surrounding areas of Seoul. Six export industrial estates, two local industrial estates, and two private industrial estates in Seoul and its surrounding areas comprised 51.1 percent of the manufacturing employment of the all industrial estates in Korea in 1975.[23]

Large scale industrial concentration in the southeastern regions has resulted in bipolar concentration of manufacturing in the Seoul and Busan areas. Government policy had no impact on industrial dispersion to peripheral areas. Rather, it provided the basis for further industrial concentration in the two largest metropolitan areas.

A key question yet to be addressed is which industrial groups should be move out of Seoul. The selection of industries to be relocated will determine, by and large, the success of the relocation policy. Identification of relocatable industries depends on the size of the firm, type of production, inter-industry linkages, the distribution of market and

---

22. Sam-Ock Park and James O. Wheeler, "Industrial Locational Policies and Manufacturing Employment Change: The Case of Seoul," in paper for Conference on Urban Planning and Regional Development in a Rapidly Changing Society, Princeton University, May 1982, pp. 2-6.
23. *Ibid.*, p. 7.

supply areas, transportation networks, and labor availability and cost.

The Korean government's new town approach is an important policy designed to reduce urban-rural income disparities and relocate industrial facilities. This policy has been a part of regional development planning for economic growth and social equity; however, it also has the objective of slowing down rural-urban migration by providing new job opportunities in rural hinterlands.

Tax exemptions have been offered to encourage firms to move their plants from Seoul to designated areas or to construct new plants in the existing development areas. There are penalties on firms that choose to remain in Seoul and other congested areas. The policies sought not only to build industrial production centers where labor supply conditions were favorable but also to transfer those factors identified as the "pulling" forces of migration from the major cities to less populated areas.

From the latter half of the 1970s, new towns in Korea were built to decentralize industry and population from large urban centers. (See Table 2.) At a time when many existing cities in Korea lack adequate water supply, drainage, sewage facilities, public transport and low-income housing, new towns compete with old cities for central government funds. High standards, high costs, low economic returns and high maintenance costs make new towns inaccessible to most of the population and are inconsistent with prevailing urban income levels.

Table 2: New Towns Under Construction

City	Planned Population	Implementing Period	Urban Function
Banweol	240,000	1977-1987	Industrial Estate
Yeocheon	100,000	1977-1986	Industrial Estate
Changweon	300,000	1977-1986	Industrial Estate
Gwacheon	45,000	1979-1983	Administrative Center
Daeduck	50,000	1974-1981	Education & Research Center

Sources: Korea Research Institute for Human Settlements, *National Land Development Planning in Korea*, 1980.

The growth center approach has been the most important Korean policy designed to encourage urban deconcentration. Its goal was to promote the growth of regional service centers to stimulate the diffusion of economic impacts in rural towns and lagging areas.

In 1977, the Korean government designated and implemented five urban growth centers (Busan, Daegu, Daejeon, Jeonju, and Gwangju) to achieve the desired reduction in Seoul's population and its redistribution to other areas of Korea over a ten-year period.

There are several reasons for the government's selection of the five regional urban centers as the major growth poles. Some research studies revealed that to achieve the highest rate of economic growth, regional investment had to be matched with characteristics of the region. Social overhead investment should be made in the "lagging areas," while economic overhead investment—investment directly supporting productive activities—should be made in "intermediate areas."[24] Some policymakers supported the construction of new cities or investment in small or middle-sized cities. However, such ideas were not readily adopted. Policymakers and planners believe that if urban growth is inevitable, many urban centers will become large metropolitan areas regardless of whether new cities are built or not. Urban policy is not considered powerful enough to affect the growth of Seoul. For this reason, the growth pole policy focused on selecting cities for national population redistribution and regional balance.[25] All of the growth pole areas are located away from Seoul in areas that are already densely populated. At the same time, several coastal areas have also been selected as heavy chemical industrial zones.

Large growth poles attract industrial firms because they can accommodate small and middle-sized industries with much less budgetary commitment than would be required in new cities. Large cities have not only attractive consumption markets but also social amenities necessary to attract industrial migrants and their families.

One of the disadvantages of this strategy is that many cities will become large metropolitan areas. Since infrastructure costs are heavy, more poles mean lower prospects of success because of sub-threshold momentum. The growth poles have been shown incapable of diffusing developmental impulses, innovations, and trickle-down effects. Another difficulty is the risk of a pole becoming an isolated enclave. For example, Gwangju, located in a depressed south western rural area, has been designated as a major pole to promote a "balanced triangular pole system" based on Seoul, Busan, and Gwangju.[26]

24. Duck-Woo Nam and Kong-Kyun Ro, "Population Research and Population Policy in Korea in the 1970s," *Population and Development Review*, Vol. 7, No. 4, December 1981, p. 655.
25. Son-Ung Kim and Peter J. Donaldson, "Dealing with Seoul's...," p. 671.
26. Bertrand Renaud, *National Urbanization Policy in Developing Countries* (New York: Oxford University Press, 1981), p. 63.

However, this approach is very ambitious in view of the differences in the size of those cities.

Industries in some growth poles are not in a position to generate backward linkages either in growth of the growth pole itself or in other major metropolitan areas. The shortage of skilled workers is a serious constraint on the expansion of industries in growth poles because it is not easy to mobilize skilled workers either from the growth center itself or from nearby rural areas.[27] Korea has a highly centralized government system. This inhibits a successful growth center strategy which would be effective in Korea only if there had been a degree of administrative and political decentralization. Growth pole strategy also may lead to the generation of urban social diseconomies, to a monopolistic industrial structure, and to persistent regional disequilibria.

During the last two decades, the Korean government has implemented and amended several kinds of urban and regional policies to promote population redistribution, balanced regional development, and industrial relocation. The Korean government has also pursued a number of measures during the mid 1970s that sought to distribute urban services and infrastructure more widely among medium-sized and larger cities. The policy had the impact of changing the spatial distribution of population among metropolitan areas and middle-sized cities.

Although all of the policies enacted to create a more balanced distribution of population and economic activities were not always strongly supported nor effectively implemented by the government agencies through which they were promulgated, these and other economic development policies seem to have stabilized Seoul's level of primacy and to have restructured Korea's rapidly expanding urban settlement system.[28]

Most of the urban and regional policies were originally implemented to remedy specific problems, particularly Seoul's high concentration of population and economic activities.[29] Programs were developed without much consideration of the interdependency among problems or the measures to alleviate them. Although the policies seemed to offer a strategy to limit Seoul's growth, there was little coordination among the agencies such as the Economic Planning Board, Ministry

---

27. Ahn-Je Kim, "Industrialization and Growth Pole Development in Korea: A case Study of the Ulsan Industrial Complex," in Fu-Chan Lo and K. Salih, eds., *Growth Pole Strategy and Regional Development Policy: Asian Experience and Alternative Approaches* (Oxford: Pergamon Press, 1978), pp. 53-77.
28. Dennis A. Rondinelli, "The Role of Intermediate Cities...," pp. 2-3.

of Construction, Ministry of Commerce and Trade, Ministry of Finance, Ministry of Home Affairs, and Seoul Municipal Government that were supposed to implement them.

Many of the policies were enacted without much research. The relationship between policymakers and planners is weak. Although the relevance of social research in population and urbanization issues has become increasingly prominent in the recent years, bureaucrats have increasingly questioned whether the government and the public are getting a reasonable return from their investment in planning research. Nam and Ro argue that:

complaints made by public officials are familiar; social scientists fail in their research to address the real problems facing the nation, and they tend to prescribe naive or politically impossible solutions. On the other hand, social scientists complain that public officials are often unaware of, or at least unappreciative of, the policy relevance of their work. Researchers argue that were their findings put to wider use, the returns of investment in social research in urbanization would be much higher.[30]

Too many laws have been made, amended and enacted by different central ministries. More than thirty urban and regional policies have been enacted to influence urban and regional development. Some measures overlap with other policies and are too complex to implement.

Evaluation of urban and regional development shows that future industrial expansion and population redistribution will take place in the immediate vicinity of the already existing industrial and urban centers. The highest returns are likely to come from investment in social overhead capital in the lagging areas to raise the local capacity to support industries rather than by attempting to industrialize these areas immediately. Besides the gains from a better interregional allocation of investment, much can be achieved through efficient urban and regional planning, policy, and strategy and better coordination among ministries.

The Impact of Urban and Regional Policies

A high concentration of population in a few large metropolitan

29. Ibid., pp. 2-3. Song-Ung Kim and Peter J. Donaldson, "Dealing with Seoul's...," pp. 651-669.

30. Duck-Woo Nam and Kong-Kyun Ro, "Population Research...," p. 651.

centers has for some time been an important aspect of urban growth in Korea. Seoul, Busan, Daegu, and Incheon grew so large in population size and share of modern industrial activities as to dominate the urban settlement system and the national economy. The geographically concentrated pattern of investment created regional disparities in income and wealth and promoted high levels of rural to urban migration, with large percentages of the rural migrants going to the large metropolitan areas. (See Table 3.)

Table 3: Population Growth in Metropolitan Areas, 1949, 1960, 1970 & 1980

Year City	1949	1960	1970	1980
Seoul	1,446,019	2,445,402	5,536,377	8,336,756
Busan	473,619	1,163,671	1,880,710	3,160,276
Daegu	313,705	676,692	1,082,750	1,607,458
Incheon	265,767	401,473	646,013	1,084,730

Source: Ministry of Construction, *Long-Range Planning of Urban Growth for the Year 2000: Data Collection,* 1980: Ministry of Home Affairs, *Municipal yearbook, 1981*

If current trends continue, the largest metropolitan centers in Korea at the end of this century will be two or three times the size of the biggest metropolitan area in some industrialized nations. Due to government policies to restrict the size of Seoul, the other metropolitan areas of Seoul and its satellite have led to a new phenomenon: the Seoul metropolitan areas. The growth of population in the metropolitan areas of Seoul was from 8.9 million in 1975 to 10.7 million in 1980. There was an 84.2 percent increase in population in Bucheon, 73.9 percent in Anyang, 32.3 percent in Suweon, 31 percent in Incheon and 31 percent in Seongnam.[31]

Busan and its surrounding region, which includes four satellite cities, has rapidly expanded to form another metropolitan area. Twenty-seven percent of the total population increase during the period between 1970 and 1975 was absorbed by this region, which comprised 9.3 percent of the national population in 1975.

The rate of population growth in Seoul has declined since the mid 1970s. It decreased from 5.3 percent in 1976 to 3.7 percent in 1981.

---

31. Ministry of Construction, *Long-Range Planning for Urban Growth for the Year 2000: Date Collection,* Vol. 1., Seoul, Korea, 1980.

Nevertheless, the absolute size of the population of Seoul continues to grow at a very high rate.

Urbanization has been strongly correlated with changes in the employment structure of cities from agriculture to other sectors. The growth of manufacturing employment is cited most frequently as the driving force behind urbanization. During the period of most rapid urbanizaton in Korea, from 1953 to 1982, the percentage of the labor force engaged in mining and manufacturing grew from less than 4 percent to more than 31 percent.[32]

The four largest cities have tended to become specialized. Busan has become a center of heavy chemical industry and harbor transportation and has the largest concentration of workers in manufacturing and the next largest in transportation and warehousing. Daegu is a regional commercial and medium-sized textile center and has the largest concentration of workers in wholesale and trade. Incheon is an industrial center of machinery and food processing and has the largest percentage of the labor force in manufacturing industry. Seoul has the smallest concentration of workers in manufacturing of the four largest cities.[33] Seoul's employment is highly concentrated in services of government, private enterprises, education, and specialized skills.

The industrial growth that occurred primarily in the Seoul and Busan regions, has led to increased regional disparities between the southeastern and southwestern regions and brought about a significant decline in the economic position of farm households relative to urban households.

Since the late 1960s, the southeastern coastal region has emerged as the country's major industry area. Much of Korea's new heavy industry is located in this region. Prominent industries are refining and petrochemicals, other chemical industries, machinery, steel and shipbuilding. The main cities in the region are Busan, Masan, Changweon, Jangseungpo, Ulsan, Pohang, and Angang. The growth of industry in this region has resulted in greater income differentials, population growth and regional production relative to the other regions.[34]

During the early 1970s, the growth of several cities in the region outstripped Seoul's. Between 1970 and 1975, Seoul's population grew

32. Ministry of Home Affairs, *Municipal Yearbook, 1981;* Samuel P.S. Ho, ''South Korea and Taiwan Development Prospects and Problems in the 1980s, *Asian Survey*, Vol. 16, No. 12, 1981, pp. 1175-1196.
33. Ministry of Home Affairs, *Municipal Yearbook, 1982,* Seoul, Korea.
34. Ministry of Construction, *Long-Range National Physical Plan,* 1980.

4.4 percent per year, whereas Busan grew 5.3 percent, Pohang 10.6 percent, Masan 13.3 percent and Ulsan 9.3 percent. Manufacturing has been the driving force behind the recent growth in the region. Between 1966 and 1973, manufacturing value added increased 34.8 percent per year in current prices in Seoul. In Busan, the annual growth of manufacturing value added was only 32.5 percent. But in Pohang it was 83.9 percent, in Masan 67.4 percent, and in Ulsan 70.5 percent.[35]

As the process of economic development proceeds, rural-urban disparities are not unusual; they are the consequence of higher productivity increases in industry than in agriculture. However, the decline in the relative economic position of Korea's rural population was made sharper by the development strategy and the relatively low level of off-farm economic activity in rural areas. The slow growth in off-farm income in rural Korea is closely related to the country's geographical pattern of industrial development. Off-farm employment accounted for 78 percent of all rural employment in 1975 as compared to 81 percent in 1960. The number of rural manufacturing workers increased, but in 1975 they accounted for only 6 percent of Korea's total rural employment and 21 percent of its total manufacturing employment.[36]

Because of numerous linkages between large industrial enterprises and small commercial, service and repair establishments, Korea's concentrated pattern of industrialization has made it more difficult for small business to develop in rural areas, which means, of course, fewer employment and entrepreneurial opportunities for rural households. Spatial concentration has eliminated the opportunities for many of Korea's rural population to participate in non-agricultural activities as "commuters" while still taking part in farm work during weekends and busy seasons.

The largest increase in the size of urban centers took place during the decade of 1965-1975. Before 1970, however, the process of urbanization was characterized by excessive population concentration of primacy. Provincial and middle-sized cities, on the other hand, grew at a much slower rate.

Some analysts such as Richardson suggest that Korea is now on the verge of "polarization reversal stage"—a process in which the level of primacy of Seoul will begin to decline and a rank-size distribu-

---

35. Edwin S. Mills and Byung-Nak Song, *Urbanization and Urban Problems* (Cambridge, Mass.: Harvard University Press, 1979), p. 54.

36. Samuel P.S. Ho, "Economic Development and Rural Industry in South Korea and Taiwan," *World Development*, Vol. 10, No. 11, 1982, p. 982.

tion of cities will begin to emerge.[37] The increasing number, size, and productivity of intermediate cities could provide greater access for people living outside of the Seoul and other metropolitan areas to non-agricultural job opportunities, educational, health, and other social services, urban facilities and amenities, and productive resources.

Growth in urban centers may occur in a number of ways: reclassification of localities reaching 50,000 population, annexation, net migration, natural increase, and industrial location.

Administrative reclassification and boundary change occurred in several cities during the 1955-1982 period. Three metropolitan areas, Busan in 1969 and Dacgu and Incheon in 1981 gained directly city status. Twenty-four areas gained city status: two in 1956, five in 1963, three in 1973, four in 1979, and ten in 1981.

During the early 1970s, the contribution of annexation and boundary change to urban growth was relatively small, about 10 percent overall. Net migration, natural increase, and industrial location played the most significant role in urban growth.

Some theorists have argued that the ability to create and sustain economically viable settlements at the middle levels of the hierarchy, to increase the productivity of town and rural areas, and to integrate the various settlements into the national economy requires the stimulation of rural economies through development of agriculture and small or middle-scale industry in Korea.[38]

Almost all Korean middle-sized cities were primarily agricultural, commercial, and service centers before 1960. Nowadays, the middle-sized cities typically have medium- or small-scale industrial and commercial enterprises; they incorporate the economic functions of both market towns and manufacturing centers. Middle-sized cities may also be important agro-industrial and primary product warehousing centers. The crucial role that middle-sized cities play in national development is vividly illustrated by Ulsan, Masan, Pohang, Gumi, Anyang, Iri, Changweon, Yeocheon, Banweol, Jangseungpo, Bein, and Bucheon, where the major industrial estates were located by the national government.[39] Changes in their economic functions and structures were facilitated by government investment in industrial estates, energy and power stations, international harbors, transportation, and warehousing and storage facilities. The urban centers

37. Harry W. Richardson, "City Size and National...", pp. 19-20.
38. Dennis A. Rondinelli and Kenneth Ruddle, *Urbanization and Rural Development: A Spatial Policy for Equitable Growth* (New York: Praeger Publishers, 1978), pp. 107-111.
39. Duck-Woo Nam and Kong-Kyun Ro, "Population Research...," p. 655.

are well linked by the national transportation networks.

The population and rank of Korea's fifty largest cities for 1960, 1970, and 1980 has seen no change in rank among Korea's six largest cities. They have reached between four and five times their 1949 population by 1980. The size distribution of cities has shown stability during the last quarter century. Almost all Korean cities have grown rapidly, but there is no tendency for Seoul, or any other city, to become increasingly dominant.[40]

Towns are crucial for transforming economically lagging rural regions because rural economies can only be stimulated by the increasing commercialization of agriculture. The greatest number of towns in Korea are both agriculture and county administration centers. Medium-sized cities in rural areas are heavily dependent on the economic health of the farm sector and their expansion is wholly dependent on the basic strategy used for the expansion of the agricultural sector.

The analysis shows that the Korean urban system has undergone substantial structural and functional changes over the past two decades. This study indicates that urban development policy in Korea should attempt to guide national urban settlement in a way that will integrate metropolitan centers, middle and small cities, and their surrounding regions.

---

40. Sung-Bok Lee, *Policies for Secondary City Development in Korea: Analysis and Implications,* Syracuse University Unpublished Ph.D. Dissertation; May 1984, pp. 89-90.

12
Rural-To-Urban Migration in Korea: A Cognitive-Behavioral Approach

Byong Man Ahn and William W. Boyer

Rural-to-urban migration in South Korea is a persistent and perplexing policy problem for its government. South Korea's urban population doubled from 1945 to 1960, while its rural population remained the same. During the period 1960-1975, the urban population more than doubled again, while the rural population actually decreased (see Table, Appendix I). Accordingly, South Korea has been experiencing momentous problems of rapid urbanization, a phenomenon attributable more to rural-to-urban migration[1] than to industrialization alone. Indeed, during the period 1945-1960, little industrialization occurred, but rural poverty nevertheless induced many to move to metropolitan areas and the places where U.S. military forces were located.[2] Unable to cope with their poverty during this earlier period, many rural people wandered around in a nomadic condition, or in what Peterson has termed a state of "primitive migration."[3]

South Korea's rapid industrialization between 1962 and 1975 was

---

* The authors wish to express their appreciation for the assistance in conducting the survey of our respondents to Professors Hong Soon Hahn, Man Ki Kim, Myong Soo Kim, and Byong Wan Suh — all of Hankuk University of Foreign Studies — and to Professor Kenneth W. Eckhardt of the University of Delaware for assisting us in our analysis.

1. See, Seyeul Kim, "The Economic and Social Determinants of Rural-Urban Migration in Korea: A Case Study of North Cholla Province," *Nong-up Kyungje Yonku* (Journal of Agricultural Economics), Vol. 17, July 1975, pp. 48-50.
2. Man-Gap Lee, "Nongchon inkue tosijunchulkwa nongchon baljon" (Rural-Urban Migration and Rural Development), a paper delivered to the First International Conference on Korean Studies, Seoul, Korea, December 7-20, 1979, p. 2.
3. William Peterson, "A General Typology of Migration," *American Sociological Review*, Vol. 23, 1958, pp. 260-266.

accompanied by an average annual economic growth rate of 9.6 percent — one of the world's highest — and by "mass migration" from rural areas which, since 1968, experienced an actual population decline despite a national birth rate in excess of two percent until 1968.

We can say then that "push" factors marked by rural poverty characterized the "primitive migration" of the earlier period, while "pull" factors marked by industrialization characterized the "mass migration" of the later period.[4]

Meanwhile, the agricultural sector of South Korea's economy remained retarded, which moved the government in 1970 to launch the New Community Movement, a rural development strategy popularly known as "Saemaul Undong." This movement was aimed at: changing traditional attitudes by infusing the so-called self-help "Saemaul spirit" among rural villages; enhancing the quality of rural life by creating a healthy, rational, and productive rural environment; and effecting over-all economic improvement of rural South Korea. Within five years, results proved this movement to be one of the most successful rural development programs in Asia.[5]

The New Community Movement by all accounts proved quite successful in inducing self-help and development attitudes toward the uplift of rural life, in substantially improving rural living conditions and agricultural productivity, and above all in drastically increasing rural income. Indeed, the average family income of farmers and fishermen for the first time surpassed that of urban laborers by 1975 (US$1,863 compared to US$1,757, or 106 percent of the latter), a superiority that has since remained.[6]

Although rapid urbanization occasioned by a decreasing rural population doubtlessly contributed to an increased urban demand for food from fewer producers, hence contributing to rural family income,[7]

---

4. Various studies in this period have demonstrated the impact of industrialization on rural-to-urban migration in South Korea. See, *e.g.*: Y. B. Choe, *A Study of the Regional Characteristics of Rural-Urban Migration in Relation to Industrial-Urban Development in Korea: 1960-1968* (Agricultural Economic Research Institute, Seoul, Korea), Research Report Series No. 36, August 1971; and United Nations, Economic and Social Commission for Asia and the Pacific, Division of Population and Social Affairs, *Migration, Urbanization, and Development in the Republic of Korea/Economic and Social Commission for Asia and the Pacific*, Population Division, Bangkok, pp. 142 (Comparative Study of Migration, Urbanization, in Relation to Development in the ESCAP Region: Country Report No. 1).

5. See, William W. Boyer and Byong Man Ahn, "The New Community Movement ('Saedmaul Undong') in South Korea," *Journal of Korean Affairs*, Vol. VI, Oct. 1976/Jan. 1977, pp. 48-62.

6. *Yearbook of Agricultural and Forestry Statistics* (Ministry of Agriculture and Fisheries, Seoul, Korea, 1975).

7. Sung Hwan Ban, Pal Young Moon, and Dwight H. Perkins (eds.), *The Republic of Korea, 1945-1975: Rural Development* (Cambridge, Mass.: Harvard University Press, 1980), p. 309.

one must conclude that the Saemaul movement was a major catalyst in effecting a more equitable distribution of national income to rural areas.

A grievous paradox nevertheless seems to have occurred. The government had assumed that substantial improvements in rural life and income would result in halting or reducing rural-to-urban migration. This has not happened. Instead, the rural-to-urban migration pattern has remained unchanged, creating vexing problems for both urban and rural areas.

In the urban areas, consequent overpopulation has severely aggravated housing, environmental, energy, and unemployment problems among others. Seoul, the capital city of South Krea is now overcrowded with a population of over 8.5 million (the eighth largest city in the world) constituting over 20 percent of South Korea's population. During the period 1973-1978, 1.2 million migrated to Seoul of whom 68 percent were from rural areas.[8] This fact has aggravated another problem — a perceived endangerment of South Korea's security — because Seoul is located only 25 miles south of the demarcation line dividing South Korea from hostile North Korea, a condition that caused South Korea's late President Park to advocate moving the administrative capital many miles south of Seoul.

Rural South Korea, on the other hand, now suffers from a paucity of agricultural labor because of the precipitous decrease of the rural population. Rural labor costs continue to increase yearly causing some farmers to have abandoned cultivation altogether. A top priority of the South Korean government, therefore, is now to consider a number of policy options for reducing rural-to-urban-migration and for promoting a reverse pattern of urban-to-rural migration.[9]

It is our contention that the unabated rural-to-urban migration since the mid-1970s cannot be explained adequately by economic "push" and "pull" factors of the "primitive" and/or "mass" migration concepts relevant to the earlier migration periods. The central question underlying our research is why the dramatic improvement in rural life apparently has not mitigated the cognitive motivations of rural people to migrate to urban areas. In the light of our research of this question, moreover, we suggest some policy options for slowing or reversing rural-to-urban migration in South Korea.

Causes of rural-to-urban migration have been explained by three

8. See, *Dong-A-Ilbo,* (Seoul Daily Newspaper), April 5, 1976.
9. See *Hankuk Ilbo* (Seoul Daily Newspaper), Jan. 28, 1982 and Feb. 8, 1982.

distinguishable types of studies: labor mobility, social demographic, and cognitive-behavioral.[10] Labor mobility studies primarily focus on the impact of urban market conditions on rural-to-urban migration by reference to wage differences between rural and urban areas, often finding a positive correlation between net migration and wage or income levels.[11] The underlying assumption of labor mobility studies is that "labor demand and supply are always in equilibrium, with the labor supply adjusting in response to the relative real-wage rates between areas."[12]

Social demographic studies, on the other hand, explain migration in terms of attributes of individual migrants, such as their life-cycle position, socioeconomic status, kinship and community ties, and psychological orientations.[13] Attributes that are positive for migration are distinguished from negative attributes. Whereas labor mobility studies treat distinguishable conditions between rural and urban areas as major explanatory variables, social demographic studies emphasize positive and negative attributes of individual migrants.

Finally, cognitive-behavioral studies emphasize the "perceived attractiveness" or the individual's perception of rural and urban areas as the critical determinant of migration and its direction. Thus, a general proposition of the cognitive-behavioral approach is that the perceived attractiveness of one's home area is inversely related to his/her migration intention, whereas one's perceived attractiveness of other locations is positively related to his/her migration intention. Some studies have verified this proposition,[14] and further attested a strong direct relationship between migration intention and actual migration.[15] The fundamental difference between cognitive-behavioral,

10. Refer to P. Neal Ritchey, "Explanations of Migration," *The Annual Review of Sociology,* Vol. 2, 1975, pp. 363-404.
11. See, J. D. Tarver and R. P. McLeod, "A Test and Modification of Zipt's Hypothesis for Predicting Interstate Migration," *Demography,* Vol. 10, 1973, pp. 259-275. Particularly for Korean studies, refer to: Y. B. Choi, *op. cit.;* K. S. Kang, "Kyongje baljunkwa nong-up inkue idong" (Economic Development and Migration of Farm Population), *Journal of Population Studies,* No. 13, Seoul, 1971, pp. 155-156.
12. P. Neal Ritchey, *op. cit.,* p. 364.
13. For an excellent study, see: L. H. Long, "Migration Differentials by Education and Occupation: Trends and Variations," *Demography,* Vol. 10, 1973, pp. 243-258. See, also: Seyeul Kim, *op. cit.;* and Seyeul Kim, *The Economic and Social Determinants of Rural-Urban Migration in Korea: A Case Study of North Cholla Province* (unpublished Ph.D. dissertation, University of Hawaii, 1974).
14. See, N. M. Hanson and R. Yukhin, "Locational Preferences and Opportunity Costs in a Lagging Region: A Study of High School Seniors in Eastern Kentucky," *Journal of Human Resources,* Vol. 5, 1970. pp. 341-353.
15. See, A. Speare, Jr., "Residential Satisfaction as An Intervening Variable in Residential Mobility," *Demography,* Vol. 11, 1974, pp. 173-188. See, also, R. L. Bach and J. Smith, "Community Satisfaction, Expectations of Moving, and Migration," *Demography,* Vol. 14, 1977, pp. 147-167.

on the one hand, and both social demographic and labor mobility studies is that the former focuses on perceptions of *potential* migrants, while the latter deal with those who have *already migrated* to urban areas.

Our research attempts to discover potential migrants among rural people and to consider possible strategies to slow and/or reverse rural-to-urban migration as means to enhance rural development. Although we acknowledge the importance of studies of those who have already migrated to urban areas, we have concentrated on what sorts of perceived attractiveness determine whether rural people will migrate or stay, and what perceptions may induce potential migrants to remain in rural areas where they may contribute to rural development.

Accordingly, we have adopted a cognitive-behavioral approach as our research framework. There is a caveat, however, to this approach, because of the very fact that it treats perception of potential movers as an *empirical* concept of migration. Besides the difficulty of operationalizing and measuring perception, there always is a problem of connecting the perceived to the real world.[16] Some studies suggest that a person's attitude to an object is not necessarily a major determinant of his behavior with respect to that object.[17] Some particular migration studies, moreover, suggest that even if it is known that motivation for migration exists, one cannot predict actual behavior until the various migration constraints — such as political, legal, economic, and social constraints — have been examined.[18] They contend, therefore, that migration intention — discoverable by a cognitive-behavioral approach — can be deemed significant or consequential only by actual migration taking place over time.

In our research effort, however, we were mainly concerned with discovering what perceptions incline rural people to want to migrate or to stay, and what strategies might be employed to influence them to stay. We could not identify before the fact, of course, those potential migrants who will actually migrate to urban areas. Considering South Korean migration patterns, however, and utilizing a cognitive-behavioral approach (which studies frequently have established a direct relationship between behavioral dispositions of rural people and their migration), we assumed that those we identify as potential migrants are more inclined to move to urban areas than those otherwise

16. David Harvey, "Conceptual and Measurement Problems in the Cognitive Behavioral Approach to Location Theory," in K. R. Cox, ed., *Behavioral Problems in Geography: A Symposium* (Evanston, Ill.: Northwestern University Press, 1969), pp. 49-62.

17. See, M. Fishbein, "Attitudes and Prediction in Behavior," in M. Fishbein, ed., *Readings in Attitude Theory and Measurement* (New York: Wiley, 1967), p. 483.

18. See, P. Uhlenberg, "Noneconomic Determinants of Nonmigration: Sociological Considerations for Migration Theory," *Rural Sociology*, Vol. 38, p. 303.

identified.

Our questionnaire was administered in 1981 to a representative sample of the adult population of Ichon-kun in Kyongki-do (Kyongki Province). Most people of Ichon-kun, a county located 40 miles south of the capital city of Seoul, are engaged in agriculture as their main living. Since our survey was confined to only one county, the sample by no means may be considered representative of rural South Korea. Ours is a case or pilot study which, we hope, will form a basis for a nationwide survey.

Our survey comprised 234 respondents from eight villages dispersed throughout Ichon-kun, including 64 village leaders (i.e., village chiefs and Saemaul leaders) who completed the questionnaire while attending class at Ichon-kun training center. All respondents were either heads of a household, spouses of a head, or representatives of a household in the absence of a head or spouse.

Our survey instrument, administered only to rural people, consisted of a questionnaire of 24 questions comprised of three parts to explain potential migration: questions aimed at identifying those respondents inclined to migrate or to stay; questions aimed at indentifying the perceived attractiveness of rural areas; and questions pertaining to the perceived attractiveness of urban areas.

The part of the questionnaire concerning the perceived attractiveness of rural areas included questions relating to the following variables: traditional rural values (i.e., degree of respect for age, ancestors, parents); the values attached to farm land; and the perceived effectiveness of the Saemaul movement. The part pertaining to the perceived attractiveness of urban areas comprised questions relating to perceptions of: urban income and job prospects; the life-style of urban relatives, educational opportunities; upward social mobility; housing and traffic conditions; urban thinking modes; plus a question concerning the frequency of visits to urban areas.[19]

Two questions of our questionnaire were aimed at identifying those inclined to become potential migrants. To one of these questions, too many (30.8 percent) gave no response for us to assign significance to those who did respond; accordingly, we have deleted responses to this question from our analysis. To the other question, however, only two persons (less than one percent of the total) gave no response. We excluded these two nonrespondents from our universe of 234 persons, thus reducing our universe to 232 respondents for this question:

---

19. To make our variables inclusive, we included in the questionnaire our respondents' perceptions of cultural-psychological, social, and economic aspects of both rural and urban living.

"Given an opportunity to migrate to an urban area, will you move?" Forty-four percent answered they will move; 28.9 percent responded they will nevertheless stay in the rural area; and 27.2 percent remained uncertain. In view of past migration patterns in South Korea, the finding that 44 percent of the respondents were potential migrants is not surprising.

Since only 44 percent of our respondents, albeit a plurality, have been fairly clearly identified as potential migrants, we have therefore interpreted *consensus* responses — which for analytical purposes we have defined as 60 percent or more — as skewed to the extent that they may contribute to our knowledge of rural peoples' "weltanschauung" (or their general perception of their dichotomous rural-urban world) but do not necessarily explain why or what variables motivate those respondents to be potential migrants. By first examining the consensus or skewed responses, therefore, to the questions pertaining to respondents' perceptions of both rural and urban areas, we gain insights of their "weltanschauung" but not explanations of migration inclination.

First, we found skewed responses to questions concerning the influence of traditional "Confucian" values, such as deference to elders and parents in making decisions, and the importance of visits to graves of ancestors, which we expected to be quite dominant among our rural respondents.[20] However, 17.5 percent of them responded they would choose to follow the advice of elders, whereas 80 percent preferred to depend on their own rationality. Similarly, 33.5 percent would follow the advice of parents as compared to 61 percent who would make up their own minds. Only when we presented our respondents with the choice of visiting their ancestors' graves or of attending to personal business, did we find a majority (56 percent) show preference for an ascriptive Confucian value, namely to visit ancestors graves. Accordingly, these data suggest that the influence of Confucian-oriented values may be eroding in rural South Korea to the extent that the perceived attractiveness of rural traditions may be too weak to keep rural people from migrating to urban areas.

Secondly, we found skewed responses to questions concerning the perceived attractiveness of the Saemaul movement which was designed to improve the quality of rural life. Of the total number of respondents, 82 percent answered that the Saemaul movement had caused them to become more diligent and comfortable, and 75 per-

---

20. Traditional Korean culture was characterized by authoritarianism and familism. See, Chong Hong Park, *Hankuk Sasang Nongo* (A Critique of Korean Thoughts) (Seoul: Suhmoon-dang, 1977).

cent answered that "both myself and my village became wealthier."
These results, however, do not mean that this high degree of perceived
attractiveness of the movement and the actual marked improvement
of rural life induced most respondents to be inclined thereby to remain in rural areas. Indeed, as we have already noted, over 44 percent of the respondents — a distinct plurality — answered they would
move to an urban area given the opportunity. Thus, our data suggest that although the Saemaul movement has definitely helped—
both in reality and perception — in improving rural life, apparently
the movement has not convinced the greater number of our
respondents therefore to remain in rural areas. Our only explanation of this seeming paradox is that the movement, by enhancing rapid
socialization and self-help attitudes, has unintendedly contributed to
the erosion of traditional ascriptive values of rural areas, on the one
hand, and the acceptance of rational achievement-oriented values of
urban areas, on the other hand.[21] We do not assert that the Saemaul
movement has actually induced rural people to move to urban areas.
We do suggest, however, that despite the movement's success, it may
not have thwarted migration inclinations of rural people as its framers
had hoped. This phenomenon of the relationship of the socializing
influence of the Saemaul movement to migration inclination clearly
deserves further research.

Thirdly, one of our questions evoked a skewed response that showed
72.4 percent (168 people) of our respondents were keenly aware that
depopulation of the rural areas resulted in too few workers to do the
necessary work in rural areas. Of these 168 respondents, however,
45.2 percent responded they nevertheless would migrate to urban areas
given the opportunity, whereas only 28.6 percent would remain.
Accordingly, though most of our respondents perceived that the quality
of their living had improved and that a larger labor force is needed
to develop their home areas, these considerations did not constrain
the migration inclination of their greater number.

The skewed responses so far discussed pertain to questions relating
to the perceived attractiveness of rural areas. Another set of skewed
responses relates to the respondents' perceived attractiveness of urban areas, from which we may similarly gain insights of their
"weltanschauung" if not explanations of migration inclination.

With regard to their perceived attractiveness of urban housing, 62
percent of respondents answered that "to obtain a house (or living
place) in an urban area is like obtaining the unattainable stars in the

---

21. For an understanding of social mobilization, see, K. W. Deutsch, "Social Mobilization
and Political Development," *American Political Science Review*, Sept. 1961, pp. 493-514.

sky" (a reference to a Korea idiomatic expression for reaching for the impossible). Fully 49 percent of those who gave this response indicated they would nevertheless migrate to an urban area given the opportunity, whereas 27.1 percent would stay. Of our total number of respondents, 30.6 percent expressed a contrary view that urban housing is not so difficult to obtain as might be expected. Those who gave this answer, however, were not thereby more inclined to migrate, for only 36.6 percent of these particular respondents answered they would migrate given the opportunity, whereas 29.6 percent would stay. These data suggest to us, therefore, that whether respondents perceive urban housing as difficult to obtain apparently offers no direct explanation of their inclinations to migrate or to stay.

Similarly, 83.2 percent of respondents answered that children living in urban areas receive a "better" education than those living in rural areas, but this favorable view of urban education has no direct relation to their migration inclination.

Finally, only one question — concerning the perceived life-style of urban relatives — evoked a skewed response that appears a factor in explaining migration inclination. Reactions to this question are analyzed in the next section.

Turning now from skewed responses that contribute to our knowledge of the "weltanschauung" of rural people, but do not necessarily explain potential migration, we were able to identify several perception variables that clearly do explain migration inclination among our rural respondents. These perception variables comprise: the value attached to farm land, and perceptions of urban income, of the life-style of urban relatives, and of the degree of "comfort" of urban living (i.e., the perceived attractiveness of the urban environment as a whole).

Although our survey results included a number of other variables pertaining to the perceived attractiveness of urban areas, none of them appeared significantly related to migration inclination and are therefore excluded from our analysis. Those excluded are perceptions concerning urban job prospects, upward social mobility in urban areas, urban thinking modes, and the frequency of visits to urban areas.

With regard to the value they attached to their farm land, we asked the respondents to choose either to sell their farm land for more profitable business or to keep their land at the expense of more profitable business. Of 232 respondents to this question, only 47 indicated a willingness to sell, whereas 119 answered they would not sell, 57 were uncertain, and 9 did not know. Among the 47 willing to sell, however, 80.9 percent were inclined to migrate, while only 35.3 percent of the 119 who would not sell were still inclined to migrate. (See

Table 1, Appendix II). Stated differently, about two-thirds of those respondents inclined to remain in the rural area also would not sell their land. Accordingly, the more attached respondents were to their land, the more likely they are to remain in the rural area, and, furthermore, the more uncertain they were about selling their land the more likely they are to be uncertain about their migration inclination. Finally, those indicating that their land is important to them only as a means of furthering their economic well-being were inclined to migrate to an urban area. Clearly, these results suggest that the desire to continue their land ownership tends to strongly deter rural people from migrating to an urban area.

A second variable explaining migration inclination arises from a meaningful disparity between perception and reality. As noted before, since 1975 the average family income of farmers and fishermen in South Korea has surpassed that of urban laborers. To the question, however, whether they believed more money was to be made in an urban area, 102 of our respondents answered affirmatively, while only 79 responded either negatively or that urban and rural incomes were not much different, and 51 answered they did not know. Although less than half the respondents can be said to have perceived urban income positively, 56 percent of these were inclined to migrate, while only 31.6 percent who had a negative or undifferentiated perception of urban income were so inclined, and 39 percent of those who responded they did not know were also inclined to migrate. With regard to the inclination of respondents to remain in the rural area, the above order is of course converse (see Table 2, Appendix II). Accordingly, we conclude that the more our respondents perceived more money was to be made in urban areas, the more likely they are to migrate. Therefore, these results suggest that — though rural perceptions of urban income may not accord with reality — the *perceived* attractiveness of urban income surely explains migration inclination.[22]

A third variable explaining migration inclination arises from our question concerning the perceived attractiveness of the life-style of urban relatives. To the question: Considering what I have learned from the life-style of my urban relatives, for me to live in an urban area would be (1) better, (2) not much different, (3) a set-back, (4) I do not know," 148 or 63.8 percent of our respondents answered "better;" only 47 chose (2) and 17 chose (3). Thus, the overwhelming majority perceived the urban life-style projected by their relatives

---

22. In terms of relative income differences between rural and urban areas, it appears very difficult for the labor mobility approach to explain why rural people migrate to urban areas when in fact the average family income in rural areas exceeds that of urban laborers.

to be attractive, and 51.4 percent of this group indicated a willingness to migrate, whereas only 31.9 percent of those who chose (2) and 29.4 percent of those who chose (3) were similarly inclined to migrate. In terms of those inclined to remain, the results are of course reverse: 64.7 percent of those who chose (3), 36.2 percent of those who chose (2), and only 23 percent of those who chose (1) indicated their intention to stay in the rural area (see Table 3, Appendix II). Consequently, the more our respondents favorably considered the life-style of their urban relatives the more likely they are to migrate. These data suggest, therefore, that the perceived attractiveness or urban relatives' life-style has a strong explnatory relationship to migration inclination.

A fourth and final variable explaining migration inclination concerns the perceived attractiveness of the urban environment as a whole. That is to say, we sought to ask a question that would provide us with a "comfort" index of how rural people perceived their future adjustment to the urban environment. Presumably, if they perceived a favorable adjustment, they would thereby be more inclined to migrate to an urban area. So we asked them this simple question: "When I think of living in an urban area, I feel (1) uncomfortable, (2) nothing much, (3) rather comfortable, (4) very comfortable." Of our total respondents, 96 answered "uncomfortable," 81 chose "nothing much," and 55 responded either "rather comfortable" or "very comfortable" (we combined the number responding to these last two choices and labeled them simply "comfortable"). Relating these three groups with our migration inclination variable, we found them clearly differentiated (see Table 4, Appendix II). Compared to other groups, those who felt they would be "comfortable" were more inclined to migrate to an urban area, and — conversely — those who felt "uncomfortable" were more likely to remain in the rural area. These results suggest to us, therefore, that the perceived comfort in the urban environment has a strong explanatory relationship to migration inclination.

Our isolation of four variables that explain migration inclination imparts an understanding of certain peculiarities of the perceived attractiveness of rural and/or urban areas that influenced our respondents' intentions whether to remain in the rural area or to migrate to an urban area. In the order they are analyzed above, these peculiarities pertain to: how much one values one's land; how one perceives urban income prospects; how much one admired the lifestyle of one's relatives; and to what degree would one feels comfortable living in an urban setting.

So far, our analysis has been confined to a technique that utilizes

Chi-square tests of associations between pairs of variables. In other words, migration inclination (the dependent variable) was related to the perceived attractiveness of farm land, of the life-style of urban relatives, of urban income, and of the degree of comfort about urban living (the independent variables). At this point, however, we are able to form a composite portrait by relating these four independent variables together and considering how they together affect migration inclination, and hence determining the strength or significance of each independent variable, respectively, in this regard. We were able to construct this composite portrait by applying a multivariate approach to the problem of analyzing determinants of migration among our rural respondents (see Tables 1 and 2, Appendix III). This log-linear approach makes use of the recent works of Goodman and others.[23]

Considering the four explanatory variables together in this composite way, we found that 89.2 percent of migration inclination (of the variance as detailed in Appendix III) can be explained. By far the most important explanatory variable is the perceived attachment to farm land, because the farm land variable alone explains 63 percent of migration inclination, whereas only 31.3 percent of migration inclination is explained by the other three variables considered together. Considered in terms of their respective strengths, we found their order of decrasing importance to be the life-style of urban relatives, urban income, and comfort in an urban setting.

Rural-to-urban migration in South Korea since the mid-1970s cannot be simply characterized as either "primitive" or "mass" migration. Substantial improvement of rural living conditions and income commensurate with an unchanging pattern of rural-to-urban migration presents a paradox requiring explanation. Utilizing a cognitive-behavioral research approach, that assumes perceptions of rural residents may influence their migration, we attempted to identify perception variables that explain migration inclination.

In the process of our analysis, we were able to discern general perceptions of our rural respondents' dichotomous rural-urban world, or their "weltanschauung" as it may be called. We found that their decision-making value system is not predominantly "Confucius" or tradition-bound, as might be expected, but is rationally oriented. Moreover, we found most respondents perceived the Saemaul rural

---

23. See: Leo A. Goodman, "A Modified Multiple Regression Approach to the Analysis of Dichotomous Variables," *American Sociological Review,* Vol. 37, 1972, pp. 28-46; and Graham J. Upton, *The Analysis of Cross-Tabulated Date* (New York: John Wiley & Sons, 1978), pp. 46-87. For excellent use of the log-linear model, see, Kenneth W. Eckhardt and G. E. Hendershot, "The 1970s Reversal in Breast Feeding Trends," unpublished article, 1982.

development movement as improving rural life and income. We believe these two findings have a connection, namely the Saemaul movement has fostered their acceptanct of rational achievement-oriented values associated with urban areas. Other predominant perceptions of our respondents that we discovered are their beliefs that a larger labor force is needed to develop their home area, that the urban housing problem is serious, and that the urban education system is superior. Unfortunately, however, none of these dominant "weltanschauung" perceptions explains why some respondents are inclined to migrate while others are not. Only one prevailing perception appears to explain the inclination to migrate, namely the belief that the life-style of their urban relatives is superior to their own.

The most significant result of our analysis is the discovery of four distinct variables that explain migration inclintion among our rural respondents, one pertaining to their perceived attractiveness of the rural area, and three relating to their perceived attractiveness of an urban area. The former is reflected by their attachment to their farm land: the greater their attachment, the less likely they will migrate; and, conversely, the less their attachment, the more likely they will migrate. The latter three variables are: their perceptions of urban income (economic variable), of the life-style of their urban relatives (social variable), and of their adjustment to — or "comfort" in — an urban setting (psychological variable). The more favorably they view these three economic, social and psychological variables, the more likely they will migrate to an urban area.

Having isolated these four distinct explanatory variables — the perceived attractiveness of farm land, of urban income, of the life-style of urban relatives, and of comfort in an urban setting — we attempted to construct a composite portrait of how they together affect migration inclination. We found that the four explanatory variables — though independent of one another — considered together do affect directly migration inclination behavior. Furthermore, we discovered that the farm land variable is the single strongest variable affecting migration inclination. In order of decreasing importance are the perceived attractiveness of the life-style of urban relatives, of urban income, and lastly of the degree of comfort in an urban environment.

An unquestioned precondition of continuing development administration in South Korea is the slowing, stopping, or even reversal of the rural-to-urban migration process. Our universe was too small to be adequately representative of rural perceptions in South Korea, and our survey was too narrow to enable us to propose sure remedies for this grievous problem. We contend that our research findings, nevertheless, are suggestive of some recommendations and/or policy implications and directions, the first of which is the recommendation that the South Korean government undertake the testing of our findings on a much broader scale.

Secondly, our research suggests that traditional Confucian values among rural people no longer bind them to rural communities. Given this finding, the degree of their attachment to their farm land appears the foremost determinant of the direction of migration inclination. It is our view, therefore, that any new policy initiative responsive to the rural-to-urban migration problem must give top priority to strengthening this land-attachment value of rural South Koreans. To do so would be to reverse the recent trend whereby wealthy urbanites have been buying up rural lands. Reactive exhortations by the South Korean government that owners should cultivate their lands by themselves are insufficient. What is needed now, if not too late, is a vigorous "return-the-land-to-the-tiller" government program with all the costs such a program would entail — namely, through government capital, the compensation of absentee owners for their land and an incentive-oriented, long-term, low-interest, loan program that will effectively transfer the ownership of rural lands to the actual cultivators.

Highlighted by the results of our research is the fact that perceptions of our rural respondents of the attractiveness of urban areas do not necessarily reflect urban realities. The perception that the average family income of urban laborers, for example, is higher than that of farmers and fishermen manifestly is false. So far as migration inclination is concerned, however, even false rural perceptions are more motivating than urban realities. Perceptions that urban income and life-style are better, and that rural residents feel they would be psychologically comfortable living in an urban setting, reflect a broadly shared desire to live in a more modern world, fantasy or not. Surely, this desire has been heightened paradoxically by the very success of the Saemaul movement itself, by easier access to urban life facilitated by urban-based mass media and transportation systems, and especially by visits to and from urban relatives. New pride-in-rural-life programs are needed to induce rural residents to remain in rural areas and for the more impoverished migrants in urban areas to be encouraged to return to rural areas.[24] Essentially, these should be incentive-

---

24. In February 1982, the South Korean government established a migration policy for the poor. To those poor people who migrate to the six metropolitan areas after April 1982, the government will not provide many of the welfare benefits, including financial aid for the education of their children and vocational training service, for at least the first two

oriented, image-building, community education programs aimed at placing the rural community at center stage in the human drama of nation building.

Finally, we recommend that rural leaders be mobilized as main actors in these endeavors, for we have found that they as a group are more attached to, and inclined to remain in, rural areas (see Table 5, Appendix II). These are the people most seriously committed to the Saemaul movement and rural development activities, and — perhaps because of their rural leadership positions — have the greatest stake in rural community development.[25] They are young and well educated — 73 percent in our sample of rural leaders are under age 40, and 79 percent have completed middle school at least. Both at the national and local levels, moreover, many Saemaul leaders' training centers already function, and these can be utilized as convenient locales for further developing rural leaders as modernizing and harmonizing rural change agents.

---

years of their staying in the urban area. Conversely, for those who have already lived more than two years in the urban area as of July 1982, the government will pay their moving expenses to a rural area, will provide vocational training service, will introduce them to new jobs, and will provide a house in case they wish to be involved in agriculture, and finally will enable them to acquire agricultural skills. For those poor people living in rural areas who will stay in the rural area, the government will provide them with more medical services so that they need pay only 20 percent of their total medical expenses, whereas under present law they are required to pay 50 percent. See, *Hankuk Ilbo*, Feb. 8, 1982. These incentives, however, are aimed at material rewards and punishments and do not include social and psychological remedies needed to thwart rural-to-urban migration.

25. See, Georges Sabagh, Maurice van Aridel, Jr., and Edgar Butler, "Some Determinants of Intrametropolitan Residential Mobility: Conceptual Consideration," *Social Forces*, Vol. 4, 1969, pp. 88-98.

APPENDIX I

Table 1: Population in South Korea

Year	Total Population (A) (in 1,000)	Urban Population (B) (in 1,000)	Rural Population (C) (in 1,000)	B/A × 100 (Percent)	C/A × 100 (Percent)
1946	19,369	2,832	16,537	14.6	85.4
1949	20,189	3,474	16,714	17.2	82.8
1955	21,526	5,281	16,245	24.5	75.7
1960	24,989	6,997	17,992	28.0	72.0
1966	29,208	9,810	19,398	35.0	66.4
1970	31,435	13,118	18,317	41.7	58.3
1975	34,682	16,771	17,909	48.4	51.6
1980	37,449	21,421	16,028	57.2	42.8

Sources: Economic Planning Board, *Korea Statistical Yearbook,* 1966; *Population and Housing Census Report,* 1975; *Dong-A Ilbo,* Jan. 24, 1981.

APPENDIX II
(Cross-Tabulation)

Table 1: The Relation Between the Value Attached to Farmland and Migration Inclination

	Migrate	Uncertain	Stay	Row Total
Sell	38	2	7	47
	80.9*	4.3	14.9	20.7
	37.3**	3.2	10.4	
Uncertain	18	25	14	57
	38.6	43.9	24.6	24.6
	17.6	39.7	20.9	
Not Sell	42	32	45	119
	35.3	26.9	37.8	51.7
	41.1	50.8	67.2	
Not Response	4	4	1	9
	44.4	44.4	11.1	3.9
	3.9	6.3	1.5	
Column Total	102	63	67	232
	44.0	27.2	28.9	100.0

X^2 = 42.3 Significance = .00
 * Row Percent
** Column Percent

Table 2: The Relation Between Urban Income Prospects and Migration Inclination

	Migrate	Uncertain	Stay	Row Total
More Money	57 55.9 55.9	23 22.5 36.5	22 21.6 32.8	102 44.0
No Difference or Less	25 31.6 24.5	22 27.8 34.9	32 40.5 47.8	79 34.1
Don't Know	20 39.2 19.6	18 35.3 28.6	13 25.5 19.4	51 22.0
Column Total	102 44.0	63 27.2	67 28.9	232 100.0

X^2 = 14.1   Significance = .006

Table 3: The Relation Between Life Style of Urban Relatives and Migration Inclination

	Migrate	Uncertain	Stay	Row Total
Better	76 51.4 74.5	38 25.7 60.3	34 23.0 50.7	148 63.8
Not Different	15 31.9 14.7	15 31.9 23.8	17 36.2 25.4	47 20.3
A Set-Back	5 29.4 4.9	1 5.9 1.6	11 64.7 16.4	17 7.3
Don't Know	6 30.0 5.9	9 45.0 14.3	5 25.0 7.5	20 8.6
Column Total	102 44.0	63 27.2	67 28.9	232

X^2 = 21.1   Significance = 0.001

Table 4: The Relation Between Psychological Comfort of Urban
        Area and Migration Inclination

	Migrate	Uncertain	Stay	Row Total
	32	26	38	96
Uncomfortable	33.2	27.1	39.6	41.4
	31.4	41.3	56.7	
	39	23	19	81
Nothing Much	48.1	28.4	23.5	34.9
	38.2	36.5	28.4	
	31	14	10	55
Comfortable	56.4	25.5	18.2	23.7
	30.4	22.2	14.9	
Column Total	102	63	67	232
	44.0	27.3	28.9	

X^2 = 11.6 Significance = .020

Table 5: Migration Inclination of Rural Leaders Vs. Rural Followers

	Migrate	Uncertain	Stay	Row Total
	19	19	24	62
Leaders	30.6	30.6	38.6	26.7
	18.6	30.2	35.8	
	83	44	43	170
Followers	48.8	25.9	25.3	73.3
	81.4	69.8	62.4	
Column Total	102	63	67	232
	44.0	27.2	28.9	100.0

X^2 = 6.6 Significance = .036

APPENDIX III

Table 1: Number of Sample Cases Used to Estimate Composite Portrait of Migration Inclination

Farmland	Urban Income in View of Rural Income	Life Style of Urban Relatives	Psychological Comfort	Migrate	Other
Sell	More	Better	Comfort	10	0
			Other	12	2
		Other	Comfort	0	0
			Other	3	1
	Other	Better	Comfort	3	0
			Other	5	3
		Other	Comfort	2	1
			Other	3	2
Other*	More	Better	Comfort	9	6
			Other	17	25
		Other	Comfort	2	5
			Other	4	6
	Other	Better	Comfort	3	5
			Other	17	31
		Other	Comfort	2	7
			Other	10	36
Total				102	130

*All "other signs appeared in this table are the collapse of those that are not positively (at least in definition) related to potential migration. For example, those people who are either "uncertain" or "certain" to keep the land are collapsed and categorized as "other," so that we are enabled to code all variables in the nominal scale for log-linear analysis.

Table 2: Goodness of Fit Tests and Adjusted Coefficient of Multiple-
           Partial Determination for Selected Log-Linear Analyses

Model[a]	Hypothesis	Chi-Square	df	R²fHn [2345]
H1. [2345][b]	Migration inclination is equally probable among all subgroups	48.6	16	
H2. [2345] [12]	Only psychological comfort directly affects migration inclination	41.2	14	.03
H3. [2345] [13]	Only life style of urban relatives directly affects migration inclination	37.1	14	.14
H4. [2345] [14]	Only urban income directly affects migration inclination	35.5	14	.17
H5. [2345] [15]	Only farm land perception directly affects migration inclination	15.4	14	.63
H6. [2345] [12] [13] [14] [15]	All of the independent variables directly affect migration inclination, but are independent of one another	3.6	11	.892
H7. [2345] [123] [124] [125] [134] [135] [145]	All of the independent variables directly and indirectly affect migration inclination with all two-way interactions	1.8	6	.90
H8. [2345] [1234] [1235] [1345]	All of the independent variables directly and indirectly affect migration inclination with all two-way and three-way interactions	.1	2	.98

a. Model Variables
   1 = migration inclination
   2 = psychological comfort
   3 = life style of urban relatives
   4 = urban income
   5 = farm land perception
b. See Appendix III, Table 1, for an explanation of this measure.

Explanation of Table 2

Table 2 shows selected log-linear models fitted in our analysis, their associated goodness-of-fit statistics, and their degree of freedom. The simplest model is model H1 which hypothesizes that none of the four independent variables has any effect on migration inclination. According to this hypothesis, all subgroups described by the four variables (e.g., those who are willing to sell the land vs. those who are not) account for equal proportions of migration intention. Model

H1 is the model against which all other models are compared.

Model H2 hypothesizes that only the psychological comfort variable directly affects migration inclination. This term is indicated by the notational convention of a [12] interaction. Actually, all models in Table 2 include a four-way interaction term among the set of independent variables [2345]. This procedure results in isolating the effects of the independent variables on the dependent variable from the known association between the set of independent variables (see, D. P. Slesinger and H. P. Travis, "A Study of Infant Mortality of Log-Linear Models," a paper presented at the Annual Meeting of the Population Association of America, Seattle, Washington, 1975). Our concern here is to examine the effects attributable to the comfort variable. The adjusted coefficients of multiple-partial determination shown in the last column of Table 2 can be used as gross indicators of such effects (in the case of the comfort variable, the adjusted coefficient is .03). This coefficient is interpreted as analogous to a multiple correlation coefficient in multiple regression analysis. All of the adjusted coefficients in Table 2 were derived by evaluating models H2-H9 against the baseline model H1 by means of the following formula:

$$[(X^2 (H1)/dfl) - (X^2 (Hn)/dfn)]/[(X^2 (Hl)/dfl]$$

Accordingly, each coefficient can be interpreted as the decrease in "unexplained" variance which results from the inclusion of the terms of each model which differ from the [2345] term in the baseline model. Models H2-H5 show the gross effects of each independent variable on migration intention. Of these models, the hypothesis that only the attractiveness of farm land is important (model H5) is most successful (R^2f.H4[2345] = .63) in accounting for the variance left "unexplained" by the base model. In other words, the attractiveness of farm land is the single strongest variable included in the analysis which impacts on migration inclination. This variable, then, is followed in order of decreasing strength by the urban life-style variable (H3), the urban income variable (H4), and the comfort variable (H2).

Model H6 hypothesizes that all of our independent variables directly affect migration inclination, but are conditionally independent of one another. In this case, we find that explanatory power (.892) meaningfully increases compared with those that are explained by any single variable. Assuming H6 as the main-effects model, when we added that two-way interaction term as shown in H7, we found that the explanatory power of H7 (.90) did not increase meaningfully. Only when we account for model H8, which assumes not only main effects but also two-way and three-way and three-way indirect effects, does the explanatory power increase to .98. But the problem with this model is that it lacks parsimony, that is — it assumes too many interactions and is difficult to interpret. This model is so complex that it does little to clarify our understanding beyond our raw observations. We concluded from this hierarchical analysis that the explanatory power of the main-effects model (H6) is substantively and theoretically meaningful.

To sum up, the farm land variable appears to be a most powerful explanatory variable about migration inclination behavior. It alone explains 63 percent of the variance left "unexplained" by the base model. And yet, we found that the explanatory power increases substantively (89 percent) when the following composite portrait is assumed: psychological comfort, the life-style of urban relatives, the urban income and farm land perceptions all directly affect migration inclination, but are independent of one another.

13

The Search for Low-Cost Land Development Techniques

Myong Chan Hwang

The main objective of the paper is to see whether the land readjustment project (LRP), an urban land development technique whcih is extensively used in Korea supplies developed land cheap enough for the low-income housing. Because it is one of the major land development techniques used by most of the urban governments in Korea, it has far-reaching implications for low-income housing in major urban areas. For instance, about 60% of the urban development in Seoul up to 1975 was done by the LRP method. The major feature of the technique is its cost-bearing method. The total project costs are borne by the land-owners who give up a certain proportion of their land for the project.

The cheapest public housing available for the low-income people in Seoul was about 2.2 million Won per unit in 1974. At that price, only 3% of the poor people could afford it. To make the public housing program more effective, every effort should be made to reduce the cost of the public housing so that more people in the lower income bracket could afford it.

Developed land is one of the most important inputs in public housing and the land prices are increasing at a rapid rate. Therefore, it is important to supply developed land at a price which is within the affordability range of the urban poor. It was found in this paper that an alternative method such as land banking could produce cheaper land than the much used LRP. The implicit profit rate of some land readjustment projects undertaken in Seoul and one other city in Korea ranges from 23% to 68% most of which go back to the original land owners. One way to achieve cost reduction is to reduce the excessive profits of the LRP. Given that land accounts for 20% of total housing costs, the 50% reduction of the land price will reduce the housing costs by 10%.

Although housing investment, in particular by the public sector, is increasing each year, housing still remains one of the most recalcitrant social problems in Korea.

As is shown in Table 1, housing shortages are quite high especially in Seoul metropolitan area which contains, in addition, a substantial number of squatter settlements. Being well aware of the problem,

Table 1. Selected Housing Indicators of Korea

% Households without own dwelling unit (1970)	
Whole country	24%
Urban areas	43%
(Seoul City)	(45.3%)[1]
Rest of the country	9.5%
Housing investment (1970)	
% of GNP	3.1%
% of capital formation	9.7%
Public sector[2]	5.3%
Private sector	94.7%
Increases in housing stocks (1966-1970)	
Whole country	13%
Seoul City	66%
Squatter housing units in Seoul (1970)	160,000
Occupancy rate (1970)	12 persons per housing unit
Living space per occupant for 58% of the housing units in Seoul and Pusan cities (1970)	41 square feet
% Single units structures (1970)	
Whole country	95%
Seoul & Pusan	87%

[1] It represents 483,600 households which account for 33.5% of the total housing shortages of the nation.

[2] It increased, however, to 15% in 1973.

Source: Tong Hu, *Study on Housing Finance*. Unpublished thesis, Kon-Kuk University, 1973, and *Korea Housing Investment Guarantee* FY 1975, USAID, Washington, D.C., 1975.

the government is allocating an increasing amount of resources for housing. As it spends more and more, the efficient use of the allocated resources within the public housing sector becomes increasingly important. It is important not only to build more houses but also to produce them at the prices within the ability-to-pay range of the people who need them.

The major objective of the paper is to evaluate whether a land development technique which is officially called land readjustment project contributes much to the solution of housing problems in urban areas by providing the developed residential sites at lower prices than other alternative land development techniques.

In the first section of the paper, the relationship between the housing cost including land prices and affordability will be briefly discussed to show the effect of cost reduction on the people's affordability.

Next the discussion focuses on the land policy instruments which are directly or indirectly used to control the speculative increase of land prices or to recapture the socially created added-value of land. Finally an evaluation of the land readjustment technique will be attempted.

The affordability of housing is determined by family income and the market prices of the houses. Each household spends a certain percent of its income for housing. For instance, the average household expenditure devoted to housing in Seoul, was 20.1% in 1972. If we, however, include other housing-related expenditures such as utilities and transport, it increases to 30.4%.[1] Given the market prices of the housing, the proportion of household income which could be devoted to the housing expenditure determines the family's affordability of housing.

What is perhaps more important to us is the determinants of the house price. If we are able to produce houses at a lower price, more families could be brought into the affordability range. The cost of housing production consists of various components: raw land, land servicing, construction materials, labor, and so on.

The cost data of public apartment for low-income families in Seoul demonstrate that the land and land servicing accounts for 19-21% of the total cost and 75-77% for construction as shown in Table 2.

There is one important intervening variable which links the house price and family affordability. The mortage loans are available for

---

1. Grimes, Jr., O.F., *Housing For Low-Income Urban Families,* The Johns Hopkins University Press, Baltimore, 1976, p. 147.

Table 2. Cost Component Per Unit of Apartments for Low-Income
Family in Seoul

	Mi-Ah Area (1974)	Young-Dong Area (1974)
Land and land servicing	21%	19%
Construction	75%	77%
Other	4%	4%
Price per unit (1000 Won)[1]	$2,170 (100%)	$2,170 (100%)

[1] The size of the unit is 13 Pyong which is equivalent of 43 square meters.

Source: *Seminar Report on Low-Income Housing,* Seoul Metropolitan Government, Seoul, 1974, p. 41.

almost all of the public housing programs, particularly for the low-income families and the terms of the loans such as the interest rate and the repayment period also influence the affordability of the housing. The lower interest rate and the longer the repayment period the more families could afford the houses they want given the house prices and their income.

For our discussion, let us concern ourselves only with the cost side of the equation assuming as givens the level of income including the proportion of housing expenditure and the mortgage terms, and see the effect of some cost reduction on the family's affordability of housing.

The sale price of one of the cheapest multi-family units built in Seoul by Korean Housing Authority was 2,170,000 Won in 1974. Given the current financing arrangement of 9% interest rate per annum and 25 year amortization, the monthly payment would be 18,210 Won.[2] If we assume quite generously that about 25% of the household income could be devoted to the housing expenditures, then the required monthly income to afford the unit would be 72,840 Won. That means that only 3% of the households without their own dwelling unit in Seoul could afford to buy the units. Income distribution data of Seoul show that 97% of them were under the monthly income of less than 68,000 Won in 1974.[3]

---

2. It is assumed that there is no downpayment. However, a certain percent downpayment is normally allowed in the housing finance.
3. *Seminar Report on Low-Income Housing in Seoul,* Seoul Metropolitan Government, Seoul, 1974, p. 110.

Table 3. Housing Cost Reduction and % Affordability in Seoul

	Current price	10% reduction	15% reduction	One-third reduction
Sales price (1000 Won)	2,170	1,953	1,844	1,454
Monthly payment (Won)	18,210	16,389	15,474	12,202
Monthly income needed (Won)	72,840	65,536	61,895	48,808
% Household able to afford in Seoul	3%	4%	5.4%	12%

Now let us assume that we could reduce the sales price by 10%, 15% and one-third. As shown in Table 3, the percent affordability of housing in Seoul would increase to 12% if the housing cost is reduced one-third.

The critical question is how to achieve the desirable cost reduction. Every effort should be made to reduce the production cost of housing. The production of the low-cost building material is one way which will ensure a great effect because of its large weight in the cost components. To develop a building technology which uses the cheap indigenous materials and labor is also important. Our major concern is, however, land prices. Although the cost proportion of land and land servicing is smaller than that of the construction, it becomes increasingly important because of the rapid price increase of land in most urban areas in developing countries.

As shown in Table 4, the land prices in Korea are increasing at a very rapid rate. In 1953-1966 period, the annual compound rate of land price increase was 42%. After 1966 the land price increase

Table 4. Annual Growth Rate of Land, Construction Materials, and Consumer Prices

	1953-1966	1962-1966	1966-1974
Whole land	41.5%	n.a.	n.a.
Construction material	n.a.	50.9%	11.6%
Residential land	n.a.	37.9%[1]	33.5%
Consumer prices	19.2%	18.7%	11.6%

[1] The growth rate is for 1962-1967.

Source: *Seminar Report on Low-Income Housing, Seoul Matropolitan Government,* Scoul, 1974, p. 40 and p. 112, and Grimes, Jr., O.F., *Urban land and Public Policy,* IBRD, Washington, D.C., 1974, p. 58.

slowed down but was still higher than the price increase of construction materials and the consumer price increase.

Although the problem of rapid increases in land price was well
known it was not until 1967 that the government started to take any
action. Starting with the legislation of Real Property Speculation
Check Tax Law in 1967, several important laws to deal directly or
indirectly with land problems were enacted.

For our discussion, the major policy instruments available for the
government to control land price increases and to facilitate the supply of developed land particularly for low-income housing may be
categorized under four broad groups: taxation, advance acquisition,
land sale regulation, and readjustment.

Although the major objective of some taxes on land such as property tax and acquisition tax in Korea may not be to control land
prices, the control effect of those taxes on land prices through tax
capitalization should not be neglected. However, the property taxes
may not be so effective to control the land price increases. The empirical evidence is not conclusive.

A tax, a major objective of which was to control the land speculation was introduced in 1967. The base of the Real Property Speculation Check Tax may be expressed as $\pi = S - (1.10C + K + T)$, where
π is net assessable marginal profit, S is the sale price of the parcel,
C is its acquisition cost, K is the value of capital improvements added by the owner, and T is transfer expenses. The tax rate is 50%
of the assessed profits.[4] However, the tax was rendered quite ineffective to control land speculation due to the generous tax exemptions.
This was one of the major reason why the tax was recently replaced
by the supposedly more effective Capital Gains Tax. In addition,
betterment levies may apply to vacant parcels at the urban fringe which
have been acquired and developed by the public authorities. For areas
at the outskirts of Seoul, the rate is currently 30% to 40%.

In several laws such as City Planning Law of 1962 and the 1972
Law of Development Encouragement for Special Areas, special tax
exemptions are allowed for the sale of developed lands, particularly
for housing. For instance, the sales of land developed under these
laws are exempt from Land Speculation Control Tax, Business Tax,
Registration Tax, Acquisition Tax, Property Tax, City Planning
Tax, and License Tax.

The government sometimes can use its expropriation power to ac-

---

4. Grimes, Jr., O. F., *Urban Land and Public Policy: Social Appropriation of Betterment*, IBRD,
    Washington, D.C., 1974, p. 56.

quire land for its public investment projects as provided in the Expropriation Law of 1962. The compensation is fixed by the government on the basis of the land values which are assessed and announced prior to the initiation of the projects. Housing construction and site development are included in the public investment projects specified by the Law. Although it is powerful, it is generally regarded as a long and time-consuming process.

There is another method to acquire land in advance of the prospective projects in the future. The Land banking method was introduced in 1974. The Korean Land Bank can purchase land which is not properly utilized by the land owners, particularly the big industrial firms which own enormous amount of land, and sell it after development. The purchase and sale prices are determined on the basis of assessment.

Some other laws such as Land Use and Management Law of 1972, City Planning Law of 1962, and 1973 Special Law for Housing Improvement have very important provisions for the negotiated purchase of land for urban development, public housing and other public projects. According to these laws, the government can appraise and announce the land values of the areas within the city planning boundaries including its vicinity and the areas for future projects such as public housing and industrial estate. The prices are adjusted annually in accordance with the general price increase of other comparable areas which are not affected by the projects, and the announced land values will be applied for compensation and for public purchases.

Under several laws such as City Planning Law, Housing Construction Encouragement Law of 1972, 1973 Special Law for Housing Improvement, and Land Bank Law of 1974, the implementors of the land development projects are required to give a top priority to housing projects when they sell the developed land. For instance, the Korean Land Bank is required to give a first priority for the sale of developed land to low-income housing. The developers of the land readjustment projects are required to sell prior to anyone else up to 50% of the total cost-equivalent land to the housing construction projects. Further, if the government owns the land in the development area, it is required to sell the land for the construction of people's housing. Sometimes, the land owned by the government is required to be available free for the housing improvement projects.

Land Readjustment Project (LRP)[5] is a land development techni-

---

5. Hwang, M.C., *Self-Help Site Development in Korea: An Overall Evaluation,* paper presented to Habitat Forum, UN Conference on Human Settlements, Vancouver, 1976. More detailed discussion and evaluation were attempted in the paper.

que which has been extensively used in Korea, especially in large urban areas. For instance, about 58% of the total developed area in
Seoul was accounted for by LRP. It has become a major source of
developed urban land, in particular residential sites for middle-income
people. In recent years, more attention is, however, given to its potential usefulness in providing serviced land to low-income housing.
Before we attempt to evaluate the role of LRP, we must understand,
first of all, what it is and how they do it.

According to the Land Readjustment Law of 1966, there are four
groups who can undertake the LRP. An individual owner or a group
of land owners can initiate a LRP with an agreement from two thirds
of the land owners in the proposed project area and with final approval from the Government.

The Korean Housing Corporation can also undertake the LRP
which is specified in the city plans. Of course, the Construction
Ministry of Central Government can always initiate the LRP when
it is deemed necessary. However, most of the LRPs have been undertaken by the local governments, in particular the municipal
governments.

There are three distinctive phases of LRP: planning, development,
and readjustment, and each phase involves several processes as shown
in Figure 1. First, the initiator should prepare the LRP plan which
includes the existing and planned land use, an outline of the public
facilities and services to be provided, the estimated revenues and expenses, the allocation method of the total costs, and assessed land
values before and after the project. Once the outline plan has been
approved by the government, the initiator of the LRP has to formulate
a more detailed land readjustment plan with a map which includes
the proposed road networks, detailed land uses, and more importantly,
the allocation of the developed land to the original owners.

A land readjustment plan is vitally important and is a major feature
of the LRP method. In fact, the land-owners bear the whole cost
of the development including required land for public uses such as
roads and parks by giving up a certain percent of their land (cost-
equivalent land) and receiving back the developed land less the cost-
equivalent land near the original location.

After obtaining a public review and an approval from the Government and announcing the approved plan, the actual development work
starts. The final phase involves the actual allocation of the serviced
land to the original owners, the title registration of the ownership,
and the sale of the cost-equivalent land.

As mentioned above, the total cost is borne generally by the land
owners. Although other funding such as government subsidies, pay-

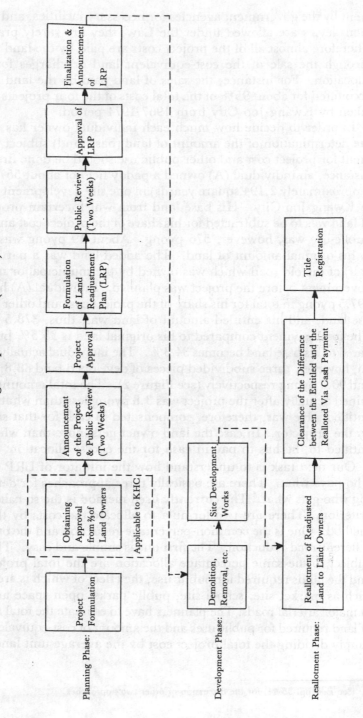

Figure 1. The Process of Land Readjustment Project for Governments and Korean Housing Corporation (KHC)

ment by the government agencies for necessary facilities, and betterment levies are allowed under the Law, they are rarely practiced.
Therefore almost all of the project costs are paid by the land owners
through the sale of the cost-equivalent land or charges for over-
allocation. For instance, the sales of land paid by the land owners
accounted for about 95% of the total costs of the four projects undertaken by Kwang-Joo City from 1967-1974 period.

In order to decide how much each individual owner has to pay,
the determination of the amount of land (base land) subject to payment for project cost and other public use should be done first. For
instance, an individual (A) owned a paddy field of about 557 pyong
(approximately 2,194 square yeards) in one site development project
in Kwang-Joo City. His base land from which certain proportion
of land was to be subtracted for his share of the project cost and other
public-use was, however, 576 pyong. About 19 pyong was added
to his original amount of land. The added land was a part (about
half) of the old road which was owned by the municipal or national
government before the project was planned. Individual (A) has paid
197.5 pyong in total for his share of the project cost and other public-
use land, and his entitled amount of land was, thus, 378.5 pyong.
The total payment compared to his original land is 35.5% but compared to his base land becomes 34.3%. The individual actually received, however, three subdivided pieces of developed land 88.8, 195.4,
and 90.5 pyong respectively (see Figure 2). The total amount he obtained actually after the project was 3.8 pyong less than what he was
entitled. He was, therefore, compensated in cash for that shortage
by the projector. In case the land owner gets more than what he is
entitled to, he has to pay in cash for the excess allocation.

Our next task is to understand how the initiator of LRP decides
who-pays-what. There are basically three approaches for determining who gets what.[6] The currently used method is the so-called area
criterion. There are two formula to allocate the costs by the area
method. One is the common-percentage-reduction and the other the
different-road-reduction. The first one is simple and easy. The costs
subject to the same percentage allocation are the total project cost
and the lands required for public use, the effect of which is areawide,
such as market site, school site, public parks, open space and part
of major arterial roads. The planners have to estimate the total amount
of land required for public uses and the amount of cost-equivalent land
simply dividing the total project cost by the average unit land vlaue

---

6. See *ibid*, pp. 36-44, for the discussion of other two approaches.

Figure 2. Reallotment of Developed Land to Land Owner A in One Project, KWANG-JOO City

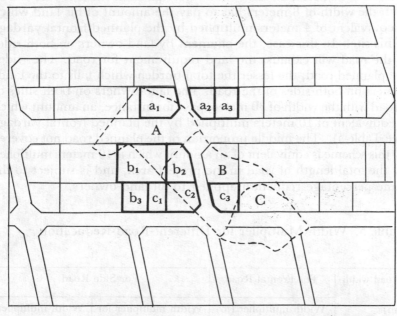

Legend

A = Original Land of Owner A

a$_i$ = Development Land Realloted to Owner A

of the area after the project. Depending upon the plan, the planner usually includes in the cost-equivalent land some of the land for public uses such as market and school sites which they can sell to the end-users.

The cost-equivalent land and the public-use land excluding the proportion of the road, the effect of which is assumed to be quite localized, comprise the land for which the same percentage reduction applies to every individual land-owner. Of course, the reduction rate is the percentage of the cost-equivalent and public-use land out of the total base land of the project.

The major proportion of the arterial roads are subject to the different reduction rate applied to the land-owner's base land through which the roads are planned to pass.

The reduction rate depends on the width of the planned road, and

the rate also varies depending whether it is a frontal or side road vis-
a-vis the planned site and whether it is in a residential or commercial
area. For instance, an individual whose planned site is to face a road
with the width of 8 meters has to pay the amount of his land which
is equivalent of 4 meters multiplied by the planned frontal yardage
of his site. In this case, the payment by land-owners on both sides
of the road will exhaust the land requirement for road. The wider
the planned road, the lesser the total burden which falls to the land-
owners on both sides of the road. The land-owners on both sides of
a road with the width of 30 meters pay, for instance, an amount which
is equivalent of 10 meters multiplied by the planned frontal yardage
(see Table 5). The middle proportion of the planned road not covered
by this scheme is equivalent of an amount which is 10 meters multiplied
by the total length of road in the project area, and is subject to the
same percentage reduction applied to all land-owners.

Table 5. Width Multiplier for Different-Road-Reducation

Road width	For Frontal Road	For Side Road	
(m)	Width multiplier (m)	Width multiplier for commercial zone	Width multiplier for other zone
6	3	1	0.75
8	4	1.333	1
10	4.5	1.472	1.104
12	5	1.667	1.25
20	7.4	2.467	1.85
25	8.7	2.9	2.175
30	10	3.333	2.50
35	11.2	3.767	2.825

Source: Sang-Bok Nam, *Reduction Rate of Land Readjustment,* Han-Yang University, Seoul, 1973 (unpublished master thesis), p. 29.

A sample survey in Young-Dong Project I in Seoul reveals that
the land-owners paid 5.9 pyong on the average for the side roads and
73.5 pyong for the frontal roads. Including the common reduction,
the total reduction of their land or payment amounts to about 40%
of their base land. The aggregated picture of all land-owners payments
and what they get after the project would look like Table 6.

One of the major reasons for the popularity of LRP as a land

Table 6. Post-Project Land Account of Am-Sa Land Readjustment

	Pyong	%
1. Land reallotted	248,784	48
2. Total payment in land	264,587	52
A. Road (different rate)	41,166	(8)
B. Same percentage reduction	223,421	(44)
(a) Cost-equivalent land	136,097	
Residential site	4,986	
Reserved site	20,000	
Land allotted over the entitled	60,000	
Apartment site (low-income)	36,000	
Market	2,000	
School site	13,111	
(b) Other public uses	87,324	
Parks	2,000	
Open space	12,631	
Water reservoir	3,177	
Road	44,049	
Road access to public uses and		
cost-equivalent land	25,467	
Total	513,371	100

(Approximately 418 Acres)

Source: *Am-Sa Land Readjustment Project Plan 1975*, Seoul City.

development technique in Korea may be that it benefits both the land-owners and the governments which generally undertake it. The LRP easily provides the needed developed land including the land for public uses such as roads and parks with no costs to the governments.

On the other hand, it creates an enormous added value to the landowners. The average land value increment after the projects undertaken in Seoul in 1967-1975 period was about seven times. Although the land-owners have to pay the project costs and public-use land by giving up some proportion of their land, most of the created value increments are returned to them through the allocation of the serviced land.

There are, however, several shortcomings and problems such as the method to determine the allocation of project costs and developed land, the participation of the land-owners in the planning process, and possible land speculation. These problems should be resolved to make the LRP more equitable as well as efficient.[7]

One more important question is: does the LRP produce the developed land cheap enough for the low-income housing? One way to answer this question is to compare the LRP with some alternative technique. For our analysis, let us suppose that the municipal governments or Korean Land Bank purchased the total area of LRP at the price before the project as shown in Tables 7 and 8 and sold the developed land.

Table 7. Sales Price of LRP Land

LRP in Seoul and Kwang-Joo City	Total area (1000 pyong)	Total land development cost (1000 Won)	Land value per pyong (Won)		Total area less public use land[1] (1000 pyong)
			Before the project	After the project (P)	
Young-Dong I	5,121	8,284,680	5,000	20,000	3,846.0
Young-Dong II	3,936	9,580,000	5,000	30,000	2,952.0
Young-Dong Addition	530	1,590,000	6,000	15,000	397.5
Chun-Ho	785	1,420,000	3,000	15,000	588.7
Kwang-Joo City Projects	2,104	1,999,748	2,105	5,100	1,578.0

[1] About 25% of the total area is allowed for public-use land

Source: Ministry of Construction and Seoul Metroplitan Government.

The expected prices of land developed in this way would be generally lower than the prices of the land developed by the LRP. For instance, the land prices of the Young-Dong II Project would be reduced about 68%. The average LRP land price of the area was 30,000 Won per pyong but if the area were developed by the alternative method, the land price per pyong would be 9,579 Won. Even if we allow for a quite modest profit rate, the expected price per pyong of the land developed by the alternative method would be substantially lower than the actual land prices of the LRP, as shown in Table 8. Given that the developed land accounts for 21% of the total cost for the public

7. See Hwang, M. C., *op. cit.*, for the discussion of these problems.

Table 8. Expected Land Price of Alternative Land Development

LRP Project in Seoul and Kwang-Joo City	Expected total cost for land purchase[1] (million Won)	Expected total development cost[2] (million Won)	Expected sales price of developed land per pyong[3] (Won)(A)	Expected sales price plus 10.5% profit per pyong[4] (Won)	Implicit profit rate of LRP $1 - \dfrac{A}{P}$ (%)
Young-Dong I	24,358.0	32,642.7	8,487	9,482.6	58
Young-Dong II	18,696.0	28,276.0	9,579	10,702.7	68
Young-Dong Addition	3,021.0	4,611.0	11,600	12,960.8	23
Chun-Ho	2,237.1	3,657.1	6,212	6,940.7	59
Kwang-Joo City Project	4,207.5	6,207.2	3,934	4,395.5	23

[1] It is estimated by multiplying the total area less the existing roads (about 5%) with the land price per pyong before the project.

[2] Expected total development cost equals the total land development cost plus the expected cost for land purchase.

[3] Expected sales price of developed land per pyong equals the expected total development cost divided by the total area less public-use land.

[4] Since no data are available, the profit rate of 10.5% is assumed on the basis of 1970 input-output table of Korea. The value added ratio other than wages and salaries, depreciation and indirect tax are 11% for non-housing construction, 10% for public works, and 10% for other construction.

housing in Seoul, the 68% reduction of the land price would be equivalent of 14% reduction of the total housing cost, and it would of course increase the people's affordability of housing.

The major reason for the relatively high land price of the LRP is that the initiator of the LRP attempts to minimize the land reduction of the land-owners and at the same time to make the project attractive by creating an enormous value increment for them. For instance, the implicit profit rates of the LRPs undertaken in Seoul and Kwang-Joo City range 23% to 68%. Although it is not required for the government to obtain an agreement on the LRP from the land-owners, they normally try to reduce the possible objections and confrontations from the land-owners involved by making the projects attractive.

Given the available policy instruments provided in the various legislation for public housing, the supply of urban land could be done at a much lower cost, either through some alternative land development method or through a modified LRP approach.

14

An Analytic Study of the Housing Policy for the Improvement of Squatter Settlements: A Case Study of Seoul, Korea

Woo Suh Park

Introduction

In a rapidly developing and urbanizing country like Korea, housing has significant economic, social, and political ramifications. Rapid urbanization has taken place primarily because the rural poor have migrated into large cities for employment opportunities and better living conditions. Consequently urban housing has become scarce in quantity, expensive in price, and overcrowded to the extent that doubling-up and tripling-up are commonplace. Coincident with these problems is that of the urban squatter settlements, which have become widespread and generate tremendous urban problems.

The Korean government has devised numerous measures to tackle the squatter problem. The government's effort has been successful only in a limited sense; it improved the city's physical appearance through slum clearance and renewal. It is, however, subject to serious criticisms; and two of them are particularly significant: inconsistency in policies which often resulted in waste of resources, and deprivation of the individual rights of those directly affected. Another, equally serious criticism, is the intolerable financial burden that relocates have to bear.

Such criticisms have forced the government to change its policy direction; and the recently considered, new policy measures are geared to selective redevelopment, rehabilitation, and immediate legalization, with reviewed housing standards for squatters. The other important feature of the new policy is its emphasis on comprehensiveness. Unlike preceding measures, it requires the city to integrate squatter programs with the city's long-range plan that has both physical and social elements. The key concept lies in gradual improvement of living conditions for the squatters.

Although it has not yet materialized, the idea is highly commendable. Obviously, more in-depth studies must be carried out; and a set of alternative courses of action generated and evaluated in terms of the legal, institutional and financial implications of each before the new policy is firmly set. Additionally, the on-going policies and programs ought to be rigorously assessed to gain insight from past experiences.

An Overview of Squatter Problems in Seoul

The first question that must be answered is, what is a squatter home? The definition should differ from one country to another, depending upon the degree of squatter settlement concentration and the definition of housing quality and/or standards.

The most difficult task in the process of defining substandard housing is to clarify the difference between a substandard unit and an illegal unit. Normally the degree of substandardness is measured in terms of qulitative housing standards, whereas illegal housing is defined simply by the absence of a legal title to the property. Generally, the major criterion for determining substandard housing is insufficiency of habitability. A.L. Mabogunje points out that[1] the first step in measuring habitability is to consider the various types of functions that standards are meant to perform in shelter provision. In reviewing the standards for shelter provision, especially in developing countries, he offered a threefold division as follows:[2]

1) Space-Use and Density Standards;
2) Health and Sanitation Standards;
3) Community Facilities and Services Standards.

According to him, the first category includes minimum lot sizes, number of buildings per unit area, building bulk per unit, number of persons per room or number of persons per area. The second grouping, technological or performance standards, is intended to define the quality of environment, particularly in terms of the quality of construction, the type of materials that must be used, the quality of services that can be offered, or tolerable levels of toxicity. The third

---

1. A.L. Mabogunje et al., *Shelter Provision in Developing Countries* (New York, John Wiley & Sons: 1978) P47-P48.
2. Ibid.

grouping defines the lower and upper limits of the size of population, and the area or distance to be served by particular amenities or community facilities.

In Korea, however, the measuring criteria for substandard housing are primarily physical and legal. The ministry of Construction (MOC) utilizes criteria somewhat a mixture of substandard and illegal housing as follows:[3]

— floor area is less than 7 pyong[4] (substandard)
— illegal housing on public land (illegal)
— housing without permission (illegal)
— housing with inadequate building materials such as shacks (illegal or substandard)
— housing without electricity, water, and sewer etc. (substandard or illegal)

The criteria used by the City of Seoul are similar to those of the MOC. The acquisition of proper title and building permission are

Figure 1: Squatter Clasifications and Pertinent Measures

	Classification	Policy Measures
	Illegally built/ improperly titled and substandard housing	- Combination of Clearnace and Redevelopment
Squatters	Illegally built, but physically sound housing	- Either Clearance or Legalization
	Legally built/properly titled, but physically substandard housing	- Redevelopment
	Scattered illegal housing	- Either Clearance or Housing Redevelopment (individually)
Blighted Housing	Legalized Old Blighted Housing	- Urban Renewal

---

3. MOC, *the Inventory of National Housing* (1976).
4. One Pyong is equal to 3.3058m² and to 35.583ft². Seven pyong are approximately equivalent to 249ft².

two major legal criteria.[5] According to these criteria, substandard housing includes both the legal but physically substandard as well as all illegally built housing. In this paper, therefore, the term (squatter) refers to both these categories of housing; i.e., legally and properly titled but substandard housing, and illegally built, improperly titled housing.[6] Figure 1 classifies squatter homes accordingly.

The total number of urban squatter units in 1979 in Korea amounted to 413,914, representing 17.3% of total housing units, 5,393,150; and 26.4% of them were concentrated in Seoul. Since Seoul is the capital city and much of the squatter improvement effort has been exerted there, this paper focuses its discussion on squatter problems in Seoul. According to the 1970 illegal housing survey, there were 187,554 squatter housing units in Seoul. Among them 13,556 units were cleared in 1970. At the end of 1970, another count found 173,998 units untouched, comprising 29% of the total housing stock. The city government executed such a strong clearance policy during 1970-1978, that the number of illegal housing units declined from 173,998 to 87,723. The latter figure was still high, given the fact that it represented almost 10% of the city's total housing stock.

Table 1: Illegal Housing in Seoul (1970-1978)

Year	Population	Number of Households	Number of Dwellings	Number of Illegal units at the end of the year	# of Cleared Illegal Units
1970	5,536,377	1,097,432	600,367	173,998	13,556
1971	5,850,925	1,151,078	624,546	166,957	7,041
1972	6,076,143	1,182,655	665,182	164,417	2,540
1973	6,289,556	1,215,538	700,754	160,085	4,332
1974	6,541,500	1,273,678	736,656	154,501	5,584
1975	6,889,470	1,410,748	763,084	134,462	20,039
1976	7,254,958	1,357,281	802,571	115,634	18,828
1977	7,525,629	1,529,323	838,514	100,715	14,919
1978	7,823,195	1,510,965	892,084	87,723	12,992
1979	8,114,021	1,713,193	936,349	160,686	7,178

Source: City of Seoul, *Housing Survey* (1978),
       City of Seoul, *City Year Book* (1979, 1980)

---

5. The City of Seoul, *City Book* (1977).
6. The definition of squatter homes excludes the illegal housing which is not in the designated housing rehabilitation area; these units are generally scattered and small in number.

An illegal housing survey was conducted in 1979; and it was extensive enough to cover traditionally excluded areas such as the resettlement area, annexed area, etc. It found the total number of illegals to be 160, 686 units. Table 1 shows the annual number of illegal housing units and units cleared.

If one closely considers the housing standard for squatter structures, it is easy to understand the necessity and the difficulty of housing redevelopment due to their location at river banks (41%) or hillside (44.1%),[7] and to their poor quality standards.

It is interesting to note the change in building materials used for squatter housing construction between 1970 and 1979. The majority of squatter units were crude shacks or board framed huts in 1970, but 83.5% of the total squatter units built in 1979 used cement bricks. Thus the recently constructed are much more sturdy and solid.[8]

The average lot size, as shown in Table 2, was 18.5 pyong which was about half of the average lot size in Seoul and in the nation. This small lot size was quite far from the required minimum size, 27 pyong. More than 70% of all squatter units fell into this category.

Table 2: Lot Size of Squatter Dwellings in Seoul (1979)

(Unit: %)

	less than 10 pyong*	10-20 Pyong*	More than 20 pyong*	Average (in pyong)*
Squatter (Seoul)	37.3	39.1	23.6	18.5
Seoul	3.1	12.1	84.7	40.9
All Cities (Nation)	2.9	11.6	88.5	44.3
Mandatory Size : larger than 27 pyong				

Source: Article 39-2, National Construction Act.
Economic Planning Board, *Population and Housing Census, 1980*.
*One pyong is equal to 3.3058 m² and to 35.583 ft²

The dwelling unit size for squatter homes follows a pattern similar to the lot size. As shown in Table 3, the average unit size of these

---

7. The City of Seoul, *Housing Survey* (1978).
8. Graduate School of Environmental Science, Seoul National University, *A Study of Housing Standards among Squatters, and the Children's Problem in Seoul* (1980).

dwellings was 15 pyong, far smaller than that in Seoul or in the nation as a whole. About one half of the squatter units were very small with a size of less than 10 pyong.

Table 3: Dwelling Unit Size among Squatters in Seoul (1979)

(Unit: %)

Area	Size less than 10 pyong*	10-20 Pyong*	More than 20 pyong*	Average (in pyong)*
Squatter (Seoul)	50.3	40.7	9.0	15.0
Seoul	7.6	38.5	53.9	24.2
All Cities (Nation)	8.9	42.8	48.3	22.0

Mandatory Size: larger than 18 pyong for single family detached unit

Source: Article 30-1, The Housing Promotion Act.
Economic Planning Board, *Population and Housing Census, 1980.*
*One pyong is equal to 3.3058 m² and to 35.583 ft²

The statistics for number of rooms per unit and per household, as shown in Table 4, were 2.9 and 1.8 respectively. Considering 5 to persons per squatter household, the average number of persons per room is estimated to be 3, so that it is easy to detect the overcrowding in squatter housing.

Table 4: Number of Rooms Per Unit and Household In Squatter Housing in Seoul (1979)

(Unit: Rooms)

	Average # of Rooms Per Unit	Average # of Rooms Per Household
Seoul (Squatter)	2.9	1.8
Seoul	3.9	2.1
All Cities (Nation)	3.4	2.2

Source: See Footnote #8

The average monthly income among the squatters varied depending upon the location. The monthly income per household in 1979 was 230,000 won, which was only half the average monthly income among nonsquatter area residents in Seoul. (Table 5)

Table 5: Average Monthly Income of Squatter Households in Seoul
          (1979)

(Unit: Won)

Distict Income	Sangke Dong	Shindang 3 Dong	Kuro Dong	Shyhung 2 Dong	Average for Squatters	Rest of the City
Income	202,500	300,700	257,500	179,400	230,700	426,700

Source: See footnote #8.

Approximately 70-75% of the their monthly income was spent on necessities and the rest was put into savings. The average living cost-income ratio for Seoul was about 80% during the same period.[9] A study done by the Research Institute for Urban Study, Yonsei University, indicated that the average saving-income ratio was 23.7% among squatter families in 1970.[10] This implies that the amount of savings among squatter families has increased since 1970 in both absolute and relative terms. It also indicates that squatter dwellers have a relatively high propensity for saving as compared to that of others.

In spite of their negative aspects, the squatter dwellings provide least-cost shelter for new in-migrants and the urban poor. Although they are physically substandard and structurally inadequate, they provide relatively easy access to public facilities and are relatively inexpensive.

Table 6: Squatter Housing Units by Location in Seoul (1966)

(Unit: Dwelling Unit)

Location	No. of Squatter Structures
Hillside	39,923
Flood Plain	13,567
River Bank	4,502
Site for Street	6,167
Private Land	60,550
Others	11,941
	136,650

Source: Graduate School of Public Administration, Seoul National University, *Administrative Cases*

---

9. Economic Planning Board, *Important Economic Indicators* (1980).
10. Institute of Urban Studies and Development, Yonsei University, *Rural-Urban Migrants, Squatter Settlements and Low-Income Housing Policy in Seoul* (1979).

Historical Perspectives of Housing Policies for Squatters in Seoul

The City of Seoul initiated the first Illegal Housing Survey in 1966 in order to formulate long-term, comprehensive control measures. As shown in Table 6, there were 135,650 illegal housing units (squatter) or 27.8% of the total housing stock of Seoul in 1966.

The following four major tools were responsible for the systematic control over, and reduction of, squatter units during this period.

1) Building Clearance Program

The government's housing policies for squatters in the early period relied heavily upon clearance and relocation. The first massive scale squatter housing clearance project was undertaken by the city in 1967. This was essentially a police action, whereby detection of newly-built units led to physical removal and tenant eviction. It relied on formal and informal systems of reporting and surveillance, including on-site inspections, aerial mapping and reporting from local administrators and community dwellers themselves. The project was overly ambitious as it attempted to clear all the squatter settlements of 136,650 units within a three-year period, with no alternative living accommodations provided for the relocatees.

2) Citizens Apartment Program

In 1968, this program was inaugurated as the first comprehensive plan for on-site, low-income housing attempted by the city. Initially designed as a three-year program involving construction of 90,000 units (1,000 structures), only 16,000 units were completed. The collapse of a building and an ensuing scandal concerning the administration of the program brought about its discontinuation.

3) Gwang Ju Satellite City Plan

The construction of 16,000 units of citizen's apartments was far too few to accommodate over 230,000 displaced families. Concurrent with the Citizen's Apartment Program, this plan, the implementation of which began in 1968, was designed to relocate existing squatter homes and thereby divert population concentration from Seoul. The large scale removals to the relocation area, located approximately 20Km southeast of Seoul, involved 320,000 people on

240,000 pyong.[11] The program was terminated in 1971 after a series of massive demonstrations took place protesting government policy on land sales and the provision of poor srvices.

The early squatter clearance project was ineffective; although half of the total squatter families were relocated by 1970, the total number of squatter settlements increased by 30% in the same year. In other words, many relocated families moved back to the city in search of job opportunities and urban services.

Up to this point, squatter settlement policy had been ill-conceived and misguided; squatter settlements were regarded simply as a social disease and the people's welfare was totally overlooked.

4) *Selective Legalization and Self-help Improvement*

Recognizing the failure of the physical clearance and relocation policy, the city government began to legalize squatter homes constructed prior to 1966. They were subject to improvement by means of the self-help method.

In addition to legalization the city conducted its second Illegal Housing Survey on June 20, 1970. In accordance with the survey findings, the city attempted to improve squatter dwellings which were located on sites where land use changes were possible in compliance with the Comprehensive Planning Act. Thos program involed site-by-site unit improvement and legalization. In order to expedite the program, the city decided to assume the cost for infrastructures in the range of 50 to 100% of the total.

Table 7: Accomplishments of Legalization and Self-help Improvement (1968-1973)

Project	Number of Project Districts	Total	Size in Pyong National & Municipal Land	Private- Land	Number of Units	Year
Legalization	49	300,367	235,901	64,466	10,161	1968-1973
Improvement	55	408,413	347,688	60,725	10,125	1972-1973
Total	104	708,780	583,589	125,191	20,286	

Source: City of Seoul

---

11. Yung-Hee Rho, *New Town Development* (Seoul, Bakyong Sa; 1973), P. 186-190.

The accomplishments of the selective legalization and self-help improvement project are shown in Table 7.

The impact of the program was measurable in respect to squatter home improvement and squatter family participation. Since the program, however, proceeded without any legal support, there were limitations to disposal of public land and legalization. In addition to these, the face-lift improvement effort failed to upgrade the structural standards for squatter dwellings, and failed to used as a permanent control measure.

Recognizing the shortcomings of on-going squatter policies, the City of Seoul enacted the Housing Rehabilitation Act in 1973[12] in order to provide legal support for housing rehabilitation. The act stipulated that local government would provide infrastructure and community services, and it allowed the governments to take full control over the rehabilitation projects of squatters. With this legal support, the city prepared the rehabilitation plan for 126,000 units by means of upgrading rather than relocation.

The basic principles manifested in this plan were:

— The municipalities reserved the right to sell the public lands in the designated project areas which were conceded by the central government, and to use the money for project costs;

— In order to imporve and recover function, and for aesthetic reasons, the Comprehensive Planning Act and Building Code would be applied to the projects;

— In order to secure open space, the squatters in those areas not eligible for rehabilitation were to be relocated in peripheral areas and to be subsidized with limited amounts of thier relocation costs or be granted a priority ticket for public housing;

— The squatter homes constructed after June 20, 1970 were to be removed no matter how sound they were.

The funds from the sale of public lands were invested to provide public services and infrastructures in project areas. The construction of community facilities was to be carried out through the joint efforts of the city and its residents. Once the necessary facilities were completed, and physical requirements had been met by all households, residents were allowed to buy their land from the government. The purchasing prices were based on prior appraisal, determined from market value before development.

During the period 1973 to 1977, the achievements of the project,

---

12. The Housing Rehabilitation Act of 1973 was a contingency act to rehabilitate squatter homes and to designate project areas by 1981.

as shown in Table 8, amounted to 32, 748 units rehabilitated and
3,727 units relocated in 88 project districts. The sum accounted for
a mere 29% of the target units.

Table 8: Rehabilitated and Relocated Units in Seoul (1973-1977)

Year	Number of Districts	Size in Pyong	Total of Units	Number of Units	
				Rehabilitated	Relocated
1973	36	700,000	20,286	20,286	—
1974	4	22,000	667	552	115
1975	10	65,000	1,418	1,236	182
1976	23	300,000	10,028	7,320	2,708
1977	15	142,000	4,046	3,354	722
Total	88	1,229,000	36,475	32,748	3,727

Source: The City of Seoul, *The City Year Book* (1978).

The impact of this project was also minor at best. Again, the project failed to relate itself to the affordabilities of low income squatter families. The majority of lots were too small to be rehabilitated, and the securing of public lands for parks and roads was also difficult. Information concerning dwelling unit size is unavailable; but, as shown in Table 2-3, more than 50% of the total squatter dwellers lived in houses of less than 10 pyong in 1979. This implies that the situation in the early 1970s was worse than in 1979. The requirement that any area legalized must not exceed one hundred meters above sea level was particularly unreasonable. This disqualified the majority of mountainside areas.

Recognizing the failure of the housing rehabilitation policy for squatters provided by the Housing Rehabilitation Act of 1973, the City of Seoul a ttempted to implement the redevelopment policy by means of clearing out squatter homes and constructing new dwelling units on the same sites. This new approach began with the premise that an efficient and effective redevelopment policy should be well coordinated with overall city functions, such as location, community facilities, etc., and consider aesthetic factors as well. The city adopted the Urban Renewal Act in 1976 (December 31), replacing the Urban Redevelopment Section of the Comprehensive Planning Act which had been established after the Korean war (1950-1953). The renewal act of 1976 provided criteria for designating a redevelopment area, the qualifications of an implementing agency and procedures, and methods and procedures for participation of private developers, etc.

As mentioned above, the redevelopment policy was implemented by means of demolishing existing housing in a designated area and constructing new housing units, mainly multi-family units. Since this policy is in effect still, this paper attempts to analyze the policy in greater depth.

With the principle of self-help development, the redevelopment policy is incorporated into the Saemaul movement. In addition to providing technical and administrative assistance and community facilities, the new policy initiated a loan and subsidy system for redevelopment, which is the major difference from the previous policy supported by the Housing Rehabilitation Act of 1973.

The principles envisaged in the new policy were:
— to enlarge the eligible redevelopment area;
— to secure maximum open space;
— to predesignate the re-allocation and lot arrangement;
— to adopt project priorities in accordance with the financial capabilities of the inhabitants.

The households in those areas not eligible for redevelopment are to be relocated on the outskirts of the city which are served with water and sewer systems. Families relocated to these areas will be able to purchase their lots at subsidized prices, with payments extended over five to ten years. The government intends to finance such areas through the sale of lots adjacent to the areas, which are expected to bring inflated prices once the program area locations have been made public. The voluntary relocation is promoted by means of issuing priority tickets for public housing.

The redevelopment procedures begin with the government's designation of areas eligible for redevelopment. Organizing the citizen's self-help redevelopment committee, demolition of existing housing, construction of community facilities prior to construction of new housing, and participation of the private developer are the main features of the procedures.

The important qualifications[13] for designation are that the areas contain a high density of squatters and are areas where the relocated families can be accommodated. Hence, the redevelopment areas are where community facilities can be constructed. Designated areas are subject to acquire land use change. The city of Seoul, however, excluded the following areas for redevelopment.[14]

---

13. Article 3, The Housing Rehabilitation Act of 1973.
14. The City of Seoul, *The City Year Book* (1978).

— All areas in which access roads of minimum specified width, water, and sewer system cannot be constructed;
— All areas which exceed the limitations of 70m in hight or 30° in slope;
— All areas in flood plains;
— All areas of strategic military use, etc.

In order to increase land use efficiency, priority is given to the construction of multi-family dwelling units meeting the public housing standard in size, i.e., equal to or below 25 pyong. In the case of apartment construction, the permitted floor-area-ratio (FAR) and open-space-ratio (OSR) are 20% to 25% and less than 150% (3 to 5 stories) respectively. For walk-up apartment construction on public lands, the permitted FAR is 35% to 40%.

The redevelopment program requires participation of a developer in order to increase the effectiveness of construction for public facilities and dwellings.

In order to maximize the effectiveness of the program, a land use plan for a designated area is required. The plan requires the reservation of public roads for up to 15% of the total area. A rearrangement and redistribution system of a lot is utilized to minimize smaller lot size problems. In other words, a minimum lot size requirements is exercised in the procedure of lot rearrangement. Once the size is rearranged, the site is redistributed to the land owners in accordance with the original ownership.

The major financial resource for community facilities comes from the sale of public lands. Costs for housing construction come mainly from Saemaul Deposit made by the squatter families, and the city

Table 9: Balance Sheet for Urban Renewal in Seoul (1979)

(Unit: 1,000 Won)

Revenue		Expenditure		Surplus
Sale of Public Land	10,904,726	Public Facilities	3,045,361	
Transfer and Others	2,605,274	Clearance of Hillside	3,716,799	
Public Housing Funds	5,600,000	Loan	11,200,000	
		Others	303,000	
	19,110,000		18,265,679	844,321

Source: The City of Seoul.

loans out the limited amount of the costs from public housing funds. As shown in Table 9, the revenue from sale of public lands accounted for 60% of the total urban renewal expenditure in 1979.

As mentioned above, in order to ease the financial burdens for squatter families, the city gives loans from public housing funds. The amounts of loans vary by the housing types. Assistance from public housing funds in 1979 totalled 11 billion Won (Table 10).

Table 10: Financial Assistance from Public Housing Funds in Seoul (1979)

Housing Type	Number of Households	Amount of Assistance (1,000 won)	Sub-Total (1,000 won)
Apartment	1,750	3,000/household	5,250,000
Walk-up Apartment	2,080	2,500/household	5,200,000
Single Detached Unit	375	2,000/household	750,000
Total	4,205		11,200,000

Source: City of Seoul.

Information regarding accomplishment in 1980 is unavailable. The city, however, had planned to subsidize 70% of the total redevelopment units (108,533 units) in 1970 with an average of 2,500,000 won per household.

In addition to direct financial assistance, the government also utilized a tax exemption scheme (national and local taxes) involving property tax, registration tax, etc., in order to ease financial burdens.

The redevelopment project was inaugurated in 1978. The pro-

Table 11: Redevelopment Plan in Seoul (1978)

Year	Number of Districts	Size in Pyong	Number of Units	Number of Units by Project Redevelopment	Clearance
1978	15	146,000	4,438	3,915	523
1979	31	580,000	14,844	12,003	2,877
1980	35	808,000	24,101	19,678	4,423
1981	30	587,000	16,142	13,196	2,910
Total	111	2,121,000	59,525*	48,792	10,733

*The number of units removed from hillsides, 34, is excluded.
Source: The City of Seoul, *The City Year Book* (1979).

ject was established to redevelop 59,525 units which in 1977, excluding rehabilitated units, remained from the inventory of the second Illegal Housing Survey of 1970 (Table 11).

The Third Illegal Housing Survey, however, was conducted in March and April of 1979, and detected an additional 72,963 illegal structures. The initial redevelopment plan had to be revised to include these additional units. As shown in Table 12, the revised plan was to redevelop 89,870 units in 227 illegal housing districts which excluded 35,503 cleared and legalized units and 61,063 units of redeveloped, legal housing.

Table 12: New Inventory for the Redevelopment Plan in Seoul (1979)

Legal Status	Number of Units to be Redevelopd	Number of Units to be Financed	Estimated Financial Assistance (in 1,000 won)
Illegal Housing	89,870	71,896	
Legal Housing	61,063	36,637	
Total	150,933	108,533	271,332,500

Source: City of Seoul, *The City Year Book* (1980).

Table 13 shows the number of redeveloped units in 1979 and the number of units to be redeveloped in 1980 and 1981.

Table 13: Revised Redevelopment Plan in Seoul (1980)

Year	Number of Districts	Number of Units
1979	23	8,471 *
1980	25	6,677
1981 and later	184	135,785
Total	227	150,933
		(5.98 million pyong)

* The figure represents the 3 years accomplishment through 1979.
Source: City of Seoul, *The City Year Book* (1980).

The revised plan will redevelop 10,000 to 15,000 units annually over the next 10-year period, and the estimated annual project costs are 40 billion won. The construction costs for infrastructure and community facilities account for 10.7 billion won, and an additional expenditure for financial assistance for 29.6 billion won.

As shown in Table 14, the project involved a total of 13 districts with 2,417 units for redevelopment. The initiation of a loan program drawn from public housing funds was introduced to the redevelopment program in 1979. The proposed loan amounted to 11.2 billion won (Table 9).

Table 14: Accomplishment of the Redevelopment Program in Seoul (1979)

	Number of Units				Costs (1,000 won)	
Total	Apt.	Walk-Up Apt.	Single Family	Total	Loan	Public Facilities
2,417	818	1,495	104	7,985,735	6,108,500	1,877,235

Source: City of Seoul, *The City Year Book* (1980).

the average construction and land acquisition costs to be charged a household for an average 15 pyong apartment in 1979 were 3 million won for an owner-occupied unit and 6 million won for a renter-occupied unit (Table 15).

Table 15: Average Redevelopment Cost per Household in Seoul (1979)

Unit: 1,000 won

	Owner-Occupied			Renter-Occupied		
	Total	Loan	Charge	Total	Loan	Charge
Land	—	—	—	3,000	—	3,000
Construction	6,000	3,000	3,000	6,000	3,000	3,000
Total	6,000	3,000	3,000	9,000	3,000	6,000

Source: City of Seoul.

The actual accomplishment data for 1980 are not available. The proposed figures for 1980, however, are shown in Table 16. The total units to be redeveloped were 6,677 in 25 districts which included 20 new ones plus 5 still in progress since 1979.

Table 16:   Redevelopment Plan in Seoul (1980)

Projects	Number of Districts	Size in Pyong	Number of Units	Project Cost (1,000 won)		
				Total	Loan	Public Facilities
Continuing from 1979	5	51,297	1,539	4,298,300	3,308,500	989,800
New	20	192,722	5,138	15,796,665	12,691,500	3,105,165
Total	25	244,019	6,677	20,583,900	16,000,000	4,583,900

Source: City of Seoul, *The City Year Book* (1980).

Evaluation of the Redevelopment Policy for Squatter Areas

The objectives of the current policy emphasize recovering the urban functions and aesthetic elements of the city by means of the physical removal and upgrading of squatter homes rather than by improving the social welfare of squatter families. Although this ill-conceived and misguided policy has contributed to improving the city's aesthetics considerably, it has brought heavy financial burdens to squatter families, destroyed community integration, downgraded living environments through relocation activities, and consequently engendered sprawls of squatter dwellings on peripheral areas of the city. It is, therefore, difficult to justify the policy objectives of the current program.

The redevelopment program, involving primarily demolition and renewal in the project areas, has some merit in its renewal of densely developed squatter areas. Furthermore the program achieves the physical improvement of squatter life by securing open space, roads, and the improvement of housing standards.

However one has to look at the negative side as well which involves aggravation of the housing shortage and the heavy financial burden on the squatters. More specifically:

1) The program weakens self-help ability due to the heavy financial burdens imposed. In the case of Wolke Dong project, Do Bong Ku, completed in late 1981, approximately 100 units were removed and apartments constructed to accommodate 136 households. The average unit size is 19 pyong. The total cost amounted to 1,245,000,000 won. The residents' share of the total redevelopment cost was 67% or 830,000,000 won, and 6,100,000 won was charged each household. The mandatory contribution of each household in the redevelopment areas was

extremely high considering the level of their incomes. The average monthly income and expenditure per household in Seoul wer 295,101 won and 236,899 won respectively in 1980.[15]

2) Uniform clearance procedures which ignored individual housing conditions increased total redevelopment costs and exacerbated the housing shortage problem.

3) The statutory requirement that any area redeveloped must not exceed 70m above sea level and a slope of 30° is unreasonable. This requirement would exclude most of the potentially designatable areas on the mountain sides.

4) Another major criticism with respect to the government criteria for selecting target areas concerns the land and house requirements. The minimum lot size and dwelling unit size required in the Construction Law are 27 pyong and 18 pyong respectively.[16] As shown in Table 2-2 and 2-4 the average lot size is 18.5 pyong and the dwelling unit size is 15 pyong. This uniform code enforcement excludes virtually all but middle and upper income housing developments.

5) The program encouraged construction of multi-family dwelling units from the standpoint of economizing land use as well as aesthetic and visual improvement. However this form of housing arrangement would destroy for squatter dwellers the sense of community they once enjoyed while living in squatter communities.

6) The upgrading and improvement of physical housing standards without income growth and change in attitude toward housing maintenance might expedite the physical deterioration of dwelling units.

As an easy physical control measure implemented in those areas not eligible for either rehabilitation or redevelopment, a relocation policy has been utilized. The procedure begins with the notification of relocation within a one year period. If the families receive the notfication to move within the required period, they are eligible for both a priority ticket for public housing accommodation and financial assistance in moving.[17] Otherwise, all families in the area will be removed by force.

The statistics for relocation, as shown in Table 17, indicate that 55,000 units were removed by the end of 1978, and 48,000 newly

---

15. Economic Planning Board, *Annual Report on the Family Income and Expenditure Survey,* 1980.
16. The required minimum dwelling size for a single detached unit is 18 pyong and for a multi-family unit is 12 pyong.
17. The amount of financial assistance for moving was 500,000 won per household in 1980.

formed units were being cleared. Since the relocation measure removed about 90% of the targeted units, it might imply the successful
achievement of the measure statistically. However, the Third Illegal
Housing Survey done in 1979 indicated that there were 30,000 additional units to be removed.

Table 17: Statistics for Relocation (1973-1979)

Year	# of Units Being Removed*	# of Newly Formed Units Being Removed
by 1973	7,183	44,953
1974	4,917	749
1975	18,621	707
1976	8,300	783
1977	10,873	777
1978	4,775	494
1979	4,761	—
Total	59,930	48,103**

* The units being removed for redevelopment are not counted.
** The number excludes the units being removed in 1979 which are not
available.
Source: The City of Seoul, *The City Year Book and Housing White Paper* (1978).

The City of Seoul, therefore, revised the relocation plan to remove
5,000 units annually for the next 6 years (Table 18).

Talbe 18: Relocation Plan by Location in Seoul (1980)
(Unit: number of units)

Hillside	River Bank	Construction Site	Land Re-arrangement District	Others	Total
2,100	607	1,205	406	609	5,000

Source: City of Seoul, *The City Year Book* (1980).

The relocation policy has many difficulties and is unlike redevelopment which provides a better living environment.
The difficulties are summarized below.

1) The subsidy for moving expenses (50,000 won/household) and the issuing of a priority ticket for public housing accommodation do not help the relocated families because of their low income levels. In the case of the Jamshil Public Housing Project,[18] 45% of total units (19,180 units), or 8,170 units were allocated to accommodate the relocated families in 1975. The majority of the families could not afford to purchase the unit despite their priority ticket. Hence, they sold (transferred) the ticket at a marginal price to a third person.

2) The majority of the families who sold their tickets moved to other places and built new squatter homes. A survey done by S.K. Lee[19] indicated that about 43% of the interviewees who lived in squatter dwellings had moved from other squatter homes. This implies that the physical removal of squatter homes does not solve the problem; instead it causes new squatter settlement in peripheral areas, and a vicious cycle continues.

3) The reckless relocation disintegratd the sense of community ties among relocated families,[20] and the moving expense subsidy

Table 19: Ratio of Housing Demolition to New Housing Construction in Seoul (1970-1979)

Year	# of Units Demolished*	# of Units Constructed	Ratio (%)
1970-1973	27,469	122,660	22.4
1974	5,584	45,182	12.4
1975	20,039	52,925	37.9
1976	18,828	55,847	33.7
1977	14,919	61,909	24.1
1978	12,992	79,574	16.3
1979	9,420	52,354	18.0
Total	109,251	470,451	23.2

*The figures include units removed not only for relocation, but also for redevelopment.
Source: City of Seoul, *City Year Book* (1976-1980).

18. Jin Ku Kim, "The Housing Project for Jamshil Complex," *Housing* (Korea Housing Corporation; 1977).
19. S.K. Lee, *A Study of Urban Squatters,* Dissertation of Graduate School of Environmental Science, Seoul National University, 1979.
20. Institute of Urban Studies and Development, Yonsei University, *Rural-Urban Migration, Squatter Settlements and Low-Income Housing Policies* (1979), P 38-40.

was insufficient compensation for the families' fincnaical losses. The families' financial burdens were doubled by moving and finding a new place to settel.

4) There is no supplementary measure to protect those who live in squatter homes as renters. Hence, the relocation might generate new squatter dwellings not only for the owners to be relocated but also for the renters in those units.

5) The redevelopment and relocation also resulted in attenuating the housing shortage problem. The number of housing units removed by relocation 1970 though 1979 was 109,000 while that of new housing construction was 470,000 during the same period (Table 19). The removed units accounted for about 23.2% of the total new housing construction. Considering the high rate of housing shortage, 38.5% of total households in Seoul in 1979,[21] the massive demolition of squatter housing aggravated the situation especially for low income families.

Mitigation Measures for Squatter Housing Policies

If one conceives only the physical improvement of squatter areas, the redevelopment approach has offered and would continuously offer great potential for accomplishing the housing policy objectives. The program was designed to clean up squatter settlements in the city core areas and build new residential complexes on them in accordance with a comprehensive plan. No other planning tool would provide the possibility for such radical change.

Although the redevelopment program has much merit for reviving the city functionally and improving its aesthetics it is nevertheless, subject to many criticizms. If the city government is to solve the problem of housing shortage, attention must be given to those segments of society that are most desperately in need of housing, and not to those already in possession of homes. Even if the government is concerned more about the quality of the urban environment, workable and reasonable measures designed to improve the status of existing houses would be more effective than wholesale removal and resettlement.

Regardless of what appears to be an obviously more realistic approach to housing policy, and regardless of the important functions that squatter settlements provide to needy residents, the government

---

21. City of Seoul, *The City Year Book* (1980).

continues to treat squatters and squatter settlements both unwisely and unfairly. Squatter areas are regarded as an embarrassment and as the breeding ground for intense political instability.

In this regard, John Turner has written:

"The reasons for the failure of conventional housing programs, or of any program for the replacement of substandard dwellings, lie in the discrepancies between people's needs and the standards for housing set by the institutions. The immense variability of individual households' needs and the inelasticity of low-income people's housing demands, creates a difficult situation for governments."[22]

The present policy lacks an appreciation for the positive functions that squatter settlements provide, and it endangers the fragile network of physical and social relationships that make it possible for the low-income squatter to survive and pursue a meaningful life in the city. It would be both more sensible and more humane to permit existing levels of squatter settlements to remain and allow the inhabitants to better their lives, than risk the potentially negative effects and high costs, both social and individual, inherent in relocation.

Much of the discussion has thus far focused on the government's failure to understand the real needs of low income, squatter families with respect to housing. Numerous attempts have been made to alleviate housing conditions of squatter families and yet many have resulted in worsening the situation.

It is this paper's recommendation that most squatter settlements in Seoul should be immediately legalized, rehabilitated, and selectively redeveloped. Although squatters comprise the lowest socio-economic group of the urban population, it has been shown that they have a very high level of developmental motivation and aspiration. In no sense are these families down-and-out slum dwellers. They are hard-working, ambitious, and achievement-oriented working class households, who, if given the opportunity, can and will contribute greatly to the overall betterment of the city.

As possible mitigation measures, some policy alternatives are proposed in this regard. These measures deal with the clarification of definition, criteria reformulation, compiling of explicit data, implementation of modified redevelopment, relocation, active participa-

22. John J.C. Turner, Housing Issues and the Standards Problem; *Rehovot Conference on Urbanization and Development in Developing Countries* (Hebrew University of Jerusalem, Israel: August 16, 1971).

tion of the Korea Housing Corporation, and financial resources.

1) *Clarification of Definition*

There should be a clarification of administrative classifications (e.g., squatter vs. illegal housing, etc.), which would give explicit meaning to each category. The classification would be of benefit to both squatters and the government.

Land ownership should also be categorized in order to recognize the differences among squatter types. These categories would be:
— those who occupy their own land but whose units are substandard;
— those who are squatters on privately owned land;
— those who are squatters on municipal land;
— those who are squatters on national land.

A clearer definition of the problem will allow for greater integration of squatter policies with the long and short-term urban development strategies of the government.

2) *Reformulation of Criteria*

Most of the criteria currently used for target area selection will have to be reconsidered, including the Comprehensive Land Use Law and the Construction Law. Conventional criteria emphasize physical standards, such as minimum lot and dwelling unit size, and the requirement to be below 70 meters above sea level. The requirements should, initially at least, be placed at much lower levels; then, perhaps, standards could be raised gradually over time, as development progresses and the residents become more and more able to attain middle-class housing standards.

3) *Compiling Explicit Data*

The conventional policies were established on the basis of inadequate and insufficient data. Also as pointed out, terms were ambiguously defined, and unable to be operationalized. The achievement, therefore, cannot be explicitly analyzed and evaluated. This ambiguity resulted in the necessity for three consecutive surveys. They were costly. Enhanced, first-hand knowledge of the situation will undoubtedly do much to encourage a thoughtful reconsideration of squatter housing policy.

4) *Implementation of Modified Redevelopment*

In the process of redevelopment, a precise determination as to which area should be designated as eligible for redevelopment is necessary. For those areas eligible for redevelopment, a comprehensive development strategy must be defined. The strategy should explicitly delineate such factors as; socio-economic and physical characteristics; present levels of community infrastructure; and a plan for each area, specifying the amount and kind of work necessary to raise the standard of community facilities to redevelopment standards, along with a precise estimation of the costs. Again, the designation of a redevelopment project area must be very selective so that the heavy financial burden to squatter families can be reduced. In other words, only selective redevelopment projects must be implemented, and the majority of squatters' housing and neighborhood standards should be improved by the method of self-help rehabilitation. The recommended measure for improving squatter areas, therefore, must be a rehabilitation with positive and significant government financial assistance in addition to community participation.

Each household would be responsible for prorating the total costs of community development. After carrying out the necessary improvements, the residents would purchase the land from the government on an individual basis. This alternative is essentially the same as the one presently in use, except that criteria have been modified and the standards have been adjusted to allow for small size housing and lots. This would reduce the net costs to each household, as well as facilitate the process of land purchase, since parcels of land could be considerably smaller.

The community would absorb the total responsibility for construction of community facilities, with only material and technical support from the government. Hence, most of the improvement work must be carried out by the community itself. The community residents should be compensated for their labor in the form of credit toward the purchase of their land.

It is also strongly recommended that the AID loan program be utilized as a financial resource to facilitate housing rehabilitation or redevelopment. The requirement of 70% or more of public land in a AID project area must also be modified to expand loan usage.

Another positive aspect of this alternative is that costless side benefits accrue; for instance, vocational training through on-site participation. Vocational programs could be structured around community construction work, such as brick-laying, carpentry, land surveying, and all the other tasks which require skills that improve the earning potential of unskilled and unemployed people in the project area.

5) *Relocation.*

Relocation areas should be as manageably small as possible. Many smaller areas would be more desirable than several large ones, as this would facilitate the integration of resettlements areas into surrounding areas. It is also recommended that the public land in the relocation area be rented out at minimum cost or at no charge to relocated families so that they could maintain the same standards of living. By the same token, the relocation subsidy should be raised and the relocation period extended.

There is another neglected sector in the relocation procedure. As resettlement occurs, high rates of dislocation can be expected to occur among rental families. In past practice, the government's failure to respond to the needs of these families was seen as the cause of the enormous amount of dislocation resulting from the Kwang Ju program. In extreme poverty, these people were forced to move around from place to place. In order to avoid this sort of tragedy, supplementary programs should be instituted for these people. Assistance could be made in several forms: provision of alternative settlement sites for renting families, or the granting of low interest loans to help obtain rental units elsewhere, or implementation of a rent supplement program.

6) *Active Participation of the Korea Housing Corporation (KHC)*

This corporation was created in 1962 to facilitate public housing construction. Article 10 of the Urban Renewal Act designated the corporation as an implementing agency; however, the corporation has never been involved in either rehabilitation or redevelopment activities due to financial uncertainty.

Since the corporation is a quasi-public agency and not a profit oriented private firm, the government should encourage its active participation in housing rehabilitation (or redevelopment) programs by means of a governmental subsidy.

7) *Financial Resources*

Given the city's limited budget, a redevelopment project must be carried out by means of the self-help method. Since the economic status of the squatter families cannot be improved overnight, it may be necessary to mobilize project funds through existing Saemaul funds. In order to accumulate a project fund for squatter families, it is necessary to permit deferral of project initiation.

Mills and Song argued for simultaneous provision of a welfare program as a long-term solution to the squatter problem.[23] The City of Seoul must come up with a set of alternatives in regard to subsidizing squatter families, financially as well as technically, in order for them to maintain minimum health and safty standards. The role of government is to help those who cannot help themselves.

23. Edwin S. Mills and B.N. Song, *Urbanization and Urban Problems; Studies in the Modernization of the Republic of Korea: 1945-1975* (Cambridge, Massachussets : Harvard University, 1979) Chapter 8.

15

Managed Urban Development or Uncontrolled Urban Sprawl?: The Case of Seoul

David S. Bell Jr. and Bun Woong Kim

Major cities in the developing world confront a myriad of common problems such as finance, housing, sanitation, transportation, land utilization and regulation, water sources and conservation, public health, law enforcement, energy supplies, social welfare, personnel, recreational facilities and so on. People problems including unemployment, educational disparities, migrant assimilation with the concomitant concerns such as communication, cultural and social isolation and political responsiveness are also acute challenges for urban administrators in the 1980s. Consequently, Seoul like other major Asian cities must seek to meet and alleviate these unrelenting challenges and demands and provide better quality urban services to its residents. It seems probable, perhaps inevitable, that this will require dramatic and far-reaching changes in urban policies and in urban management. Clearly, patchwork or piecemeal legislation—the pattern for the last two decades—will not suffice. Nor will the continued traditional concentration of managerial elites preoccupied with their own organization's operations meet the requirements of this and succeeding decades. However, before addressing the requisites of current and future urban policy and urban management, we must first briefly describe the development of the primate city, Seoul, and identify the major issues and problems.

Seoul has a history extending over 2000 years but its designation as the capital and its corresponding growth in importance as an administrative center begins after the founding of the *Yi* dynasty in 1392. King Yi Sung-gye, the founder of the *Yi* dynasty, issued an official decree in 1394 designating Seoul as the capital. In the following year the King commissioned the *Hansung-bu* (a city hall) for the administration of his new capital. The Hansung-bu was headed by a *Panyoon* or magistrate, comparable in rank to a minister in the national government.[1] Since the city was maintained for military and administrative reasons, interactions between the populace and the royal court were minimal and the population remained relatively stable at approximately 100,000 for five centuries. However, in the late nineteenth century with the establishment of trade posts and Christian missionary centers in the capital city, the population began to increase, reaching an estimated 250,000 in 1913.[2] Japanese colonization and the ensuing modernizing of the country subsequently resulted in significant increases in population; from 600,000 in 1936 to 940,000 by 1944.[3]

The burgeoning population added to the administrative requirements and in 1946 Seoul was designated a special city under the direct control of the Minister of Home Affairs in the central government. This was in contrast to the usual classification of cities as administrative appendages of the provincial administration. By 1949, the capital of the Republic of Korea had a population of 1,600,000 and a total administrative region of 268.35 square kilometres. A temporary halt to the growth of the population and the accompanying administrative requirements occurred during the Korean War (June 25, 1950—July 27, 1953). Seoul was devastated and rehabilitation did not begin until the government returned to the city after the ceasefire.

Already buffeted by severe economic, political and social problems following the disruptions of the War, the government of Syngman Rhee found itself swamped by thousands of widows, orphans, farmers, ex-military personnel, university graduates and laid-off or unemployed workers, many of whom flocked to Seoul seeking relief from proverty and access to work opportunities, glamour and excitement. Despite the enormity of the economic, political and social problems, they came to the capital to make good in the material sense. Seoul inexorably recorded population increases. By 1960 the capital had 2,450,000 inhabitants.[4]

In part, the continuous growth of Seoul can be attributed to the remarkable achievements of the Korean economy as it progressed from

1. *Seoul Metropolitan Administration 1980* (Seoul: Seoul Metropolitan Government, 1980), p. 9.
2. Rhee, Chong-Ik, "Administration and Financing of Metropolitan Seoul: Challenges for the Year 2000" (paper presented at the International Conference The Year 2000: Urban Growth and Perspectives for Seoul, Seoul, October 13-18, 1980), p. 2.
3. Rhee, Jon-Mo, "A Study of Population Problems in Seoul—Reference to Labor Force", in *Aspects of Social Change in Korea*, ed., by C.I. Eugene Kim (Kalamazoo, Mich: Korean Research and Publications, Inc., 1969), p. 130.
4. *Seoul Metropolitan Administration 1980*, p. 13.

the import-substitution phase to the export-led growth phase. From 1960 to 1975, for example, the urban population grew at a rate of 6.1 per cent per annum in contrast to the national annual population growth rate of 2.2 per cent. According to Renuad, the rapid urban growth was the result of the rapid expansion of employment in the urban sector.[5]

Labor intensive manufacturing created innumerable opportunities for employement and this in turn led to an expansion in the service sector. A second factor seems to be integrally related to the growth of Seoul. As the capital city, Seoul, is the nation's image to the outside world. It is the nerve conter of the nation; the center of industrial, commercial and trading enterprises, political organizations, educational and cultural activities. To the rural people, the capital is the symbol of success, opportunity and the good life. The conclusion is inescapable; the only way to share in or obtain the benefits of this cornucopia is to migrate to the capital and become a Seoulite.[6]

The increasing concentration of economic activities and population in Seoul produced many negative side effects and overloaded the administrative structures. Traffic jams, insufficient transportation facilities, housing shortages, shortages of water supplies, inadequate sanitation systems, overcrowded schools, and pollution are a few of the all too familiar by-products of rapid urbanization. Governmental emphasis on economic development and rapid industrialization also created an urban mass psychology that accepted the necessity of transformation without any serious concern about the costs to the residents of the primate city. National economic growth was used as the justification for the construction of innumerable industrial complexes, housing estates, hotels, shopping centres and so on. The results are now painfully obvious: the cost of acquiring land for reconversion into open spaces may have to be delayed for several decades, perhaps, forever.

Administrative changes were imperative if the municipality were to attempt to meet the increasing demands in the public service sector. In February 1962, Seoul was made responsible to the Office of the Prime Minister. Undoubtedly, the move enhanced the prestige and position of the city but it did not result in more favourable treat-

---

5. See:
   Betrand Renaud, "Economic Structure, Growth and Urbanization in Korea" (paper presented to a Multi-Disciplinary Conference on South Korean Industrialization, Honolulu, June 14-17, 1977), p. 19.
6. Ham, Euiyong, "Urbanization and Asian Lifestyles", in Paul Meadows and Ephraim H. Mizruchi, eds., *Urbanism, Urbanization, and Change: Comparative Perspectives* (2nd ed.; Menlo Park, California: Addison-Wesley Publishing Company, 1976), pp. 226-227.

ment or in more attention to the growth pains of the metropolis.[7] In 1963, in a readjustment of the city's administrative region, the physical holding capacity was expanded from 268.35 to 613.04 square kilometres. Recognition of the physical limitations of absorbing more residents was manifested in 1964 when the cabinet adopted a policy to alleviate population concentration in the metropolitan area. Briefly the policy consisted of the following measures: (1) the decentralization of secondary government agencies; (2) the development of new towns away from the primate city; (3) the regulation of industrial development in the metropolitan areas; and (4) the location of educational and cultural facilities in non-metropolitan areas.[8] Clearly, the cabinet had boldly identified remedies to correct the serious overconcentration of people and activities in Seoul. However, the adaptation and implementation of the policy was passive; that is, urban administrators did not seek to direct urbal development but rather sought to accommodate existing developments or those that were taking shape. The results were increasing centralization and concentration of people and activities in the capital.

As the overconcentration of economic activities and population continued, additional laws were enacted to restrain further metropolitan Seoul development and channel people and industrial enterprises to designated areas. For example, the Local Industrial Development Law was enacted in 1969. Under the provisions of the law, the government designated local industrial estates and allowed exemptions from income and corporate taxes for industries locating in the designated estates. Eleven local industrial estates were created and between 1969-1975, 602 manufacturing plants were located there employing 55,700 workers.[9] The law was partially effective but the overall impact was hardly noticeable as the agglomeration of peoples and activities in Seoul continued to increase.[10]

In 1970, Seoul's population totalled 5,520,000 and an executive guideline was issued to control population concentration. Basically the guideline provided for: (1) the adoption of a comprehensive na-

---

7. See:
   Rhee, "Administration and Financing of Metropolitan Seoul: Challenges for the Year 2000", pp. 11-12.
8. Hwang, Myong Chan, "A Search for A Development Strategy for The Capital Region of Korea", in *Metropolitan Planning: Issues and Policies,* ed. by Yung-Hee Rho and Myong-Chan hwang (Seoul: Korea Research Institute for Human Settlements, 1979), p. 7.
9. *Ibid.,* p. 7.
10. See:
   Hwang, Myong-Chan, "Planning Strategies for Metropolitan Seoul" (paper presented at the International Conference The Year 2000: Urban Growth and Perspectives for Seoul, Seoul, October 13-18, 1980), p. 4.

tional land development plan which would encourage the location of educational facilities in non-metropolitan areas and the balanced development of both urban and rural sectors to decrease the attractiveness of relocating in the capital; (2) the identification and establishment of green belts, stimulation of local industrial developments, delegation of administrative functions to local offices, and the relocation of public corporations in other areas; and (3) decentralization within the metropolitan region. The guidelines were aimed at correcting severe socio-economic problems which, if left unresolved, would jeopardize national objectives and cause political instability. A few examples will illustrate the nature and magnitude of the crisis. Economic polarization in the capital area had created inter- and intra-regional imbalances in income distribution. Other regions suffered as the limited resources could not accommodate equitable development and as a result the inexorable centripetal influence of the capital attracted additional migrants from other areas. In other words, what was occuring was the expansion of the primate city at the expense of the other regions. Additionally, population increases had been so large and so constant that urban services could no longer be adequately provided. The demands for such basic services as housing, transit services, water supply, utilities, sewage disposal, education facilities, health and sanitation services, parks and recreational certers and pollution controls, far exceeded the already overburdened capabilities of the capital. Housing is an excellent illustration. In 1967 there was a housing shortage of 46 per cent; eight years later the rate was still 46 per cent! According to one authority, "... the housing supply has never outpaced newly created housing demand, and the housing shortage rate has never improved.[11] Unfortunately, the same could be said for the other basic urban services.

One of the major impediments to meeting the basic urban services needs of the residents is financial. For example, in 1980, revenues for the municipal government's general account were derived from the following sources: municipal taxes (77.5 per cent); property incomes (9.6 per cent); rents and service fees (7.3 per cent); subsidies (1.5 per cent); and other (4.1 per cent).[12] It ought to be noted that the capital is almost totally financially independent; its dependence

11. *Ibid.,* p. 4. See also:
    Chu, Chong Won, "Issues in Housing and Urban Development in Seoul" (paper presented at the International Conference The Year 2000: Urban Growth and Perspectives for Seoul, Seoul, October 13-18, 1980), p. 11. Professor Chu addresses the questions of housing needs and supply in Seoul for the next two decades and concludes that there will be no housing shortage.
12. *Seoul Metropolitan Administration 1980* (Seoul: Seoul Metropolitan Government, 1980), p. 17.

on subsidies as indicated is a miniscule 1.5 per cent. This is not an aberration but rather a typical breakdown of revenue sources. Financial independence may be laudable but financial independence has constrained the city's ability to meet resident demands for basic urban services. Citizen demands for more services and greater responsiveness and equity in their distribution push urban policy makers in many directions. Urban administrators, therefore, must seek to strike a balance between the fiscal capabilities of the city on the one hand and the service expectations of the citizenry on the other. Effective and efficient delivery of basic urban services depends upon adequate revenue sources and, given the current financial base of the municipal government, there is no conceivable way to provide those service at even a minimal level. Obviously, an expanded revenue base is imperative if the capital is to meet its obligation to provide basic urban services. Identifying areas or items for new or extended taxation could be hazardous, but it appears that current tax bases could be strengthened, large state subsidization could be solicited, the management and collection of current taxes could be more effectively carried out, and finally, non-tax revenues could certainly be enlarged. Seoul plays a key role in Korean national development and yet this integral function has received niggardly financial support. For example, Seoul is lauded for its modernity and its ability to meet the exigencies of the highly competitive and complex international and domestic market systems. It is the center of the academic, business, economic, government and research communities; in other words, it is the fountainhead of the Republic of Korea. Countless billions of *won* were spent and are spent cultivating that image. National support must become a reliable revenue source; the national government must recognize its financial obligations to Seoul especially in view of the environmental problems caused by national policies. The environmental pollution problem in Seoul is the inevitable outcome of short-sighted planning, lack of comprehensiveness and neglect of environmental and health concerns. The scarcity of human and financial resources are major reasons for the current situation; but so also is the lack of awareness of the impact of economic growth at any cost.

Government planners and urban managers, academics, foreign scholars and others all addressed the question of managing the heretofore unmanageable and largely unrestrained growth of Seoul in the 1970s. Numerous plans, laws and amendments were adopted, but space does not permit comprehensive analysis and summary of each enacted measure. Substantive enactments, however, will be discussed.

In 1971, the *Ten Year Comprehensive National Land Development Plan*, containing numerous elements of the executive guideline of 1970, described above, such as the adoption of green belt areas to check urban sprawl and the creation of large industrial estates, were adopted. Another measure *The National Land Use and Management Law* Provided the government with the authority to establish a standard land price system. An amendment of the *Urban Planning Law* authorized the government to expand the designation of green belts to all major urban centers. A *Building Law* amendment empowered the government to set density controls and restrict building construction in areas designated special districts. To control the migration of people and new industries the government passed tax penalties in 1973. People moving to Seoul were to be subject to a citizen tax. Differential property and acquisition taxes were applied to newly established factories in metropolitan areas. For example, newly established industries in large metropolitan areas were subject to triple property taxes and acquisition taxes five times the normal tax for five years. The reverse was also the practice, viz., favorable tax rates and, in some instances, outright tax exemptions were granted to factories relocating in non-metropolitan areas. Educational decentralization was also an objective of legislation and examples include: (1) the application of differential school fees; (2) the introduction of pre-college entrance examinations; (3) the introduction of professor exchange programs; and (4) the strict control of expansion of existing universities and new schools.[13] These piecemeal efforts to manage the growth of metropolitan Seoul were not sufficient and merely cloaked continued urban sprawl with a governmental seal of approval.

As mentioned previously, enactments in the 1960s and 1970s to stem the overconcentration, overdevelopment and overcrowdedness of Seoul were ineffectual. By 1977, the capital had grown to 7,500,000 and there appeared to be little prospect of change unless more vigorous remedial policies were adopted and rigidly but fairly applied. All previous planning efforts addressed the problems of physical planning with a veiw towards the maximization and acceleration of national economic growth. As a consequence the growth problems of Seoul were surbordinated to the objectives of accelerated national economic growth. However, the promulgation of the *Basic Plan for the Population Redistribution* of the Capital Region seemed to change the emphasis. The Basic Plan provided specific programs to: (1) control the expansion or new establishment of factories in the capital and en-

---

13. Hwang, "A Search for A Development Strategy for the Capital Region of Korea", p. 8.

courage existing factories to relocate; (2) create population absorption centres in designated regions in the southern part of the country—Daejun, Taegu, South East Shore Industrial Zone, Masan, Junju and Kwangju; and (3) restrict expansion of educational institutions and encourage redistribution. To encourage compliance with these decentralization programs, financial incentives and infrastructure development techniques were to be applied. In addition, the Basic Plan called for the establishment of a new administrative capital. Using population projections, the government forecast Seoul's population at 11,400,000 in 1986 and decided that overconcentration was unacceptable. Therefore, an absolute population ceiling of 7,100,000 was to be enforced and the population absorption centers listed above and the new administrative capital were to accommodate the excess 4,300,000. However, there were some doubts expressed about the target population for the capital city. According to Dr. Myong-Chan Hwang, Research Director of the Korea Research Institute of Human Settlements, "it may not be feasible to depopulate Seoul ... it may seriously damage the very foundation of economic growth in Korea."[14] Thus it was clear that though there appeared to be concern about the overconcentration, overdevelopment and overcrowdedness of Seoul, remedial measures such as those implemented under the *Basic Plan* and previous statutes were conditioned by the constraint of sustained economic growth. In other words, if decentralization or the construction of a new administrative capital conflicted with the paramount goal of national economic growth, the highest priority would be given to economic growth and the conflicting programs would be unceremoniously terminated.

Managed growth demands an intricately integrated and efficient system where choices and decisions are made with full knowledge of all the variables, constraints and trade-offs and where the programmes and policies are synchronized for effective and timely execution. A comprehensive, coordinated and functionally integrated plan seemingly consistent with national economic and urban development goals was prepared through the joint efforts of the city of Seoul and the Korean Planners' Association. The *Long Range Seoul Metropolitan Plan* subdivides the metropolitan region of 12,489 km² into five concen-

---

14. *Ibid*, p. 10. See the full article for the specifics of the *1977 Basic Plan for the Population Redistribution of the Capital Region*. An Jae Kim also asserts that since there is not enough spatial space capacity to accomodate continuous growth, relevant strategies should be employed to limit Seoul's population to 9,500,000—10,000,000. See:
Kim, An Jae, "Population Perspectives and Socio-economic Development Planning of Seoul for the Year 2000" (paper presented at the International Conference for the Year 2000: Urban Growth and Perspectives for Seoul, Seoul, October 13-18, 1980), pp. 17-19.

tric areas and applies discriminatory development strategies in each
of the sub-regions. (See Figure 1 and Table 1).

Figure 1. Development Zoning for Metropolitan Development

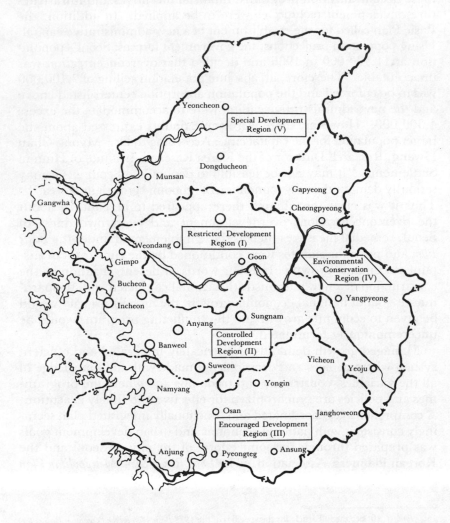

Table 1: Development Guidelines for Subregions

Subregion	Administrative Jurisdictions	Location	Development Guidelines
I. Restricted Development Subregion	Seoul, Euicheongbu, Goori, Weondang	Core areas of inner ring with radius of 15km, located North and South of Han River. Matched with the Seoul administrative boundary	Dispersal, Decongestion, Decentralization 1. Disallowance of new factory construction 2. Relocation of pollution-generating firms 3. Dispersion of population and prevention of immigrants 1. Population growth control 2. Denial of new factory construction 3. Accommodation of portions of displaced industries from Seoul 4. Suspension of disorderly land use practices 5. Expansion of existing cities. 6. High density development
II. Controlled Development Subregion	Incheon, Suweon, Anyang, Banweol	Suburban areas of middle ring with radius of 35km. Incheon as the subregion's centre	Intensive and extensive development 1. Development of urban centres 2. Expansion of existing cities and towns 3. Development of industrial estate in Ah San Bay. 4. Minimization of pollution problem and of loss of agricultural land.
III. Encouraged Development Subregion	Pyeongteg, Yicheon, Ansung, Janghoweon	The fringe areas of the outer ring with radius of for peripheral development for peripheral development	
IV. Environmental Conservation Subregion	Cheongpyeong, Yangpyeong, Yeoju, Gapyeong	The fringe areas of the outer ring located on the basin of upstream Han River	Preservation, Conservation, Protection 1. Prevention of upper Han River basin from pollution to maintain water quality 2. Water resources development 3. Natural resources preservation and promotion of recreational and outdoor activities 4. Promotion of dairy and vegetable farming
V. Special Development Subregion	Gangwha, Munsan, Dongducheon, Pocheon	The fringe areas of the outer ring located North of Seoul and South of DMZ. Sparsely developed	Reserved for Future Development 1. Buffer for national defence 2. Limited development 3. Conservation of forestry and other natural resources 4. Promotion of city-oriented farming and recreational and outdoor activities

*Source: Hwang, "Planning Strategies for Metropolitan Seoul", pp. 16-17.

The Metropolitan Plan is an attempt to manage the growth of the region for the next twenty years, that is 1981-2001. Its basic premises are: (1) Seoul remains the nation's capital; (2) the green belts continue in effect to contain urban sprawl and preserve the natural environment; (3) the major mode of transportation will be the private automobile; (4) decentralization will be pursued and five growth centers, namely Taegu, Masan, Kwangju, Junju and Daejun will accommodate relocated industries and people; and (5) the government will develop the Ah-San area as the second largest industrial estate.[15]

As evidenced by the developmental guidelines in Table 1, this is a very ambitious project. Its successful completion is not assured and several obstacles remain to be resolved. First, the size, relative dominance and specialization of function cause the primate city to be the nation's crossroads both for domestic political and economic administration, and for the principal interactions with other nations. Thus all the actions that improve the situation in Seoul or in the Metropolitan area make the *whole area* even more attractive to migrants (firms and employees). The actions could, therefore, create more problems in the future and this would call for even more rigidly structured guidelines in the future.

The city administration's successful attempt to host the Asian Games in 1986 and the Summer Olympics in 1988 seems certain to attract migrants and resources from other regions thus aggravating the chronic problems of overconcentration, overdevelopment and overcrowdedness. These two events have already received intense publicity in the press with reports of "industries gearing up to meet tourist demands" and "local sport equipment manufacturers producing all the sports equipment for the Olympics." The chance to cash in on the expected bonanza will act as an immense magnet and additional thousands will be added to the metropolitan rolls. This was further reinforced by the creation of a new Ministry of Sports on March 20, 1982. The new addition to the national government will handle matters relating to sports and provide assistance for the 1988 Olympics. Though this sports' mania may be temporary and will probably pass after the 1988 international event, great symbolic importance is attached to it. Both the 1986 Asian Games and the 1988 Olympics represent political successes for the government over their North Korean

---

15. *Ibid.*, p. 10. A subway system has been in operation since 1975 and additional segments are scheduled to come on line in 1983 and before the 1986 Asian Games. Subway stations are important economic stimuli, in value and in development intensity. However, the economic, social and environmental consequences of subway construction have not been evaluated.

rivals for the Asian Games and over Japanese competitors for the Summer Olympics.

Second, the developmental guidelines of the metropolitan plan require extensive government supervision and intervention. Given a submissive political culture that tends to legitimize the moral authority of the upper strata, culture that tends to legitimize the moral authority of the upper strata, perhaps the economic and social disruptions likely to occur during the plan's twenty years will not cause political instability. Much will depend upon the method of application: government controls can be used to serve as well as to abuse the public.[16]

Third, government control and regulation necessitates expansion of the administration to meet the needs of the metropolitan region. Seoul's municipal administration in 1970 included fourteen bureaus and bureau-level offices, nine administrative districts *(Ku)* and 20,000 municipal workers.[17] In 1982 there were thirteen bureaus and bureau-level offices and fifty-eight divisions under the direction of the Mayor and the assistance of the Vice-Mayor, seven project offices under the Mayor and seventy other project offices under bureaus of the city administration, seventeen administrative districts *(Ku)* with 417 subdivisions-dongs, the administrative units closest to the people, and 44,000 municipal workers.[18] The administrative structures grew in a discordant fashion much like the city itself with patchwork additions of bureaus, bureau-level offices and projects to meet perceived needs. In the next twenty years, the demands will be even greater owing to the increases in administrative responsibilities and a projected metropolitan area population of 16,304,000. By contrast, the metropolitan population in 1980 was only 11,886,000.[19]

Fourth, the addition of new personnel in the metropolitan administration will not assist in the realization of the objectives of the metropolitan plan. What is necessary is a fundamental change in administrative style. Such chronic problems as an excessive degree of centralization, discontinuity of programs, nepotism, favoritism, lack of cooperation and coordination among administrative agencies involved in the execution of public policy, substantial discrepancies

---

16. For a discussion of the political attitudes and behavior patterns of the Korean people see: Kim, Bun Woong, "The Korean Political Psyche and Administration", in *Korean Public Bureaucracy*, ed., by Bun Woong Kim and Wha Joon Rho (Seoul: Kyobo Publishing, Inc., 1982), pp. 117-132.
17. Rhee, "Administration and Financing of Metropolitan Seoul: Challenge for the Year 2000" *op. cit.*, pp. 6-7.
18. Interviews.
19. Hwang, "Planning Strategies for Metropolitan Seoul", p. 1.

between formally prescribed rules and regulations and the highly personalized power pattern of the public adminisrator have to be terminated. The future urban administration will require: (1) more dynamic leadership including the ability to delegate authority; (2) more effective supervisory techniques to facilitate coordination; and (3) an improved control system.

Finally, managed growth requires an intricately integrated and efficient system where choices and decisions are made with full knowledge of all the variables, constraints and trade-offs and where programs and policies are synchronized for effective and timely execution. Perhaps the most perplexing problem in the development of the primate city has been overspecialization which led to the current phenomenon in which people, consultants, or public officials, working in a special field within one overall environment do not coordinate their activities with each other. Coordination of the myriad of problems related to urban development can only be achieved through the establishment of a Ministry of Urban Affairs in the national government. The Ministry would have exclusive responsibility for managing urban growth nationwide and coordinating growth policies with the objectives of national development plans. To facilitate the development of policy alternatives, an exploratory urban development research center should be established as an integral part of the Ministry of Urban Affairs. Adequate policies, staff and financial support are crucial to the interrelated problems of urban growth, land use, housing, water supply, treatment of municipal sewage and industrial wastewater, transportation and so on. The Ministry should also have the authority to set the requirements, administer the examinations, and monitor the performance of urban administrators. This might assist in the eradication of the chronic traditional problems of the Korean bureaucracies, at least in the urban management sector. A positive dynamic urban administration would be an asset to the solution of growth problems in the metropolitan region. If a transitory phenomenon such as competitive sporting events (the 1986 Asian Games and the 1988 Olympic Games) requires national attention, can recognition of the seriousness of managing urban growth be far behind? We hope not, because the alternative is the continuation of uncontrolled urban sprawl.

16

The Challenge of Urban Overpopulation and Public Policy: The Case of Metropolitan Seoul

Yong Hyo Cho and Young Sup Kim

I. Introduction

During the past two decades, Korea has undergone a massive change in social structure caused by its rapid urbanization. This change is a part of the larger process of modernization in economy, technology, and global outlook. Not surprisingly, the gorwth of Seoul has been the center of attention, politically and otherwise. In 1960, Seoul had a population of 2.5 million. In October, 1982, the population of Seoul exceeded 8.9 million, thus becoming one of the super-cities in the world. This amounts to an average annual population growth of 300,000, a phenomenon perhaps unprecedented elsewhere.

The growth of population in Seoul was also accompanied by the growth of political, economic, social, and cultural activities. The growth of the entire nation was led by Seoul and oriented to Seoul. Public policy dealing with overpopulation and congestion in Seoul is based on the premise that population growth must be restrained and the existing population must be dispersed. Beginning in the mid-1960's, the government developed various programs and adopted a variety of policies to respond to the overpopulation problem in Seoul.

The objective of the present paper is four-fold: (1) to examine the social policy implications of the population increase and concentration in Seoul; (2) to review the past population trend and to attempt to project the future growth of population in Seoul; (3) to make a systematic analysis of factors contributing to the population growth and concentration in Seoul: and (4) to review and evaluate the existing policy measures that are designed to restrain the growth of population and to disperse the existing population from Seoul to other cities, while seeking to develop a set of alternative policy approaches.

II. Population Concentration in Seoul: Past Experience and Future Prospect

Following the Korean War, particularly since the 1960's, Korea has been swept by a drastic shift toward modernization. Along with the industrialization of economy, the sophistication of technology and science, and the popularization of education at all levels, the social structure has been transformed from rural to urban at a dramatic speed.[1] In view of the data shown in Figure 1, it is evident that the urbanization process of Korea has been much faster than in the industrialized countries. It took more than 100 years for Great Britain's urban population to grow from 20 percent of total population of the nation to 60 percent. It took the United States about 80 years for the same change to take place, while it took Japan about 45 years.

Figure 1. Urbanization Trend: Korea and Selected Industrialized Nations

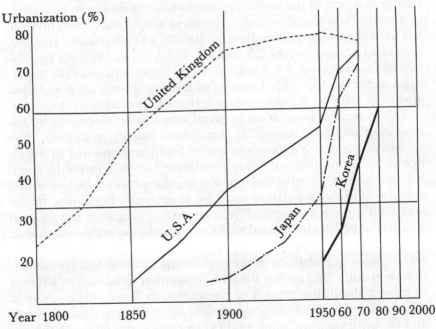

1. "Urban" in this study is meant to be synonymous with "City" as an administrative unit of urban area with population of 50,000 or more. There are 50 cities in Korea as of 1983.

In contrast, Korea took approximately 30 years for its urban population to grow from 20 percent to 60 percent of its total population.

Thus, the urbanization of Korea is characterized by two distinctions; it is a post-World War II phenomenon and its speed has been extraordinarily fast. This rapid urbanization process has caused a regional imbalance in national development and excessive concentration of the population in a few cities like Seoul. If the rural-to-urban movement of population had proceeded at a slower pace, the urban capacity to accomodate the population growth and in-migration could have expanded adequately to meet the challenge.

As Table 1 shows, the total population of the nation grew 77 percent from 1955 to 1980 (from 21.5 million to 38.1 million), while city population was increased by 314 percent (from 5.28 million to 21.89 million). The growth rate of urban population was four times as fast as that of the total population and in fact, the urban population in 1980 was larger than the total population of the nation in 1955. What this implies is that the population settlement pattern of Korea has been drastically reshaped, mainly due to the urban migration from rural areas accompanied by a steady growth of population.

Table 1: Population Trend of the Entire Nation and Urban Areas, 1955-1981

	National Total (000)	Annual Growth Rate (%)	Urban Pop. (000)	Urbanization Rate (%)	Annual Growth Rate (%)
1955	21,502		5,281	24.5	
1960	24,954	2.88	6,997	28.0	5.51
1966	29,160	2.71	9,805	33.6	5.96
1970	31,435	1.90	12,929	41.1	7.16
1975	34,679	1.98	16,794	48.4	5.37
1980	38,124	1.82	21,890	57.6	6.07
1981	38,723		23,186	59.8	5.92

Source: The Korea Research Institute of Human Settlements, *The Second Comprehensive National Development Plan (Tentative), 1982-1991* (Seoul: KRIHS), p. 39.

Table 2 shows that the population of Seoul was increased by 440 percent between 1955 and 1980. This growth rate is somewhat higher

than that of all cities combined. However, the population growth
rate of the Capital Region is rather modest with a 245 percent increase.[2] What is evident from this growth rate is that the population
growth in the areas outside Seoul has been sluggish, but the trend
has been changing since the 1970's. For example, between 1973 and
1980, the average annual growth rate of the population in Seoul was
4.3 percent compared with 5.3 percent in the Capital Region outside
Seoul and 8.1 percent in cities of the Capital Region other than Seoul.[3]

Table 2: Population Trend of Seoul and Capital Region for Selected
          Years from 1955 to 1982

	Capital Region Pop. (000)	Annual Growth Rate (%)	Ratio of National Total (%)	Seoul Populat. (000)	Annual Growth Rate (%)	Ratio of National Total (%)
1955	3,929		18.3	1,575		7.3
1960	5,194	5.5	20.8	2,445	8.7	9.8
1966	6,911	5.0	23.7	3,803	7.9	13.8
1970	8,878	6.5	28.2	5,525	9.8	17.6
1975	10,929	5.3	31.5	6,889	4.5	19.9
1980	13,542		35.5	8,518	4.7	22.3
1981	13,779		35.5	8,676	1.9	22.4
1982				8,916	2.8	

The population growth trends of Seoul and the Capital Region
demonstrate that their proportions relative to the total national population have become increasingly greater. The population of the Capital
Region accounted for 18.3 percent of the nation's total population
in 1955, but this proportion grew to 35.5 percent in 1980. The land
area of Seoul accounts for only 0.6 percent of the national total, but
its population accounted for 22.3 percent of the total population of
the nation in 1980. In short, more than one out of five Koreans lives
in Seoul and more than one out of three Koreans lives in the Capital
Region.

---

2. For the purpose of this paper, The Capital Region is defined as the total area of Gyonggi
    Province in the center of which Seoul is located.

3. The data is derived from Table 1-9 in *The Basic Settlement Plan (Tentative) of the Capital Region,
    1982-1991* (The Korea Research Institute of Human Settlements), 1981, p. 18 (A translation
    from Korean).

1. Population Projection-Seoul

A number of research institutes and government agencies have estimated the future population of Seoul and the Capital Region. Eleven estimates made by nine agencies are brought to our attention and they are shown in Table 3. The estimate figures show a considerable difference. For example, the estimated population for the year 1991 ranges from a high of 11.9 million (the one made by the planners of the Second Comprehensive National Development Plan) to a low of 8.5 million (the one made by the City Government of Seoul). The estimated population for the year 2001 ranges from a high of 14.25 million (as estimated by the United Nations) to a low of 7 million (as projected by the City Government of Seoul).[4] The

Table 3: Population Projection for the City of Seoul for Selected Years through the Year 2001 (See next Table)

(in thousands)

	1981	1986	1991	1996	2001
Korea Institute of Science and Technology	8,072	8,813	8,991		
Korea Development Inst.	7,610	8,260	8,970		
Korea Research Inst. for Human Settlements 1	8,250	8,800	9,150	9,350	9,450
2	8,770	10,330	11,900		
3	8,628	9,200	9,600		
Economic Planning Board	8,367	10,474	11,961	13,808	15,583
City of Seoul	8,300	9,100	8,500	7,800	7,000
SNU Regional Planning Research Center	8,645	9,313	10,008	10,702	11,336
Ministry of Construction		9,200	9,600		
The United Nations	8,490		11,845		14,246
1st Minister without Port.	8,645	9,313	10,008	10,702	11,336
Cho-Kim Projection	8,676	9,900	11,150	12,450	13,700
	(actual)				

Sources: The Office of the First Minister without Portfolio, *Policy for an Effective Redistribution of Population in the Capital Region,* 1980 and KRIHS. *The Second Comprehensive National Development Plan (Tentative), 1982-1991,* 1981.

---

4. The population figure estimated by the Economic Planning Board is the highest although the target years for the estimate do not coincide with the rest of the projections.

Table 4: Population Projection for the Capital Region for Selected
Year through the Year 2001

(in thousands)

		1981	1986	1991	1996	2001
KIST		12,984	14,310	15,121		
KRIHS	1	13,156	14,794	15,385	15,933	16,304
	2		14,847	15,720		17,700
	3		15,170	16,560		18,550
City of Seoul		13,072	14,563	15,053		
Environmental Planning Research Center		13,577	15,721	17,864	20,007	22,149
Office of 1st Minister without Portfolio		13,577	14,794	15,718	16,808	17,841
Cho-Kim Projection		13,779 (actual)	15,200	16,950	18,600	20,350

Source: The Office of the First Minister without Portfolio, *Policy for an
Effective Redistribution of Population in the Capital Region*, 1980.

reasons underlying the variance of the projected population of Seoul
come from the different assumptions on which the estimates are based: namely, (1) the effect of public policies designed to constrain the
population growth and to disperse population from Seoul, and (2)
the birth rate.

The future population projected by the City Government of Seoul
is a target population, not an projection. This target population was
originally to be attained by building a new Capital City. It was expected that all of the central administrative functions of the three branches of government and the central management functions of business
corporations would move to the new Capital as its capacity would
grew to accomodate them. However, this plan to build a new Capital
City has long been scrapped, and the target population set by the
City Government of Seoul is now totally irrelevant.

The future population figures developed by the Korea Research
Institute for Human Settlements (KRIHS) include the population pro-
jected as well as the population planned for the future dates. The
KRIHS projects a rather moderate growth in population in the future.

This projection is based on the assumption that the national development plans will have the effect of reducing the growth rate of Seoul and that the birth rate will decline significantly.

In this study, we based our projection on a number of different considerations. First, we used past population trends as the basic of the future population projections. Second, we took into consideration the current and future economic conditions. Third, we considered the effect on population of various public policies. Fourth, we considered the role of Seoul in the economic, social, political, educational, and cultural spheres of national life. Fifth, we took into account the effect of public policies directed toward the population problems in the Capital Region.

The most important is past population trends as the basis of future population projections. The population trend between 1955 and 1982 in five or six year intervals has been extended to the year 2001 with every possible combination of the intervals. The population growth rate based on the years between 1966-1980 is the highest, while the rate based on the 1980-82 trend is the lowest. Thus, we set the projection based on the former as the upper limit and that based on the latter as the lower limit. The upper and lower limits of the projected population for the City of Seoul for the selected years from 1982 to 2001 are as follows:

		1982	1986	1991	1996	2001
Upper Limit	(000)	8,916	10,200	11,800	13,500	15,000
Lower Limit	(000)	8,916	9,600	10,500	11,400	12,400
Probable	(000)	8,916	9,900	11,150	12,450	13,700

The projection based on the 1980-82 trend is believed to be unrealistically low for the following reasons. First, the period of 1980-82 was characterized by an unusually serious economic depression in Korea and the urbanization of population during this period was negatively affected. Seoul is considered no exception to this general pattern.[5]

Second, when the economy begins to have a upward swing, the economy in the Seoul region wil respond more quickly than most other areas of the country, thus acting as an inducement to population

---

5. A more dramatic example is the industrial cities in the North Central region in the U.S., where population decline and factory closings created a so-called "rust bowl."

growth. The government is seeking to develop a plan which will make it possible to have a second take-off in Korea's economic growth. The economic growth induced by the development policy of the government will strengthen the Seoul's attraction to the population.

Third, the current government policy for Seoul is to transform Seoul into a modern, pleasant, international city. The government has spearheaded the effort to relocate those pollution-producing factories away from Seoul, while improving facilities necessary for safety and convenience such as the subway system and sewer system.[6]

Fourth, Seoul will be the host to international events of historic significance such as the Asian Games of 1986 and the Olympics of 1988. In addition, more than 100 sizeable international conferences are hosted by Seoul each year. The City of Seoul, as well as the central government, places emphasis on these international events and it is not too difficult to expect that government investment in Seoul is proportionate to the importance of the city.

Fifth, Korea will continue to urbanize and Seoul is expected to draw a fair share of the urban population. One estimate suggests that the urban population in 1986 will account for 72.9 percent of total population and in 1991 it will account for 76.9 percent.[7] The urbanization is likely to reach a saturation point in the early part of the 21st century.

Sixth, the Seoul-oriented population movement will continue so long as the freedom to choose residence and freedom to move are guaranteed by the consitution as is now the case. As long as Seoul retains those unique valued opportunities which it now has, such as access to political power, high quality education, economic success, and the benefits of modern convenience, Seoul will continue to remain enchantingly attractive.

For these reasons, we predict that the most probable population growth rate will fall somewhere between the two extremes, the lower limit of the average annual growth of 2.27 percent and the upper limit of the average annual growth rate of 8.4 percent. The projection we present here is the midpoint between the two extremes.

2. Concentration of Economic, Social, and Cultural Activities in Seoul

The concentration of economic activities in Seoul is much greater than that of the population as shown in Table 5. Seoul's share in

---

6. For example, currently only 68.8 percent of the households in Seoul is hooked up to the sewer system. The City Government is planning to expand the sewer connection to 100 percent of the households by 1987, the year before the 1988 Olympics.

7. KRIHS, *The Second Comprehensive National Development Plan (Tenntative), 1982-1991*, 1981. p. 59, Table 12.

financing (bank deposit and loan), tourist hotels, and export firms ranges between 50 percent to 60 percent of the national total. Except for the export firms and manufacturing firms, the degree of Seoul's concentration in other economic activities tends to decrease slightly.[8]

Table 5: Concentration of Economic Activities in Seoul

	Unit	Year	Nation	Seoul	Share of Seoul
Land Area	Km²	1980	98,992	627	0.63
Population Thou,	persons	80	38,197	8,518	22.3
		76	35,860	7,255	20.2
Corporate Hqs.	No.	1979	5,887	3,888	66.0
		75	2,733	1,891	69.2
Manufacturing Firms	No.	1980	33,681	14,335	42.6
		76	22,355	9,451	42.3
Manufacturing Employees	No. in Thousands	1980	1,998	541	27.1
		76	1,504	516	34.3
Export Firms	No.	1980	3,372	1,880	55.8
		76	2,244	595	26.5
Bank Deposits	Billion Won	1981	15,117	9,592	63.5
		76	3,760	2,417	64.3
Bank Loans	Billion Won	1981	15,000	9,306	62.0
		76	3,725	2,453	65.9
Gross Retail and Whole Sale	Billion Won	1979	11,038	4,033	36.5
		76	5,759	2,623	45.6
Rooms of Tourist Hotels	No.	1980	18,547	10,541	56.8
		76	11,300	6,952	61.2

Source: The Seoul Chamber of Commerce, *A Survey Report on the Concentration of Economic Activities in Seoul,* 1982.

---

8. If Tokyo serves as a model for Seoul, it is likely that manufacturing firms will decline in Seoul. Instead, those functions of central administrative control of government and industries will expand further in Seoul. See Masahiko Honjo, "Metropolitan Problems in Post-Industrial Societies: Case of Japan," in Yung-Hee Rho and Myong-Chan Hwang (eds.), *Metropolitan Planning: Issues and Policies* (Seoul: Korea Research Institute for Human Settlements, 1979), pp. 59-82.

Education, culture and other public amenities are also heavily concentrated in Seoul. As shown in Table 6, 54 percent of all passenger cars is concentrated in Seoul. The concentration of universities and university students is 43.5 percent and 42.7 percent, respectively. Modern services and urban amenities such as medical facilities, doctors, telephone, water supply and sewer services are as equally con-

Table 6: Concentration of Educational and Cultural Facillities in Seoul

	Unit	Year	Nation	Seoul	Share of Nation
Automobiles	No.	1980	498,232	206,778	41.5
		76	207,006	85,407	41.2
Passenger Cars	No.	1980	240,667	130,505	54.2
		76	86,125	46,265	53.1
TV Sets	No. in	1981	5,800	1,048	18.1 (B & W)
	Thousands		1,014	455	44.8 (Color)
		1976	2,809	994	35.4 (B & W)
Rate of Newspaper Readership	%	1980	38.9	61.8	
Rate of Water Supply	%	1980	86.7	92.7	
		1976	76.0	89.3	
Telephones	No. in	1980	2,705	1,015	35.7
	Thousands	76	1,271	512	40.3
Beneficiaries of med. ins.	Persons in	1980	9,113	4,408	48.4
	Thousands	76	3,203	1,771	55.3
Medical Doctors	No. of Persons	1980	22,307	9,053	40.6
		76	18,214	6,721	36.9
Medical Service Organizations	No.	1980	13,324	4,785	35.9
		76	12,823	4,697	36.6
College Students	Persons in thou.	1980	403	172	42.7
		76	230	134	58.2
College	No	1980	85	37	43.5
		76	72	36	50.0

Source: The Seoul Chamber of Commerce, *A Survey Report on the Concentration of Economic Activities in Seoul,* 1982.

centrated in Seoul as are higher education activities. As in the case of economic concentration, some of the cultural concentration in Seoul has tended to decline in recent years. This tendency may suggest that a diffusion of modernization is taking place in the rest of country.

III. Problems Resulting from the Population Concentration in Seoul

The simple fact that 22.4 percent of the nation's population is packed in to 0.63 percent of the nation's land area does raise policy questions in relation to such matters as high density living environment and a balance in the land use policy. Here, we will only examine those policy problems most often cited by policy analysts and urban experts. They include: (1) the issue of national security; (2) the issue of regional balance in national development; (3) environmental quality; (4) amenities, public services, and diseconomies of scale; and (5) social problems.

The National Security Issue—It has been often pointed out that the concentration of population and economic activities, particularly those activities essential to national defense, in Seoul (which is only 50 Km away from the DMZ) is considered detrimental to national security in case of armed conflict with North Korea. When the policy to build a new capital city was adopted in 1977, the concern about the national security was one of the factors which influenced the decision. It is believed that the target population of seven million set by the City Government of Seoul is also related to the national security consideration.

However, what is sorely lacking is the views of military strategists supporting this national security-based argument for population control in Seoul. All those assertions in favor of reducing population in Seoul for national security reasons are made by non-military experts. In view of the delivery range and destructive power of contemporary weaponry possessed by the both sides of the DMZ, these security-related arguments do not seem convincing even to a layman in military affairs.[9]

A Balance in National Development—Korea is a densely populated country whether it be a mountainous or coastal area. Korea has not yet developed a comprehensive and systematic land use policy for its entire territory. Under these circumstances, a dense and disorderly

---

9. This debate is moot without contribution from the experts in military strategy.

development of Seoul implies that only a limited area of the nation's land is abused by an excessive concentration in Seoul. The case in point is the development of the area south of the Han River in the 1960's and the 1970's. In spite of the fact that this development housing more than 4 million population has taken place at the threshhold of the 21st century, the development resembles an urban form of the pre-industrial revolution era. There is no consistency in the land use pattern and street layout, both evidence of lack of planning. In a sense, it is fortunate that urban development of the kind experienced in Seoul did not take place evenly throughout the country. If it had, damage would have been evenly inflicted upon the entire land area of the nation. In the absence of a systematic, comprehensive, consistent, and long-range paln for national development and land use, the disorderly development of the kind experienced by Seoul may be considered a way of avoiding nationwide abuse of the land.

Environmental Qualty—The problems affecting the living environment are important policy issues and they are wide-ranging. Here, we will only consider a few selected problems such as pollution, traffic, and public health hazards. The level of air pollution and water pollution in Seoul exceeds the safety standards far above the level acceptable. Noise is also a serious problem affecting the quality of life.

Traffic congestion is a chronic problem, causing delays and discomfort. It is not unusual to leave home one or two hours ahead of the starting time of school or work in the morning to be on time. The fact is that only 15 percent of the land area in Seoul is allocated to streets. The city is utterly unprepared for this automobile transportation era. A recent case study makes the point abundantly clear. That is, to run the main thoroughfare in the center of Seoul, Chongro, from Kangwha-moon to Tong-dae-moon, it will take 3 minutes 22 seconds to travel 2.8 Km distance at a speed of 50 Km per hour However, it is common for a taxi to take 25 minutes to travel through the thoroughfare during a rush hour.[10]

Traffic congestion in Seoul is likely to become worse in the future. Although the subway system will play an increasingly greater role as it is completed and great expectations are held for it, the system has a limited service capacity. As the level of personal income rises, the ownership of passenger cars will increase. The impact on traffic congestion will be detrimental.

Public Health, Recreation, and Housing Problem—The level and type of public services necessary to support the lives of some nine million

---

10. *The Tong-A Ilbo*, Feb. 2, 1983, p. 9.

people living and visiting Seoul daily are enormous. The most critical of all include services to prevent public health hazards, to provide recreation facilities, and to make housing available.

Water supply is available to 92.7 percent of the households, but its quality is debatable. Sewer service is available to 66.8 percent of the house-holds, but 80 percent of the sewage is released into the Han River without treatment, thus polluting the river and coastal waters.[11]

Providing housing for the growing population is a challenging policy issue. Since 1966, an annual average of 49,000 units of housing have been constructed, and the housing shortage has been considerably ameliorated. The housing shortage was 50 percent in 1966 and it declined to 38 percent in 1980. Still, more than one-third of the families in Seoul are not properly housed, but an increased supply of housing is likely to compound the problem by further stimulating the growth of population.

Social Problems—The population concentration in Seoul brings about the concentration of the poor requiring public assistance, the incidence of crime, and unemployment. However, poverty and unemployment are not caused by the size of population, but the structure of economy. The size of population and the density of population do not necessarily have a decisive effect on the rate of crime in cities as evidenced by a systemeatic study of American cities.[12]

Social Cost and Diseconomies of Scale—The rapid rate of economic development and population growth generates the problem of social costs and diseconomies of scale due to overpopulation. Air pollution, water pollution, traffic congestion, and a dreadful city-scape without adequate green spaces or parks are the products of the economic development and urban expansion which has taken place without being guided by a set of well thought-out plans or standards. The builders and manufacturers certainly would have saved construction and pro-duction costs, but the social costs imposed on the community at large are massive and they have a lasting effect. During the expansionary period of the 1970's, the manufacturing firms and related economic activities concentrated in Seoul were believed to offer the benefits of the economies of scale.

However, in recent years, the opposite view is gaining acceptance, i.e., that the over-concentration inflicts diseconomies of scale due to traffic congestion and the rising price of land, thus contributing to the cost increase of manufacturing and transportation. The

11. *The Tong-A Ilbo*, March 14, 1983, p. 9.
12. Yong Hyo Cho, *Public Policy and Urban Crime* (Cambridge: Ballinger Publishing Com-pany, 1974), pp. 144-161.

diseconomies of scale are also considered a significant factor in the delivery of public services. A recent study reported that the marginal cost of public services per person in Seoul is ₩ 674,200 per year. This cost include that for housing, education, water supply transportation, public health, and social welfare.[13] Since there is no time series data available, it cannot be determined whether the marginal cost for public services is increasing or decreasing and at what rate.

Difficult problems abound in Seoul, but not all of these problems are generated by the excessive population concentration. The lack of adequate plans and policies plays no small part. However, in the country where economic development claims the highest priority in the national policy, any regulatory policies which may adversely affect economic development are likely to be ignored. Undersirable byproducts will follow.

IV. Factors Contributing to the Population Concentration in Seoul

The forces underlying the population growth in Seoul resemble those underlying urbanization in Europe and America, while maintaining some uniqueness. The urbanization of Korea and the population growth in Seoul are significantly influenced by economic factors in the same way as are European and American cities. But in the case of Seoul, the influence of political factors was also decisive. Korea has a highly centralized political system; distribution of economic and social values is primarily controlled by political power. In addition, education claims a top priority in the value system of Korean life. Therefore, those distinguished universities located in Seoul have a magnetic power in attracting people to Seoul.

Economic Factor—Two sets of empirical data were brought to our attention. One is the data compiled by the City Government of Seoul in each year by ascertaining the reasons for moving to Seoul by the immigrants. The other is a set of data collected by the Korea Research Institute for Human Settlements. Two major common variables for these two sets of data are economic and educational factors. The data compiled by the City Government of Seoul covers the period from 1965 to 1981 and they are summarized in Table 7. The KRIHS data are shown in Table 8, but the data for the data is not specified, though believed to be recent. The two sets of data are distinct in that the

---

13. KRIHS, *The Basic Settlement Plan of the Capital Region (Tentative)*, 1981.

subject for the City data is all immigrants to Seoul, while that for the KRIHS data is a sample of residents of the city.

Table 7: The Reasons for Moving to Seoul as Given by the Immigrants

(Percent)

	Seeking Jobs	Found Jobs	Job Changes	Educational Reasons	Accompany Family	Others
1981	6.39	8.09	9.85	9.00	62.04	4.63
1980	8.00	7.10	10.38	18.01	54.83	1.67
1979	12.00	8.3	12.3	10.9	50.8	5.7
1978	11.2	7.5	11.3	9.4	52.1	8.5
1977	13.8	8.3	9.7	7.9	54.2	6.1
1973	18.6	10.9	7.7	11.2	47.0	4.7
1972	28.6	9.6	7.9	5.4	—	48.2
1968	29.4	17.9	—	6.0	38.5	8.3
1965	13.3	4.6	5.9	6.2	0.9	69.2

Source: The City of Seoul, *Statistical Annual.*

Table 8: The Reasons for Living in Seoul by Income Classes

(in Percent)

	Average	Low Income	Middle Income	High Income
Hometown	23.9	17.2	23.5	38.2
Jobs and Related	42.5	46.0	43.2	34.4
Education	17.9	17.8	17.9	17.8
Others	15.7	19.0	15.4	14.6

Source: The Korea Research Institute for Human Settlements.

According to the City data, those who moved to Seoul to be with their families account for the largest proportion of the migrants, followed by those who moved for job-related reasons. However, the proportion of those moving to Seoul for jobs tended to decline over the years. As shown in Table 7, the job-related move declined from 47.3 percent in 1968 to 24.3 percent in 1981, the latest year for which the data are available. Of those moving to Seoul for job-related reasons, the number who came to Seoul in search of jobs has declined drastically from 29.4 percent in 1968 to 6.4 percent in 1981. The percentage of those who moved to Seoul because they found a job has remained relatively unchanged, while the percentage of those moving to Seoul because they were reassigned shows a modest increase.[14] Those who accompany their families to Seoul may also be considered job-related migration because the family members they accompany are most likely to move to Seoul because of their jobs. Both sets of data clearly demonstrate that the economic factor is a key determinant of immigration to or living in Seoul. What this implies is that there is an economic superiority in Seoul in terms of job opportunities, which are more plentiful and better paying than elsewhere in the country, thus the higher standard of living than elsewhere in the country.[15]

There is a considerable difference in per capita income between Seoul and the entire nation as shown in Table 9. However, the data for the years 1980 and 1976 are so deviant from the general trend that their accuracy is questionable. In 1975, per capita income in Seoul was 42 percent higher than the nation, but in 1976 the difference was increased to 105 percent. In the following year, the difference dropped to 38 percent. In 1979, per capita income in Seoul was 36 percent higher than the nation as a whole but in 1980 the difference was reduced to only 16 percent. Except for the year 1976, the income difference between Seoul and the entire nation is rather modest. In a modern industrial economy, the nature of economic base causes a vast variance in the income level from city to city and from region to region.[16] The more industrialized a country becomes, the more even the pattern of income distribution among different cities and regions becomes. The American experience attests to this pattern of income distribution and this trend is certainly understandable in the sense that industrialization takes place selectively in the beginning and spreads gradually throughout the country, thus creating the

---

14. The pattern of migration to and from cities in the United States is sensitive to the expansion or shrinkage of economic activities, thus job opportunities in the cities. This point is stressed in Frank Costa and Yong Hyo Cho, "Frontiers and Civic Leadership," in G. Gappert and R. Knight (eds.), *Cities in the 21st Century* (Beverly Hills, Cal.: Sage Publications, 1982), pp. 271-284.

15. Son-Ung Kim and Peter J. Donaldson, "Dealing with Seoul's Population Growth: Government Plans and Their Implementation," *Asian Survey*, Vol. 17, No. 13 (October, 1979), pp. 660-673.

16. In the case of the United States, where the industrial economy is highly advanced, the income level in Connecticut, where a high income population is heavily concentrated, is nearly twice as high as that in Mississippi, where the economy is still agriculture-based. For example, in 1980, per capita income in Connecticut was $11,720 while that in Mississippi was $6,580.

equalizing effect of income level.[17]

Table 9: Per capita Income for the Entire Nation and Seoul: 1975-1980

(in thousands of Won)

	Nation (Won)	Seoul (Won)	Ratio of Seoul (%)
1980	900	1,049	116
1979	649	881	136
1978	504	707	140
1977	377	521	138
1976	200	411	205
1975	228	324	142

Sources: The City of Seoul, *Production and Income Distribution Within the City of Seoul,* 1975-1981; and The Economic Planning Board, *The Statistical Annual of Korea,* 1981.

Educational Factors—Education is another factor widely acknowledged as influencing the choice of Seoul as residence. The KRIHS data shows that some 18 percent of the residents in Seoul admit that they live in Seoul because it offers better quality education for their children. The City of Seoul data indicates that some 10 percent of the new migrants into the city admit that they move to Seoul for educational reasons.

Unlike these two sets of data, another survey conducted in the middle of the 1970's suggests that nearly 51 percent of those moving to Seoul are motivated by the educational opportunities.[18] Education occupies a top place if not the top place in the value hierachy of Korean society. Therefore, it is quite possible to assume that most of those who move to Seoul for jobs are also motivated to locate in Seoul because of the educational advantages that Seoul offers for their children. In this sense, jobs and education are mutually reinforcing factors in motivating people to move to Seoul, thus creating a massive population concentration.

17. If the income level is compared between Seoul and the rest of the country excluding Seoul, the difference will certainly stand out much more than the comparison between Seoul and the entire country including Seoul as is the case in Table 9. Even if this computation problem is taken into account, the difference is surprisingly low.
18. Choon-hee No, "The causes of population concentration in the Capital Region and its dispersal methods," *Urban Problems* (September, 1975), pp. 8-18 (A translation from Korean).

Political Factors—It is indisputable that political power occupies the pinnacle of the traditional value system in Korea. All other social values are attainable when political power is achieved and this tradition is still more or less intact. The unprecedented economic development during the late 1960's and the 1970's was led by the government. Government support and regulations have affected the corporate operations in every aspect. Therefore, corporations engaged in all kinds of economic activities found it preferable to locate their operations, or at least their headquarters, in Seoul so as to maintain intimate relationships with the government agencies in charge. Because of the wide-ranging influence of the government over coporate operations, information about the government's policy changes or new regulations has critical importance to the success of any business firm. To be part of the grapevine of information flow, it is essential to be located in Seoul.

Since Seoul is the capital of the highly centralized government, economic activities, particularly corporate headquarters, and educational institutions and students are attracted to Seoul. The reason that education is so highly valued is that an excellent education is a prerequisite to obtaining promising positions in government and business. Therefore, political power, economic factors, and educational motivation in combination constituted a sort of triad which powered the incredibly rapid population growth in Seoul.

V. Public Policies to Restrain Population Concentration in Seoul

Since the mid-1960's, it has been sustained as the basic policy of the government to restrain the growth of population in Seoul and to disperse the existing population and economic activities. Here, we would like to review those policies and plans adopted and implemented so far in order to specify the nature of those policies and to ascertain the effect of those policies. Further, we would like to seek to outline a set of polic directions which are based on reality rather than hopeful thinking dictated by necessity only.

Several policies and plans dealing with population growth problems in Seoul and the Capital Region have been adopted or developed by the Blue House, The Economic Planning Board, the Ministry of Construction, the First Minister without portfolio, and the City Government of Seoul. Some of the more important policies and plans are listed below in a chronological order.

Policies and Plans to Control
Population Growth in Seoul

Year

1964 Policy to Prevent Population Concentration in Large Cities (Prepared by the Ministry of Construction and Adopted by the Cabinet Meeting)

1969 Policy Proposals to Restrain Population Concentration in the Capital Region (the Blue House and the Ministry of Construction)

1970 Adoption of the Basic Policy Guidelines to Control Excessive Density and Population Concentration in the Capital Region (The Cabinet Meeting)

1972 Completion of Research Proposal on Controlling Population Concentration in Seoul (Seoul City)

1973 Completion of A Policy Proposal to Disperse Population in Large Cities (The Economic Planning Board)

1974 Proposal for Land Use Policy and Urban Planning: Policy to Reduce Density in Large Cities (the Blue House)

1975 • Policy Proposal for Land Use and Urban Development: Policy to Reorder the Settlement Pattern in the Capital Region (the Ministry of Construction)
      •Policy to Reduce Density in Seoul (EPB)
      •Plan to Reduce Density in Seoul (Seoul City)

1977 Policy to Redistribute Population in the Capital Region, Confirmed as the Basic National Plan

1981 The Basic Plan (Tentative) to Reorder the Settlement Pattern in the Capital Region, 1982-1991 (KRIHS).

The existing public policies to control population growth and density in Seoul or the Capital Region can be classified into two categories based on policy scope and policy direction. Based on geographical scope, the policies can be grouped into two categories: first, those policies and plans that deal with Seoul or the Capital Region: second, those that deal with the entire nation. Based on policy directions, those policies and plans may be grouped into four categories: (1) suppressing development in Seoul and the surrounding areas such as prohibiting construction of new factories and removing the existing factories and setting up green belts around the city: (2) directing the growth pressure in Seoul into the outlying areas within the Capital Region: (3) constructing the sites for industrial parks in selected areas throughout the country to stimulate balanced growth; and (4) systematically balancing development by establishing selected cities as population growth poles and by encouraging community development of farming and fishing villages to prevent migration to cities in general and to Seoul in particular.[19]

In spite of these policies and plans, it is evident that the objective of controlling population growth in Seoul has not been successful. In 1964, the population of Seoul barely exceeded three million, but in 1982 it was very close to nine million. Even in 1977, the City Government of Seoul was planning to stabilize its population at the level of seven million by the year of 2000, though such an objective was rendered unrealistic long ago.

However, it is unfair to be overly critical in evaluating the existing policies to control population growth in Seoul for the simple reason that the population of Seoul exceeded the targeted level. Two things much be taken into account. First, the growth rate of Seoul is largely similar to the long-term urban growth rate of the entire nation. The population of Seoul increased by 242.2 percent between 1960 and 1980 from 2.44 million to 8.37 million, while that of all the cities was increased by 206.5 percent during the same period, from 7 million to 21.44 million.

Second, the more systematic and comprehensive policies are of recent vintage and in the initial stage of implementation. Specifically, the 1977 Plan to Redistribute Population in the Capital Region is in the early phase of implementation and the Second Comprehensive National Development Plan was launched in 1982. If the 1977 Plan to Redistribute Population in the Capital Region achieves the desired objectives, the entire Capital Region is likely to become a vast megalopolitan region: namely, a phenomenon of enlarging Seoul throughout the Capital Region may take place. In this case, the urban problems in the Capital Region will become even more difficult to manage.

The Second Comprehensive National Development Plan is much more rational than those preceding policies and plans from the perspective of population distribution. This plan considers the population problem of Seoul as a part of national population problem. Instead of attempting to suppress population growth in Seoul, it seeks to strengthen regional cities. Instead of seeking short-term effects, the policy is seeking a step-by-step and long-term effect. Whether this ambitious policy is to become successful in relieving population growth

---

19. This point is the main policy focus of the Second Comprehensive National Development Policy launched in 1982 and to be completed in 1991.

pressure on Seoul and enhancing a balanced development throughout the country or not is dependent upon the future efforts in refining the policy and in implementing it with consistency. More specifically, the success of this plan will depend upon the priority it commands in the national budget allocation, the ability to mobilize private capital for the implementation of the plan, and how effectively the capital made available from public and private sources is invested in the development processes.

In the past twenty years, urban policies and national development policies have been criticized for lack of consistency in strategy as well as the means employed. Further, additional criticisms are that policy implementation lacked the staying power in the sense that the effort to implement a policy has tended to be discontinued without seeing it through to the final stage. However, the basic objectives of these policies remain unchanged; i.e., to limit the population growth is Seoul, better yet to reduce population in Seoul and to stimulate the growth of cities in the outlying region and to achieve a better balance in the national development pattern and population distribution. These policy objectives are still a dream.

1. Population Policy for Seoul: Alternatives for the Future

The less than impressive records of those population control policies in place may not necessarily suggest that these policies were ill-conceived, but that it is difficult to reverse the population trend of a great city like Seoul. Here, an attempt is made to outline a number of alternative policies which are anchored in broad perspective and based on the factual data. A set of conceptual premises underlying these alternative policies are advanced as follows.

First, the population will continue to grow in Korea. The growth rate may decline in the future, but the era of zero growth may not come in the foreseeable future, even in the 21st century. Second, an increasingly greater proportion of the increasing population is likely to be absorbed by the cities. In the beginning of the 21st century, the urban population of Korean is expected to reach the level of 80 percent as in the United States, the United Kingdom, and Japan. Third, the economic structure will continue to change, most likely from labor-intensive to capital-intensive production system. This change will be hastened as those countries with surplus labor like China become increasingly more active in international competition. More specifically, the post-industrial economic activities, particularly service economy, that require highly advanced knowledge and skills are likely to gain greater significance. Fourth, the society will face the unavoidable challenge to transform from a society of inequity to one of equity. The differences between cities and rural areas, between large and small cities, between occupations, and between regions that characterize social inequity are likely to be brought to the forefront as policy targets.

Korea is a nation with limited land area and a high population density. From a policy point of view, it is more meaningful to judge the density of population based on social-economic carrying capacity rather than on a physical standard. So considered, the excessive density of population is not limited to Seoul. Rather, it may be correct to view the continuous growth of population in Seoul as indicative of its greater carrying capacity.

In fact, the key indicators of the carrying capacity of population of Seoul are far stronger than the rest of the country, including water supply, sewer service, communication facilities, employment opportunity, medical service facilities, etc. The carrying capacity in Seoul is likely to further outdistance the rest of country as Seoul is transformed into a more modern and international city and a proud window of Korea. The population policy for Seoul seeks conflicting objectives. On the one hand, it seeks to control population growth and disperse the existing population away from Seoul. On the other hand, a variety of policies are employed to expand the capacity to accommodate more population in Seoul, thus stimulating a further growth of population there.

Now we turn to some of the policy alternatives considered more rational, comprehensive, long-term oriented, and fact-based.

2. National Population Policy

Korea has relied on birth control policy to control population growth for nearly two decades. The birth control policy has been focused on physiological and medical aspects, but lately a social welfare aspect of birth control is brought into policy consideration. A case in point is a policy adopted recently limiting the educational expense allowance for government employees to two children. The birth control policy may become more effective when it is built into the economic incentives and disincentives of a broad range of public policies as follows.

First, only two children may be allowed as income tax exemptions. Second, the care for the older persons may be guaranteed by public support when they do not have their own children, particularly sons. A predominant majority of Koreans tends to plan dependency on their children when they become old.[20] Since old age dependence on their own children means more than economic dependence, for example companionship and love, the government guarantee of livelihood for the older persons without children, particularly sons, may not eliminate families with multiple children, but such policy may certainly help reduce such families.

Third, when middle and high school education becomes compulsory, the tuition may be waived for no more than two children per family and the full educational cost may be charged to the parents for all the additional children. This type of financial disincentive may also be applied to elementary education system. This responsibility for educational expenses for children beyond a given limit may discourage parents from having too many children.

3. *Environmental Protection Policy*

The pollution of the rivers, air, land, and coastal waters is becoming increasingly worse, thus making them less suitable as living environments and less valuable as natural resources. Agricultural pesticides, fertilizers, raw sewage from homes, toxic waste from industrial plants, auto emission, emission from factory smokestacks, pollute the land, water, and air in the urban as well as rural areas throughout the entire country. The growing pollution threatens to destroy the natural space for human habitation and the natural resources for economic activities, thus resulting in the reduction in the carrying capacity of population of the land.

Environmental protection must be a high priority item in the national population policy, including the growth control policy of urban population. The sewage collection and treatment system, which is sufficient to assure public safety, must be provided for all cities and towns. Considering the alarming degree of farmland pollution due to pesticides, it is urgent to develop pesticides that are not harmful to humans and animals. It is also essential to enforce a stringent set of air pollution control standards and apply them natiom-wide. The massive economic development in recent years will be rendered meaningless unless the nation succeeds in protecting the environment from pollution and recovering the environment already polluted.

It has been planned for Seoul to extend the sewer connection to all households and to build plants to treat all sewage by the year of

---

20. According to a recent survey by the KDI, 52.8 percent of parents reported that they will depend on their sons when they become old. This propensity to depend on a son is often the cause of having many children. *The Hankook Ilbo,* February 11, 1983, p. 3.

1987. A pollution control plan of this sort must be extended to all types of pollution and to the entire nation as a long-term plan and implement it step-by-step.

4. Policies to Reduce Imbalance in Locational Advantages Between Seoul and Other Areas

Being the capital of the nation, Seoul offers political advantages unsurpassed by any location in the nation. All the ˧ ˖itical powers of the nation are centralized and controlled in Seoul. The massive efforts to modernize the nation's economy and social structure are led by the government located in Seoul. The advantages enjoyed by Seoul as the seat of political powers are as much a deep-rooted tradition as a contemporary phenomenon. Therefore, it is unlikely to find an answer to the challenge to develop a policy or a set of policies to reduce the differentials between Seoul and other areas caused by the concentration of political powers in Seoul.

To move the second level government offices out of Seoul, government office buildings have been built in Gwachon, a newly developing town outside Seoul. However, relocating the second level government offices to Gwachon office buildings will not disperse the locational advantages of Seoul because the policy-making and administrative decision-making powers will continue to remain in the headquarters. Therefore, a policy of this nature will not affect the location of those economic and social activities closely attached to political powers. Although it cannot be expected to eliminate the differences in locational advantages caused by political power superiority, the implementation of a local self-government system and the transformation of an economic develoment system from the government-dominated to the private-controlled one are likely to lessen the differences.

Local Self-Government System — The implementation of a local self-government system is synonymous with the decentralization of political powers to localities, thus dispersing the unique advantages offered by political power to other areas. The effect of this policy will go beyond the level of powers transferred from the central government to localities, provided that the local self-government system is made into a political mechanism to promote the community consciousness, community pride, and the desire to build one's own community into a better place to work and live in instead of looking for an opportunity to move out. A community spirit, the conviction of the people that they can have a happy life by preserving and developing their own communities with their own hands, should accompany the implementation of local self-government system to create the desired effect. This kind of community spirit can grow in a social climate where leaders of all walks of life demonstrate such spirit in their daily lives.

Transformation of the Economic System from the Government-Dominated to the Private-Controlled One—During the past twenty years, the central government thoroughly controlled the economic development policy of Korea. The entire range of major economic policies including capital formation, technology import, product export, and the labor-management relations were directed by the central government. The government-controlled economy has accentuated the locational superiority of Seoul. Relinquishing government control over the economy and transferring it to private control is likely to reduce the dependency on Seoul.

Recently, the economic system has begun to change in the direction of privatization. The case in point is the privatization of commercial banks. Currently, the Korea Development Institute, an economic thinktank supported by the government, argues that free competition should govern the economy instead of government control, and as a specific step toward this direction, the KDI proposed removing restrictions on foreign imports. The private-controlled, free competitive economy will make it less necessary, if not unncessary, for the corporations to depend on political powers, thus expanding the targets of locational choices for their operations throughout the country in search of a place where production costs can be reduced and productivity can be increased.

5. Other Measures to Reduce the Difference in Locational Advantages

Policies to develop cities and communities in the Outlying Areas—The Second National Comprehensive Development Plan is a long-term national development policy to be refined and implemented step-by-step, and this plan is premised upon the development of cities and communities in the outlying areas away from Seoul and other large cities in order to restrain the population growth. The plan designates which cities will serve as the primary growth poles and those which will act as the secondary growth poles. Those cities designated as the growth poles are dispersed throughout the country and their ability to absorb population and economic activities will promote a balance in the national development. The development of these cities and other communities of all sizes should be carefully planned and carried out to be consistent with the Comprehensive Naitonal Development Plan.

The development of regional cities and outlying communities should safe-guard environmental quality by installing sewer and waste treatment facilities and other pollution-preventing systems and should provide a high quality infrastructure attractive to production and service industries in this technologically advanced era, including transportation, communication, and public services. Particularly, capital infrastructure will require a huge investment. The capital budget must be financed creatively in a way satisfactory to the tax payers and users.

Incentives to Industries to Locate in Outlying Cities—In order to attract industries and firms to cities away from Seoul, these cities must offer more advantages than Seoul can, both economically and socially. In case the location·itself does not offer economic advantages, the government must compensate these disadvantages.

The economic compensation must be equitable for the corporations and the tax payers, but it is difficult to determine the level of equitable compensation. It must also be recognized that the level of compensation for locational disadvantages will differ from one industry to another. In order to offer equitable yet attractive incentives, the losses and gains caused by locational differences must be carefully studied.[21] Economic incentives to locate industries in cities away from Seoul and other large cities could take a variety of forms including the following: (1) to provide the land for factories or part of the site acquisition cost; (2) to subsidize a part of the construction cost of factories; and (3) to offer tax abatement. Tax reduction is likely to be effective in inducing industrties at desired locations, provided that the tax system of the country is highly sophisticated and efficiently administered. Most important of all, the tax benefit will become a critical factor in determining the industrial location when the balance between profits and loss is dependent on it. Otherwise, tax incentives will prove unproductive.[22]

---

21. In the United States, a differential tax credit has been offered to firms investing in the declining and high unemployment areas including the metropolitan central cities. However, little research has been done to determine the business cost differentials due to the locational disadvantages.

22. In the United States, tax incentives are often used to influence the corporate investment behavior whether it be to encourage the level of reinvestment or the location of investment.

Disincentives to Industries Locating in Seoul—To relocate industries from Seoul to a desired location or to discourage firms interested in locating in Seoul, a policy of imposing economic penalty may be employed. For example, special taxes may be imposed on those industries generating pollution or attracting population. The extra burden of taxes may force such industries to relocate from Seoul to other less congested places or discourage such firms from locating in Seoul. The revenues from taxes may be used to control pollution or to provide subsidies to those industries locating (or relocating) in certain designated places.

Educational Policies—In view of the influence of superior quality of education in attracting people to Seoul, educational quality must be equalized to succeed in dispersing population to the growth-pole cities. In order to overcome the difference in educational quality between Seoul and the rest of country, educational policies need to emphasize measures to improve educational quality in the outlying areas, to reduce educational expenses for parents in the outlying areas, and to provide preferential treatment for students graduating from schools and universities in the outlying areas for college entrance or government and business recruitment.

The measures to improve educational quality include faculty, facilities, and curriculum. For example, the quality of faculty in local universities can be improved by attracting capable and ambitious faculty members to local universities. To do so, the faculty positions in local universities must be prestigeous and well paid. Government consulting and advisory positions may be assigned disproportionately in favor of local university faculty as well as favoring local university faculty in the awarding research grants. The local universities may need to be supported more generously regarding library, laboratory, faculty office, and assistants to faculty for research and teaching.

Financial incentives may be offered to those attending universities and high schools in the outlying areas so as to make schools outside Seoul, financially attractive. Such inventives may include a disproportionate allocation of available scholarships to those students in local universities and a substantial difference in tuition and fees in favor of students attending universities outside Seoul. Furthermore, the tuition-free public high school education being considered for the future may begin in those areas for which population growth is desired and then may be extended gradually to the large cities as additional financial resources become available.

The most critical factor that affects the choice of education is the differential opportunity for jobs after graduation. The graduates from the universities in Seoul, particularly from those prestigious universities, have been preferred by the government and corporations in recruitment. A public policy designed to give preferential treatment to local university graduates in the government and corporate recruitment processes is essential to provide incentives to choose the less developed areas for education and residence. In the United States, many cities and local governments maintain so-called residency requirements for employment in the local government so as to reserve the government jobs of the locality for their own residents. When the local self-government system is implemented, a variety of residency requirements may become a useful means for population dispersion, though that is not necessarily an ideal policy approach. It may be imperative to adjust the corporate recruitment process to include the regional balance as a criterion in order to avoid recruitment excessively biased toward Seoul.

IV. Summary and Conclusions

The population of the Capital Region approaches 14 million and accounts for nearly 36 percent of the nation's total population. The population of Seoul alone is nearly 9 million and accounts for 22.4 percent of the total population. The degree of Seoul's concentration in political, economic, and social activities far exceeds that of the population. The political, economic, and social distance between Seoul and the rest of hte country is striking, and this distance places Seoul in a superior position to pull regional population to it.

Public policies developed and implemented in the past to slow down population growth, if not reduce population, have not produced the desired effect as evidenced by the population trends of Seoul during the past twenty years. Those policies employed are perfectly sensible as far as their directions are concerned. They have pursued three policy directions in various combinations: (1) those policies seeking to remove population-attracting industries and firms from Seoul to other areas; (2) those policies speeding up urban development in the Capital Region outside Seoul to accomodate the excess population flowing over from Seoul; and (3) policies pursuing a balanced development throughout the country. The reasons that these policies have failed to reduce population in Seoul do not seem to come from the illconceived policies, but from the lack of consistency and persistence in the efforts to refine and implement them. The balanced development policies are of recent origin and will take time to put into full operations.

The balanced development policies manifested as the national goal have been considerably compromised in the sense that the actual policy measures put to work are biased toward accelerating the development of Seoul, thus further outdistancing the other regions. The development of urban infrastructure associated with the 1988 Olympics and the 1986 Asian Games and other major international events hosted in Seoul turn out to have an adverse effect on the population distribution policy of the nation, particularly between Seoul and the rest of the country. Under the present conditions, the population of Seoul will continue to grow and social and economic activities will concentrate in Seoul more than ever.

In this paper, we propose two sets of policy approaches which are mutually complementary, though distinct. First, we believe that policy priority must be placed on the overall population growth and natural environment of the entire nation, since Korea is a small country with a very high population density. Korea has a limited carrying capacity of population. Therefore, the carrying capacity must be maximized by protecting the natural enivronment from pollution and destruction, while birth control should be encouragd to reduce the rate of population growth to eventual zero growth level. The zero growth of population or a negative growth will relieve the nation of the mounting population pressure.

Second, we believe that a variety of policy measures must be desiged and implemented to reduce the differences in political, economic, social, and cultural activities between Seoul and the rest of the country. These differences are the major factors influencing population movement from the rural areas and small cities to Seoul since it is believed that Seoul offers a chance for ordinary people to have a better life and for talented people to have greater success.

Is it possible to control the population growth in Seoul? The answer is affirmative, but the actual result will depend on the policy priority that this particular problem commands now and in the future. A firm commitment must be made to address this problem by developing a set of long-term and systematic policies and implementing these policies consistently and persistently. The past two decades in Korea have been the era of economic development at any cost. The next two decades will hopefully be a new era of development which will enhance the quality of life.

Part Five

Social Development

17

New Dynamics for Rural Development: The Experience of Saemaeul Undong

Young Pyoung Kim

Introduction

In 1970 a visitor to a South Korean village would have found only a small cluster of simple thatched huts, each enclosed by a rough straw fence. The narrow lanes would scarcely accommodate even a small cart, and he would have stepped carefully as he walked through the village, mindful of the open drainage ditches along his path. In the fields surrounding the village he would have seen peasants laboriously cultivating traditional crops, using techniques that differed little from those used generations ago. This was the situation in no less than 35,000 villages, typically consisting of 25 to 75 houses, scattered across the nation.

Today things have changed in rural South Korea, however. Many villages now display dramatic evidence of new outlooks and heightened economic vitality. Slate roofs top many houses. Straw fences have given way to neat enclosures of concrete block. Unpaved lanes have become sound roads, and culverts have replaced open ditches. In the fields an extraordinary change has taken hold. Farmers are growing new crops, employing new production patterns and using technology rarely seen a decade ago. Korean villages are voluntarily undertaking a wide range of cooperative development projects— and they seem to be working.

The source of this new dynamism is the saemaeul* ("new village")

---

*Pronounced Sa(as in "cat")-ma-ool. Korean government documents give the name of the New Village movement as "saemaul," but this spelling tends to be pronounced in two syllables in spite of the name's three syllables. Therefore, I prefer the "sae-ma-eul" spelling.

movement. It was launched in 1971 to lessen the gap between the urban and rural sectors resulting from government emphasis on industrialization and relative neglect of agriculture during the prior decade. The changes wrought by saemaeul are evident not only in attitudes but also in living standards. The average farm household earned $813 in 1971; in 1975 the figure reached $1818, and two years later it had exceeded $3,000.[1]

The remarkable jump in household income cannot be attributed solely to the saemaeul movement, of course, for the striking industrialization of the 1960's itself played an important role. Before 1960 agriculture was the primary industry in Korea, with more than 60 percent of the population engaged in farming. However, the rural population decreased as industrialization opened wide opportunities in urban areas, until by the late 1970's Korea's rural population had dropped to less than 35 percent of the total. Not only the proportion but also the absolute numbers of rural population have been declining, a factor in reducing rural underemployment and "disguised employment," which in turn increases the *per capita* income of the agricultural sector. Industrialization has also stimulated rural development by improving market conditions through increased urban income and resultant growth in demand for agricultural products.

Favorable conditions for agricultural development require the backing of sound policy. In Korea that policy has been provided by the saemaeul movement. The difference in the growth rate in the agricultural sector between the saemaeul period and immediately prior years—only 2.5% from 1967 to 1971, rising to 5.9% from 1972 to 1976—cannot be ignored as evidence of the effectiveness of saemaeul policies. This study is an effort to understand what makes saemaeul work.

Context and Emergence of Saemaeul

The Rural Context

Most Koreans outside urban areas work the land, not so much due to an affinity for farming, but because of lack of alternative employ-

---

1. The household income figures are in many documents issued by the Korean government. Farm household income actually overtook urban salary and wage earner income in 1975. See *A Handbook of Korea*, Korean Oversea Information Service, Seoul, 1978, pp. 532-535; *Saemaul Undong*, Korean Background Series, Korean Oversea Information Service, (KOIS) Seoul, 1977, p.55; *Korean Statistical Yearbook From 1971 to 1978*, Economic Planning Board, Seoul.

ment. Agriculture has rarely been very profitable; at times it has barely reached even subsistence levels. Meager plots—less than one
hectare for the average household—have hampered land management
and discouraged investment in land improvement. Poor techniques
and crude tools have kept farmers tied to a life of poverty and of painfully hard work. To add to the sheer physical difficulty of peasant
agriculture, Korean economic policy has often worked to the farmer's
disadvantage. Low prices of agricultural products compared poorly
with the prices of manufactured goods the farmer purchased. Inadequate water control systems left fields exposed to flood and drought.
Where irrigation facilities existed they were poorly built and carelessly
administered. The lack of rural roads complicated nearly every farm
chore and discouraged the farmer from using agricultural machinery.

It is not surprising that the peasant's resentment of his station in
life has been a perennial theme in Korean culture. In recent history,
peasant aspirations for a better life produced two broad social
movements: education and rural-urban migration.

Education offered peasants he hope that their children might escape
the hardships of virtual serfdom on the land. When opportunities
for schooling began to expand at the end of Japanese rule in 1945,
peasants who could manage without their children's help sent them
to school in the cities. This drive for education, rooted in the hope
for a better life, has dramatically boosted the average level of education in Korea.

Education and urbanization are closely linked. While some
educated youths did return to their villages, such homecomings implied a failure to succeed in the city; therefore, most young Koreans
drawn to the cities for schooling stayed there. Education was not the
only urban appeal. Rich peasants migrated with the intent, and often
the resources, to establish shops and businesses. Noteworthy, too,
were those landless peasants and other economic refugees who headed for Korea's cities with neither clear plans nor prospects, only the
conviction that urban life must be better than what they were leaving behind.

Rapid, wholesale demographic changes have blurred the distinction between city and village cultures. A large segment of Korea's
population is in social transition—no longer rural, not yet urban.
Many new city dwellers retain close ties with their home villages,
creating important town-and-country dynamics. Urban workers often
return home for the New Year and the Moon Festival (chusok),
cultivating ties with relatives and participating in ancestral
ceremonies. More mundane but equally important are the economic
exchanges facilitated by this hybrid culture. Peasants often send part

of their crops to family members living in the city, while urban Koreans obtain various manufactured necessities for their relatives on the land.

Not only people and goods but ideas and expectations flow between cities and villages. In recent years education and the mass media have broken down rural isolation, improvements in transportation systems have made cities more accessible, and visits from relatives provide vivid models of urban life. Young villagers are altering their perceptions of the possibilities. They sense that village life is harder and less productive than it might be. They are ready for change.

A range of circumstances make Korean villages fertile ground for innovation. The overall literacy rate of the peasantry is high. Village youth generally attain an educational level well beyond minimal literacy; many are graduates of high schools or technical schools. In addition, the almost universal experience of compulsory military service gives young Korean men an active and progressive orientation and ensures that a significant segment of the populace is familiar with technology and organized undertakings.

These factors profoundly influenced the social setting for the saemaeul movement. During the 1960's rising urban incomes and the requirements of an industrial labor force created an imperative for rural development, while the competent and motivated rural population acquired a potential for change. But needs and possibilities are not sufficient conditions for rural development. *Policy* was needed to initiate action, and in the 1970's an appropriate policy was established.

Emergence and Refinement of the Saemaeul Concept

Korea's rural sector suffered from official neglect prior to the saemaeul movement. Officials had little enthusiasm for programs promoting agricultural innovation, and market arrangements generally worked to the farmer's disadvantage. The government's emphasis was on urban policies.

In the early 1970's executive attention turned to the imbalance between urban and rural Korea. President Park knew of villages where seemingly spontaneous self-help efforts had produced striking transformations in the quality of rural life. Inspired by these models he proposed a strategy: rural development through cooperative village self-reliance. At a provincial governors' conference in 1971 Park introduced the saemaeul idea and called for efforts to translate it into action.

The essence of the saemaeul plan was simply to promote cooperative development efforts by villages, guided by competent and motivated village leaders, with judicious government aid through technical and financial assistance and the training of local leaders. Successful cooperation in one project would create experience, organizational capacity, and the motivation for more ambitious self-help efforts.

Realizing the vision[2]

The first stage of the saemaeul movement ran from 1971 to 1973. It was intended as a foundation for further growth. The cooperative theme dictated a concentration on building public facilities and village infrastructure.

The President's personal support of the movement supplied an impetus for building saemaeul institutional arrangements within government organizations and at local levels. The Ministry of Home Affairs (MHA) integrated and coordinated government policies. A new Saemaeul Movement Central Consultative Council promoted and managed overall planning. Special divisions were created in ministries involved in rural matters—such as Home Affairs, Agriculture and Fisheries, Commerce and Industry, and Education—and in local governments. Organizations patterned after the Central Consultative Council were set up at each level of local administration: province *(do)*, country *(kun)*, township *(myon)*, and village *(maeul)*. The two most significant official innovations were the opening of the Saemaeul Leaders' Training Institute and the creation of a system for classifying villages. These marked the beginning of the institutionalization of rural development in Korea.

The saemaeul ideology and its associated policies were not fully formed in the first stage of the program; they evolved out of a trial-and-error process. Officials quickly discovered, for example, that imposing projects on villages invited disappointment. This became clear as early as 1971 in saemaeul's first major undertaking when villages were offered cement to build common wells, laundries, compost plots, and other public facilities. Only one-third of Korea's 35,000 villages responded positively. On the basis of this experience the government shifted its focus from centrally-developed projects to the encouragement of village initiatives. Saemaeul has since concentrated its efforts on those villages that display the will and the competence to carry out development projects in accordance with the program's

---

2. The three stages of the movement's progress coincides with the Korean government classification. See *Saemaul Undong: From the Beginning to the Present (1976 and 1977)*, (in Korean) Ministry of Home Affairs. However, the perspective of this paper is not necessarily that of the government.

ideals of self-reliance and cooperation.

The second stage of the movement (1974-76) aimed at improving rural living standards and disseminating the saemaeul concept throughout Korean society. Income-generating projects received priority, particularly those dealing with food production, regional crop specialization, and cooperative production. Other projects to improve village environments—houses, roads, drainage, and mountain woodlands—were also emphasized. Community wells and laundary places were lined with cement for sanitation. The assumption was that visible "environmental improvement" projects would accelerate momentum for further efforts.

Village-level associations were established where they did not already exist, to encourage projects for generation of income and environmental improvement. These organizations, including women's leagues, youth clubs, and saemaeul production units, exercised considerable autonomy in selecting projects; they also received outside guidance and assitance. Such village institutions channeled spontaneity and made possible the continuity of cooperative efforts. Many of them have been effective in promoting improvements in village marketing and technical innovation.

As the movement grew and evolved, attempts were made to spread the saemaeul concept throughout Korea. The saemaeul training program was expanded to include leaders from government and society at large. Ministers and legislators were invited to attend training programs, and most government officials were required to participate. Trainees were introduced to the underlying spirit and ideology of the movement and briefed on its concepts and strategies. There are currently 15 institutions in Korea modeled on the Saemaeul Leaders Training Institute at Suwon.[3]

---

3. The saemaeul training has played an important role in disseminating the concept of saemaeul not only among rural leaders but also among the influential classes throughout Korean society—the bureaucrats, technocrats, and professionals. In fact, the majority of saemaeul training programs are primarily for person who are not directly related to the saemaeul movement but are prominent in society at large.

The saemaeul training has a military-like aspect. All trainees live in dormitories, isolated from their normal contacts during the training period of a week to ten days. Activities are thoroughly programmed. The daily training starts with collevtive singing of the national anthem and exercising for physical fitness. Daytime sessions include lectures on national security and the economy or on the saemaeul spirit, field tours, and report and narratives by selected saemaeul leaders. Evening sessions, until the military-style roll call at 10:00 p.m., include group discussion about personal concerns regarding the saemaeul, group singing of saemaeul songs, meditation about "what I will do for the nation," and writing in diaries to be presented to the training institute on completion of the course. These meetings are in some ways very similar to religious proselytizing. There are also many occasions for self-confession by saemaeul leaders and selected trainees about per-

Table 1: Basic Statistics of the Saemaeul Movement*

	Unit	Total	1971	1972	1973	1974	1975	1976	1977
Participating Villages	village	—	33,267	22,708	34,665	34,665	36,547	36,557	36,557
No. of Projects Implemented	thousand	7,845	385	320	1,093	1,099	1,598	887	2,463
Average Projects per Village	one	215	12	14	32	32	44	24	67
Investment for Saemaeul Movement	million won	1,359.7	12.2	31.3	98.4	132.8	295.9	322.6	466.5
Government Assistance	million won	6,361	41	33	215	308	1,653	1,651	2,460
Investment per Project	thousand won	173	32	98	90	121	185	364	189
Investment per Village	thousand won	37,197	367	1,378	2,839	3,831	8,096	8,825	12,764

Source: *Saemaul Undong: 1977*, Ministry of Home Affairs, Korean Government, pp. 142-143.

*A word of caution about the numbers of projects and amounts of investment shown in this table. Village saemaeul projects range from small and simple ones like haymaking, cleaning village streets, purchasing farm machinery, repairing ditches and lanes, and cleaning wells, which can be accomplished in a day's time, to full-scale remodeling of village structure. The numbers of projects do not represent *initiated* projects but the ones *implemented* during the year, regardless of size. Therefore, continuing projects like the Village Nursery Operation would be counted as "implemented" projects each year. The implemented projects include both cooperative ones and individual ones for personal benefit. The astonishing number of projects in 1977, the year when emphasis on saemaeul was probably at its height, simply means that many small, unsystematic activities were implemented under the name of saemaeul. A second observation is that large amounts of investments are based on calculations of labor offered free by the villagers.

The third stage, from 1977 onward, has been concerned with rein-forcing self-help initiatives. Unassisted, spontaneous development efforts are now emphasized. Villages are encouraged to accumulate capital by designing and managing projects independently. The scope of projects for generating income now includes such non-farm sources as small-scale village industries. Villages that have failed to advance satisfactorily receive special attention and assistance.

Table 1 shows the general trend of the saemaeul movement. In the beginning (1971-72) the movement was cautious and experimen-tal. The numbers and scale of project investments expanded as the government learned from experience, and increased its assistance and investment per village.

The Project Process in the Saemaeul Movement

The Korean Administrative System and Saemaeul

Though centered on the village, saemaeul is shaped and guided by Korea's strongly centralized administrative system.[4] This section of the study traces saemaeul's organizational structure and examines the relationships between public agencies and between different levels of government. It also examines elements of the movement that are at variance with the centralized Korean administration.

The saemaeul movement is too vast a program to be implemented by any single government agency. Its scope and diversity are such that some part of the movement falls within the jurisdiction of vir-

---

sonal contributions, accomplished and intended, to the saemaeul movement. Throughout the training runs a philosophy that could be put in these words: "The saemaeul is the savior of the nation, and I must devote myself to the saemaeul more than ever."

In my judgement, the impact of saemaeul training is ambiguous, except for the benefits of propagating the saemaeul concept among bureaucrats and technocrats. One may argue that the training has been the major factor in providing actual and potential saemaeul leaders with a rigorous conception of the movement, the managerial skills for village develop-ment, and the positive vision of national development. The contrasting view is that the saemaeul training has been a kind of "brainwashing" program intended to enhance the political legitimacy of President Park's *Yushin* (rehabilitation) government. For further information about the saemaeul training program, see Kim, Hae-Dong (et.al.), *An Evalua-tion and Field Experimentation of Saemaeul Movement in the Republic of Korea*, Graduate School of Public Administration, Seoul National University, Seoul, 1979, pp. 67-101.

4. Students of Korean public administration agree that the Korean government has a cen-tralized administrative system. See, for example, Kim, Hae-Dong, "Relationships be-tween the Central (Government) and the Local (Government)" and the following discussion (in Korean) *Korean Development Policy Studies*, v 2, 1975, Graduate School of Public Administration, Seoul National University, pp. 73-95.

Figure 1: Coordinative System for the Saemaeul Movement

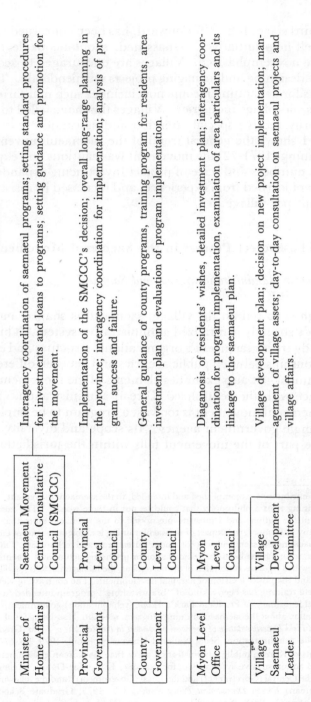

		Functions
Minister of Home Affairs	Saemaeul Movement Central Consultative Council (SMCCC)	Interagency coordination of saemaeul programs; setting stardard procedures for investments and loans to programs; setting guidance and promotion for the movement.
Provincial Government	Provincial Level Council	Implementation of the SMCCC's decision; overall long-range planning in the province; interagency coordination for implementation; analysis of program success and failure.
County Government	County Level Council	General guidance of county programs, training program for residents, area investment plan and evaluation of program implementation.
Myon Level Office	Myon Level Council	Diaganosis of residents' wishes, detailed investment plan; interagency coordination for program implementation, examination of area particulars and its linkage to the saemaeul plan.
Village Saemaeul Leader	Village Development Committee	Village development plan; decision on new project implementation; management of village assets; day-to-day consultation on saemaeul projects and village affairs.

Source: *Saemaeul Movement: From Beginning to Present*, Ministry of Home Affairs, 1973, p.37, and Kim, Hae-Dong (et.al.), An Evaluation and Field Experimentation of Saemaeul Movement, op.cit., pp.20-34.

tually every public organization. Yet all saemaeul programs take place in villages, and the integration of agencies' activities is a key theme.

To say that no ministry bears exclusive responsibility for the saemaeul movement does not mean that there are no formal and informal hierarchies. At higher levels of administration various ministry programs are coordinated by the State Council (a constitutional institution) or the Vice-Ministers' Council (a conventional interministry coordinating group) or both. The Economic Planning Board examines the budget proposals of each ministry, though it usually refrains from modifying the substance of ministry decisions.

The Ministry of Home Affairs (MHA) is responsible for local government; it designs the basic framework for saemaeul and is charged with implementing the program. The MHA design is not a final blueprint, but a working proposal to be discussed by the Saemaeul Movement Central Consultative Council, chaired by the Minister of Home Affairs and composed of vice-ministers from 16 ministries and the directors of seven independent offices. The Council examines the projects proposed by each ministry, reviews implementation reports, and guides the development of overall direction and strategy.

While the Council generates principles, resolves conflicts and coordinates policies, implementation falls to the program ministries. Each ministry is responsible for saemaeul activities within its jurisdiction. In the case of joint projects and cooperative activities, the importance of each ministry is generally proportional to its accountability for a specific project, and to its role in initiating an activity.

Since the saemaeul movement affects political change in rural areas, presidential control is a strong factor. Noteworthy during the Park regime was the relationship between the Presidential Office (Blue House) and the operating ministries. In contrast with the dispersion of policy-making authority among ministries, the line of control between the ministries and the Blue House was unmistakable and strictly maintained. While the Blue House did not initiate or design programs, its judgements on ministry proposals were potent. An official could solicit Blue House guidance on particular problems, but disagreement with Presidential policy was taboo. The Blue House did not attempt to guide the decision-making process within ministries; rather, it identified and acted on matters that reached a point of potential impact on the political system, and judged proposed ministry programs before they were put on the agenda for the State Council or the Saemaeul Movement Central Consultative Council. (The writer assumes, in the absence of up-to-date information, that these policies continue in much the same way.)

The central government lays down policy but local governments

Figure 2: Administrative System for the Saemaeul Movement

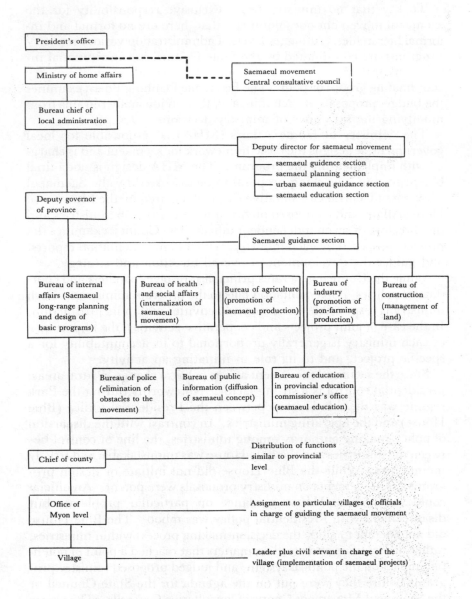

Source: *Comprehensive Directions of the Saemaul Movement.* The Saemaul Movement Central
        Consultative Council, Seoul, 1973, p. 12, and Kim, Hae-Dong (et. al.)
        An Evaluation and Field Experimentation of Saemaeul Movement, op. cit., p. 34.

are responsible for implementing the projects.[5] Saemaeul's requirements are reflected in formal institutional relationships between the two levels of government. Local governments, which are the responsibility of the MHA and may be considered an extension of that ministry, have little opportunity for autonomous decision-making. They have no representative institutions, only an executive branch composed of central government appointees and their subordinates. Most higher bureaucrats are appointed by the central government. Lower bureaucrats, are generally recruited and controlled by central government appointees.

In principle, a local government may carry on independent programs. In practice, the central government can interfere with virtually any program through several "levers": the personnel system, program recognition, subsidies, audits, demands for reports, or some combination of these.

Personnel management and subsidy allocations are the MHA's most effective tools with which to control local government. The ministry has the power to replace local officials. Since a local government head cannot prevent his subordinates from being replaced, he cannot ask them to follow his policies in opposition to those of the central government. MHA subsidies are another control. Only about 10% of a local government's appropriations depend on its own revenue sources.[6] All other local funds come from the central government in the form of MHA subsidies and program funds from other ministries.

Local government operations are not completely controlled by the MHA. Central government program ministries have counterpart units in local governments. If a program ministry wants to undertake projects, it must give the local government funds and detailed instructions for implementing the project. A program ministry usually acts as a patron, providing technical guidance and funds. But im-

---

5. The term "local government" in this paper is used according to the definition employed in the Korean "Law of Government Organizations." The term refers to agencies whose jurisdiction affects local territories. Actually, no Korean local governmet is "a political unit able to make autonomous political decisions" on the basis of "constituency power." Thus the term "local government" as used in this paper would not correspond to the conventional meaning in Western societies. It refers more to levels of government than to units of government. However, the Korean local governments are not simply the equivalent of field agencies in Western Political Institutions. In many respects the Korean local government system is similar to the French prefectoral system, but without any consitutional institutions for autonomous politics at the local level.

6. Choi, Jongho, "The Finance of Koean Local Governments," (in Korean) *Korean Developemnt Policy Studies*, v.2, 1975, pp. 96-115.

portant decisions about program priorities and resource allocation are made by the program ministries according to their own criteria, and they retain the power to make final decisions. Little discretion is given to local government agents. On the other hand, it is a time-honored pattern in Korean government that local officials seldom try to exercise discretion. When confronted with a choice, they find it prudent to obtian legitimation from a patron organization. Centralized administration thus allows field offices to avoid responsibility; they are held accountable yet they lack effective control.

The discretion that a local government retains varies with the program category. Some ministries dominate local governments more than others. By tradition, the MHA and the Ministry of Agriculture and Fisheries are apt to exercise tight control. The Ministry of Construction, on the other hand, gives local governments considerable discretion.

A counter-tendency has arisen since the saemaeul movement was introduced in 1971. In the early stages of the movement central government planners tried to enforce agricultural development programs. This did not elicit the deisred response: voluntary participation of local peasant. Planners then attempted to revise the process and more discretion was granted to local governments, still within the centralized administration. Program implementation came to depend on judgments in local offices, based on information about specific situational factors, which central offices generally lack. Officials in the central administration recognized that local government agents had to deal with rural peasants face-to-face to persuade them of the merits of government policies. When local officials receive peasants' questions and demands they must have some discretionary authority if their responses are to be acceptable.

The saemaeul administrative system is intended to raise responsiveness in local level organization. The design not only expands local discretion, it also creates a deputy-chief at the county level who is explicitly responsible for saemaeul project administration. (The position of deputy chief is discussed in more detail below.) Field organization responsiveness was enhanced by President Park's emphasis on the movement.

Relationships between Government Agencies and Villagers

Traditionally, local government in Korea has been limited in the ways it can represent local interests. Without a formal apparatus for articulating local claims there is no way of determining whether programs truly reflect local desires and demands. Programs have customarily been regarded as largesse from the central government, rather than as the political responses to local needs.

The dominance of bureaucrats over the common people has deep roots in Korea. In dynastic times when Confucianism was the political principle, government officials had absolute power. Japanese colonial bureaucrats maintained a similar position. Within this tradition modern Korean bureaucrats command formidable authority in society.

In the past officials working in the field were seldom involved in local activities. Maintaining an authoritarian posture required keeping some distance from the local inhabitants; the status of local government officials was little enhanced by popularity with the people. Moreover, it was generally thought that wise management of bureaucratic offices meant minimizing interest in local activities and minimizing the expansion of formal responsibility. Officials met with local people only when necessary to impose government edicts.

Rural people found ways to assert their interests in the absence of formal channels. They made connections with persons in important positions in the central government or in political parties, usually natives of the area or old friends. These patrons give a person what is called by the local people "a line" or "background." A decision-maker in the local government is vulnerable to the demands of people with powerful "backgrounds." But these personal linkages do not necessarily work to further local interests, for people with "background" are likely to pursue particular personal interests. Common people without patrons have little influence with bureaucrats in central and local governments.

The traditional relationship between local bureaucrats and the people has changed with government efforts to increase field office responsiveness. Organizational status has been linked to the achievements of saemaeul projects; local officials who seek advancement must devote themselves to rural development. Only those officials who induce rural people to undertake successful saemaeul activities enjoy promotion and better placement. Now a bureaucrat's career depends on how well the local people have done in their saemaeul projects.

This observation is derived from informal personal interviews by the author, who has met hundreds of Korean civil servants and rural villagers. Most saemaeul leaders agreed that Korean rural peasants have received more frequent visits than ever before by senior central and local government officials. The newly created position of deputy county-chief has also helped make local government more accessible to the peasants. Most deputies are young senior officials who have not yet been molded by long bureaucratic experience.[7] They tend to have a more progressive and idealistic orientation than their elders.

Even minor alterations in formal structure can produce significant behavioral changes. One example is the new policy of appointing a civil servant to take charge of a village in addition to his regular job. This provides the villagers with an informal contact with the bureaucracy. No longer required to cope with bureaucratic red tape, the peasantry can deal with government agencies through their "civil servant in charge." The latter tends to be sympathetic to the villagers, because they are the key to his own success. This relationship contributes to mutual understanding. Civil servants have an opportunity to explain the government's positions and constraints on choices, while villagers can explain their situation to government agencies.

Government agents do not contact individual peasants at random. They usually meet village leaders at regular business meetings to discuss development strategy problems, and plans. Thus government agencies can limit the number of contacts and the diversity of demands, which keeps their workload manageable. By and large government agents deal only with consensus positions of a village. The broader the range of common perspectives, the more easily offcials and villages can agree on solutions to problems.

The Project Cycle

To guide slection and implementation of projects, villages are classified as *basline, self-help,* or *self-sufficient.*[8] Government support for a baseline village is aimed at demonstrating the benefits of cooperative projects. When the village is elevated to the self-help stage, government agencies assist it with income generating projects. Finally, a village is defined as self-sufficient when its residents are able to turn their attention to such community welfare projects as health facilities. The Ministry of Home Affairs evaluates the performance of each village periodically. (The following tables show how a village is classified and promoted.)

Villagers are urged to select projects from program packages

---

7. The Korean Government annually recruits college graduates as senior civil servants. Government service is a popular career, especially among those graduates with a social science background. The recruits are assigned to each ministry according to staffing needs and individual preferences. For those who are placed in the Ministry of Home Affairs it is quite common to be appointed a deputy county-chief for one's first civil service position.

8. For details of the village classification scheme, see *Saemaul Undong,* KOIS, *op. cit.,* Appendix I, pp. 71-79.

Table 2: Criteria for Village Classification and Promotion

A. Required Minimum Criteria

Projects	Moving from baseline to self-help	Moving from self-help to self-sufficient
1. Village road	Completion of main road	Completion of main and feeder roads
2. Farm road	Feeder farm road into the village	Main farm road to the village
3. Bridges	Small bridges (10 meters or more)	20 meters or more
4. River control	Small streams passing through village territory	Small rivers near the village
5. Irrigation	80%	85%
6. Common facilities		Village hall or workshop
7. Roof improvement	50% of all houses	75% of all houses
8. Village fund	Over $600	Over $1,000
9. Savings in cash	Over $20 per household	Over $40 per household
10. Income, annual	Over $1,400 per household	Over $1,600 per household

B. Project Weighted Points

Classification	Full Points	Weighted Points by Projects			
		Production Infrastructure	Income Generation	Environment Improvement	Spiritual Enlightenment
Baseline	1,000	300	200	400	100
Self-help	1,000	300	300	300	100
Self-sufficient	1,000	400	400	100	100

C. The Following Actions are Taken Based on the Evaluation

Points	Grade	Action
800 or above	Good	Promotion and support
600-800	Fair	No promotion but support
Below 600	Poor	No promotion but special guidance

D. Items Rated in Evaluating Village Performance

A. Projects for Building Production Infrastructure (10)
   1. farm road construction
   2. small bridge construction
   3. small river control
   4. irrigation facilities
   5. cooperative production facilities
   6. cooperative warehouse
   7. erosion control
   8. pier and port facilities
   9. rural electrification
   10. rural communication facilities

B. Income-Generation Projects (7)
    1. cooperative rice farming
    2. increased barley production
    3. increased production of organic fertilizer
    4. cooperative income-generating activities
    5. village afforestation
    6. village seedling nursery
    7. sideline income-generation activities

C. Environmental Improvement Projects (6)
    1. improvement of village roads
    2. roof improvement
    3. drinking water facilities
    4. village hall
    5. drainage control
    6. village well .

D. Spiritual Enlightenment Projects (7)
    1. self-defense activities
    2. saemaeul training
    3. women's club activities
    4. village fund
    5. village credit union
    6. broadcasting facilities
    7. maintenance of existing facilities

Source: *Saemaul Undong: Korean Background Series,* Korean Oversea Information Service, Seoul, 1977, pp. 75-79.

prepared by the government. Each ministry develops projects linked to rural development within its own jurisdiction. Program packages of projects are divided into four categories: (1) Production Infrastructure, (2) Income Generation, (3) Welfare and Environment, and (4) Spiritual Enlightenment. The villages choose projects according to thier classifications. Baseline villages concentrate on infrastructure projects, self-help villages focus on income generation, and self-sufficient villages consider welfare and environmental projects. Spiritual enlightenment projects are initiated only by government agencies.

The extent of government support for a saemaeul project is determined by project type and village classification. For xample, technical assistances, but no financial grants, are provided for projects in which the beneficiary is an individual farmer. Government resource support—materials, cash, and techniques—is given to cooperative projects and intervillage projects where the whole community benefits and such assistance covers more than half of the project expenses.

Table 3: Progress of Village Promotion

Village Classification	1973		1974		1975		1976		1977	
	No.	%	No.	%	No.	%	No.	%	No.	%
Baseline	18,415	53	10,656	30	6,165	18	4,046	11	302	1
Self-help	13,943	40	10,763	57	21,500	62	20,936	60	19,049	54
Self-sufficient	2,307	7	4,246	13	7,000	20	10,049	29	15,680	45
Total	34,665	100	34,665	100	34,665	100	35,031	100	35,031	100

Source: *Saemaul Undong: Korean Background Series*, Korean Oversea Information Service, Seoul, 1977, p. 79.

The rest of the investment is provided by village funds and villagers' voluntary, unpaid labor. Thus commumity consensus is a precondition for installing a new cooperative project. Peasants are also aware that the government concentrates assistance on those villages that appear to have the greatest chance to succeed. Potential competence is evaluated on the basis of past performance and villagers' willingness to undertake new responsibilities within saemaeul, while the suitability of a village project is reviewed in terms of natural conditions, technical manpower, and locally available resources.

Initially, cooperative projects are emphasized. Attention shifts gradually to individual projects as a village reaches the self-sufficient stage. The purpose of postponing individual projects until a general consensus on village improvements has been reached is to avoid prematurely advancing individual benefits at the expense of the common good. This strategy greatly reduces the possibility of opposition to the self-help movement.

The basic assumption is that if villagers can improve their standard of living with government assistance and their own motivation, they will continue to maintain these standards without outside assistance. A self-sufficient village is expected to run development projects for itself, and saemaeul's goal is to make every village self-sufficient. We can see indirect support for this assumption in Table 3, Progress of Village Promotion. Self-sufficient villages were only 7 percent of the total when the village classification system was introduced in 1973; by 1977 almost half of the Korean villages had achieved the level of self-sufficiency. To my knowledge, there has been no serious report of backsliding among advanced villages.

The formal codes of government guidance are in accord with the fundamental goal of rural self-reliance. "No directing, only suggesting" is a cardinal rule. In the early period of the movement there were some abortive attempts to impose projects on villages. Now government agents use persuasive and suggestive teaching methods rather than authoritative directions. The most often used and the most influential method of field guidance consists of frequent visits to the viallage, not only by the civil servant-in-charge but by the county-chief and higher officials.

Local Institutions and the Saemaeul Movement

The family is the basic unit for social action in Korean rural life. An individual acts as a family member rather than as an independent figure: collectivity comes before individuality. The concept of family is extended to other social collectives. A community such as a village is an extension of the family. Even without literal blood relationships villagers use kinship terms among themselves, such as "aunt," "uncle," "brother," or "sister." These affective ties encourage strong commitements to village activities.[9]

The family is dominated by a patriarchal model creating a sense of rank-order. This is also extended to other social collectives. As the father is the central figure in family decisions, so is the chief of an association granted a dominant position. The patriarchal rank-ordering also consolidates seniority rule. The elder's domination often gives old ways of doing things more legitimacy than new ones. This principle is observed in the collective activities of rural peasants, and discipline is generally maintained without explicit regulations. In the light of this tradtion, the success of saemaeul in shifting initiative to young saemaeul leaders is remarkable.

The saemaeul movement is not designed to alter existing patterns of social interactions, but to promote an institutional approach to village development efforts. Emphasized in the working of saemaeul are the *saemaeul leader,* the *Village Development Committee,* the *village organization,* and the villagers' *general meeting.* The saemaeul leader is responsible for implementing village saemaeul projects; in this his role is distinct from the village-master's, who traditionally acts as a liaison

---

9. May N. Diaz and Jack M. Potter, "Introduction: The Social Life of Peasants," in J. M. Potter, M.N. Diaz, and G.M. Foster (eds.), *Peasant Society,* Boston: Little Brown, 1967, pp.154-167.

between the people and local government. The Village Development Committee, composed of influential residents, provides village support for the movement. The various local associations which make up, in an informal, unsystematic way, the village organization, further the common interests of their constituencies.[10] Finally, a general meeting may occasionally be called by the saemaeul leader to vote on controversial problems and to try to achieve a village consensus. The saemaeul leader and the village organization are generally the most active elements in the movement. The Village Development Committee and the general meeting are support activities.

The saemaeul leader, who must be an inhabitant of the village and who serves without pay, is the main figure at the village level. Some leaders are recommended by the village elders or local government, and others volunteer; but a saemaeul leader is always selected by the villagers' vote. He is not a government official and he holds no formal position. His authority is a function of his own contributions to the village and his ability to mediate between government agencies and the community. He can exercise considerable influence in village affairs through the government's support and confidence. Government agencies provide the saemaeul leader with a foundation for obtaining assistance and support from the outside, for gaining access to necessary information and techniques, and for transmitting villagers' demands to the government. The government also gives saemaeul leaders frequent opportunities to communicate with local government agencies. Leaders receive distinctive recognition from local institutions such as government field agencies, local bank branches, and agricultural cooperatives. The central government encourages saemaeul leaders by awarding honors, holding an annual convention, and inviting selected leaders to Presidential luncheons. The village saemaeul leader is seen as the torch-bearer for the movement.

Within the village the saemaeul leader relies on the Village Development Committee to provide support and legitimacy. The Committee is usually composed of the elders and the village organizations'

---

10. The properties of village organizations described here are similar to Milton Esman's concept of constituency organizations, the main features of which are formal equality of individual members, accountability to the constituency, opportunities for participation, and exercise of influence by individual members. "Development Administration and Constituency Organization," *Public Administration Review*, Mar/Apr, 1978, pp.168-192. The village organizations described in this paper are an example of intermediate organization developed by Martin Landau. See "Linkage, Coding, and Intermediacy: A Strategy for Institution Building," in Joseph W. Eaton (ed.), *Institution Building and Development: From Concept to Application*, Beverly Hills, Calif.: Sage, 1972, pp. 91-109.

leaders. It sometimes includes people who are not directly involved in farming, like school teachers, businessmen, or religious leaders. The Committee examines possible projects among the government's program packages and approves the saemaeul leader's proposals for implementing projects. It then drafts a village development plan.

Typically, the Committee generates village agreement and support for the saemaeul leader's initiatives. But the Committee's decisions are not always compatible with the leader's proposals. Some saemaeul leaders introduce new village projects on their own initiative and at their own expense, risking significant loss if they fail to gain approval of the Village Development Committee. When the Committee does not approve a project the leader can appeal to the villagers' general meeting.

The third element in the local saemaeul program is the informal village organization, which brings together such local groups as the women's league, the Village Forestry Association, the youth club, etc. These associations have existed in villages for decades,[11] but were ignored by the government before the saemaeul movemnet. When the need arose for institutionalizing rural development these village organizations came into their own, because they gave momentum and continuity to development efforts. The government has encouraged the establishement of even more associations, believing that an organized group is more likely to accept challenges and to explore new enterprises than are individuals. Village organizations also make it easier to mobilize manpower and skills.

These associations have no rigid regulations, nor do they act to increase systematic, formal relations within their membership or with other groups.[12] Most members only occasionally participate in organizational activities; continuity is provided by the leadership. Relations based on personal sympathy, favors, and kinship background are the foundation for village organizations.

In summary, village organizations make it easier for government agencies to reach and interact with peasants; they can relay selectively the information, technology, and resources that formal agencies supply

---

11. Korean rural society has long had various forms of voluntary associations in order to share the benefits of cooperation. Peer groups of villagers usually combine their labor for farming, weeding, haymaking, etc. Mutual saving associations are also created which can help members with familial ȯbligations calling for extra spending, such as marriages, funerals, and the 60th birthdays of parents. These traditional forms of village associations have been more diversified in recent years to help villages achieve self-reliance. *Saemaul Undong*, KOIS, *op. cit.*, pp.10-18; and Diaz and Potter, *op. cit.*, pp.154-167.

12. Martin Landau, *op. cit.*

on a "wholesale" basis.[13] The village organizations also articulate the interests of the peasants, a vital function in a country that has no other local political institutions.

It is the village organizations that actually implement collective projects. (Projects for individual benefit such as telephone installation, and introduction of new crops and techniques are not subject to action by village organizations. These projects are often recommended by village leaders, but final decisions are made by individual farmers in principle, even if accepted under social pressure in practice.) The Village Nursery Operation, for example, is managed by the Village Forestry Association. Village organizations play a critical role in mobilizing manpower for cooperative projects, since decisions on new projects must be legitimated by consensus. Without this legitimacy the peasants refuse to cooperate. Thus when a new porject is being introduced village leaders try to get full support from their constituency by explaining, persuading, compromising, and bargaining. It is necessary that all constituents understand and accept the project before it is adopted.

When the villagers approve a project the leaders make a detailed project management plan, including the formation of work-teams and the coordination of activities among village organizations. Once the plan is set the leaders act without detailed consultation with the villagers. The saemaeul movement thus operates under a hybrid leadership, demorcratic in decision-making and authoritative in implementation.

Yet implementation is possible only with voluntary participation, and village leaders use various incentive strategies to encourage it.[14] The most potent incentive, of course, is the prospect of increased income and improved living standards; thus the saemaeul emphasis on income-generating programs.

Cooperative projects, where profits are not directly linked with individual income, receive generous government assistance, and collective-minded villagers understand the link between common benefits and individual interests. Cooperation among the villagers is a behavioral goal of the movement and group incentives are built into saemaeul projects. Profits from cooperative projects are usually put into such undertakings as farm machinery pools, nursery schools,

---

13. Esman, *op. cit.*
14. They are trained in scientific farming, agricultural machinery, health, housekeeping, and family planning. But the emphasis is on the saemaeul spirit, project management and implementation, field tours, and case studies through group discussion. Kim, Hae-Dong (et. al.), *op. cit.*, pp.76-79.

or credit unions. Quite often cooperative projects are carried out alongside projects geared to personal income, and some cooperative projects also distribute proceeds directly to individuals. But it is village-units rather than individuals that usually receive incentive awards for excellence, especially financial awards.

The growing opportunities for community participation add to these incentives, particularly for women and young people. In a society dominated by men, it is encouraging to note that organizations such as the women's league and the youth club are beginning to have more influence in village affairs. At the same time, allowing women and the young to participate in village organizations reinforces cooperation, since each member desires to be identified as a part of the group.

Conclusion

Since the saemaeul movement began in 1971 rural Korea has undergone tremendous change. An attempt has been made to institutionalize rural development through the peasantry. Village development projects are no longer imposed by a distant government but instead are directed through village organizations. These processes tend to be imperfect; but this experimental, redundant approach is essential for institutional development. It increases the possibility of success.[15] Institutionalized activities support spontaneity while providing some continuity for development efforts. In addition, village institutions have domonstrably helped to increase government responsiveness to peasant demands.

One way to increase agricultural productivity on farms that average less than one hectare is through cooperative activities. The saemaeul movement has introduced a new pattern of cooperative production, largely because of village organizations. In cooperative farming, a village is able to apply technology and machinery that would be inefficient on smaller individual plots. The village has access to government assistance and other sources of support not available to the individual farmer. Cooperative production also offers advantages for nonagricultural income projects, in terms of capital accumulation and labor mobilization. The new pattern of cooperative production is reinforced through village institutions that provide organized activities of, by, and for the villagers.

---

15. Martin Landau, "Redundancy, Rationality, and the Problem of Duplication and Overlap," *Public Administration Review*, v. 27, August 1969. See also his "Linkage, Coding and Intermediacy," *op. cit.*

The saemaeul movement has brought changes in the relationships between government bureaucrats and the peasantry. Government measures, such as the new personnel motivation system reflect the orientation of the movement. The system increases the peasants' opportunities to communicate with top policy-makers, and this is slowly altering the traditional role of bureaucrats. If an official's future depends on the cooperation of his clientele, he will be responsive rather than authoritarian. This change in orientation has also brought about a shift in the way peasants deal with bureaucrats. The peasantry used to respond to the bureaucrats' domineering manner with indifference. As they become effective partners with officials in development efforts, they come to value government guidance.

Saemaeul has been responsible for these transformations, but only because of a set of crucial preexisting conditions. It is difficult to isolate conclusively the most important of these. Certainly high levels of aspiration among peasants, as well as access to technology and markets for agricultural products, have been important to the success of the movement.

The saemaeul movement does offer lessons. Some of them may be applicable to rural development projects in other countries. The first concerns the contradiction between the need for village autonomy in decision-making and the peasants' actual capacity to decide. It is believed in many developing countries that rural people lack the ability to prepare technical plans for development programs. They are seen as passive in initiating new projects. The government usually designs rural development programs and imposes them on rural inhabitants regardless of local desires, with the typical result that the peasantry ignore these imposed goals. Yet the essential basis for decision-making is neither accuracy nor logical soundness, but legitimacy.[16] The most urgent task in rural development programs, is to create legitimacy. There remains a contradiction between the imperative of participation and the imperative of efficacy.

A solution to this contradiction may be the "program package" system, of which saemaeul stands as a good example. From a variety of projects provided by government authorities for rural areas, peasants can select those relevant to their needs. This system assumes that rural inhabitants know their own village better than do outsiders. If villagers have the responsibility for selecting projects themselves,

---

16. William J. Siffin, "Discussion" of Nicolaas Luykx, "Rural Governing Institutions," in Melvin G. Blase (ed.), *Institution in Agricultural Development*, Iowa State University Press, Ames, Iowa, 1971, p.210.

they may tend to choose those they understand best in terms of cost, benefits, techniques, available resources, and linkages with other projects. They may also choose on the basis of a step-by-step, incremental approach. It is not, of course, certain that they will choose the best "package." Program packages should accordingly include means for government agents to test the feasibility of projects selected.

The second lesson from the saemaeul program concerns incentives for rural development. Limited resources for development mean limited rewards for individual peasants. In a situation where the larger part of the available resources must be directed to infrastructure projects which do not produce direct and immediate economic benefits, profits may be too small to allow any sizable distribution among contributors. Yet the saemaeul movement has been based on local energy, mobilized and channeled through a system of incentives and supports. Cooperative projects usually create, by their nature, common properties with community-wide distribution of benefits. Some income-generating saemaeul projects emphasize collective operations in which the profits are distributed according to the degree of individual contribution. Even though the promise of individual reward tends to be modest, the saemaeul incentive system seems to have motivated peasants.

Moreover, the fact that village leaders are not paid, either by the government or out of village assets, is of considerable symbolic importance in encouraging their fellow villagers. Village leaders tend to be teachers of farming and organizers of new activities, motivated by social recognition and community respect, and are seen by the rural people as helpers rather than as exploiters of opportunities.

The saemaeul strategy fits well into the Korean socio-cultural context. The incentive system is based on a relatively egalitarian approach, which reflects an important aspect of Korean culture with its collective-minded villagers. (Most of those who presumably would have least chance to benefit, i.e., the landless and poorest peasants, have emigrated into the urban areas.)

The saemaeul experience provides another lesson concerning motivation: incentive systems for rural development must reflect the rural people's calculations of benefit rather than those of planners or policy-makers, especially where a high degree of voluntary participation is necessary. The critical factor is the peasants' perception of incentives. They should conclude that participation will improve their own living standard and involve limited risk. Incentive systems for rural people must be simple and clear so as to allow simple calculation.

In this calculation, the comparison of rewards with contributions is probably less important than the sense of fairness. In a short-term perspective, fariness may be judged in terms of relationships with a leader or government bureaucrats. One of the most obvious requirements is that rural leaders or "development catalysts" be perceived as devoted to rural development more for the community than for their individual interest. Rural people are likely to form their calculations on the evidence of everyday life rather than on any comprehensive analysis. The most compelling evidence is the behavior of the development catalysts and their relationships with the peasants. Thus incentives are not simply rewards. Rather, they form an "energy reproduction" system for development which can fuel future efforts.

18

Popular Participation in Community Development Projects
— Search for Alternative Approaches —

In Joung Whang

1. Introduction

The purpose of this paper is to identify and analyze the factors and conditions underlying popular participation in the process of planning and implementation of Korea's community development activities with a view to searching for alternative approaches to citizen's participation. The Saemaul Undong, or the "new village movement," has brought about significant changes, physically and socially, in rural communities for the more than ten years since its inception in 1970. It is a nation-wide community development movement organized on the basis of positive participation of village members whose main purpose is to promote community development projects such as construction of roads and bridges, small-scale irrigation projects, sanitary water supply projects, and production of other public goods. Specific projects using government-donated materials are selected through discussion among community members in the village assembly. In addition, a major objective of the movement is to foster the spiritual enlightenment of rural people in regard to development-oriented values such as diligence, self-help, cooperation, and participation.

In light of its major inputs, process, results and impact, the Saemaul Undong can be considered Korea's version of integrated rural community development.[1] The major factor in the success of this movement was undoubtedly the maintenance of a high level of popular

---

1. In-Joung Whang, *Management of Rural Change in Korea: The Saemaul Undong* (Seoul: Seoul National University Press, 1981), pp. 20-21.

participation in local development activities. Approximately 36,000 rural villages participated in the Saemaul Undong every year throughout 1971-82, meaning that most rural villages in Korea have taken part in the movement for community development. Participation in rural community development programs has also increased greatly, from 7 million man-days in 1971, to a level of 184 million man-days in 1978, and to 159 million man-days in 1982. The degree of participation in each rural village has also increased from 216 man-days in 1971, to 5,274 man-days and 4,501 man-days respectively in 1978 and 1982 (Table 1). Considering that most Saemaul Undong programs were undertaken in rural communtities during the off-farm season, usually from December to next April, the degree of participation is quite impressive.

The extensiveness of rural participation is also demonstrated by the contributions to the Saemaul Undong made by the rural residents, including donations of labor, cash, land and other materials. Although they have declined recently, the value of these contributions increased more than 20 times between 1971-78, while the government's con-

Table 1. Expansion and Diffusion of the Saemaul Undong, 1971-82

	No. of Participating Village	No. of Participants	Total Investment	No. of Participants per Village
Unit	each	million man-days	billion Won	man-days
1971	33,267	7	12.2	216
	(33,267)*	(7)	(12.2)	(216)
1973	34,665	69	98.4	1,999
	(34,665)	(67)	(98.4)	(1,948)
1978	36,257	271	634.2	7,472
	(34,815)	(184)	(603.5)	(5,274)
1981	36,792	258	702.9	6,971
	(35,100)	(124)	(672.9)	(3,533)
1982	36,894	273	866.6	7,392
	(35,327)	(159)	(814.0)	(4,501)

*The numbers in parentheses indicate corresponding figures for rural areas.
Source: Ministry of Home Affaris, *Saemaul Undong: From Its Inception Until Today* (1975, 1978 and 1982).

tribution increased only about 12 times (Table 2). In fact, the gross amount of private contributions to Saemaul projects during 1971 was two times greater than that of the government's. The ratio of private to public Saemaul investment increased to 3.3 in 1978, and still remains as high as 1.8. Clearly, private contributions have been the major source of funding for the Saemaul Undong. This implies that popular participation increased consistently during the seventies. During the last three years, on the other hand, the poor harvest, economic recession and political instability had a strong negative impact on the pursuit of rural community development. Since inter-village development projects, which are larger in terms of investment and regional coverage than single village projects, have been encouraged in recent years, the extent of popular participation has declined slightly as the mode of participation has had to be readapted.

It is also interesting to note that the major part (77%) of the citizen's contribution during 1972 was in the form of labor. With time, this proportion dropped rapidly, and by the mid-1970s cash had become the major type of private contribution (Table 3). This fact implies

Table 2: Increase in Saemaul Investment, 1971-82

Unit: million won in 1971 price

Year	Total Investment	Gov't Budget	Rural* People	Others
1971	12,200	4,100	8,100	—
	(1.0)**	(1.0)	(1,0)	
1972	27,714	3,141	23,989	583
	(2.3)	(0.8)	(3.0)	
1975	134,988	56,979	73,351	840
	(11.0)	(13.8)	(9.0)	(1.4)
1978	211,962	48,698	163,047	218
	(17.4)	(11.9)	(20.1)	(0.4)
1981	116,476	30,961	83,922	4,575
	(9.5)	(7.6)	(10.4)	(7.8)
1982	142,318	51,788	89,791	739
	(11.7)	(12.6)	(11.1)	(1.3)

*Includes loans by the government and other organizations.
**Figures in parentheses indicate the number of times.
Source: Ministry of Home Affairs, *The Saemaul Undong: From Its Inception Until Today* (in respective years).

that the people's commitment as well as their concrete contributions to self-help development projects grew as their confidence in the Saemaul Undong increased.

Table 3: People's Contribution to the Saemaul Undong

Unit: million won

Year	Total	Cash	Labor	Materials	Land
1972	27,348 (100.0)	—	21,116 (77.2)	5,238 (19.2)	994 (3.6)
1974	98,738 (100.0)	32,622 (33.1)	54,139 (54.8)	10,089 (10.2)	1,888 (1.9)
1975	169,554 (100.0)	94,261 (55.6)	63,876 (37.5)	8,646 (5.1)	2,771 (1.6)
1978	487,835 (100.0)	306,034 (62.7)	102,437 (21.0)	42,803 (8.8)	36,561 (7.5)
1981	281,721* (100.0)	87,926 (31.2)	252,405 (54.1)	40,208 (14.3)	2,072 (0.7)
1982	298,087 (100.0)	112,690 (37.8)	144,694 (48.5)	39,231 (13.2)	1,382 (0.5)

*Excluding ₩890 million donated by the private business sector.
Source: Ministry of Home Affairs, *Saemaul Undong: From Its Inception Until Today* (in respective years).

At this point, then, we should consider several questions: What was the particular mode of citizen's participation in the Saemaul Undong? What factors motivated such strong participations and what social and cultural conditions are most conducive to private participation? What lessons can be drawn from the Korean experience in community development in terms of the government role in encouraging local and popular participation?

Participation is an action process undertaken by individuals and/or groups to further their own interests, or to contribute their energies and resources to, the systems which govern their lives.[2] Hence, par-

---

2. Sherry Arnstein, "Eight Rungs on the Ladder of Citizen Participation," in E. Chan and B. Passett (eds.), *Citizen Participation: Effecting Community Change* (New York: Praeger Publishers, 1961), pp. 69 91.

ticipation can be activated at the individual and/or the organizational level. Unless individual participation is channelled into collective organizational action, it could hardly make any real impact upon the community development process. Therefore, a thorough analysis of participation would require close examination of factors promoting participation at the individual as well as the organizational level.

Conceptually, there are two different approaches to the initiation of citizen's participation: (a) the top-down approach, in which government acts as the initial motivator of participation in community development, and (b) the bottom-up approach, in which citizens voluntarily participate in community development activities.[3] Participation through either the bottom-up or top-down approaches is often absent in most developing countries, because both the motivation of the people and the administrative capability of the government are not substantive enough to generate success under either approach. In most successful cases, both approaches have been utilized together.

Clearly, both the level at which participation is activated and the approach to the initiation of participation are important determinants of the extent of community participation. Therefore, this paper attempts to take a close look at critical factors in participation by analyzing the role of these two variables in the case of the Saemaul Undong. Chart A indicates the four major factors which have an impact upon community participation in rural development. They are:

(a) individual motivation,
(b) the role of leadership in responding to the people's needs and in providing support for development projects,
(c) the development of grass-root organizations which can accomodate individual motivation at the community level and properly aggregate and articulate community interests, and
(d) government mobilization of both human and material resources for community change and regional development.

Positive improvements in each of these four factors are highly correlated or associated with greater levels of participation in community development. Thus, it is important to examine both how and to what extent these four factors are brought to bear in Korea to realize popular participation in the Saemaul Undong. In addition, it is necessary to analyse what social and cultural prerequisites, if any, which had been established before the Saemaul Undong was launched.

---

3. Theodor Dams, "Development from Below and People's Participation as Key Principles of Integrated Rural Development," presented at Seoul National University, Internaional Research Seminar on the Saemaul Movement, Seoul, 8-13 December, 1980.

Chart A. Critical Factors Affecting Community Participation

Level at which participation is activated	Approach to initiation of participation	
	Top-down approach	Bottom-up approach
Individual level	Leadership role	Motivation
Organizational level	Government mobilization and inducement	Participatory organization at grass-root level

2. Motivating Mechanisms

The extent of participation in the Saemaul Undong depends on the commitment to community development. So far, three major programs have motivated rural Koreans: (a) rigorous implementation of Saemaul training programs, (b) extensive programs for public information, education and communication (IEC) for community self-help projects, and (c) the expansion of formal education.

In the case of Korea's rural development program, training deserves special attention. The Korean approach to rural development training seemed unique in its objectives, participant mix, curricula, training methods and eventual impact. Conducted in a "closed oven" situation, Saemaul training focused on changing the values of village leaders, both men and women. This strategy rested on the assumption that these leaders will eventually encourage rural people to participate in the community activities which will imporve their lives. Accordingly, a series of case studies, success stories and group discussions was included in the training program to augment the images, hopes, expectations, self-confidence and self-awareness of community leaders, as well as rural people.

Beyond the motivational impact, the training had brought about significant changes in perceptions, attitudes and group dynamics of those involved in the rural development process. The Saemaul Undong provided different sectoral elites with the common conceptual framework necessary for the nation-wide participation of rural people. It also induced the participants to make a collective commitment to the achievement of rural development projects. Furthermore, the training program has facilitated the coordination of different policies and programs. The training course enabled political and urban elites to better understand the rural situation and its development needs. This process has consequently created support for an active partnership between political and social elites and local people.

The extensive mass media campaign has greatly improved public awareness of the Saemaul Undong. Acting through government-hired change agents and village leaders, political leaders and local government officials have advocated the ideas and program activities of the Saemaul Undong. The face-to-face communication sponsored by the Saemaul Undong has also made a positive impact on the attitudes of members of the village community. Furthermore, the ideas and program activities of the Saemaul Undong have also been adopted in the educational programs at both primary and secondary schools for better understanding of the movement and encouraging wider popular rural participation.

While the Saemaul training and IEC activities have had a short-term impact on the process of community change, the cumulative effect of the massive formal education drive at the primary school level and above has definitely enhanced the motivational level of rural people. The importance of formal education as a prerequisite for popular participation will be discussed in Section 6.

3. The Role of Leadership

Another important factor in promoting people's participation has been the firm commitment of leadership at all levels to the success of Saemaul Undong. Analysis of the results of the first year of Saemaul Undong showed that the role of village leadership was a key determinant of popular participation.[4] The study found that more able village leadership produced greater participation. In turn, more extensive participation led to a more successful implementation of community projects. This finding justified the institution of the Saemaul Leadership Training Program since 1972.

The training program contributed to the formation of village leadership all over the nation. According to a recent interview survey,[5] the Saemaul leaders, men and women, played a key role in coordinating community participation. They also acted as the nexus of

---

4. In-Joung Whang, *Hangug eui Jonghab Nongcheon Gaebal* (Integrated Rural Development in Korea) (Seoul: Korea Rural Economics Institute), Research Series No. 2, p. 114.
5. Whang, *Management of Rural Change in Korea*, pp. 75-85.

local communications for village development projects. Most were so dedicated to the development of their villages, that they sacrificed their own time, energy, and sometimes money to community projects without any compensation. A majority of 1,497 community members in the sample survey agreed that Saemaul leaders are those who really dedicated themselves entirely to the development of their villages. Indeed, the strong commitment and dedication of village leadership to community development inspired the positive participation of villagers in these projects.

The strong support of top government leaders undoubtedly encouraged community participation in local development activities. Major presidential speeches, such as annual messages and budget speeches, the allocation of financial and material resources, and the necessary changes in the legal as well as the administrative framework in favor of the rural sector testify to the extent of this commitment. Besides political and international affairs, one of the most frequently raised issues in presidential speeches was rural and agricultural development. It received as much attention as industrial development and trade.[6]

Besides the explicit concern expressed through speeches on important occasions, the President has demonstrated his commitment to rural innovation and balanced regional development by making frequent visits to local communities. These visits served not only to encourage people's participation in the Saemaul Undong but also to highlight rural problems. Field visit also provided special occasions for the President to make specific instructions and to establish guidelines for coping with problems as well as for monitoring program performance. He expressed his personal interest in this movement for new community development by personally awarding prizes to the two best Saemaul leaders. These prizes were presented during the monthly national economic progress report of the Deputy Prime Minister, in front of the economic ministers of the cabinet and leaders of the business community.

The mobilization of broad social support for the Saemaul Undong reinforces the values and ideas of rural community development. It also contributed to getting the ruling elite, including party leaders and urban intellectuals, to understand the ideas and changes implied in the Saemaul Undong.

Furthermore, the commitment of leadership reoriented government programs at all levels towards regional and community development, and eventually towards th grass-roots level and greater rural popular

---

6. *Ibid.*, p. 43.

participation. The details of the government reorientation will be discussed in the next section.

4. Government Inducement and the Role of Local Administration

The government plays an important role in mobilizing rural people to participate extensively in development activities at the community level. In turn, the political system determines the extent of, and means with which, governments mobilize human and material resources. Under the "mobilization system" of a country like Soviet Russia, genuine popular participation tends to be minimal, while under the "reconciliation system" often found in Western countries, participation is rather encouraged. However, most developing countries belong to a third category, namely that of "modernizing autocracy".[7] In developing countries, "mass participation has been essentially a new form of mass response to elite manipulation," although "even such limited participation has a role to play in nation building".[8]

For the sake of analysis, one may identify three broad patterns of participation in terms of the extent of government mobilization, namely (1) *voluntary participation,* arising from the people's own initiatives, (2) *induced participation,* which is stimulated by government or elites through incentive systems, and (3) *forced participation,* or total mobilization by the government. Voluntary participation of a people is highly correlated with that people's level of education and training. Forced participation is achieved through the exercise of authority in a hierachically organized society. In between these two patterns is induced participation in which psychological and material incentives are offered to the people.

In general, the pattern of popular participation in the Saemaul Undong belongs to the category of induced participation. To wit, the government offered a donation of 335 bags of cement and steel bars to each rural village at the inception of the Saemaul Undong. This government offer served as a challenge to previously static communities, creating an identity crisis, participation crisis, integration

---

7. David E. Apter, "System, Process, and Politics of Economic Development," in Bert F. Hoselitz and Wilbert E. Moore, (eds.), *Industrialization and Society* (The Haque, UNESCO: Mouton, 1963), pp. 143-147.
8. Lucian Pye, "Armies in the Process of Political Modernization," in Johnson (ed.), *The Role of the Military in Underdeveloped Countries* (Princeton: Princeton University Press, 1965), pp. 8-9.

crisis, leadership crisis, and management crisis all at once for the village. That it took some 2-3 weeks for villagers to reach a consensus with regard to what projects should be undertaken with the donated cement and steel demonstrates the power of this challenge. Eventually, however, the painful and protracted process of decision-making induced wider participation among the village members. Thus, the subsequent participation of rural people was partly a response to the inducement. Since then, the village general assembly has been a major mechanism for people's participation, decision-making, and consensus building on major communal issues.

In addition to donating material assistance over the course of the last ten years, the government has created a variety of social and economic incentives. The principle that "the better village should receive the first support" stimulated competition between neighboring villages to achieve better performance in implementing the Saemaul projects. The competitive mood between neighboring villages stimulated substantially greater participation in village projects. A series of citations, and especially the Presidential Awards given to outstanding community workers, served as incentives to encourage citizen's participation.

To make government inducement more effective, the efficiency of local administrative systems in delivering development services to the community has an important role to play. Historically, local government in Korea was oriented to "law and order" and served the central elite by controlling local resources. Therefore, the reorientation of local governments to local needs was an essential prerequisite for the introduction of profound change at the community level.

Improving the relationship between local governments and their constituents increased the effectiveness of local government support of the Saemaul Undong. Discord due to the traditionally bureaucratic and colonial attitude of local officials has gradually evaporated, thanks to the consistent support of development by local governments. Indeed, the credibility of local government allowed it to sponsor rural innovations in the process of Saemaul Undong.

Throughout the 1960s and 1970s, extensive management training in planning service delivery, monitoring work performance, communications, coordination and other techniques improved the managerial competence of local officials. The timely and accurate delivery of materials and services to villages according to planned schedules is an indicator of the outstanding performance and commitment of local administrators. The remarkable discipline of local government officials also strengthend the credibility of government.

The package of government support is coordinated between dif-

ferent agencies of government and integrated into the total scheme
of village development. Preventing conflicts and the unnecessary
duplication of village activities, the coordination of local government
helped develop community spirit. These sentiments encouraged rural
people to participate in local development activities.

The commitment of local government is also reflected in arrangements for the special assignment of local officials. Each staff
member is assigned to a village to monitor and assist popular participation in community development projects. The promotion of local
officials on the basis of this monitoring of their work performance
for Saemaul projects is almost institutionalized. In addition to their
competence in the relevant technical subjects field workers are able
to build a fresh image of "service men." They can efficiently deliver
required services, contact and communicate with people easily, and
stimulate, motivate, and encourage community members. The
managerial and technical competence as well as the fresh image of
the local officials tends to bring about a synergistic effect, causing
local people to make positive responses to government inducements
by actively participating in community development projects.

5. Participatory Organization

The encouragement of successful popular participation requires the
proper organizational structure at the village level. Organized in each
community, the Village Development Committee consisted of ten or
twelve members selected from among the villagers. The Saemaul
leader chaired the group in each village. Participatory organization
at the community level required village leadership, which was provided by selecting both Saemaul leaders (men and women) from village
members. They acted as the agents of change, introducing attitudinal
changes toward cooperation, participation and rural innovations. They
performed their leadership role in collaboration with the village chief,
a semi-official person appointed from village members by the township
office. The incorporation of women leaders into village leadership[9]
helped mobilize the talents and energies of women for community
action programs,[10] and so reinforced the trend of increasing participation. The grass-roots level organization became more conducive to

---

9. Brandt, Vincent and Man-Gap Lee, "Community Development in South Korea" (Seoul:
    Seoul National University, 1977), mimeo.
10. Whang, *Management of Rural Change in Korea*, pp. 103-110.

Chart B: Organizational Arrangement for the Saemaul Undong

Organization	Functions	Membership
Central Coordinating Committee	Coordination and overall policy formation	Chaired by Minister of Home Affairs, with membership of vice-ministers of Economic Planning Board, Ministries of Education, Agriculture and Fisheries, Commerce and Industry, Construction, Health and Welfare, Communication, Culture and Information, Finance, Science and Technology and Minister without Portfolio (Economic Affairs); Office of Rural Development, Office of Forestry, Office of Supply
Provincial (or Special city) Coordinating Committee	Functional responsibility, regional coordination, and liaison	Chaired by Governor, with membership of vice-Governor of province, Superintendent of Education, provincial representative of Agricultural Cooperatives; Regional Directors of Agricultural Development Reserve Army; college professors, teachers in agricultural high school, directors of the Provincial Bureau of Education and Bureau of the Forestry Federation, Korean Electricity Corporation and the Communication Department.
County (or city) Saemaul Undong Coordinating Committee	Integrated guidance and promotion	Chaired by major (or county chief), with membership of police chief, county agricultural cooperative, principal of agricultural high school, chief of post office, Saemaul leaders and others
Myeon Saemaul Undong Promotion Committee	Specific guidance and assistance	Chaired by chief of Eub (or Myeon) with membership of police, branch post office, agricultural cooperatives, extension service and Saemaul leaders
Village Development Committee	Planning and implementation of village development	Chaired by village chief (or Saemaul leader), with 10-12 members, including village opinion leaders and some elected villagers

Source: In-Joung Whang, *Management of Rural Change in Korea* (Seoul, SUN Press, 1981), p. 120.

the extensive participation of community members in thier development projects since the inception of the Saemaul Undong activated
the Village Development Committee.

Organizational arrangements in the central government sector have
also been conducive to citizen's participation in local-level development activities. Specifically, the Saemaul Undong Bureau, which
is responsible for developing the overall strategies and policies of the
Saemaul Undong, was established within the Ministry of Home Affairs after the inception of the Saemaul Undong. At the provincial
level, the establishment of the Saemaul Planning Division in the provincial government provided support and guidance for local governments at the county level. A Deputy County Chief was added to every
county office with the sole responsibility of managing support and
assistance to the Saemaul Undong. Added to each township office,
a new administrative unit assumed responsibility for planning and
guiding local Saemaul projects.

In addition to setting up line organizations, the government made
special arrangements for the planning and coordination of Saemaul
projects. A series of Saemaul consultative councils at all administrative
levels of local government were established. Extending from the central level down to the village level, this series of councils and committees was set up to facilitate coordination between the ministries
and agencies concerned with rural development, and to provide diversified planning perspectives for Saemaul projects (Chart B). It should
be noted, in this connection, that Saemaul leaders participate as
members in both county and township-level councils. The Saemaul
leaders were given the privilege of meeting with the county-chief or
governor whenever they wanted to do so. These measures obviously encouraged Saemaul leaders to participate in the decision-making,
implementation and evaluation processes of the Saemaul Undong.
Such a series of organizational arrangement promotes popular participation in local community affairs, as well as providing better information about the interests and ideas within each village.

6. Socio-economic Prerequisites for Popular Participation

The pattern of participation in the Saemaul Undong belongs to
the category of induced participation. The effectiveness of induced
participation in Korea is related to the infrastructural reforms which
took place in the 1950s and 1960s, before the Saemaul Undong was
launched. The prerequisites for the effective participation of rural
people in the Saemaul Undong include the following: (a) relatively

equal access to land ownership among rural farmers through the land reform of 1950-53; (b) equal opportunities in education, offered to the people since the Liberation from Japanese colonial rule in 1945; and (c) organizational and leadership training provided through military service.

A. Equity in Land Ownership

The Land Reform Act of 1949 provided the Korean government with the legal basis to redistribute farmland according to the principle of "land-to-the-tillers." Out of approximately 601 thousand hectares subject to land reform, 470 thousand hectares (79% of the target) were redistributed during 1949-52. As a consequence, 953 thousand households (95% of the planned 1,022 thousand households) obtained farmland during this period.[11] The three-hectare ceiling on land ownership per farm household rather helped to reduced average farm size (Table 4), and in so doing, delayed agricultural modernization in terms of productivity and farm mechanization. In fact, the average size of household farms in Korea has remained almost constant at 0.9-1.0 hectare for the last thirty years. The land reform also increased

Table 4. Number of Farm Households by Size of Land Ownership

Unit: thousand (%)

	1965	1970	1975	1980
Total No. of Farm Households (1)	2,507	2,483	2,379	2,155
Landless Farmers (2)	—	72	94	69
Farm Household (1-2)	2,507(100)	2,411(100)	2,285(100)	2,086(100)
0-0.5 ha	901(36)	788(33)	710(31)	635(31)
0.5-1 ha	794(32)	824(34)	809(35)	769(37)
1-2 ha	643(26)	639(27)	618(27)	569(27)
2-3 ha	140(6)	123(5)	112(5)	88(4)
3 ha & over	29(1)	37(2)	36(2)	26(1)
Average Size of Land Ownership	0.9 ha	0.93 ha	0.94 ha	1.0 ha

Source: Ministry of Agriculture & Fisheries, *Nongjung Soochup* (Handbook of Agricultural Administration), (in respective years).

---

11. S.W. Lee, "Land Reform in South Korea: Macro-level Policy Review," Inaytullah (ed.), *Land Reform* (Kuala Lumpur: UN/APDAC, 1980), pp. 331-335.

the financial burden on small farmers, since they were obliged to pay 30 percent of their average annual yield for five years thereafter for the redistributed land. Because the law prohibited the transfer of redistributed land for the five years necessary to pay these installments, farmers' livelihoods were tied to these small pieces of land. Accordingly, their social mobility was reduced.[12]

In spite of such restraints, the reform provided more or less equal access to production assets and also motivated farmers to work hard.[13] The land reform also promoted egalitarianism in rural communities in terms of land ownership and facilitated the disappearance of class consciousness between landlords and tenants. Nevertheless, it should be noted that it took almost one generation following the land reform to make farmers receptive to real cooperation. These favorable attitude toward participation formed only after farmers became aware that the differences in their land ownership and living standards were insignificant and that they could expect equal benefit from their participation in community projects.[14] Indeed, the belief that all will benefit equally is an important basis for any cooperative effort. Thus, the land reform provided the social and psychological groundwork necessary for cooperation among farmers and active participation in community projects. The redistribution of production assets in the rural sector by the government fostered fraternal sentiments between Korean farmers, especially those of the younger generation.

B. Improvement in General Education

After Liberation, the prevailing ideology of equal opportunity led to the introduction of a massive educational drive. Free and compulsory education at the primary school level was provided. None of the many changes in the rural sector was more widespread and far-reaching than the education of rural youngsters. The immensity of the educational effort since Liberation is reflected in the sheer magnitude of the school population. It increased from 1.5 million in 1945 to 8.0 million in 1970, the year that Saemaul Undong began. As a share of the total population, the school population rose from 9% to 26% during the same period (Table 5). The existence of

---

12. Ki-Hyuk Pak, et. al. (1966), *A Study of Land Tenure System in Korea* (Seoul: Korea Land Economic Research Institute, 1966), pp. 93-96.
13. Hans W. Singer and Nancy O. Baster, *Young Human Resources in Korea's Social Development* (Seoul: Korea Development Institue, 1980), pp. 3-5.
14. Whang, *Integrated Rural Development in Korea,* pp. 92-96.

Table 5: Number of Enrolled Students

Unit: thousand

School	1945	1955	1965	1970	1975	1980
Elementary	1,382	2,959	4,941	5,749	5,599	5,658
Secondary	85	748	1,276	2,060	3,369	4,169
Higher	8	87	135	177	236	611
Sub-total (a)	1,475	3,794	6,352	7,986	9,204	10,438
Total Population (b)	16,000	21,500	28,700	30,900	34,700	37,400
(a)/(b) %	9	1ɛ	22.1	25.9	26.5	27.9

Source: Adopted from Ministry of Education, *Annual Report of Education* (in respective years), and Economic Planning Board, *Statistical Yearbook* (in respective years).

Table 6: Rate of School Attendance and Illiteracy

Unit: thousand

	1960	1966	1970	1975	1980
Persons 5 years old & over (a)	19,672 (14,066)*	23,710 (15,499)	26,261 (15,278)	29,540 (15,264)	32,812 (14,122)
Never Attending (b)	7,765 (6,452)	6,033 (4,932)	5,125 (4,003)	4,215 (3,083)	3,871 (2,595)
(b)/(a)%	39.5 (45.9)	25.4 (31.8)	19.5 (26.2)	14.3 (20.2)	11.8 (18.4)
Illiterate (c)	4,454** (n.a.)	2,605 (2,105)	2,299 (1,830)	n.a.	n.a.
(c)/(a)%	22.6** (n.a.)	11.0 (13.6)	8.8 (12.0)	n.a.	n.a.

*The numbers in the parentheses indicate corresponding figures in the rural sector.

**Indicating the number of persons 10 years old and over in 1960. Therefore, this percentage is only an approximate figure. "Illiterate" means those who can not read and write the Korean alphabet, *Hangul*.

Source: Economic Planning Board, *Population and Housing Census Report* (in respective years).

Hangul, the indigenous alphabet invented in the middle of the fifteenth century by King Sejong, expedited the spread of education. Due to the social political repression of colonial rule, the full potential of *Hangul* was only exploited after Liberation.

The educational drive brought a great increase in literacy in the rural sector. Specifically, 46% of all persons 5 years old and over in the rural sector had never attended any regular educational institution at any level in 1960. By the time Saemaul Undong started in 1970, that figure dropped drastically to 26% in 1970 before falling further to 18% in 1980. The trend of the illiteracy rate, though based on inconsistent data, also suggests a significant improvement in the educational level of the rural population during the same period (Table 6).

The improvement in the educational level as well as the increase in the number of literate people in the rural sector has enabled rural farmers to become active participants in community decision-making. The impact of educational drive has facilitated communication between government officials and village people as well as between development field workers and community members. Indeed, communication skills, improved through general education, have expedited the efficient dissemination of rural innovations, such as the introduction of high-yielding varieties of rice.

C. Training in Leadership and Organization through Military Service[15]

The catastrophic impact of the Korean War of 1950-53 on social institutions was immense. Life, physical and social, was never the same in both urban and rural areas. The large number of wandering refugees, estimated at about 5.5 million during 1951-53, testified to the wide-spread social disintegration produced by the war. Another immediate impact of the war on Korean soceity was the physical damage to buildings, industries, roads, bridges and equipment.

Nevertheless, the impact of the Korean War may have facilitated future national modernization in some respects. For example, one positive aspect of the family disintegration caused by the war was growth in the number of social marginals, whose newly acquired "empathy"[16] would take on many different manifestations in the course of subsequent development. Another direct consequence of the war

---

15. Hahn-Been Lee, *Korea: Time, Change and Administration* (Honolulu: East-West Center Press, 1968), pp. 54-60.
16. Daniel Lerner, *The Passing of Traditional Society* (Princeton: Princeton Univdersity Press, 1958), pp. 47-52.

was the enormous expansion of the Korean armed forces. This had an important effect, the "socialization at a rapid tempo of millions of young men who were mostly from the rural communities. Recruitment in the army exposed them to a sense of national and ideological identity (anti-communism and democary) together with common symbols such as letters, numbers, signals, and modern techniques in handling weapons and vehicles. All these new experiences gave them empathy—that is, interested perception of other people, other places, other ideas and techniques"[17] (Lee H.B., 1968, 60).

Military service was beneficial to the social education of rural people and, to some extent, to the development of community leadership years later, since those who had served were experienced in efficient modern organization, in target-oriented managerial systems, and in modern science and technology. The experience promoted "social mobilization"[18] in rural communities. As most farmers had also served in the army as part of their national duty, their decision-making patterns, organizing methods, communication skills, interaction patterns, and modes of participation in projects implemented under village leadership were inevitably adopted from the military sub-culture. The basic technical training of farmers and their experience of modernity through military service have indeed influenced not only farmers' perceptions and attitudes toward cooperation, work ethics, participation and community innovations, but have also indirectly contributed to the basic sociocultural infrastructure of rural communities so necessary for their development.

7. Conclusions

The extensive and positive participation of the rural populace in community development projects has had a significant impact on results of these efforts. Participation has had a "hands-on" training effect as rural people solve their problems together, determine their priorities, practice the dynamics of group decision-making and democracy, and learn to appreciate the value of self-reliant collective action. Moreover, popular participation has helped to develop self-confidence among the people as well as collective sense of power. By virtue of its immediate impact on the village environment, participation in the Saemaul Undong enabled community members to realize

17. H. B. Lee, *op. cit.*, p. 60.
18. Karl W. Deutsch, "Social Mobilitization and Political Development," *American Political Science Review*, LV, 1961, pp. 498-505.

the benefits of concerted effort carried out in league with government officials. Thus, indirectly, it also lent credibility to the government.

Participation effected profound changes in individual behavior and attitudes via group dynamics. Through continued participation in the Saemaul Undong, the people's attitudes became more positive towards social change and more cooperative toward government officials. Participation in collective decision-making made them more democratic, more achievement-motivated, more rational in their way of life, and more future-oriented with respect to both farming and their children.

Participation also helped the community to exert control and influence over its residents and institutions. Community members became able to mold their village into instrument for improving their living standard. Therefore, the relationship between local officials and village people became both more harmonious and interdependent. The exploitative attitude of bureaucrats, a holdover of the old days, was transformed into a cooperative attitude, to the point where government officials have come to feel responsible for the successful implementation of Saemaul projects. Indeed, the promotion and transfer of local officials has become tied up with the success of community projects.

What are the lessons which can be learned from the Korean experience in popular participation in community development? The Korean experience demonstrated the synergetic effect of the four instrumental factors as they are mutually inclusive in nature. The cumulative process of social change indeed contributed to the positive formation of socio-cultural prerequisites for active participation of citizens at the community level such as socio-economic conditions, perceptual basis, communication skills, institutional framework etc. From the analysis of Korean experience, however, one can still indicate that to establish effective participation in community-level activities, governments should:

(a) utilize the par-bureaucratic personnel such as village chiefs and Saemaul leaders as "change agents" based in the community. Governments should establish, and give positive and systematic support, to self-reliant grass-roots organizations which consist of community people:

(b) organize the training program as a strategic instrument for leadership formation at the grass-roots level and for motivating rural people to participate in community programs:

(c) induce or promote active participation of people in the entire process of community development projects, from the stage of problem identification and project planning up to final evaluation;

(d) institutionalize moral support from local officials to the maximum extend by improving the service delivery capacity of local governments; and

(e) mobilize the energies and social support of the urban elite for citizen's participation based in local communities.

So far, the extent of community participation in village development projects in Korea has been satisfactory and the social and cultural conditions for popular participation have been favorable. However, popular participation in the future seems to face new challenges because the intervillage projects which are predomiant in the 1980s require more extensive participation of people from different villages. Hence local administrators and planners may have to develop new channels to identify local interests and projects and also to organize popular participation on a scale appropriate to the needs of regional development.

19

Future Demands and Supplies of Health-Care Personnel in Korea: The Case of Medical Doctors

Young Sup Kim

Introduction

As Korea enters into an advanced stage of economic development, the effective nationwide delivery of medical services will become a more critical factor in maintaining social stability. Policy makers are now recognizing this, and an increasing amount of emphasis is being placed on social welfare issues, particularly the supply of trained medical manpower. The major purpose of this paper is to forecast future needs and supply capabilities of medical manpower, both of which are essential in designing the nation's plan for health care services.

The types of critical medical manpower include doctors, dentists, nurses, pharmacists, radiological technicians, and dental technicians. Although the research from which this paper is derived analyzes the future demand and supply of each of these medical professionals, only the part dealing with demand and supply estimates of medical doctors is reported here to conserve space.

Determinants of Medical Manpower Needs

There are many important factors involved in determining the demand for medical manpower, e.g., size of population and its structure, state of the nation's economic development, level of income and education, and medical delivery system, most of which are easily measurable. However, there are other important variables which are difficult to quantify and, therefore, cannot be included in quantitative studies, e.g., technical innovation in medical services and ecological change of human diseases.

The factors which are regarded as primary determinants and treated in this study are the following:

(a) **Structural change of population:** The structure of the population in Korea has been changing as average life expectancy has lengthened. Average life expectancy was 56, 65, and and 67 years in 1960, 1970, and 1976, respectively.[1] As average life expectancy increases, the proportion of elderly population increases and creates more demand for medical services. Declining mortalit rates in general will contribute to an increase in health care demand.

(b) **Decreasing tendency of persons with disease:** The number of persons with diseases per 1,000 persons was 242 in 1965 and 166 in 1973. The average number of days in hospitals per person per year also decreased from 8.1 in 1965 to 5.5 in 1973.[2] Consistent improvement of nutrition (2,000 calories per person in 1960, 2,390 calories per person in 1976)[3] will enhance general health conditions and thus may result in decreases in medical demand. On the other hand, industrial pollution and population concentration in urban areas have resulted in increased incidence of respiratory and circulatory diseases.

(c) **Improvement in income and educational level:** There factors will contribute to an increasing demand for medical services.

(d) **Improvement in the medical delivery system:** The rate of increase in the number of persons demanding hospital service among the insured has been much faster than the rate of increase in the number of persons insured. The medical insurance system has influenced health care demand significantly upward since 1977 when Korea first introduced the system. At the end of 1978, the total number of persons insured was 1,421,030 and during 1978 the total number of hospital users among the insured increased to 2,889,112. These figures indicate that each insured person on an average visited the hospital almost twice. The evidence illustrates that the medical insurance system will increase the number of patients calling on hospitals in the future.

---

1. Korea Development Institute (KDI). *Long-Term Prospect for Economic and Social Development,* Seoul, Korea, 1977-81, p. 162.
2. Ministry of Health and Social Affairs, *A Study of Medical Insurance and Use of Medical Resources,* Seoul, Korea, 1977, p. 56.
3. KDI, *op. cit.,* p. 162.

Method of Demand Estimation

(a) From the 1970-1978 data the numbers of in-patients and out-patients for every two-year interval were calculated separately. These were then converted into the ratio of in- and out-patients to total population and this ratio was called "in- and out-patient rate".

(b) Trend curves of these in- and out-patient rates were drawn separately. From these curves a best-fitting regression model was derived—dOLT and dILT (see Equations 2 and 3). The flow chart shown in Figure 1 summarizes the process through which the equation to estimate the demand for doctors was derived.

$$Dt = \frac{OLt}{Odt} + \frac{ILt}{Idt} \tag{1}$$

(c) By method of regression analysis, coefficients of separate regression equations for in-and out-patient rates were determined and extrapolation of future patient rates (1981-2001) was estimated.

(d) Total number of patients in the year "t" was calculated by multiplying pre-estimated population with the rates of in- and out-patients in the year "t".

(e) To estimate how many patients a medical doctor can handle in year "t", Delphi-type questionnaires were administered to doctors. The key question asked was: "How many patients can a doctor handle per day at present and ten years later?"

(f) The time-service data of in- and out-patient rates from 1970-1978 shown in Table 1 were regressed against time and the regression equations so derived to estimate out-patient rate and in-patient rate at any given time were developed as follows:

$$dOLT = 24.86 + 1.18^t \tag{2}$$
$$dILT = 12.52 + 1.68^t \tag{3}$$

(g) The numbers of in- and out-patients per doctor in year t were calculated by using the Delphi method for doctors. Under the assumption that the difference between the current number of patients a doctor can handle and that number ten years later is either a diminishing or progressing relationship, the number of patients a doctor can handle in year "t" was calculated according to the following equations:

$$O = O_1 + \frac{O_{10} - O_1}{(10)t} \tag{4}$$

Table 1: Annual Patients Rate

Year	Population	$(OL_t + IL_t)$ Annual No. of Patients			$(dOL_t + dIL_t)$ Annual Patients Rate (%)		
		Total	Out-Patients	In-Patients	Total	Out-Patients	In-Patients
1970	31,435	10,656	7,131	3,525	33.89	22.68	11.21
1972	33,505	8,652	5,583	3,069	25.82	16.66	9.16
1974	34,692	11,796	7,774	4,022	33.99	22.40	11.59
1976	35,860	14,637	10,009	4,628	40.82	27.91	12.91
1978	37,019	21,472	14,915	6,557	57.94	40.23	17.71

Patient rate = (No. of patients/population) × 100.

Source: Population: EPB, *Korean Statistic Year Books*, every year; number of patients: Ministry of Health and Social Affairs, *Statistic Year Book*, 1979.

Figure 1: Flow Chart for Estimating Total Number of Doctors Demanded

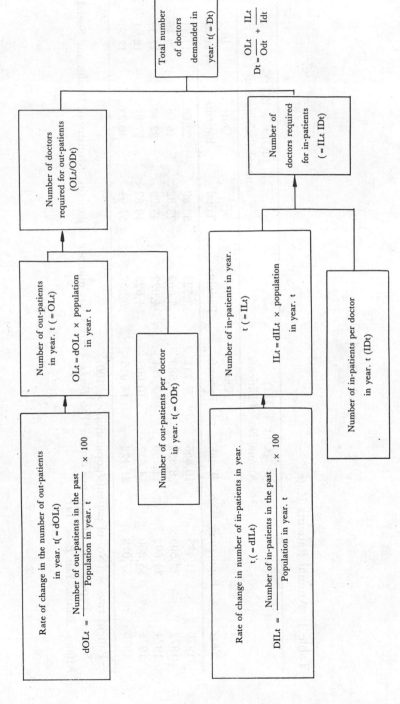

$$I = I^1 + \frac{I_{10} - I_1}{(10)t} \tag{5}$$

O = number of out-patients per doctor to be handled a day in year t

O^1 = number of out-patients per doctor to be handled a day in 1979

O^{10} = number of out-patients per doctor to be handled ten years later

I = number of in-patients per doctor to be handled a day in year t

I_1 = number of in-patients per doctor to be handled a day in 1979:10

I_{10} = number of in-patients per doctor to be handled ten years later

(h) Reference values O and I are to be converted into numbers of in- and out-pataients a doctor can handle (Odt, Idt) in any year, and then, by dividing these values by the corresponding total numbers of in-patients (ILT) and out-patients (OLT), respectively, we can estimate demand for medical doctors in any year (see Fig. 1).

The Projected Demands

Based on the estimating equations (1), (2), (3), (4), and (5), the patient rate, the number of patents, and demand for doctors were projected for selected years through the year 2001. The results of these projections are presented in Tables 2, 3, and 4. Where:

number

O = number of out-patients per doctor to be handled a day in year t

Odt = number of out-patients per doctor to be handled in the year t

I = number of in-patients per doctor to be handled a day in year t

Idt = number of in-patients per doctor to be handled in the year t

OLt = total number of out-patients in year t

ILt = total number of in-patients in the year t

$\dfrac{OLt}{odt}$ = required number of doctors for out-patients in the year t

$\dfrac{ILt}{Idt}$ = required number of doctors for in-patients in the year t

Dt = total demand for doctors in the year t

TP = total population

TDt = population per doctor

G = GNP per capita

Table 2: Estimation of Patient Rate

	1981	1986	1991	1996	2001
dOLt	44,251	67,122	101,926	153,635	232,192
dILt	18,369	22,566	26,754	30,941	35,129
Total	62,620	89,688	128,680	184,576	267,321

Patient rate = (number of patients/population) × 100(%)

Table 3: Estimation of Number of Patients

	1981	1986	1991	1996	2001
Total population	38,807	42,088	45,251	48,282	50,950
Total patients (OLt + ILt)	24,300,943	37,747,885	58,228,986	89,116,984	136,200,049
No. of out-patients	17,172,485	28,250,307	46,122,534	74,178,051	118,301,824
No. of in-patients	7,128,458	9,497,578	12,106,452	14,938,933	17,898,225

O and I were calculated from the results of the Delphi questionnaire and application of equations (4) and (5). For example, when t = 2 (1981), the decreasing rate of out-patients per doctor in ten years will be 1.6.

$$O = O_1 + \left(\dfrac{O_{10} - O_1}{10}\right) t = 8.1 + \left(\dfrac{1.6}{10}\right) \times 2 + 7.78$$

The demand for doctors in 1979 can be calculated by using equation (I) as follows:

$$Dt = \dfrac{OLt}{Odt} + \dfrac{ILt}{Idt} = 6,639 + 4,302 = 10,941$$

Table 4: Estimation Process for Future Demand of Doctors

	1979	1981	1986	1991	1996	2001
*O	8.1	7.78	6.98	6.18	5.38	4.58
Odt	8.1 × 263	7.78 × 263	6.98 × 263	6.18 × 265	5.38 × 263	4.58 × 263
	= 2,130	= 2,046	= 1,836	= 1,625	= 1,415	= 1,205
*I	4	3.9	3.65	3.4	3.15	2.9
Idt	4 × 365	3.9 × 365	3.65 × 365	3.4 × 365	3.15 × 365	2.9 × 365
	× 1,460	= 1,428	= 1,332	= 1,241	= 1,150	= 1,059
OLt	14,140,016	17,172,485	28,250,307	46,122,534	74,178,051	118,301,824
ILt	6,281,507	7,128,458	9,497,578	12,106,452	14,938,933	17,898,225
OLt/Odt	6,639	8,393	15,387	28,383	52,423	98,176
ILt/Idt	4,302	5,006	7,130	9,755	12,990	16,901
Dt	**10,941	13,399	22,517	38,138	65,413	115,077
TP	37,605,000	38,807,000	42,088,000	45,251,000	48,282,000	50,950,000
TDt	3,437	2,896	1,869	1,187	738	443
G		1,386	2,342	3,665	5,296	7,636

Manpower Supply for Health Care

In order to appraise the supply of health care manpower, the following information was obtained: sex, age, level of income, educational background, occupation, expertise, and field status characteristics. In particular, age and sex distribution among physicians is believed important in determining the supply level of doctors.

For example, the predominance of doctors in the age bracket 55-60 indicates that there will be a sharp decrease in the supply of doctors as doctors of this age group reach retirement age in five to ten years. With respect to sex, the working life of female doctors will be affected by marital status and childrering.

In Korea, 77 percent of doctors, dentists, and Chinese medical doctors are concentrated in urban areas. The concentration of medical specialists in urban areas means that rural areas face severe shortages of manpower in some medical services.

Data used for estimating the supply capacities of health-care man-

Table 5: Supply Projection for Doctors

	1979	1981	1986	1991	1996	2001
Supply[1]	18,183	20,048	24,709	29,371	34,033	38,695
Licensed	21,121	23,287	28,702	34,117	39,532	44,947
Abroad[2]	1,478	1,630	2,009	2,388	2,767	3,146
Deaths[3]	87	95	118	140	162	184
Retired & unemployed[4]	1,373	1,514	1,866	2,218	2,570	2,922
Newly licensed	1,369	1,548	1,958	2,120	2,120	2,120
Graduated	1,429	1,576	1,940	2,100	2,100	2,100
Population per medical doctor	2,068	1,936	1,703	1,540	1,419	1,334

$Sr = 17,872 + 1,083t.$

[1] Actual number of doctors = licensed doctors − (abroad + deaths + retired + unemployed).

[2] 7% of licensed doctors.

[3] 0.41% of licensed doctors.

[4] 6.5% of licensed doctors.

Source: Number of deaths, emigration, retired and unemployed are based on *Citizens' Health and Conditions of Medical Facility (1978), A Study of Korean Medical Insurance and Use of Medical Resources (1977),* Committee for Social Security Council, Ministry of Health and Social Affairs.

power are from various sources including professional licenses and occupational registration. The 1970-1979 trend data on doctors were used to develop regression equations to estimate the projected supply of doctors in the future. The estimating equation is:

$$SDt = 17,872 + 1,083,$$ (6)

The number of doctors estimated based on this equation is shown in Table 5. This projection indicates that the number of doctors will grow from 18,183 in 1979 to 38,695 in 2001. At the same time, the population/doctor ratio will decline from 2,068 persons per doctor in 1979 to 1,334 persons per doctor in 2001.

Matching the Demands and Supplies Projected

Table 6 shows the projected demands and supplies of doctors for selected years from 1979 to 2001. The demand/supply relationship changes radically dfrom heavy surplus to heavy shortage as time progresses. In 1979, demand for doctors was 10,941, while the supply was 18,183, a surplus of 7,242 doctors. Around 1987, the demand and supply is expected to reach an equilibrium. From that point on a shortage in the supply of medical doctors is expected to grow, reaching a shortage of 66.4 percent by the year 2001.

Table 6: Comparison of Supply with Demand for Doctors

Year	Demand	Supply	B – A = C	IC/A × 100
1979	10,941	18,183	+ 7,242	+ 66.2
1981	13,399	20,048	+ 6,649	+ 49.6
1986	22,517	24,709	+ 2,192	– 9.6
1991	38,138	29,371	– 8,767	– 22.9
1996	65,413	34,033	– 31,380	– 47.9
2001	115,077	38,695	– 76,382	– 66.4

Some factors presently unforeseen may stimulate even greater increases in demand for medical services in the future. An unexpected increase in per capita income or sudden change in public policy, such as public financing for the medical services of the lower income families, are two examples. Since the supply of medical professionals is largely inelastic, there is a concern as to whether such unanticipated developments can be dealt with effectively.

Another problem anticipated in the delivery of medical services is the spatial distribution of projected medical professionals. As discussed earlier, there is an increasing tendency for doctors to be concentrated in urban areas. Like other white collar workers, they prefer to work in large metropolitan areas where amenities exist. However, this is leading to critical shortages of medical doctors in rural areas. Since the initiation of the medical insurance program, this problem of spatial maldistribution of doctors has beocme particularly serious.

Conclusions

To effectively match the demand for and supply of health care professionals whose roles are critical for social welfare, the following points should be considered.

1) Here the demand and supply of medical manpower are projected through the year 2001 based on analysis of empirical data. If public policies and social conditions continue to follow the established trends, they are likely to result in a crucial shortage of health care manpower. Because of the overconcentration of medical professionals in metropolitan areas, the overall equkilibrium between demand and supply could arrive at a much earlier date than predicted.

2) The supply of medical manpower is characterized by inelasticity. Therefore, supply cannot respond quickly to changes in demand; time is needed to train health-care manpower, e.g., doctors and dentists require six years of medical school and two years of intemship and pharmacists and nurses require four years of college education before practicing their professions. Thus, in forecasting the supply and demand for health-care manpower, the projection of supply and demand must be made at least ten years in advance in order to develop a workable plan to bring future demands and supplies into balance.

3) As experienced in many other countries, when the supply is projected too generously, health care manpower tends to show shortages in reality. When the disadvantages of oversupply and undersupply are compared, it is believed easier to deal with oversupply than undersupply although neither is desirable.

4) It is estimated that the oversupply of health care manpower will disappear within the next six or seven years. Before entering the nineties, demand will accelerate; thus medical school facilities should be gradually expanded now in order to cope with future demand. Until now, the supply trend curve of health care personnel has followed

a linear pattern, not elastic enough to cope with changes in demand. Therefore, policy makers should take into consideration that supply must be increased exponentially to match demand so that shortages caused by time lag can be avoided.

5) To improve the overall effectiveness of health care, a policy of redistribution is urged to ease the overconcentration of health care manpower in metropolitan areas. To do so, government subsidy, tax exemption and other forms of incentives for medical personnel to move into rural areas deserve serious consideration as a policy option.

6) To attract qualified professors to medical schools, incentives such as research funds and monthly allowances might be provided.

7) To bring back prominent Korean scholars from abroad, professional and economic incentives such as housing and research opportunities should be considered as a policy strategy.

20

Testing Perceptions of Distributive Justice in Korea

Yong Duck Jung and Gilbert B. Siegel

There is a growing body of evidence that Koreans seek a more equitable distribution of wealth in their society. While economic growth has been substantial since the 1960's, sharing of the proceeds has not been widespread, and inequities have worsened as development has accelerated. Korea's level of income inequality has not been as severe as that of other countries,[1] therefore, it cannot be considered a primary causal factor in demand for income redistribution. Nevertheless, there has been a demonstrable demand for some form of redistribution of wealth.[2] Rising expectations have been stimulated to some extent by diffusion of information on governmental policies of other nations, and also by growing popular awareness of political favoritism resulting from government domination of the political and economic systems of the country.

This article examines three alternative models of distributive equity tested for conformity with expectations and beliefs of the Korean people. The effects of public policy extant in Korea are considered, and policies are examined without reference to governmental priorities. For example, government may favor export over domestic consumption and, accordingly, give preferential treatment to exporting industries over those which serve domestic markets. Our public policy

---

1. B. Renaud, "Economic Growth and Income Inequality in Korea," World Bank Staff Working Paper, No. 240 (1976), p. 11; H. Chenery, et al., *Redistribution with Growth* (Oxford University Press. 1975), pp. 8-9.
2. Hoon Yu, "Hankuk Sahoe Kaebal Chungchaek ui Banghyang Moseak," *Koean Journal of Public Administration,* 17:1 (1979), p. 45; Seoul National University, Social Science Research Institute Survey of Korean Citizen Values, reported in *Dong-A Ilbo* (American Edition), January 5, 1980, p. 4.

concern is with outcomes (e.g., impact on the industrial work force), regardless of political priority, in order to test the effects of policies from the perspectives of the three models of distributive justice. Results of empirical tests of the three models, employing the methodology developed by Rossi and others[3] with American samples, are presented; some modifications were made for societal differences between Korea and the United States.

MODELS OF DISTRIBUTIVE JUSTICE AND THE KOREAN EXPERIENCE

Norms of justice evolve in all societies; each society may differ substantially from others in perceptions of fairness and equity. We posit that the concern with equity in Korea is related to (a) specific, popularly held conception(s) of distributive justice. As detailed below, there are at least three different principles, including egalitarian, meritarian, and needs-based conceptions of distributive justice. An egalitarian value system for income distribution requires equalization of economic benefits regardless of level of personal need or merit. A more meritarian value system will probably focus less on the level of income equality and more on the fairness of distribution. On the other hand, need based on fundamental deficiencies may be the value system. We have defined these values for operational purposes as: (1) equal distribution, (2) unequal distribution based on merit, and (3) unequal distribution based on need.[4]

The Engalitarian Principle of Distributive Justice

The principle of perfect equality appears to have a place in an adequate social ethic. But many, including Aristotle, have considered equal justice to apply to general human rights rather than economic rights.[5] Every human being is equally a human being, and that

3. Peter H. Rossi, et al., "Measuring Household Social Standing," *Social Science Research* 3 (September 1974), pp. 169-90; Jasso Guillermina and Peter Rossi, "Distributive Justice and Earned Income," *American Sociological Review* 42:3 (1977), pp. 639-51; Wayne M. Alves and Peter H. Rossi, "Who Should Get What? Fairness Judgments of the Distribution of Earnings," *American Journal of Sociology* 84:3 (1978), pp. 541-64.

4. For example, see M. Rein and S. Miller, "Standards of Income Redistribution," *Challenge* (July-August, 1974), pp. 20-26.

5. Aristotle, *Nicomachean Ethics*, reprinted in T. Schwartz, *Freedom and Authority: An Introduction to Social and Political Philosophy* (Belmont, Ca.: Dickenson Publishing Company, Inc., 1973), p. 34.

minimum qualification entitles all equally to certain human rights which usually are not economic goods. However, to egalitarians general human rights are not enough. In addition to "civil" rights, such as freedoms of speech, press, and assembly, they argue that people are entitled to economic rights such as food, shelter and education.[6] Accordingly, a strict egalitarian would apply Aristotle's formula of proportionate justice, which is that "distributive justice is accomplished between A and B when the following ratio is satisfied":

$$\frac{A\text{'s share of P}}{B\text{'s share of P}} = \frac{A\text{'s possession of } Q^7}{B\text{'s possession of } Q}$$

where P stands for economic goods and Q is humanity or a human nature; since every human being possesses Q equally, it follows that all should share society's economic wealth equally. Implicit in this equal shares model is the idea of equality of opportunity—both to act and to develop abilities or potential through exposure to various outputs which government affects or delivers, such as nutrition, education, culture, etc.

Korea's experience in the light of this criterion may be seen by examining a measure known as the "Gini coefficient." The lower the Gini coefficient, the more equitable the society. Korea, with a Gini coefficient of .36 in 1971 and .4 in 1978, has been more equitable than the Philippines (.49) and Malaysia (.52), and has been less equitable than Sri Lanka (.35), Yugoslavia (.35), Taiwan (.28) and Japan (.29).[8] As for the trend of inequality, Korean society has become less equitable since the 1960's, in that its Gini coefficient has increased from .34 in 1966 through .36 in 1971 to .40 in 1978.[9]

To date, the Korean government's record in equalization of wealth has not been extensive through measures such as social security and educational or technological research/training policies, as well as more direct initiatives such as the imposition of minimum wages, the limitation of dividends, and so forth.[10] Taxation in Korea is mainly indirect and so tends to be regressive in effect.

On the expenditure side, the Korean government has provided

---

6. J. Feinberg, *Social Philosophy* (New Jersey: Prentice-Hall, Inc., 1973), p. 89.
7. *Ibid.*
8. *Dong-A Ilbo*, June 26, 1980; and S. Jein, *Size Distribution of Income* (Washington, D.C.: World Bank, 1975).
9. *Ibid.*
10. J. Tinbergen, *Income Distribution: Analysis and Policies* (Oxford: North-Holland Publishing Company, 1975), pp. 137-42.

various programs and services in education, public health, and welfare supports, but its investment in these programs has not been emphasized during the 1960's and 1970's.[11] Expenditures for social security programs were only .8 percent of GNP in 1966. Total expenditure for social development, including education and social security, was at 3.4 percent GNP.[12] In spite of the Korean government's pronouncement that it would promote social development in the mid-1970's, change of policy direction has not occurred; to the contrary, the ratio of government expenditure for social development to total national expenditure decreased during the late 1970's.[13]

The Meritarian Principle of Distributive Justice

Another candidate rule to achieve distributive justice is the principle of merit: justice is achieved by distributing benefits so that everyone gets the share he or she deserves. Distribution of the goods of society according to merit is an idea which dates to Socrates and the Old Testament. Later, Aristotle reaffirmed this meritarian notion of distributive justice by arguing the principle, "To each according to his desert," which may be described through the previously stated formula, with the change that Q stands for merit or desert.[14] But what are the characteristics of merit or desert? A first distinction can be made between objective (i.e., individual native ability and acquired skills) and subjective (i.e., individual effort) criteria.[15] Effort and achievement appear to have a strong claim as criteria of merit. But, considering that effort and achievement depend on prerequisite ability, the ability criterion also is a relevant basis of desert, at least to the

11. C. K. Park, *Social Security in Korea* (Seoul: Korean Development Institute, 1975), pp. 116-18.
12. See Yong-duck Jung and Gilbert B. Siegel, "Distributive Justice in Korea: Searching for a Policy Criterion for Social Development and Income Distribution," paper presented at the Annual Conference of the American Society for Public Administration, Honolulu, March 1982, Table 16. Table 16 is titled "Social Security Expenditures as a Percentage of Gross National Product, 1966" and is derived from C. Lindblom, *Politics and Markets: The World's Political-Economic Systems* (New York: Basic Books, 1977), p. 29, and Bank of Korea, *Kyungche Tongkye Nyunbo*, 1966.
13. *Ibid.*, Table 15. Table 15 is titled "Expenditure for Social Development: 1960—1981," and is derived from Bank of Korea, *Kyungche Tongkye Nuynbo* each year for FY 1960—1980, and *Dong-A Ilbo*, for FY 1981.
14. This formula for calculating whether or not individuals are in a just relationship was proposed originally by Aristotle and has been utilized by some social scientists, such as J. S. Adams, "Inequity in Social Exchange," in L. Berkowitz, ed., *Advances in Experimenteal Social Psychology*, Vol. 2 (New York: Academic Press, 1965), pp. 267-99.
15. R. Veatch, "What is a 'Just' Health Care Delivery?" in R. Veatch and R. Branson, eds., *Ethics and Health Policy* (Cambridge: Ballinger Publishing Company, 1976), p. 129.

extent that it contributes to achievement.

In general, for the meritarians the end-state of size distribution of income is not the focus of concern. What is important is the question of whether the "return of contribution" principle works in a society. However, it is not easy to identify the comparable degrees to which individuals have contributed to social wealth or to measure the causal factors in the production of social wealth. Instead, it is easier to focus on the *procedures* of income distribution. Just income distribution is concerned with fairness of the procedure by which every person has an equal chance to develop his abilities and capacities and to succeed through effort.[16] Thus, in evaluating a country's income distribution, the principle of equality of opportunity can be applied, for example, to the extent to which there are illegitimate barriers to improving incomes, or to which opportunities are available to some groups but not others. Government policies would be aimed at eradicating such barriers and opportunities.

Since the beginning of the Republic in Korea the government has reiterated principle of freedom of and respect for initiative in private enterprise as its institutional philosophy.[17] However, the Korean economic system has been one of mixed capitalism in that the government will either directly participate in or indirectly render guidance to basic industries and other important sectors.[18] Especially since the early 1960's, the government's role in the economy has become more influential through measures such as economic planning, public enterprises, fiscal and monetary policies, and economic regulations favoring certain industries. Most government activities have been conducted in the name of economic development, and many agree that Korea's rapid economic growth during the 1960's and 1970's was engineered by the public sector employed on behalf of guided capitalism.[19] In addition to the positive effects on economic growth, however, intervention in the Korean economy may have had redistributional impacts

For example, the Korean government has permitted large firms to conduct monopolistic pricing in the name of encouraging economies of scale and enhancing competitive power in international markets, but has restrained prices for labor and agricultural products in the name of preventing inflation and (again) improving large-firm inter-

---

.   A. Goldman, "Limits to the Justification of Reverse Discrimination," *Social Theory and Practice,* 3:3 (1975), p. 291.

17. Republic of Korea, *Summary of the First Five-Year Economic Plan, 1962—1966* (Seoul, 1962), p. 28.

18. *Ibid.*

19. G. Caiden and Y. Jung, "The Political Economy of Korean Development under the Park Government," *Journal of International and Public Affairs,* 2:2 (Spring/Summer 1981), pp. 173-183.

national competitive position. As a consequence, the share of national income to business enterprises has been rising since the early 1960's, whereas that of combined agricultural income and employee compensation has been declining and in fact has been growing less rapidly than GNP.[20] Additionally, overall tax policies have disadvantaged wage earners and individual consumers more than manufacturers and the export companies. Monetary policies, including loans, have been more beneficial for firms than households, profit earners than wage earners, export-oriented than domestic-consumption-oriented industries, large than small or medium-sized enterprises.

Perhaps more worrisome has been the reeemergence of corruption and favoritism and their possible impact on income distribution. The name of the Rhee regime has been synonymous with corruption in Korea.[21] After the military coup in 1961, steps were taken to reduce corruption and punish offending officials for inefficiency and negligence. Howevre, this campaign had limited success as evidenced by the so-called "four scandals" in the Democratic Republican Party: the rigging of the stock market, the excessive profits on imported taxicabs, the diversion of foreign exchange to construct the Walker Hill resort, and imported pinball machines. More recently there have been complaints of favoritism in awarding government contracts. Officials have been tempted to extract forced payments in return for favoritism.[22] The Daewoo group started with modest capital and amassed billions within ten years. Illegal loans were obtained by the head of the Yulsan group of companies to finance exports through government influence.[23] Moreover, the dominance of government over economic policy in the 1960's and 1970's has invited abuse. The government had power to put firms out of business by shutting off their credit. It could restrict them from some fields and force them into others through its control of investment funds. Since the country's independence, it has been widely believed by Koreans that political linkage exists between the government and the *chaebol* (defined as a few groups of large enterprises).[24] It has also been accepted that

20. S. Ban, "The Community Movement," in C. Kim, ed., *Industrial and Social Development Issues* (Seoul: Korean Development Institute, 1977), p. 232.
21. See G. Henderson, *Korea: The Politics of Vortex* (Cambridge: Harvard University Press, 1968).
22. N. Pearlstine, "How South Korea Surprised the World," *Forbes*, April 30, 1979, pp. 53-61.
23. W. Chapman, "South Koreans Uneasy with Changes Spawned by New Wealth," *The Washington Post*, June 13, 1979, pp. A19, A22.
24. L. Jones and I. Sakong, *Government, Business, and Entrepreneurship in Economic Development: The Korean Case* (Studies in the Modernization of the ROK: 1945-1975) (Cambridge: Harvard University Press, 1980), p. 269.

the expansion in new enterprises has resulted more from the founding of "offspring" firms by existing enterprises than from entry of new entrepreneurs into the market.

Another factor with regard to fair competition and equal opportunities in Korean industrial organization has been the lack of influence of labor unions on economic policy-making. While labor unions exist, they are so weak that not only do they not provide much opinion input, but their potential reaction is seldom considered as a constraint.[25] In this context, it is quite understandable that the growth rate of real wages had been lower than that of labor productivity since the early 1960's.[26] Finally, social status was of greater weight than occupational status in determining individual incomes in Korea during the mid-1970's.[27]

Need as a Principle of Just Distribution

A third candidate principle of distributive justice is human need. In this case economic resources should be distributed on the basis of individual needs. This principle is seen again through Aristotle's formula, previously described, but where P stands for economic benefit and Q is personal need.

Need, too, is subject to various interpretations. In most of its forms the criterion shares the same ground as either of the extreme principles of criterion shares the same ground as either of the extreme principles of distributive justice: equality or merit. First, need can be regarded as a mediating way to achieve more equal distribution of income. However, what does perfect equality mean? Equality may mean identical treatment. For example, "We can provide equal rations of food for each member of the community," J. Lucas writes, "but at the cost of satisfying appetites unequally, leaving boys still hungry, and old women overfed."[28] The idea of equality can be achieved not necessarily by treating persons in an identical manner, but by treating them with due attention to different individual needs. However, the principle more often appears as a requirement to lessen inequalities or to have levels of tolerable or acceptable inequalities

25. *Ibid.*, p. 268.
26. EPB, *Kyongche Paekso* (Economic Whitebook), 1976, pp. 261 and 431.
27. H. Koo and D. Hong, "Class and Income Inequality in Korea." *American Sociological Review,* 45 (August 1980), pp. 610-26.
28. J. Lucas, "Equality," in R. Flathman, ed., *Concepts in Social and Political Philosophy* (New York: Macmillan, 1973), pp. 347-51, especially pp. 348-49.

even though perfect equality may be held as the orienting goal.[29] As an intermediate step toward perfect equality, minima are improved by raising the minimum of basic services, etc. The objective of the so-called "social minimum" or "floor of protection" approach is that no one should fall below some minimum level of income and service. Where to place that floor is a subject of disagreement, but the principle is accepted that poverty should be eliminated.

On the other hand, the principle of personal need can be considered as a way of mediating the applicaiton of the meritarian principle of distributive justice. The meritarians assume that the pattern of income distribution is determined by the competitive equilibrium between firms, individuals, and prices of factors and commodities. Such a competitive equilibrium model implies a unique income distribution with economic efficiency. However, some economic activities in the name of competitive equilibrium and economic efficiency may in the long run be inconsistent with this efficient competition. For example, if some people are to lose their health or job due to uncontrollable events, they do not have the necessary opportunity to exercise certain basic rights. Consequently, perfect competition and economic efficiency are difficult to achieve. Accordingly, it is argued that some basic needs must be provided for the sake of maintaining the pure meritarian principle of justice. Thus, distribution should be achieved through the competitive meritarian principle, but accompanied by minimum income and allotments of basic needs such as food and medical care, etc.

The first step for the public policies is to define and measure basic need. The Korean government has attempted to determine the size of its poor population. The "absolutely poor" group was about 40 percent of the total population in the mid-1960's and was reduced to about 15 percent in the mid-1970's.[30] This reduction was attributed to rapid economic growth during the period. However, there have been problems with both government policies for the alleviation of poverty and with methods for measuring the level of the absolutely poor.

First, we examine the government's policy. Using 1978 data, there were about 4.05 million absolutely poor people or 12 percent of the total population in Korea.[31] However, only 1.99 million (about 5.9 percent of the total population) were included in this category of the

29. M. Rein and S. Miller, *op. cit.,* pp. 21-25.
30. *Dong A Ilbo,* June 26, 1980, and August 8, 1979.
31. *Ibid.*

government's assistance program.[32] Roughly half of the absolutely poor (i.e., more than two million) were not covered by the government's program. Thus, about six percent were left to fall below the minimum standard of living level in the late 1970's.

Measurement standards have also been inadequate. According to the social security law in Korea, the Minister of Health and Social Affairs is to decide the minimum standard of living. However, it has been reported that the government authority did not provide the public with any "rational standard to measure the minimum costs of living" or "the number of the poor" in Korea.[33] In 1978, the categories of "absolutely poor" or "the public assistance needy" included the people whose monthly incomes fell below about $10 for rural residents or $11 for urban residents. The basis for these standards is not known, and many critics have argued that they were neither realistic nor reasonable.[34]

Programming the provision of assistance to the needy may take a number of alternative approaches. Government can attempt to alleviate or eliminate the conditions of poverty by providing various goods and services (food, shelter, clothing, medical care, etc.). Most governmental programs under the title of "public assistance" in Korea are include in this category and aim at "providing a minimum level of subsistance to certain categories of needy"[35] adults and children. In additin to the alleviation strategy, it is necessary to develop more of a preventive approach. Social insurance concepts in Korea can be included in this category in that they aim at "preventing poverty resulting from unemployment, old age, death of a family breadwinner, or physical disability." etc.[36] Another attack on the causes of poverty is to improve individual productive capacity and earning power through education and training programs. Also, the approach of increasing individual earning capacity must be accompanied by monetary, fiscal, and industrial policies which increase demand for labor and assist the immigration of workers out of poorly paid agricultural pursuits and break down restrictive or discriminatory

---

32. C. Son, "Gong Jok Bucho" (Public Assistance), *Guk Hoe Bo* (National Assembly Review) 165 (July-August 1978), pp. 39-44.
33. *Ibid.*, p. 44.
34. For example, see a special series of articles on Korea's social welfare system in *Guk Hoe Bo* (National Assembly Review) 165 (July-August 1978), pp. 33-56.
35. See C. Son. *op. cit.*, and T. Dye, *Understanding Public Policy* (New Jersey: Prentice-Hall, 1972), p. 97.
36. See C. Park, "Sahoe Bohom Chedo" (Social Security System), Guk Hoe Bo 165 (July-August 1978), pp. 45-49; and U.S.HEW, *Social Security Programs in the United States* (Washington, D.C.: HEW, Soual Security Administration, 1968).

practices.[37]

In general it can be said that these programs and services have not been emphasized in comparison to those for economic growth and national defense. The Korean government has not implemented comprehensive social insurance programs, except for some civil servants, military personnel, and industrial employees.[38] During the late 1960's expenditures for social security, health, and social welfare were small in relation to total GNP or total government expenditures.[39] It should be acknowledged, however, that government expenditures for education have increased since 1960 to more than 15 percent of the budget.[40] Also the high rate of labor absorption has contributed significantly to improving income levels of urban residents, and growth in the urban labor market has made regional differences in wages decline steadily.[41]

MEASURING CONCENSUS ON DISTRIBUTIVE JUSTICE

We have identified three alternative conceptions of distributive justice—equality, merit, and need—and the state of Korean society relative to each model; we now wish to determine what principle(s) of justice prevail in Korean society with regard to distribution of economic resources. An empirical survey was conducted in Korea to determine upon which of the three there is broad-based concensus. Operationally:

1. the first hypothesis to be tested is that people think income distribution ought to be equal;

2. if the first hypothesis is rejected, then, two additional hypotheses are considered: people think income ought to be distributed unequally based on individudal merit, and people think income should be distributed unequally based on personal need.

37. See J. Tobin, "On Improving the Economic Status of the Negro," in E. Budd. ed., *Inequality and Poverty* (New York: W. W. Norton and Company, Inc., 1967), pp. 194-214.
38. C. Park, *Social Security in Korea: An Approach to Socioeconomic Development* (Seoul: Korea Development Institute, 1975), p. 116.
39. *Ibid.,* p. 117.
40. *Long-Term Prospect for Economic and Social Development: 1977-1991* (Seoul: Korea Development Institute, 1978), p. 138.
41. E. Mason, et al., *The Economic and Social Modernization of the Republic of Korea* (Studies in the Modernization of the Republic of Korea: 1945, 1975) (Cambridge: Harvard University Press, 1980).

Research Methods and Procedure

The research strategy is to elicit from a representative sample of respondents a set of judgments about the justice of the earnings enjoyed by a variety of fictitious individuals and families.[42] These judgments were obtained in household interviews by presenting to the respondents a set of descriptions of individuals and families (called vignettes). The set of vignettes presented to each respondent had certain important features. The distribution of earnings across the vignettes is random and rectangular to maximize the earnings variance. Earnings are random with respect to all other characteristics, thus assuring a test of the relative importance of the various justice rules. The overall patterning of judgments about such a set of vignettes allows inferences concerning collectively preferred earnings distributions.

Vignette Construction

A first step was to develop vignettes: a set of descriptions of fictitious individuals and families. We settled upon some key characteristics as measures of merit, need, etc.

Merit: Four characteristics were employed as measures of merit: educational level, occupational prestige, length of employment, and level of capital investment. These are described and scaled as follows:

Educational level. A seven-point credential scale was used instead of years of education: (1) no or some elementary school, (2) completed

---

42. Recently there have been some attempts to study the question of "Who should get what?" at the empirical level. For example, Joseph Berger et al., (1972), George Homans (1974), Guillermina Jasso and Peter Rossi (1977), Wayne Alves and Peter Rossi (1978), and J. Rohrbaugh and G. McClelland (1980) have tried to develop research methods to answer the question, "What is actually considered 'just' by individuals and societies?" Among them the survey method designed by Jasso and Rossi (for the population of Baltimore City) and Alves and Rossi (for the total U.S. population) can be considered a useful approach to the issues raised in this research. Thus, this study relies mainly on their research design and methodology with some modifications. See J. Berger et al., "Structural Aspects of Distributive Justice: A Status-Value Formulation," in J. Berger et al., eds., *Sociological Theories in Progress*, Vol. 2(1972), pp. 119-46; G. Homans, *Social Behavior: Its Elementary Forms*, revised ed. (New York: Harcourt, Brace, Jovanovich, 1974); G. Jasso and P. Rossi, "Distributive Justice and Earned Income," *American Sociological Review* 42 (August 1977), pp. 639-51; W. Alves and P. Rossi, "Who Should Get What? Fairness Judgments of Distribution of Earnings," *American Journal of Sociology* 84:3 (1978), pp. 541-64; J. Rohrbaugh and G. McClelland, "Measuring the Relative Importance of Utilitarian and Egalitarian Values," *Journal of Applied Psychology* 65:1 (1980), pp. 34-49; and P. Rossi, "The Presidential Address: The Challenge and Opportunities of Applied Social Research," *American Sociological Review* 45 (December 1980), pp. 889-904.

elementary school, (3) completed junior high school, (4) completed senior high school, (5) some college or two-year college graduate, (6) college graduate, and (7) post-college.[43]

Length of Employment. Years of employment are categorized in the following intervals: (1) about 5 years, (2) about 10 years, (3) about 20 years, (4) about 30 years, and (5) about 40 years.

Occupational Prestige Level. Sixty-one different occupational titles were chosen from the titles for which occupational prestige scores are available in Treiman's standard international occupational prestige scores and selected with probabilities roughly proportional to appearance in cohort census categories in the Korean labor force.[44]

Level of capital Input. Four rough categories of capital investment are used, ranging from no capital input (0), small property ownership (1), small level firm ownership (2), middle level firm ownership (3), large firm ownership (4).

Personal Needs: Personal needs are measured by the number of dependent family members.

Number of Dependent Adults. (parents, spouse, and brothers/sisters, etc.) ranging from zero to three.

Number of Dependent Children. (children or dependent siblings) ranging from zero to six.

In addition to merit and need, there may exist other variables which can influence fairness judgments with regard to income earnings. In general, "sex" and "ethnicity" play an important role in stratification theory and were included in the studies by Rossi and his colleagues in the United States. But since Korea is a racially homogeneous society and it is difficult to define ethnicity, it is not included in this study as a variable.

Sex: Female (0) and Male (1)

Average monthly earnings. This was considered to be a measure of

Each respondent was handed a sample of 50 vignettes among the 500 vignettes and a box with nine slots, each labeled with a number

---

43. Although strictly speaking it is not an interval variable, treating it as such would not violate common research practice in social science. In the following analysis it is used as an interval variable.

44. See Daniel J. Treiman, *Occupational Prestige in Comparative Perspective* (New York: Academic Press, 1977), pp. 235-60; H. Koo and D. Hong's research, which was conducted to determine the validity of SIOPS in the context of Korean society, shows that there is a high product-moment correlation between Treiman's socres and their own (.75); therefore, it should not matter too much if Treiman's is used. Also, Treiman's measure has merit for a comparative study. However, we found some score that did not make sense considering Korean standards; there were modified by asking Korean students and visiting scholars in the Boston area.

income for each individual in a household: average monthly earned incomes ranged from W60,000 to W1,500,000 for a household in increments of W20,000 between W60,000 and W120,000; in increments of W30,000 between W120,000 and W300,000: in increments of W50,000 between W300,000 and W500,000; in increments of W100,000 between W500,000 and W1,000,000; and in increments of W500,000 between W1,000,000 and W1,500,000.

The vignette were generated by a computer program which selects a value for each characteristic described above at random. Thus, for a household vignette, occupation was randomly selected, then length of employment, education, capital input, number of dependent adults, number of children, sex, and finally an earnings amount was selected. Restrictions to eliminate nonsensical combinations (e.g., a physician or a university professor with less than college education) were imposed a priori. Among the vignettes generated by the computer program, only 500 were selected randomly for the research.

Variables

The vignette characteristics described as measures of merit, need, earned income, and others are regarded as independent variables. The income-fairness rating is treated as a dependent variable. This research design assumes that individuals make judgments about the fairness or relative unfairness of economic distribution. Further, following Aristotle, it assumes that personal justice may be conceptually viewed as a continuum with a mid-point of justice and two extreme poles of injustice—one of excess and the other of deficiency—that are contrary both to each other and to the mid-point; and that these may be treated as degrees of variation. Using a nine-category fairness-ratings scale, we attempted to uncover the underlying continuum of perceived relative unfairness with a minimum of bias and a maximum of field utility.

Sampling and Interview Methods

The date were collected through personal interviews with a sample of 302 adult respondents residingin urban and rural areas in Korea in spring 1981. Block quota sampling methods were used to choose a respondent sample of 302 adults living in the capital city of Seoul for urban data, and in Yichon County, Kyunggi Province, for rural data. Interviews, lasting about half an hour each, were conducted by experienced research assistants of the Research Institute of Public Affirs, Graduate School of Public Administration, Seoul National University.

and a description corresponding to a level of the justice evaluation variable, ranging from 1 for the "extremely overpaid" through 5 for "fairly paid" through 9 for "extremely underpaid."

The basic tasks set before respondents were to judge how fairly each of the 50 household vignettes described wre paid; to place each vignette, described on a 3 × 5 card, in the slot corresponding to their judgment; and to provide standard background and demographic information about him/herself and his/her household, including occupation, dependents, income, and age.

Data Analysis and Findings

Testing the First Hypothesis, Equal Distribution of Income: In order to test the first hypothesis (i.e., Koreans think income distribution ought to be equal), the nature of the distribution of income-fairness ratings produced by the survey for all the vignettes was analyzed. The distribution of ratings received by the approximately 14,900 vignettes rated by 298 Korean respondents is shown in Table 1. Since earnings are rectangularly and randomly distributed among the vignettes, the ratings must also be rectangularly distributed among the nine categories if the respondents consider equality as just or equitable distribution of income.

Table 1: Frequency Distribution of Income-Fairness Ratings

Income-Fairness Rating	Frequency	Percent
1. Extremely Overpaid	1,161	7.79
2. Much Overpaid	1,210	8.12
3. Somewhat Overpaid	1,254	8.42
4. Slightly Overpaid	1,551	10.41
5. Fairly Paid	2,712	18.20
6. Slightly Underpaid	1,562	10.48
7. Somewhat Underpaid	1,607	10.79
8. Much Underpaid	1,918	12.87
9. Extremely Underpaid	1,889	12.68
Mean Frequency	1,651.6	
Mean Rating	5.39	
Total Ratings	14,864	
% Rated	99.76	

In statistical terms, each of the nine categories of ratings must have the same frequency distribution of the rated vignettes, if the hypothesis is true. That is:

H_0: $f_1 = f_2 = f_3 = f_4 = f_5 = f_6 = f_7 = f_8 = f_9 = 14864/9$
H_1: Not $f_1 = f_2 = f_3 = f_4 = f_5 = f_6 = f_7 = f_8 = f_9 = 14864/9$

where f_i = the number of vignettes distributed in each category, and $i = 1 \sim 9$.

The null hypothesis is tested using the χ^2 statistic at the significance level of .01.

$$\chi^2 = \Sigma(0 - E)^2/E$$

where E = expected frequency (14864/9), 0 = observed frequency, and d.f. = $9 - 1 = 8$.

The observed χ^2 for Table 1 is 1129.7 and is significant beyond $\chi^2_{99 \cdot 8}$ (= 20.1). Thus, the null hypothesis is rejected; the results do not support the first hypothesis that Koreans think income distribution should be equal. Instead, Koreans show some degree of tolerance for variations in earnings, 18 percnet of the vignettes being rated as "fairly paid." It can be said that the Korean respondents are endorsing a somewhat laissez-faire outlook, expressing approval of the same range of earnings levels for persons of widely varying characteristics. However, their approval of income variations is not as strong as that of Americans, who rated 28 percent of the vignettes as fairly paid in the research of Rossi et al.[45]

Testing the Second and Third Hypotheses, Merit versus Need: In order to test the second and third hypotheses, it is necessary to uncover the structure of justice rules that guided the respondents, i.e., what characteristics of people in the vignettes influenced the judgments of respondents about fairness or unfairness of earnings? What weights are given to the different characteristics in arriving at such judgments? To answer these questions, multiple regression analysis was employed, regressing the ratings on the characteristics displayed in the vignette description.

The multiple regression equation was found by stepwise procedure regressing dependent variable Y (income-fairness ratings) on all the independent variables of vignette characteristics and their interaction

---

45.   If respondents were simply endorsing an extreme laissez-faire outlook, the rating would be expected to pile up in the category. See Alves and Rossi, *op. cit.*, p. 547.

terms.[46] It was decided that the final regression equation would include all the vignette characteristics except that adults and children were added together and two interaction terms, (length of employment)* (occupation) and (length of employment)* (education), were employed as in equation (1).[47]

Y(Fairness-Rating) = a + b_1 Occupation + b_2 Length of Employment + b_3 Earned Income + b_4 Capital Input + b_5 Sex + b_6 Education + b_7 (Length of Employment)* (Occupation) + b_8 (Education)* (Length of Employment) + b_9 Dependents   (1)

Table 2: Descriptive Statistics for Vignette Characteristics and Fairness Ratings

Variable	N	Mean	Standard Deviation
Y (Fairness-Rating)	14,860	5.387	2.451
Occupation	14,900	44.095	19.167
Length of Employment	14,900	20.245	12.705
Income	14,900	45.167	38.221
Capital	14,900	0.420	0.856
Sex	14,900	0.549	0.498
Education	14,900	3.942	1.741
Occupation *Length	14,900	942.186	795.645
Education *Length	14,900	75.258	60.095
Dependents (adult + children)	14,900	4.352	2.269

---

46. It is notable that the unit of analysis is not the respondent but the vignette. There are about 14,900 vignettes, each of which has been rated by a respondent. The correlations among the independent variables are of little interest since they are design outcomes of this study, in which vignette characteristics were almost randomly associated with each other. But the column of Y (fairness-ratings) which presents correlations between the fairness-ratings and other variables contains empirical findings and can be useful in data analysis with regression statistics.

47. In the first analysis, two of the interaction terms, (length of employment)* (occupation) and (length of employment)* (education), achieved statistical significance and were included in the model. Among the vignette characteristics, education, dependent adults, and dependent children did not achieve statistical significance. To see whether the number of dependents (our measure of need) had any influence on the fairness ratings, the numbers of dependent adults and children were added together (total dependents) and included in the analysis by stepwise procedure again. This time, total dependents achieved statistical significance and was included in the model. All other variables included in the model were the same as in the first analysis. Though education did not achieve statistical significance, it was also included in the final equation to compare its regression coefficient with other variables.

Table 3: Correlation Matrix of Vignette Characteristics and Income-Fairness Ratings

	Occup.	Length	Income	Capital	Sex	Education	Occup* Length	Educ.* Length	Depend.	Fairness-Rating
Y (Fairness-Rating)	0.249	0.081	-0.590	0.082	0.028	0.101	0.173	0.127	0.120	1.000
Occupation		0.203	-0.046	0.179	0.117	0.510	0.636	0.472	0.044	0.249
Length of Employment			0.011	0.042	0.057	-0.205	0.821	0.707	-0.055	0.081
Income				0.048	0.018	0.010	-0.011	0.019	-0.002	-0.590
Capital					-0.032	-0.080	0.097	-0.014	0.043	0.082
Sex						-0.027	0.129	0.013	-0.038	0.028
Education							0.107	0.454	-0.045	0.101
Occup. *Length								0.805	0.001	0.173
Education* Length									-0.062	0.127
Dependents (adults + children)										0.020

Table 4: Regression of Income-Fairness Ratings on Vignette Characteristics

Parameter	Understandardized b value (b)	Standardized b value (b*)	t for H_0 Parameter = 0	Standard Error of b
Intercept	5.406	0.000	55.53	0.097
Occupation	0.027	0.212	14.27	0.002
Length	0.014	0.074	4.02	0.004
Income	− 0.038	− 0.587	− 92.28	0.0004
Capital	0.223	0.078	11.75	0.019
Sex	0.112	0.023	3.50	0.032
Education	0.016	0.011	0.69	0.022
Occup. *Length	− 0.0002	− 0.074	− 2.98	0.0001
Educ. *Length	0.002	0.041	1.92	0.001
Dependents (adults + children)	0.016	0.015	2.28	0.007

Note: R^2 = .405806, F = 1127.17, N = 14863

b = unstandardized regression coefficient, b^* = standardized regression coefficient

The descriptive statistics for variables, correlation matrix, and regression statistics for the final model are shown in Tables 2, 3, and 4.

To determine whether merit (or need) considerations appear to be important in the judgments, we need to explore how much and in which direction the charactcristics considcred as measures of merit or need) affect the fairness-ratings. As shown in Table 4 merit characteristics of higher occupatinal attainment, seniority, capital input, and higher educational level, coupled with seniority, are seen as justifying a judgment tending in the direction of underpayment, regardless of the level of earnings involved.

---

48. Among them, occupational prestige level appears to be the most important in the fairness judgments, affecting fairness-ratings in the direction of underpayment. Also, length of employment an capital inputs tend to affect ratings in the same direction. However, the interaction term between occupation and length of employment shows a contradicto:y result with a negative coefficient. It is now known why the interaction term has a negativ value in view of the positive b values of the two variables separately. However, it has a relatively small b value (0.0002) and a positive correlation with fairness-rating (Y) in the correlation matrix (see Tables 3 and 4). Educational attainment by itself does n:t achieve a statistically significant regression coefficient, although the signs of the coeff:-cient of regression and correlation are in the direction of underpayment. However, the interaction term of education and length of employment does have a significant coeffi-cient which indicates that high education coupled with seniority affected fairness-rating: in the direction of underpayment. That education alone is not significant is worth mentioning in view of its importance in popular belief and for occupational success. Again, it should be noted that respondents were reacting to vignettes, not individual values. Therefore, thre is a strong interactive effect among vignette elements as noted for education and seniority.

The measures of need included in the vignettes were numbers of dependent adults and children. As mentioned earlier, the variable of adults and children did not achieve any significant regression coefficients separately. But, when they were included in the equation in a combined term, the sum showed a statistically significant and positive regression coefficient. Therefore, need can also be considered as playing a role in judgments, affecting fairness ratings in the direction of underpayment. That is, the more dependents a householder has, the more income he/she is justified in receiving.

To determine which of the two factors—merit or need—is more dominant in fairness judgments, we compared the standardized regression coefficients ($b*$ values) for the variables of merit and need. As Table 4 indicates, the standardized regression coefficient for dependents (measure of need) is lower, with a value of .015, than any $b*$ values of merit characteristics with statistically significant regression coefficients. Therefore, merit seems to be considered as more important than need in fairness judgments in our respondents, though both appear to be significant.

Besides the variables for merit and need considerations, two other variables included in the vignette characteristics, i.e., earned income and sex, achieved statistical significance in the regression equation. In particular, income has the highest $b*$ value (.587) among all the variables in the whole equation, indicating that the fairness ratings are most sensitive to the level of income earnings. Further, the negative sign indicates that there is a tendency toward judging the higher income earnings as overpaid and the lower income ernings as underpaid despite the other qualifications—e.g., occupation, capital inputs, etc.—of the individual described in the vignette. This result indicates that the Korean respondents consider the principles of social maxima and minima as important criteria in fairness judgments. That is, holding all merit and need criteria constant, lower (or higher) income appears to be unfair, relative to the perceived level of maximal "fairness."

Sex also plays a role in income fairness ratings, indicating that females are given scores higher in the direction of overpayment. Thus, Koreans considered that males must be paid more than females, regardless of the person's other characteristics. This result contrasts with that of the United States, where sex was not a statistically significant variable influencing the fairness of income.[49]

The Issue of Consensus: Another question in our study is whether

---

49. See Alves and Rossi, *op. cit.,* p. 551.

any consensus exists among respondents on distributive justice concepts. In this research consensus is considered to exist in a population when there is no significant amount of structured disagreement among socially recognizable subgroups of the population in question. To this end both respondent and vignette characteristics were included in the regression equation of fairness ratings of all the vignettes to see if any respondent characteristic has significant influence on the judgment.

A new multiple regression model was developed which includes all the variables of equation (1) and the nine respondents'

Table 5: Regression of Income-Fairness Ratings on Vignette and Respondent Characteristics

Parameter	Unstandardized b value	t for H_0 Parameter = 0	Standard Error of b
Intercept	5.405	46.08	0.117
Vignette Characteristics			
Occupation	0.027	14.23	0.002
Length	0.014	3.94	0.004
Adult + Children	0.014	2.01	0.007
Income	−0.038	−92.66	0.0004
Capital	0.226	11.93	0.019
Sex	0.113	3.53	0.032
Education	0.103	0.66	0.022
Occup. *Length	−0.0002	−2.88	0.0001
Length *Educ.	0.002	1.91	0.001
Respondent Characteristics			
Occupation	0.103	6.22	0.017
Length	−0.021	0.82	0.026
Dependent	0.014	1.65	0.009
Income	0.0001	0.25	0.0004
Capital	−0.153	−6.35	0.024
Sex	−0.421	−9.86	0.043
Education	−0.040	−2.48	0.016
Age	0.044	−2.88	0.0001

Note: R^2 = .412096, $F = 612.14$, $N = 14863$

characteristics.[50] As shown in Table 5, the R^2 statistic of the new equation (.412096) increased by only .00629 over the equation (1) (.405806). In other words, there is only a tiny difference in R^2's whether or not respondent characteristics are entered into income-fairness regressions. This fact strongly suggests that the determinants of income-fairness judgments are not rooted to any great extent in respondents' demographic characteristics.[51]

To explore further possible structured disagreement among the subgroups of respondents, we conducted additional regression analyses. The subgroups chosen were based on the five respondent characteristics which achieved statistical significance in the new equation: occupation, capital, sex, education, and age. Each of the five characteristics of respondents was divided into two groups.[52] For each of the subgroups, the regression equtions of fairness ratings on vignette characteristics were made. The regression results showed little difference between the two subgroups on each of the respondent characteristics of sex, age and education. Only results for low-and high-occupational prestige respondents and for low-and some-capital input respondents indicated some significant differences between the subgroups.

As shown in Table 6, the coefficients for occupation are larger in the high-occupational prestige respondents' regressions, while the coefficients for length of employment and capital input are larger in the low-occupational prestige respondents' regressions. One interpretation of these results is that high-occupational prestige respondents place greater weight on occupational prestige than low-occupational prestige respondents, while low-occupational prestige respondents give length of employment and capital input more weight. To support this suggestion, the differences in coefficients for length of employment (and capital input) are two (and four) times as large as the standard errors of any of the individual coefficients. But the differences for occupation are smaller than the standard errors of any of the individual coef-

---

50. The new equation is: Y(Fairness-Ratings) = $a + b_1 V$-Occupation + $b_2 V$-Length + $b_3 V$-Income + $b_4 V$-Capital + $b_5 V$-Sex + $b_6 V$-Education + $b_7 V$-Occupation* V-Length + $b_8 V$-Education* V-Length + b_9 V-Dependent + $b_{10} R$-occupation + $b_{11} R$-Length of Employment + $b_{12} R$-Dependent + $b_{13} R$-Income + $b_{14} R$-Capital + $b_{15} R$-Sex + $b_{16} R$-Education + $b_{17} R$-Age

where b_1—b_9 = vignette characteristics, and b_{10}—b_{17} = respondent characteristics.

51. The analysis of income fairness regressed on respondent's characteristics showed only that the regression equation had the R^2-value of .008.

52. These include: (1) low occupation versus high occupation, (2) male versus female, (3) no capital input versus some capital input, (4) low educations versus high education, and (6) young respondents versus old respondents.

Table 6: . Regressions Income-Fairness Ratings on Vignette Characteristics by Respondent Subgroups
(A) High-and Low-Occupational Prestige Respondents

Parameter	Low-Occupational Prestige Respondents			High-Occupational Prestige Respondents		
	b value	t for H_0 Parameter = 0	Std. Error of b	b value	t for H_0 Parameter = 0	Std. Error of b
Intercept	5.410	44.38	0.122	5.398	33.88	0.159
Occupation	0.027	11.14	0.002	0.028	9.04	0.003
Length	0.019	4.33	0.004	0.007	1.27	0.006
Adult + Children	0.013	1.54	0.009	0.019	1.68	0.011
Income	−0.037	−73.10	0.001	−0.039	−57.06	0.001
Capital	0.245	10.28	0.024	0.192	6.22	0.031
Sex	0.123	3.08	0.040	0.097	1.83	0.053
Education	0.013	0.46	0.028	0.019	0.52	0.037
Occup. *Length	−0.0003	−3.59	0.0001	−0.0001	−0.54	0.0001
Educ. *Length	0.002	1.59	0.001	0.002	1.11	0.001

Note: Low-occupational prestige respondents are those with the occupational prestige score below 40 and high-occupational prestige respondents are those with the score above 40. $N = 8685$, $R^2 = 4197$ for low-occupational prestige respondents regression equation and $N = 6177$, $R^2 = .3917$ for high-occupational prestige respondents regression equation.

Table 6: (Continued)
(B) No- and Some-Capital Input Respondents

Parameter	No-Capital Input Respondents			Some-Capital Input Respondents		
	b value	t for H_0. Parameter = 0	Std. Error of b	b value	t for H_0. Parameter = 0	Std. Error of b
Intercept	5.404	40.97	0.132	5.407	39.62	0.136
Occupation	0.023	8.90	0.003	0.033	12.45	0.003
Length	0.015	3.13	0.005	0.012	2.60	0.005
Adult + Children	0.017	1.87	0.009	0.014	1.46	0.010
Income	−0.032	−57.51	0.001	−0.047	−80.85	0.001
Capital	0.216	8.43	0.026	0.239	8.91	0.027
Sex	0.061	1.42	0.043	0.174	3.83	0.045
Education	0.017	0.55	0.030	0.015	0.49	0.032
Occup. *Length	−0.0003	−2.49	0.0001	−0.0002	1.61	0.0001
Educ. *Length	0.002	1.68	0.001	0.001	0.93	0.001

Note: $N = 8886$, $R^2 = .3091$ for no-capital input respondents, and $N = 5976$, $R^2 = .5649$ for some-capital input respondents.

ficients. Therefore, we can say that there are some variations, at least for capital and length of employment, in the structure of judgments about income-fairness due to respondent characteristics.

In addition, the coefficients for length of employment are larger in the no-capital input respondents' regressions, while the coefficients for occupation and capital inputs are larger in the some-capital input respondents' regressions. Accordingly, it appears that the no-capital input respondent tends to place greater weight on seniority, while the some-capital input respondent places more weight on capital and occupation. However, the differences in coefficients for capital and length of employment are smaller than the standard errors of any of the individual coefficients. Therefore, variation on the structure of judgments of income-fairness due to respondent chararacteristics seems to exist only for occupational attainments.

Also, the results show that there are some differences in R^2 between the regression equations of the low- and high-occupational prestige respondents ($.4197 - .3917 = .028$) and between those of no- and some-capital input respondents ($.5649 - .3091 = .2558$).

In short, there are some variations in the structure of judgments of income-fairness due to the levels of capital input and occupational prestige of respondents. However, the differences appeared only in the priorities among merit considerations (i.e., length of employment, occupation, and capital input, etc.), not in the priorities between merit and need.

CONCLUSIONS

The survey results show that the Korean population does not consider egalitarianism as a justice criterion for economic distribution; hence the first null hypothesis, that "income distribution ought to be equal," was rejected. Instead, Koreans support a strong meritarian principle of distributive justice, by choosing occupational and educational attainments, work experience, and capital investment as the major criteria for an individual's earnings. Though individual needs appear to be important for income distribution, the regression was dominated by merit, except for education, rather than the need criterion.

Public policy implications of this research have been considered elsewhere.[53] Briefly, however, application of the meritarian principle requires reduced government intervention in the economy and

---

53. Jung and Siegel, op.cit., passim.

more of a free market-oriented economic system. Such a transformation of the Korean economy must be accompanied by measurs to secure fair competition and equality of opportunity. These measures may include elimination of political and administrative corruption and favoritism, and equalization of opportunities between large and small corporations and between employees and employers.

Need-based distribution is important also. In spite of the rapid economic development during the last two decades, a population of more than four million "absolutely poor people" (or 12·percent of the total population in Korea in the late 1970's) has persisted. Public policies of basic-need satisfaction can help to foster a competitive market system, contributing eventually to merit-oriented redistribution.

21

The Bureau of Auditing and Inspection, and its Role in Soical Development

Myoung Soo Kim

Introduction

The traditional role of state audit institutions is characterized by a conservative nature, i.e., they check the legality of agency expenditures. More recently, however, their role has changed. Today they have begun to evaluate the efficiency and effectiveness of executive action, namely program evaluation. However, this docs not mean they neglect the job of determining whether or not an audited entity has complied with all applicable laws and regulations. Determining the legality of agency transactions comprise a major part of the auditor's work.

Whether or not to include program evaluation as a part of auditing has been hotly debated in several quarters.[1] Nevertheless, an underlying assumption of this article is that program evaluation is an integral part of auditing, and that auditors should carry it out. It should also be remembered, however, that program evaluation is not the sole responsibility of the state audit unit. It may be carried out by special evaluation units within an organization, by independent research organizations, contractors engaged for the purpose, or by auditors.

The very fact that an audit includes evaluation of executive action as well as developmental policies and programs, indicates the positive role that state audit institutions play in the process of national and in particular, social development. That is, it is by means of evalua-

---

1. Ellsworth H. Morse, Jr., "The Auditor Takes on Program Evaluation", *Federal Accountant*, Vol. XXII, No. 2, June 1973, p. 18.

tion of social policies and programs that state audit institutions contribute to social development.

Concern about social development was raised by the new understanding that economic growth alone (as reflected in the gross national
product) is not sufficient for national development unless it is accompained by equitable distribution among the people.

Social development is viewed in this paper as any improvement
in such areas of life as income, employment and manpower, education, health, housing and environment, family life and leisure, and
public safety. That is to say, if the indicators of respective sectors
move in a right direction, ceteris paribus, we know that social conditions have been developed.

It is well known that the agencies in the executive branch of government have been instrumental in the development of many developing countries. It is found that state audit institutions can oversee the
bureaucracy. Consequently, they can play a supportive role in the
social development process through evaluation of developmental
policies and programs in the social sectors. The reasons for this are
as follows: First, the fact that the state audit system conducts program evaluations at all implies that it values program outputs more
than program inputs. This surely causes operating agencies to be
more output oriented in their operations which in turn contributes
to development. Second, the role of the state audit unit as evaluator
forces the operating agencies to either initiate policy planning processes or refine what has already been instituted. Third, the findings
of a program evaluation provide a clear basis for feedback and control. That is, state audit institutions can make recommendations about
the future of any audited programs based on the program evaluations. If they are judged to be unsuccessful, those programs can be
modified, eliminated, or their funding decreased.

In the meantime, since auditors can not and need not evaluate all
the social programs, they have to be given a guideline on how to initiate program evaluation. It is suggested that evaluation efforts focus
on programs within those social sectors where the responsible system
looks as if it is failing with regard to the quality of life level. But how
do we know whether the system is failing in performance? In this
respect, social indicators which involve quantitative descriptions, and
analyses of social conditions and trends,[2] can do the job. By observ-

2. David Nachmias, *Public Policy Evaluation* (N.Y.: St. Martin's Press, 1979), p. 80; Eleanor
    Sheldon and Howard Freeman, "Notes on Social Indicators: Promises and Potential,
    Policy Sciences, 1 (Spring 1970), p. 97; Thomas R. Dye, *Understanding Public Policy* (N.J.:
    Prentice-Hall, 1978), p. 324.

ing the time-series information of a relevant social sector, we are able to make a reasonable appraisal of conditions within the sector in question.

However, there are limitations to using social indicators directly for assessing the conditions and trends of society. Because they are expressed in the form of averages, and because they are not usually broken down based on income classes, in many cases we are not able to capture a full picture of the disadvantaged.

Social indicators can also play another part in the evaluation process. An auditor can use them to define the objectives of a social program, and to measure the extent to which they have been achieved. Figure 1 depicts the underlying themes which have been discussed so far.

Figure 1: Relationships among social indicators, auditing, and social development.

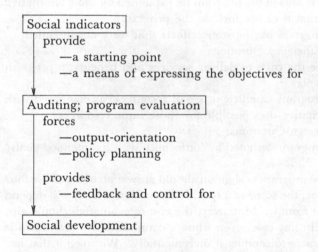

In this article I will first outline program evaluation and social indicators with respect to their recent development in Korea. Next, how and to what degree program evaluation and social indicators have been utilized by the Bureau of Audit and Inspection (BAI) will be examined. Finally, a plan of action will be presented which is geared to improving the role of the Board of Audit and Inspection of Korea (BAI) in the process of social development. Problems involved in implementing strategies and possible solutions will also be discussed.

Program Evaluation and Social Indicators

1. Program Evaluation: Its Rationale and Areas of Concern

Program evaluation is necessary because "no longer do we assume that once we pass a law, establish a bureaucracy, and spend money, the purpose of these acts will be achieved and the results will be what we expected them to be."[3] More specifically, program evaluation must be performed in order to meet one or more of the following decision needs of decision-makers:[4]

(1) Program Monitoring Questions:
   — Is the program reaching the persons, households, or other target units to which it is addressed?
   — Is the program providing the resources, services, or other benefits that were intended in the program design?

(2) Impact Assessment Questions:
   — Is the program effective in achieving its intended goals?
   — Can the results of the program be explained by some alternative process that does not include the program?
   — Is the program having some effects that were not intended?

(3) Economic Efficiency Questions:
   — What are the costs to deliver services and benefits to program participants?
   — Is the program an efficient use of resources, as compared with the alternative uses possible for those same resources?

(4) Program Design Questions:
   — Is the program designed in conformity with its intended goals?

A comprehensive program evaluation should answer all of the above four questions. However, the scope of a specific evaluation activity will depend on who wants what from it. Moreover, the cost of evaluation should also to be considered. In any case, even when a comprehensive evaluation is required, it is desirable to conduct it incrementally. We suggest that implementation be examined first, then impact, and then if it is efficacious, a cost-benefit or cost-effectiveness evaluation should be undertaken. If it is not effective, program redesign should be considered.[5] But we must

---

3. Thomas R. Dye, *Policy Analysis* (University, Ala.: University of Alabama Press, 1976), p. 95.
4. Cf. Peter Rossi, Howard E. Freeman and Sonia Wright, *Evaluation: A Systematic Approach* (Beverly Hills, Calif.: Sage Publications, 1979), p. 33.
5. See *Ibid.*, pp. 45-46.

remember that the most important task of program evaluation is to assess the impact of a program. When providing answers to questions about the impact of a social program, social indicators must be utilized. Let us now turn to social indicators.

2. Social Indicators: Their Types and Development in Korea

Social indicators are classified in various ways. For example, Kenneth C. Land makes a distinction among three types of indicators: (1) output descriptive indicators, (2) other descriptive indicators, and (3) analytic indicators.[6] The last category refers to 'components of explicit conceptual models of the social processes which result in the values of the output indicators." The United States Department of Commerce uses another classification scheme:(1) indicators of system performance, (2) indicators of well-being, and (3) indicators of public perceptions.[7] The following three types of social indicators are offered for our purpose:

(1) Indicators of system inputs: These are measures of the input resources and governmental activities, i.e., what the government does (e.g., public expenditure on public education). They correspond to the indicators of system performance used by the U.S. Department of Commerce.

(2) Goal output indicators: These are measures of specific national goals attained (e.g., median earnings of individuals). They roughly encompass Land's first category, and the last two categories set forth by the U.S. Department of Commerce.

(3) Other general output descriptive indicators: These are more general measures of the social conditions of human existence and the change taking place therein (e.g., total population). They are the same as Land's second category.

This tripartite classification is aimed at relating what governments do with what effect their actions have. Schneider argues that social indicators research should "try to accurately relate changes in carefully specified societal conditions to the actions of government and its agencies."[8]

The Korean government has evolved a system of social indicators ever since 1978 and has since then annually published Social Indicators

---

6. Kenneth C. Land, "Social Indicator Models: An Overview," in K.C. Land and S. Spilerman, (eds.), *Social Indicator Models* (N.Y.: Russell Sage Foundation, 1975), pp. 17-19.
7. U.S. Department of Commerce, Bureau of the Census, *Social Indicators 1976*, p. xxiv.
8. Mark Schneider, "The Quality of Life and Social Indicators Research," *Public Administration Review*, May/June 1976, p. 304.

Table 1: Number of Social Indicators by Social Sector

Social Sectors	Number of Indicators Include in		
	1978 Version	1980 Edition	1983 Edition
Population	14	18	18
Income and Consumption	9	11	16
Employment and Manpower	23	32	44
Education	17	22	27
Health	23	26	30
Housing and Environment	13	19	26
Family Life and Leisure	7	15	17
Public Safety	8	8	9
Total	114	151	187

Source: Korea Economic Planning Board, *Social Indicators in Korea 1980*, p. 29; *Social Indicators in Korea 1983*, pp. 22-30.

in Korea, the editions of which are becoming progressively more detailed. The 1978 version contained 114 indicators; the 1980 edition 151, and the 1983 edition 187.[9] As shown in Table 1, social indicators appear for eight social sectors: (1) population, (2) income and consumption, (3) employment and manpower, (4) education, (5) health, (6) housing and environment, (7) family life and leisure, and (8) public safety.

All these indicators have been compiled from the files of operating agencies existing within the executive branch of government and other public organizations.

Upon examining the social indicators, we note the following characteristics:

(1) They are mainly either goal output indicators, or general output descriptive indicators;

(2) There are only a few indicators of system inputs. This is also the case with *Social Indicators 1976* in the United States.

(3) There first began to appear a few indicators of public perceptions in the 1980 edition, and their number increased a great deal in the 1983 edition.

---

9. See Korea Economic Planning Board, *Social Indicators in Korea 1980* and *Social Indicators in Korea 1983*.

Utilization of Program Evaluation and Social Indicators by the Board of Audit and Inspection of Korea

1. Use of Program Evaluation[10]

Since its birth in 1963, the Board of Audit and Inspection of Korea (BAI) has conducted audit and inspection of government operations with a major emphasis on checking the legality of financial transactions.[11] In 1971, a major change took place in the BAI method of audit and inspection. That was the first year that the BAI put a balanced emphasis on both audit of accounts and inspection function, of which performance evaluation of government activities, programs, functions and operations is a part. As a result, as shown in Table 2, almost half the man-days were given over to the latter function in 1980.

Table 2: Man-days Involved in Audits of Accounts and Inspection Function

	Audit of Accounts		Inspection Function	
	Man-days	%	Man-days	%
1977	41,784	65.8	21,732	34.2
1978	46,501	68.2	21,673	31.8
1979	44,367	62.3	26,795	37.7
1980	31,159	51.0	29,938	49.0

Source: Board of Audit and Inspection of Korea, *National Government and Auditing,* 1983, p. 438.

This shift in the emphasis of audit and inspection should be praised, for it helped to reinforce the efforts of the Korean government in the area of social development. This shift, of course, was clearly manifested in the Third and Fourth Five-Year Economic Development Plans which began in 1972 and 1977, respectively, and in the Fifth Five-Year Socio-Economic Development Plan which began in 1982. As of today the basic policy of the BAI remains unchanged.

---

10. Hereafter program evaluation refers to evaluation of the developmental programs within the social sectors of our concern.
11. Until 1970, examining the legality of financial transactions occupied over 80 percent of the total cases handled by the BAI. See BAI, *History of the Board of Audit and Inspection* (Korean), December 1973, p. 187.

It would be worthwhile to take a closer look at what Korean auditors are directed to examine when conducting a program audit, and how thoroughly they have actually performed their task. The *Audit and Inspection Manual,* published in 1975 by the BAI, instructs them to pay attention to the following points, despite some variations from program to program:[12]

(1) Are the program goals and objectives in conformity with relevant laws and government policies?

(2) Was the right priority taken into account in choosing the programs?

(3) Were all relevant factors considered when formulating the plans?

(4) Were all necessary measures taken before implementing the program plans?

(5) Were efficiency and economy taken into account in implementing the program plans?

(6) Were adequate investment resources secured?

(7) Was the fund alloted at the proper time?

(8) Was the program management well organized?

(9) Was the program effective?

(10) Was the method for measuring the program's effectiveness appropriate?

(11) Was the program worth the cost?

(12) If the program was a failure, were its problems identified?

In this connection, an examination of both program audit reports and the Inspection Consultation Conference material, which were prepared by the BAI auditors during 1972-1983, reveals that they have been primarily concerned with the process of program implementation, economy and efficiency, and that they have not paid much attention to measuring the effectiveness of the programs, but, rather, have been more concerned with determining the validity of methodologies that the audited entities used in measuring the program's effectiveness, i. e. , metaevaluation. [13]

2. Use of Social Indicators

Until recently, BAI auditors did not utilize social indicators in the

---

12. BAI, *Audit and Inspection Manual,* June 1975, pp. 985-1064.

13. For discussion of metaevaluation, See Thomas D. Cook and Charles L. Gruder, "Metaevaluation Research," *Evaluation Quarterly,* Vol. 2, No. 1, February 1978, pp. 5-51.

process of auditing. This policy was a direct result of the fact that they paid scanty attention to the overall effectiveness of developmental programs. However, since they are attempting to determine whether those programs are achieving the desired results or benefits as well as a preventive audit, they will have to utilize social indicators more and more when auditing social sector agencies and programs.

This contrasts with the practice of certain other agencies of the executive branch of government. Those agencies use social indicators in two ways. First, they observe the movement of those social indicators which merit their concern and then try to determine what problems underline the signals, positive or negative, that they perceive. For example, the Ministry of Health and Social Affairs regularly inspects changes of direction among 15 major indicators (e. g. , infant mortality rate, protein intake, etc.). Through this inspection they better understand the problems they may have to face, and can better judge how well they have been performing their duties. [14] Second, the agencies use social indicators to set specific objectives for their programs. For example, in order to improve maternity and infant health, the Ministry set their objectives as follows:[15]

(1) To reduce the infant mortality rate from 38 per thousand in 1975 to 20 in 1981;

(2) To decrease the maternal mortality rate from 5.6 per ten thousand births in 1975 to 3.0 in 1981.

To summarize, we may characterize the approach taken by the Korean auditors as "a passive approach. " Passive in the sense that the auditors themselves are not the ones who uncovered problems within the agency, or its programs. When conducting a program audit, the auditors paid more attention to the question of legality, economy, and efficiency than to program effectiveness. Consequently, a change in the auditing practice is necessary. We will discuss this question next.

Strategies for Improving the Role of the BAI in the Process of Social Development

1. Strategies

No one would argue the fact that by auditing governmental develop-

---

14. Health and Social Security Planning Unit, the Republic of Korea,Government, *Fourth 5-Year Economic Development Plan: Health and Social Security Plan 1977-1981*, 1976, p. 24.
15. *Loc. Cit.*

ment programs, the BAI has played a part in the process of social development. However, in order to play a more supportive role in the process of social development in Korea, the BAI is expected to seek a way to transform its passive approach to ''a positive approach.'' Positive in the sense that the auditors themselves will be able to uncover questionable social sectors or agencies, pay more attention to the question of program effectiveness and deal with the intended objectives of a whole set of programs implemented in a particular sector or agency. In order to adopt such an approach, the BAI will have to pursue three goals:

(1) Better utilization of social indicators in planning an audit and inspection;

(2) More attention to program results; and

(3) More attention to the theories linking programs with their goals and objectives.

Utilization of social indicators in planning an audit and inspection. In order to play a positive role in the process of social development, BAI auditors will have to utilize social indicators in the following way:

1) Choose an array of social indicators which are deemed to represent a certain sector.

2) Scrutinize those representative indicators to see whether they are moving in the right direction, that is, in a way that suggests amelioration is taking place.

3) If the indicators are uniformly positive, the program should be left alone. If they are not satisfactory, then is it time for the auditor to mvoe into that particular sector and apply his auditing skills?

In addition, auditors might direct their attention to a particular sector or sectors where citizen complaints arise most frequently.

More attention to the program results. It is very important to check the legality of financial transactions, and to check whether an audited entity is using its resources in an economical and efficient manner. And even more important than that, auditors must determine what the entity achieves with those resources in terms of the desired resutls or benefits it was supposed to meet. Upon knowing the effectiveness of a program, the auditors are in a better position to suggest what the audited entities should do next. With such information in hand, the latter would know how well they have heen performing their job and to what extent they meet the objectives of the developmental programs they implemented.

More attention to the theories linking programs and their goals and objectives. Programs, social or industrial, are by definition, the planned means to meet specific government goals and objectives. It is possible that a program may be implemented in order to achieve more than one objective, or that more than one program may be put into effect in order to meet a specific objectrive, or complex of objectives. In the latter case, it is essential to examine the whole series of programs in relation to their intended goals and objectives and to decide whether or not unnecessary or ineffective programs have been implemented.

There are of course problems with putting these three assertions into effect so that the BAI may play a positive role in the process of social development. These problems as well as solutions for them are presented categorically as follows.

2. Problems and Possible Solutions

Problems and solutions with regard to the utilization of social indicators in the BAI

Because a) operating agencies have used social indicators for a long time, and b) the Korea Economic Planning Board has compiled a system of social indicators, the utilization of social indicators by the BAI may not raise any problems, once top management decides to use them. However, problems will arise when the system of social indicators is not able to meet the needs of the BAI auditors. In other words, the auditors may not be able to find the right indicators in the existing system which can measure the variable (or a specific objective) with which they are most concerned.

In such a case, the auditors will have to consult the operating agency personnel, and persuade them to collect the relevant information. Although obtaining cooperation from them will be a difficult task, it is essential.

Problems and solutions with regard to putting more emphasis on program results

Determining whether a program achieves its desired results raises some real problems. Perhaps, the foremost is political. In this regard, two political problems can be distinguished. One is resistance on the part of the audited entities.[16] People generally do not want their performance evaluated, especially when the results can be used as a basis for punishing poor performers. The knowledge on the part of operating personnel that the value of program evaluation lies primarily

---

16. Larry B. Hill and F. Ted Hebert, *Essentials of Public Adminsitration* (Mass.: Duxbury, 1979), pp. 388-390.

in its use as a tool for meeting accountability needs, and facilitating corrective action may help reduce resistance.

The other problem refers to the territorial question. As mentioned in the first section of this article, whether or not auditors should perform a program audit, which includes determining the effectiveness of a program, has been debated in several quarters. In Korea both the Office of Planning and Management in each ministry, and the BAI are authorized to perform program evaluation. Therefore, there exists a possibility of conflict on the issue of who should take charge of it. Somewhere a line should be drawn. The BAI is best suited to evaluate a) evaluations done by operating agencies, and b) controversial major programs. Along these lines then, revision of the relevant laws, such as the Board of Audit and Inspection Act, should be undertaken.

Methodology also presents difficult problems. Measuring program effectiveness necessitates two requirements: (1) that the problem addressed, the program intervention implemented, and the anticipated outcome of that intervention on society be sufficiently well defined to be measurable, and (2) that the logic of assumptions linking expenditure of resources, implementation of program intervention and the immediate outcomes of that intervention, be understood clearly enough to permit testing them.[17] Generally, however, this is not the case. And even if these requirements are met through use of an experimental design, (which is regarded as the most powerful way to assess the causal relationship between a developmental policy and its goals), it is still not easy to come up with an accurate assessment. Social, political and ethical considerations may prevent experimentation.[18] This calls for the construction of alternative research designs. These are generally referred to as "quasi-experimental designs."

Another problem is the limited number of the trained auditors in this field. They need a broad interdisciplinary background and a thorough understanding of social science methodology.[19] Provision for education and training is the only solution for this problem.

Problems and solutions with regard to theories which link programs with their goals.

In order to examine linking theories, the auditors should be pro-

17. See Pamela Horst, Joe Nay, John Scanlon and Joseph Wholey, "Program Management and the Federal Evaluator," *Public Administration Review,* (July/August 1974), pp. 301-304.
18. Nachmias, *op. cit.,* p. 16.
19. See Frank P. Scioli, Jr., "Problems and Prospects for Policy Evaluation," *PAR,* (January/February 1979), pp. 41-42.

vided with a record of why a certain program or programs were chosen initially. If not the theories, at least the assumptions underlying those chosen programs should be made known. This might be too much to expect at the present time. However, it is important to require that operating agencies keep such records. It is beneficial for them as well, because it is the most appropriate tool for meeting accountability needs.

Conclusion

In following the line of thought presented in the first section, the writer has examined both the basic policies of the BAI and its auditing practices as they relate to social development. As a result, a gap between the two has been identified. Through a diagnostic approach, he has developed strategies for improving the role of the BAI by means of program evaluation and social indicators. He has also discussed ways of putting the suggested measure into effect. He strongly feels that the strategies, if put into effect, will greatly contribute to enhancing the quality of life in Korea, thereby helping to achieve the goals of our national policy, i.e. to build a welfare state and a just society.

Some of the main points discussed in this article are summarized below.

(1) Program evaluation should be an integral part of an audit.

(2) State audit institutions can play a supportive role in the process of social development by evaluating social programs and polciies.

(3) Social indicators may be utilized in planning an audit, and in auditing programs.

(4) The BAI has long been concerned with the performance of developmental programs. However, until recently, the major concern was legality, economy and efficiency.

(5) The BAI auditors have not utilized social indicators in the process of auditing. However, since they are going to take on program evaluation fully, it is expected that they will increasingly utilize social indicators when auditing social sector agencies and programs.

(6) The BAI has to seek a way to change its approach to a positive approach. In order to take such an approach, it will have to do the following:

(a) Utilize social indicators in planning audits and inspections;

(b) Pay more attention to program results; and

(c) Pay more attention to the theories linking programs and their goals and objectives.

(7) The writer fully understands that the problems faced in im-

plementing such strategies are not easy to overcome. The suggested solutions should not be regarded as a panacea.

Index